HUMAN NEEDS AND POLITICS

**edited by
Ross Fitzgerald**

PERGAMON PRESS

Pergamon Press (Australia) Pty Limited, 19a Boundary Street, Rushcutters Bay, NSW 2011
Pergamon Press Ltd, Headington Hill Hall, Oxford OX3 OBW
Pergamon Press Inc, Maxwell House, Fairview Park, Elmsford, New York 10523
Pergamon of Canada Ltd, 75 The East Mall, Toronto, Ontario M8Z 2L9, Canada
Pergamon Press GmbH, 6242 Kronberg/Taunus, Pferdstrasse 1, Frankfurt-am-Main, West Germany
Pergamon Press SARL, 24 rue des Ecoles, 75240 Paris, Cedex 05, France

© Ross Fitzgerald, 1977

Cover design by Allan Hondow
Typeset in Australia by Savage and Co
Printed in Hong Kong by Dai Nippon Printing Co

Fitzgerald, Ross, 1944-.
Human needs and politics.

Index.
Bibliography.
ISBN 0 08 21402 9.
ISBN 0 08 021401 0 Paperback.

1. Political science — Addresses, essays, lectures.
I. Title.

301.59208

Acknowledgements

In the course of preparing this collection I have incurred many debts. I would like to thank all contributors for their co-operation and promptness in meeting what, for many, was a very difficult deadline. I am especially grateful to Douglas McCallum, Donald Horne, Conal Condren and Angelo Loukakis for their encouragement and advice, to Libi Nugent and Eryl Brady who typed much of the final manuscript, and to Averil Condren for compiling the index. In particular I would like to thank Irina Dunn for her extremely helpful and efficient editorial assistance. My greatest debt is to Lyndal Moor, whose love, friendship and creativity continue to sustain and enrich me.

Ross Fitzgerald

ERRATUM

Human Needs and Politics
Edited by Ross Fitzgerald

p 46, lines 11–14 should read as follows:

insurmountable problems. It is clear that, in so far as a potentially verifiable aspect can be abstracted from this ambiguous amalgam, Maslow's theory of human needs has not been empirically established to any significant extent.

A major difficulty with his theory is that Maslow, like Fromm, does

v

Contributors

CHRISTIAN BAY	*Department of Political Economy, University of Toronto, Canada*
CONAL CONDREN	*School of Political Science, University of New South Wales, Australia*
JAMES C. DAVIES	*Department of Political Science, University of Oregon, USA*
ROSS FITZGERALD	*School of Humanities, Griffith University, Brisbane, Australia*
ANTONY FLEW	*Department of Philosophy, University of Reading, England*
DAVID HOLBROOK	*Cambridge, England*
JEANNE N. KNUTSON	*The Wright Institute, Los Angeles, California, USA*
NEIL MCINNES	*Paris, France*
C.B. MACPHERSON	*Department of Political Economy, University of Toronto, Canada*
KAI NIELSEN	*Department of Philosophy, University of Calgary, Canada*
STANLEY A. RENSHON	*Department of Political Science, Herbert H. Lehman College, City University of New York, USA*
M. BREWSTER SMITH	*School of Psychology, Division of Social Sciences, University of California, Santa Cruz, USA*
PATRICIA SPRINGBORG	*Department of Government, University of Sydney, Australia*

Contents

Introduction

Ross Fitzgerald

Talk about human needs has traditionally had considerable currency in common language and in political rhetoric. Recently, however, there has been a marked revival of need theory, especially in relation to politics, by many contemporary scholars, a number of whom are included in this collection.

The recent resuscitation of the notion 'need' can best be interpreted in the context of a reaction against the allegedly value-free or value-neutral approach in the social sciences. In this sense the work of Christian Bay, James C. Davies and C.B. Macpherson, for example, can most usefully be seen as part of the return to a valuing political and social science that has followed on from the writings of C. Wright Mills, Gunnar Myrdal, Abraham Maslow and Erich Fromm. Contemporary need theory itself echoes the cries for relevance, significance and action made in recent years.[1]

It seems clear that during the late 1950s and early 1960s in the West many scholars in the social and behavioural sciences were in fact inhibited from normative utterance because of the orthodoxy of value-neutrality, their image of what comprised philosophy and science and their belief that

---

1 See for example *Apolitical Politics: A Critique of Behavioralism*, eds. C.A. McCoy and J. Playford, Thomas Y. Crowell, New York, 1967, and *The Dissenting Academy*, ed. T. Roszak, Penguin Books, Middlesex, 1969.

there was no way to overcome what was perceived to be 'the fact/value problem'.[2] While there is no *logical* reason why drawing a distinction between 'is' and 'ought' statements should inhibit normative utterance, in practice it tended to do so.[3] Certainly there was an inbuilt reticence, especially on the part of professional students of political behaviour, to talk normatively or prescriptively because they believed that if they did so as political or social scientists they would be engaging in fraudulent and unscholarly activity.

Resurrection of the concept 'need', especially when dressed in empirical or behavioural garb, was a device supremely suited for an attempt to bridge the gap between empirical and normative inquiry and in some way to 'overcome' the so-called problem of the separation of 'fact' and 'value'. For the ambiguous notion 'need' amalgamates and confuses 'is' and 'ought' and in this special sense itself links 'fact' with 'value'.[4]

Significantly even if contemporary theorists are not always prepared to *ground* political prescriptions on the basis of an empirical theory of human needs, there has been a recent attempt by some of them to *connect* and *relate* value-statements in an intelligible way to allegedly empirical evidence about human needs and their priorities. Such theorists (most notably Christian Bay whose essay opens this collection) have constantly and consistently related talk about human needs not only to the study of political behaviour, but also to the evaluation of political ends and purposes.

Contemporary need theory, particularly in relation to politics, draws its 'inspiration' from the younger Marx, from Maslow, Fromm and Marcuse.

The notion of 'needs' is central especially to Marx's early writing. Thus he claimed that 'Private property does not know how to change crude need into human need ...' Crude needs are inhuman, unnatural, illusory and

---

2 See Conal Condren, this collection, Chapter 14. For the notion of 'objective' science, see David Holbrook, Chapter 10, and M. Brewster Smith, Chapter 7.

3 Central to academic orthodoxy was a general acceptance of the need to avoid the 'naturalistic fallacy'. While there are difficulties with the current usages of the term they all clearly refer to Hume's famous 'Is'/'Ought' distinction. (*A Treatise of Human Nature*, Book III, Part I, Section I.) In broad outline this thesis holds that there is a class of statements of fact which are logically distinct from a class of statements of value and that no set of statements of fact by themselves entails any statement of value without the addition of at least one evaluative premise. To believe otherwise is to commit an illicit transition from what *is* to what *ought* to be. The actual use of the term 'the naturalistic fallacy' derives from G.E. Moore's *Principia Ethica*, (Cambridge University Press, Cambridge, 1956, first published 1903). Moore appears to have meant a number of different things by the 'naturalistic fallacy' and it is not clear that in each of the several meanings a fallacy is involved.

4 See my essay 'The Ambiguity and Rhetoric of "Need" ', this collection, Chapter 11.

imaginary appetites. By contrast human needs are expressions of our deepest natures, especially those that set us apart from brute animals. They are not 'depraved'; rather man only truly becomes himself when he satisfies all his distinctly human needs. The satisfaction of these needs is, for Marx, the pre-condition of a 'fully unalienated life', and the appearance of the true realm of freedom.[5] In the *1844 Manuscripts* and elsewhere Marx distinguished between 'true' and 'false', 'real' and 'artificial' needs. Marx claimed that 'real' needs were objective and that man only realises himself when his true needs are satisfied and his 'false', unreal and artificially created needs (especially the need for money and possessions) are rendered redundant.[6] Man's distinctly human needs emerge when the realm of necessity is sloughed off by way of a liberating revolution which purges away 'the muck of ages' and transforms the nature of man. While Marx's view of human needs is often presented indirectly, it is made abundantly clear in the *Theses on Feuerbach*, for example, that for Marx the ideal society is that which fulfils man's real and authentic needs.[7] Consequently it has been claimed that Marx's account of human needs is not only tied to a notion of what is truly human but also provides him with a standard by which to evaluate various social orders.[8] Thus when he prescribed 'From each according to his ability, to each according to his needs', the needs referred to, it can be argued, are human needs in Bay's and Marcuse's sense of the term.[9]

Abraham Maslow, whose need-hierarchy (that is, physical, safety, affection, esteem, and self-actualisation needs) is the source of much contemporary theory, explicitly proclaimed '. . . we are working up what amounts to a scientific ethics' on the basis of our knowledge of human needs.[10] Maslow claimed to have demonstrated 'the possibility that a *scientist* could study and describe normality in the sense of excellence, perfection, ideal health, the fulfilment of human possibilities'.[11] Similarly Erich Fromm claimed that it was for psychology to discover the principles of a 'universal

---

5 See G. Duncan, *Marx and Mill: Two views of social conflict and social harmony,* Cambridge University Press, Cambridge, 1973, pp.56-75.
6 *Economic and Philosophical Manuscripts of 1884,* tr. Martin Milligan, Foreign Languages Publishing House, Moscow, 1959, pp.116-17.
7 For the above see *Marx's Early Writings,* ed. T.B. Bottomore, McGraw-Hill, New York, 1964, pp.168, 174 and 155.
8 See G. Duncan, *op.cit.,* especially pp.56-7 and 61-3.
9 But compare Patricia Springborg's analysis, this collection, Chapter 9. Also see C.B. Macpherson, Chapter 2.
10 *Motivation and Personality,* Harper and Row, New York, 1954, p.366.
11 *ibid.,* pp.342 and 346. My emphasis.

ethics' tuned to the universal needs of man.[12] The sane society, he suggests, is that which 'corresponds to *the needs of man*, not necessarily to what he *feels to be his needs* — because even the most pathological aims can be felt subjectively as that which the person *wants* most — but to what his needs are objectively, as they can be ascertained by the study of man'.[13]

Both Maslow and Fromm argued that a knowledge of human needs can enable us to establish values which have objective validity.[14] It is not accidental that, of all contemporary theorists, the 'humanistic psychologists', primarily influenced by Maslow and Fromm, come close to considering themselves a school of social scientists who share a belief in the importance of relating their work to a conception of human needs. There is, in the forefront, *The Journal of Humanistic Psychology* founded by Maslow before his death and *The Journal of Transpersonal Psychology*.[15]

Herbert Marcuse makes the notion of needs central to his analysis of the defects of advanced industrial society.[16] Marcuse distinguishes between 'true' and 'false' or 'alien' needs. The former, he claims, begin with 'the vital ones — nourishment, clothing, lodging at the attainable level of culture', while 'False needs' are those 'which are superimposed upon the individual by particular social interests in his repression: the needs which perpetuate toil, aggressiveness, misery and injustice'.[17] Marcuse further holds that the existence of needs is a matter of truth and falsehood and that their satisfaction

> involves standards of *priority* — which refer to the optimal development of the individual, of all individuals, under the optimal utilisation of the material and intellectual resources available to man.[18]

These resources, he maintains, are calculable. The 'truth' or 'falsehood' of needs, Marcuse asserts, designate objective conditions 'to the extent to

12 See *Escape from Freedom*, Holt, Rinehart and Winston, New York, 1961 (first published 1941), and *Man for Himself*, Rinehart, New York, 1947.
13 'The Psychology of Normalcy', *Dissent*, Vol.1, 1954, p.43. My emphases.
14 See Maslow and Fromm's contribution to *New Knowledge in Human Values*, ed. Maslow, Harper and Row, New York, especially pp.123 and 151.
15 In psychiatry there are similar orientations developing especially among those influenced by Erikson, May and Winnicott, and the anti-psychiatry of R.D. Laing. The same applies to 'deschooling educationalists' such as Illich and Freire and 'valuing sociologists' like Gouldner and O'Neill. Further, in social philosophy there is the work associated with Lewis Feuer, Kurt Baier, Kai Nielsen and Nicholas Rescher. See entries in Selected Bibliography.
16 See especially, *One Dimensional Man*, Routledge and Kegan Paul, London, 1964, Chapter 1 and pp.241-5, and *Eros and Civilization*, Beacon Press, Boston, 1955, pp.96ff.
17 *One Dimensional Man*, pp.4-5.
18 *ibid.*, p.6. His emphasis.

which the universal satisfaction of vital needs and, beyond it, the progressive alleviation of toil and poverty are universally valid standards'.[19]

Marcuse holds that individuals are not necessarily the arbiters of what they truly need.

> In the last analysis, the question of what are true and false needs must be answered by the individuals themselves, but only in the last analysis; that is, if and when they are free to give their own answer. As long as they are kept incapable of being autonomous, as long as they are indoctrinated and manipulated ... their answer to this question cannot be taken as their own.[20]

This position, as with Christian Bay's, raises the charge of elitism and allows the possibility of an authoritarian 'forcing men to be free' or of 'indoctrinating a *real* consensus', for while men know what they want or desire they may not know what they need. Like Bay, Marcuse focuses on autonomy and connects 'need talk' to freedom theory. He, too, relates statements about human needs to a normative model of man and to the possibility of attaining a truly human existence. In this, it can be argued, Marcuse is following on from Marx.[21]

In recent empirically oriented studies the notion of needs has become an especially significant item in the explanation of political behaviour. James C. Davies has drawn on Maslow's hierarchy to argue, particularly in regard to Third World countries, that one cannot expect human beings to participate in political activity until basic needs have been satisfied.[22] In *The Human Basis of the Polity*, Jeanne Knutson, in many ways like Davies' *Human Nature and Politics*, connects political behaviour to a theory of human needs. What the book attempts is to subsume all existing work on the relation between personality and political behaviour under one master theory. Significantly, the theory selected is Maslow's. Knutson endeavours to show that, in the United States at least, there can be a significant correlation between levels of fulfilment of basic needs and the incidence (and type) of political participation.[23] Stanley Renshon's new work *Psychological Needs and Political Behavior*, which also employs Maslow's need hierarchy, centres on 'the need for personal control'. Renshon seeks to

---

19 *ibid.*
20 *ibid.*
21 But again compare Patricia Springborg's analysis, this collection, Chapter 9. Also see C.B. Macpherson, Chapter 2.
22 *Human Nature in Politics*, Wiley, New York, 1963. See Davies, this collection, Chapter 5, which centres on human needs and the stages of political development.
23 Jeanne N. Knutson, *The Human Basis of the Polity*, Aldine-Atherton, Chicago, 1972. See Knutson, this collection, Chapter 6.

demonstrate empirically that there exists in human beings a need for a sense of personal control which has a profound impact on political behaviour.[24] Renshon regards personal control as an aspect of Maslow's postulated need for security.[25] Several other theorists have also related Maslow's need-hierarchy to the field of political psychology.[26] However, with the conspicuous exception of Robert Lane's lengthy discussion of the application to politics of Maslow's need hierarchy, and of need theory in general[27], all of these authors, like Bay, Knutson, Renshon and Davies, use 'needs' and Maslow's model as though it were essentially trouble-free.[28]

Need theory (and especially Maslow's hierarchy) has not only been used to *explain* political behaviour but also to provide the basis for political morality, for judging polities and political institutions. C.B. Macpherson, for example, charges that liberal democracies choose 'to make the essence of man the striving for possessions, thereby making it impossible for many men to be truly human − to acquire and satisfy human needs'.[29] And in his sweeping indictment of American culture, Charles Reich observes that 'neither the work people do nor the goods and services that are produced are judged by human needs'.[30]

The Caucus for a New Political Science − a dissident group within the American Political Science Association with a marked antipathy toward formal and value-free political science − focuses on the satisfaction of human needs as opposed to wants and desires. The Caucus is a group of colleagues who share a general commitment to a critical political science. For many this implies commitment to general notions of human needs

---

24 Stanley A. Renshon, *Psychological Needs and Political Behavior*, Free Press, New York, 1974. Cf. Richard de Charms, *Personal Causation*, Academic Press, New York, 1968. Also compare R.K. White's claim for 'a need for competence' ('Motivation Reconsidered: The Concept of Competence', *Psychological Review*, Vol.66, 1959, pp.297-333) and the work of Milton Rokeach (especially *Beliefs, Attitudes, and Values*, Jossey-Bass, San Francisco, 1969, and *The Nature of Human Values*, Free Press, New York, 1975, pp.5-21).

25 Renshon, *op.cit.*, pp.1-11 and 43-58. See Renshon, this collection, Chapter 4.

26 See my essay, 'Abraham Maslow's Hierarchy of Needs: An Exposition and Evaluation', this collection, Chapter 3.

27 *Political Thinking and Consciousness: The Private Life of the Political Mind*, Markham Publishing House, Chicago, 1969, especially Chapter 2, 'Human Needs, the Energising Sources of Political Thought', pp.19-47.

28 See David Holbrook's essay on 'The Need for Meaning', this collection, Chapter 10. For criticisms of Maslow see Macpherson, Chapter 2, Fitzgerald, Chapter 3, M. Brewster Smith, Chapter 7, and Neil McInnes, Chapter 13.

29 *The Real World of Democracy*, Clarendon, Oxford, 1966, p.54. See Macpherson, this collection, Chapter 2.

30 *New Yorker Magazine*, October 1970, p.69. Also see Reich, *The Greening of America*, Random House, New York, 1970.

as a source of criteria for judging political institutions. At the forefront of the Caucus' position is the prescription of 'Taking "human needs" seriously'. The dominant suggestion is that political science research ought now to alter priorities; and 'the new priorities of a new political science' in effect means priorities in terms of serving human needs. Likewise the Caucus maintains that 'We need a different set of standards for judging regimes'. The fundamental standard, it is suggested, is to be found in the satisfaction of basic human needs.[31]

The notion of a politics in the service of human needs is best exemplified by the work of Christian Bay. According to Bay's normative position, '. . . the only acceptable *justification* of government, which also determines the limits to its legitimate authority, is its task of *serving human needs* — serving them better than would be done without any government. The only acceptable justification of a particular form of government, which again also determines the limits on its legitimate demands on the individual's obedience and loyalty, is that it serves to meet human needs better than other forms of government'.[32] To Bay, once we develop a conception of man and his needs, the natural consequence is to insist that a political system should have our allegiance only if and to the extent that it serves human needs in the order of their importance to individual survival and growth, and does so better than alternate systems. Thus he submits that 'To meet human needs is . . . the ultimate purpose of politics'.[33] Bay suggests that Maslow's need-hierarchy be tentatively adopted for the purpose of indicating what the priorities of politics should be, assuming that the most basic needs have prior claim on political guarantees.[34]

*   *   *

Human Needs and Politics is a collection of original articles by scholars from a number of disciplines and countries written independently of each other from a variety of viewpoints. These essays require neither brief nor abridgement. However two central themes manifest themselves throughout the collection.

1 Although many contemporary theorists emphasise universal human

---

31 For a summary of a typical Caucus election platform see Lewis Lipsitz, 'Vulture, Mantis and Seal: Proposals for Political Scientists', *Polity*, Vol.III, No.1, 1970, especially pp.16-21.

32 'Needs, Wants and Political Legitimacy', *Canadian Journal of Political Science*, Vol.1, September 1968, pp.241-2. My emphases.

33 *ibid.*, p.241.

34 *ibid.*, pp.242 and 248.

needs, some (like Bay) attempt to do so with reference to a distinction between needs and wants[35], while others (like Marcuse and Nielsen) wish to distinguish between 'true' and 'false', 'real' and 'artificial' needs.[36] To many of these theorists, basic human needs are characteristics of the human organism, and they are less subject to change than the social or even physical conditions under which men live. Wants are sometimes manifestations of real needs but we cannot always infer the existence of needs from wants. Wants are often artificially induced by outside manipulation, or they may be neurotically based desires whose satisfaction fails to satisfy needs, or both. Thus it is necessary for such an enterprise to distinguish conceptually between needing and wanting and to differentiate 'true' or 'real' from 'false' and 'artificial' needs. But the fundamental question remains. How can the genuine internally rooted needs of persons and groups be established empirically? Wants, desires and demands can be ascertained by way of asking people or directly observing their behaviour. But this is not so with needs. And even if one can determine criteria whereby 'needs' can be differentiated from 'wants', 'desires', and 'demands', and 'true' from 'false' needs, there is the problem of conflicting and competing 'needs' within or between individuals and groups which itself presupposes that one can distinguish between human and personal needs.

There are enormous difficulties involved in conceptualising needs. The very expression 'human needs' is problematic and emotionally loaded. And even if 'fundamental human needs' could be ascertained by empirical inquiry, there is the quite separate issue of whether such statements would validly enable us to prescribe what we ought to do, or what ought to be done, especially in politics.

2 There is much disagreement between theorists over placing primacy on the satisfaction of 'needs', rather than 'wants', 'desires', or 'demands'. Traditional liberal-democratic theory has always stressed the latter, while radicals aiming at the transformation of man and society have given priority to needs and interests. To oversimplify, the division between scholars over 'needs' is often itself a political division. In the main, radical theorists are 'pro-needs' arguing that the prime legitimating purpose of government is the satisfaction of human needs, while conservatives are uniformly 'anti-needs', stressing instead that the function of government ought to be to satisfy expressed wants and demands and arguing that an emphasis on needs

35 See Christian Bay, this collection, Chapter 1.
36 See Kai Nielsen, this collection, Chapter 8.

has profoundly authoritarian, even totalitarian, implications.[37] In fact positions on human needs closely correspond to Sir Karl Popper's famous Utopian Engineer/Piecemeal Engineer distinction — Plato's approach to politics representing the former, pragmatic reformism the latter.[38] The Radical/Reformist dichotomy is intimately connected with the distinction between optimists and pessimists which reflect fundamentally different views of the nature of man, of human possibilities, and of ways of seeing the world.[39] Radicals, ever hopeful of achieving ideal ends and of transforming human nature, tend to regard a commitment to needs as a blueprint for the establishment of the good society. Conversely, piecemeal reformists and conservatives, pessimistic about prospects for human perfectibility, perceive the doctrine of needs as being a prime contemporary example of moral and political evasion[40] which, moreover, is fraught with the enormous dangers associated with Platonic experts and the erosion of individual autonomy.

The revival of need theory in relation to politics is clearly of the utmost contemporary relevance. Now some of the protagonists in the needs controversy, and some uncommitted observers, can speak for themselves.

---

37 See Antony Flew, this collection, Chapter 12, and Neil McInnes, Chapter 13.

38 *The Open Society and its Enemies*, Vol.1, Routledge and Kegan Paul, London, 1966, fifth revised edition (first published 1945), Chapter 9, pp.157-68.

39 Compare and contrast Bay, Chapter 1; Macpherson, Chapter 2; Renshon, Chapter 4; Davies, Chapter 5; Brewster Smith, Chapter 7; Holbrook, Chapter 10; Fitzgerald, Chapter 11; Flew, Chapter 12; and McInnes, Chapter 13.

40 See K.R. Minogue, *The Liberal Mind*, Methuen, London, 1965, pp.103ff.

Human Needs and Political Education

Christian Bay

Human need priorities must be the ultimate basis for distinguishing legitimate from illegitimate public policies: do these policies serve the most pressing needs better than other, possibly available alternative policies? In principle the same kind of test must determine how legitimate, how deserving of loyalty and support, is a government, or a regime.

But this kind of test is not a simple one to carry out. In this paper the most I hope to accomplish is to raise some relevant issues, with particular reference to the relationship between 'radical humanism' (a shorthand term for the basic assumption just outlined) and political education. My approach will not be to attempt a description and analysis of human propensities in the spirit of scholarly detachment; nor do I aspire to a comprehensive analysis of practices and options that go under the name of 'education'. Instead, I shall be concerned with developing certain *conceptions* of human needs which in my view will be most likely to be optimally useful toward facilitating *liberating* political education.

One trouble with 'humanism' and 'humanistic' in a political context is that while these terms suggest lofty aims and reassuring values they offer scant guidance regarding strategies and constraints. For one thing, such terms beg the question about what is essentially, or ideally, *human*. What is the basic nature of human beings, beneath their various cultural and subcultural garbs? What are the most valuable among potential alternatives to currently prevailing human characteristics; alternatives that would seem not entirely out of the question in our historical context? We must, if we want to mobilise all human resources potentially available for combat against corporate domination, develop empirically viable conceptions of what human potentialities can in fact be mobilised, in our kind of society, at this time.

In this paper I shall focus on some of the accumulating empirical knowledge that can aid the efforts toward political liberation within the First World; that is, in North America, West Europe and other relatively rich countries, all of them committed to liberal economic systems and to constitutional, allegedly democratic political systems.

I Human needs and related concepts

Let us begin with a clearly empirical observation: that most people will seek to protect their lives, their health, and their freedom. I shall interpret such behaviour as evidence that most people *want* to live free and healthy lives.

'Want' will in this paper refer to any demonstrable predisposition to desire or prefer something, whether expressed in words or by nonverbal behaviour. 'Want' in this sense requires no philosophical assumptions and raises no necessary ontological issues. Wants are facts. Whether or not a particular want ought to be satisfied is an issue quite separate from noting that it exists, for a particular person at a given time. Depending on your philosophical perspective, any particular want, for a person P in a situation S, may be constructive or destructive, in the sense that the desired satisfaction may tend to benefit or harm the person, or other persons.

'Need' in our sense must at this stage remain basically a hypothetical construct. Needs cannot be measured, in the way of wants, by way of preference scales or the like. We cannot even prove, strictly speaking, that particular needs, or needs in general, as distinct from wants, actually exist. Yet, anyone who has ever dealt with young children must for practical purposes recognise that what children must have, or need, may or may not correspond to what they demonstrably want. Clinical psychologists and social workers in their work routines know that the same can be true of adults. Only liberal social scientists, plus the vast constituencies of citizens who have been taught that constitutional democracy should always prevail, appear to be blind to this particular part of common sense. Plato saw clearly that the might of numbers does not make right; in fact he went much further, charging that what appears most palatable to the non-philosophical majority is least likely to meet their needs; candy will routinely be preferred over foul-tasting medicine, not only among children. But Plato is dead, and is, moreover, dismissed as a totalitarian by influential liberal writers of our time.

In a liberal-democratic civilisation it remains a vexing problem, to be sure, how to achieve a serviceable definition of 'need' in relation to 'want', without being cast in the role of an authoritarian who announces by *fiat* the one and only acceptable conception of Man as he or she 'really' is, or ought to be, constituted.

Let us first consider Marcuse's rather reckless approach: he distinguishes *true needs* from *false needs**. What is seen or felt by most people to be their needs, beyond biological necessities, tends to be primarily determined by the predominant interests in a given society, according to Marcuse; it is an aspect of political domination.[1] Marcus Raskin goes further than Marcuse in the specificity of his diagnosis of political domination in the United States; Raskin considers the American people a colonised population, programmed by industrial interests, by the military and their patriotic supporters, by the educational apparatus, and by all the mass media; programmed to define personal needs and projects, even personal identities, in terms of service to duties and careers constructed *for* them, without their participation, even without their questioning.[2]

But this very insight into the powerlessness of man-the-consumer as well as man-the-producer (whose alienation Marx had analysed so profoundly in his Paris manuscripts), when we express it in terms of a critique of allegedly democratic institutions, and on that basis question our political obligation to those who rule over us on false pretences, is precisely what leaves us open to liberal charges of elitism, or even totalitarianism. If we follow Plato's critique of democratic rhetoric as self-serving careerism to take advantage of a gullible citizenry, must we not automatically opt for Plato's Republic, or even for Stalin's Politbureau?

I think Marcuse is right in arguing, in effect, that an ostensibly democratic order responding mainly to the more salient among the induced wants ('false needs') of corporate ideology-programmed individuals is hardly a democratic society in fact; and I share his assumption that a prerequisite for achieving democracy in any real sense is an end to the prevalence of externally imposed needs and self-perceptions. Unlike his more superficial,

---

* See Introduction, p.xi [Ed.]
1 Herbert Marcuse, *One-Dimensional Man*, Beacon Press, Boston, 1964, pp.4-9.
2 Marcus G. Raskin, *Being and Doing*, Random House, New York, 1971.

easier to please (regarding criteria for democracy) liberal critics[3] Marcuse insists on a democracy that is not a mere cover-up for domination.

But as long as we remain mired in a social order falsely advertised as democratic, our first practical objective must be to establish and to communicate in clear terms what is going on. In this situation I think of my needs/wants distinction as didactically and also for empirical research purposes more useful than Marcuse's true/false needs distinction. My approach has the advantage that there are no difficulties involved in establishing the incidence of wants. While each want may or may not be motivated by or correspond to a need, this uncertainty in no way handicaps continuing advances in the study of human behaviours relative to wants, including studies of values and attitudes and belief systems. Compared to how wants relate to values (in Rokeach's sense; see below, pp.14–16), we may never achieve equally firm findings on how to draw inferences about needs from the study of wants. But we are sure to come closer than we are now.

For purposes of political education Marcuse is surely right: the more people are enabled to take control over their own lives, and achieve independence from bureaucratic or corporate programming, the less the psychological necessity of distorting (falsifying) their perceptions of their own needs, if one uses Marcuse's terms; in my terms, the more closely will their wants *on the whole* come to correspond to their personal needs and to their objective requirements. In other words, the more he or she will become capable of achieving authentic growth toward wholeness, autonomy, and realistic insight into one's own needs and those of others. And to the extent that political education can be made to work, on the basis of a clearer understanding of the psychological processes of domination, we must expect more people not only to take charge of their own lives but to achieve a clearer insight into their own authentic, 'inner nature's' basic need priorities, so that their most salient wants may truly come to serve their needs.

It must be stressed that there is no firm empirical data-basis as yet for asserting that wants and needs will tend to converge, with reduced domination. This is in part because needs can at best be inferred, never directly observed, unlike wants. But is is also in part because the social sciences have become predominantly behaviour-oriented rather than concerned with authentic action. In fact, the want/need dichotomy can well be seen as related to the considerably broader behaviour/action dichotomy.

---

3 See especially Alasdair MacIntyre, *Marcuse*, Fontana, London, 1970; and David Spitz, 'Pure Tolerance', *Dissent*, Vol.13, 1966, pp.510-25.

The variety of human activities may be said to encompass, at one extreme, purely reflexive behaviours, like swerving to avoid a sudden collision; and, at the other extreme, acts that have been prepared for and planned for over long periods of time. By *behaviour* will be understood habitual or conventional activities, responses to situations and events, activities that do not require much thought, or initiative, or choice; by *action* will be understood activities that involve some conscious decision to choose one course rather than another, and to persist beyond the immediate situation. Action normally is in pursuit of given or chosen objectives, while behaviour tends to be fairly automatic and independent of purpose. Robert Pranger has coined a corresponding set of terms to refer to qualities of participation: participants are people who behave as they are expected to in situations that call for certain types of responses, like voting on election day; while participators contribute creatively, and therefore to some extent unpredictably.[4] They don't just behave; they act. Their activating wants are not mere reflections of external contingencies.

Naturally, those who dominate a given social order are best served, as C. Wright Mills has taught us so well[5], by social scientists who interpret and study human activities exclusively in terms of behaviour rather than action. Behavioural research has on the whole tended to reduce human beings to automatons; and the massive results that have accumulated over the years, with numerous hypotheses confirmed and re-confirmed with subsequent data, have demonstrated that this is, alas, a good part of the truth. What is less frequently conceded, however, is that conventional behavioural research itself may powerfully reinforce the tendencies toward automatic behaviour rather than self-fulfilling prophecy: how we are induced to perceive ourselves is how or what we tend to become — increasingly flexible, if not plastic, objects of political domination.

And of commercial domination, too. In his new book, *The Limits to Satisfaction,* William Leiss analyses the processes by which men and women as consumers are induced to behave in ways optimally useful to the dominating industrial and financial interests in our society. The very difficulty of pinning down empirically what our real needs are makes it possible for 'the system' (Leiss does not support any conspiracy theory) to program most people into assuming that every need requires a com-

---

4 See Robert J. Pranger, *The Eclipse of Citizenship*, Holt, Rinehart and Winston, New York, 1968.

5 See especially his *The Sociological Imagination*, Oxford University Press, New York, 1959.

modity for its satisfaction. Even a fundamental need like, for example, social acceptance is felt by increasing numbers of people to require a variety of de-odorizing sprays or perfumes; even different ones for every part of the body, it would seem to some. Commodities, meanwhile, are being manufactured for limited satisfaction only, so that always additional kinds of commodities, with allegedly new bundles of characteristics, will be in demand. The over-all result, apart from greasing the wheels of industry and business, turns out to be seriously disappointing in at least three ways: needs are not satisfied in any complete or lasting ways by the commodities purchased; human relationships tend to become impoverished when commodity fetishism gets in the way of spontaneous, simple togetherness; and our planet's non-renewable resources are fast being wasted in the affluent countries, with potentially catastrophic consequences for the Third World, and for our own descendants as well.[6]

Leiss, however, chooses to make no conceptual distinction between needs and wants; nor between true and false needs. In his view all manifest needs are historically determined, including those that are biologically determined as well. However obvious it may be that a given sense of need is artificially induced, say by a massive advertising campaign for a new product, and however clear it may be that the corresponding commodities are harmful to our environment, or even to the person himself or herself; if the sense of need is real in the person, then Leiss wants to think of the need as real.

A want/need distinction would to Leiss suggest that needs are objective and in principle quantitative, while wants are subjective and ephemeral, liable to ebb and flow in rhythm with satisfactions. He rejects all attempts in the literature to establish either lists of or hierarchies of needs, or to distinguish cultural from biological needs, and adopts this position: 'To understand the problem of satisfaction in the high-intensity market setting we require only one hypothesis about the structure of human needs. The hypothesis is quite a simple one, namely that every expression or state of needing has simultaneously a material and a symbolic or cultural correlate . . . in other words, the experience of needing is inherently a multidimensional activity.'[7]

Quite so. And I do not quarrel with Leiss's analysis to the effect that the structures of domination tend to dissolve our perceived need-structures into response-sets that serve the short-term requirements of corporate

---

6 William Leiss, *The Limits to Satisfaction*, University of Toronto Press, Toronto, 1976, p.64.
7 *ibid.*, p.64.

interests. I find his analysis profoundly convincing. But that is all the more reason, I think, to insist on the necessity of confronting this virtual abolition of man[8] with a new model of man which focuses on an inner nature, a basic need structure that must be recovered, at least conceptually, from the weight of external domination. What propensities and potentialities would be there, but for all these external pressures? This admittedly speculative conception of an elemental 'inner nature', not shaped by corporate-ideological programming, can be thought of as a conceptual beachhead for a humanist position in search of psychological grounding. To put it more carefully, we may at least think of man's biological requirements as constituting the most elemental needs, with which under given circumstances of alienation a person's wants may be poorly matched, to the detriment of the human organism, and therefore surely in some measure to the detriment of the psyche as well.

Abraham H. Maslow in a classic (1943) paper develops a skeletal need theory that even today, more than thirty years later, in my view provides the best beginning toward a perspective on basic needs that is independent of history and politics, and therefore can provide a partial basis toward a politically critical humanistic psychology. According to his initial formulation, there are at least five basic human needs which constitute a hierarchy, in the sense that those first on his list, the 'lower' needs, require some measure of satisfaction (or past experience of satisfaction) before the next, the 'higher' needs become motivationally activating. Firstly, the physical, biological needs; secondly, the safety needs; thirdly, the affection or belongingness needs; fourthly, the self-esteem needs; and fifthly, the self-actualisation or self-development needs.[9]

In later works Maslow has referred to the first four need categories as D-needs or Deficiency needs, while the fifth category is said to include a variety of B-needs, or Being needs, in which Maslow toward the end of his life took a particularly strong interest. This was followed up by a whole new line of literature referred to as 'humanistic psychology' — often much too idealist, much too far removed from conceptual rigour and from empirically specific implications to suit the purposes of the present paper.[10]

---

8 The phrase is borrowed from C.S. Lewis, *The Abolition of Man*, Collier, New York, 1962 (1947).

9 Maslow's 1943 paper is Chapter 5 in his *Motivation and Personality*, Harper and Row, New York, 1954.

10 Maslow's most central subsequent books, for my purposes, are *Toward a Psychology of Being*, Van Nostrand, Princeton, 1962; and his posthumous work, *The Farther Reaches of Human Nature*, Viking Press, New York, 1971.

II Objective requirements and the need for perceived freedom

Psycho-social inquiry to establish prerequisites for a liberating approach to political education must move beyond Maslow's largely speculative hierarchy of five basic needs. I shall recommend that we seek empirical enlightenment mainly in three directions, which I believe will add up to a coherent and fruitful perspective, in which Maslow's need theory will achieve added plausibility.

First, we must discuss some general objective constraints on human options; requirements for collective survival that neither the rulers nor the ruled can violate without potentially catastrophic consequences. Secondly, there is probably a kind of basic need, in addition to Maslow's five, that should be postulated: a need for perceived personal freedom, or sense of efficacy or power to influence the course of one's life. If I were to speculate on its relative prepotency, I would place it as need number four in a Maslow-type hierarchy of six basic needs: that is, probably between 'belongingness' ('love') and 'self-esteem' (see below, p.12). Thirdly, in the next section (III) I shall discuss some empirical work that bears on phenomena and concepts related to 'human needs': belief systems, values, attitudes, and wants; *and* to the probable need for perceived personal freedom. For this latter need, if we can call it that, seems closer to being empirically established than Maslow's five needs, as we shall see.

Let me begin here with the category of objective requirements. In our age of post-industrial technology it can be said with near-certainty that there are environmental constraints that effectively remove certain political options as, for example, ecologically disastrous. Thus, President Nixon a few years ago ordered the destruction of all U.S. bacteriological weapons and the dismantling of all war-related bacteriological research laboratories, once a part of the nation's military preparedness arsenal but now seen to involve unacceptable risks even as a wartime supply of options.

On the subjective side of the objective requirements I want to step carefully. It is possible to adopt an extremist individualist position and argue that the individual may well choose to have no concern at all about mankind's relatively distant future. Robert L. Heilbroner has dramatised this ultimate caricature of liberal contract-oriented wisdom in the question 'What Has Posterity Ever Done for Me?'[11] The person is real who asks the following kind of question: 'Suppose that, as a result of using up all the world's resources human life did come to an end. So what? What is

---

11 See the Postscript to Heilbroner's *An Inquiry Into the Human Prospect*, Norton, New York, 1975 (first published in 1974, without the Postscript).

so desirable about an indefinite continuation of the human species, religious convictions apart ... Do I care about what happens a thousand years from now?'[12]

This outlook strikes me as insane, but understandable as the *reductio ad absurdum* of liberal individualism. Marx's charge that exploitation under capitalism tends to alienate Man from his species-being could hardly be more strikingly confirmed: 'estranged labour estranges the *species* from man. It turns for him the *life of the species* into a means of individual life. First it estranges the life of the species and individual life, and secondly it makes individual life in its abstract form the purpose of the life of the species, likewise in its abstract and estranged form'.[13] In psychological terms it would seem clear that most reflective people are *not* indifferent to the issue of whether or not mankind is doomed. *Hope* for a future, even a better future, for humankind is a demonstrable want, I believe; and possibly as well a requirement for optimal health and freedom, in other words a need, too.

Yet I shall stick to the language of *requirement* for collective survival; the opprobrium given to the antonym of survival for all peoples, genocide (more strictly, the word for deliberately *causing* non-survival for a category of persons), suggests that this basic aim or constraint on legitimate political behaviour and action is nearly universally shared, at least in principle. But it is necessary to ask, survival for precisely what? A distinction must be made between survival for mankind, or for a given nation or ethnic group, on the one hand; and on the other hand survival for a given cultural or economic system. B.F. Skinner, who is otherwise so exacting in much of his reasoning, is surprisingly loose in this crucial issue area.

Having first made the valid point that we do not need to explain the origin of a cultural practice in order to account for its contribution to the survival of that culture, Skinner proceeds to make the following remarkable pronouncement: 'Survival is the only value according to which a culture is eventually to be judged, and any practice that furthers survival has survival value by definition'. And responding to his own rhetorical question, why should anyone care about the survival of a particular economic system, Skinner states: 'There is no good reason why you should be concerned, but if your culture has not convinced you that there is, so

---

12 Wilfred Beckerman, 'The Myth of Finite Resources', *Business and Society Review*, No.12, Winter 1974-75, pp.21-5, at p.22.
13 From the 'Economic and Philosophical Manuscripts of 1844: Selections', in *The Marx-Engels Reader*, ed. Robert C. Tucker, Norton, New York, 1972, pp.52-103, at p.61.

much worse for your culture'.[14]

In contrast to Skinner's position, I believe that our socio-cultural and economic system, with its enormously wasteful and alienating exploitation of natural and human resources, ought not to survive; that indeed it will soon have to be scrapped and replaced even to meet essential objective ecological requirements for the survival of our peoples and our human species. To assert baldly that there are no values beyond our present culture's or social system's survival, as Skinner does, may suit the thesis that freedom, dignity, and humanism are epiphenomena; but so much the worse for that thesis. Surely a scientist who sees survival as the only value ought to be very precise about *what* is to survive: particular cultural traditions; or a mankind capable of creating new and better adaptations to changing goal priorities and to a changing natural and technological environment. In this paper I assume, quite dogmatically, that the second choice must be made, and needs no philosophical justification.

Yet Skinner surely is right in his contention that vast changes in human behaviour are required, even to preserve our familiar social order of rich and poor, of masters and servants, of cultural designers and objects. Even more immense changes in behaviour, and action, are required if we ever want to achieve a liberated humankind, a social order as envisioned in the *Manifesto*, 'in which the free development of each is the condition for the free development of all'.[15] I go along with Skinner also in his practical contention that 'What we need is a technology of behavior'[16]; but only, mind you, in two areas of application.

Firstly, there is the area of behaviours directly bearing on the protection or destruction of our natural environment. While democracy and individual freedom in general indicate important values to aspire to, they must yield in contexts in which either majorities of voters or individual citizens now go about destroying or wasting living and non-living nature at will, without any necessity for human sustenance and survival. To the extent that Skinner and those who are reinforced by his teachings are able to develop effective aversive conditioning against such behaviours or, as Skinner would prefer, effective reinforcing conditioning toward more careful and constructive behaviours, I would like to see our schools and mass media cooperating in seeking to induce all of us to adopt better habits in this context.

14 B.F. Skinner, *Beyond Freedom and Dignity*, Bantam/Vintage, New York, 1972 (1971), pp.130 and 131.
15 See Tucker, *op.cit.*, p.353.
16 Skinner, *op.cit.*, p.3 and *passim*.

Secondly, with respect to behaviours affecting our natural as well as our social and political environment, I would like to see Skinner and his kind of psychologist go to work on how to make corporations behave, if or when political governments have the actual power and motivation to make the public interest prevail. M. Brewster Smith puts this point well: 'To control the behavior of corporations, those pseudopersons in the eyes of the law, Skinnerian principles may be especially appropriate. Corporations seem typically to be pigeon brained. Suitable legislation could alter the reinforcement contingencies of costs and profits to shape the behavior of modern industry toward acceptable environmental practices'.[17] And, I would add, toward acceptable economic, social, and political practices; beginning, of course, with a requirement that all books and business correspondence be made available for public scrutiny.

Outside these two applications I would, however, resist Skinner's call for new uses of behaviour technology. There is in my view far too much control of behaviour now; relatively few, privileged people already have enormous powers and influence over the lives of others. That is the basis for talking about political domination as the all-pervasive historical fact to contend with (above, p.2). The struggle for liberation must in large part be a struggle *against* the many manipulative uses of Skinnerian and other kinds of behavioural knowledge. I ask again the same question that I have tried to tackle before: 'How can increased insights into human behaviour be employed in the service of sheltering the growth of individuality and freedom in the modern society?'[18]

I come now to the problem of personal freedom. Once again I want to hedge on whether or not personal freedom should be construed as a human need, but I have postulated that the values of freedom and of health are inextricably tied in with the ultimate value of human life itself (cf. above, p.2).

Perceived personal freedom, on the other hand, I shall in this paper postulate as a need, to be located within a Maslow-type basic need hierarchy. 'Perceived personal freedom' will refer to a broad range of need-attributes, all having to do with the person's sense of being a chooser and a maker of decisions that do have some probable influence and benefit affecting at least one's own life. A whole range of specific kinds of wants may be motivated by this need, including the desire for freedom of choice, for

---

17 M. Brewster Smith, *Humanizing Social Psychology*, Jossey-Bass, San Francisco, 1974, p.203.
18 See my *Structure of Freedom*, Stanford University Press, Stanford, 1970 (1958) p.3.

power to affect one's social and natural environment, and for competence in handling one's affairs and directing one's life.

Richard de Charms goes further than I do in this paper: *'Man's primary motivational propensity is to be effective in producing changes in his environment'.*[19] This certainly does not appear to be true of all men, let alone of all women. Surely we all know persons who seem so afraid of life's vicissitudes that what they most want is a sense of security, if not a place in which to hide, rather than a sense of personal freedom or power. In fact, perceived freedom in this sense seems to fit particularly well into Maslow's sequential scheme, in which 'the basic human needs are organized into a hierarchy of relative prepotency'.[20]

Though the precise delimitation of each need concept at this stage must remain speculative and somewhat arbitrary, and the exact ordering as well, beyond the clear prepotency of physiological and safety needs, it would seem reasonable to place the need for a sense of freedom after the need for love or belongingness, the first need-attribute of the *human* animal; but before the need for self-esteem. Self-esteem would seem to require both being loved (or at least accepted as a valued person) and having a sense of being more than a pawn, more than an object, capable of acting rather than merely behaving, going along, doing as one is told.

This assumed need for perceived freedom must be taken to include a sense of personal power and of competence[21] as well. Unless one can believe, whether correctly or wrongly in fact, that one's acts can have some appreciable impact, and most often in the directions desired, the freedom to choose and act would be meaningless, even a fraud. For example, it may well be argued that the freedom to vote is nearly meaningless for the underprivileged, if in a given society all successful politicians must placate the corporate interests at the expense of the poor. Moreover, the same freedom may

---

19 Richard de Charms, *Personal Causation*, Academic Press, New York, 1968, p.269. His italics.

20 Maslow, *op.cit.*, p.83. 'It is quite true that man lives by bread alone — when there is no bread. But what happens when there *is* plenty of bread and when his belly is chronically filled? At once other (and higher) needs emerge and these, rather than physiological hungers, dominate the organism.' *ibid.*, same page.

21 In an influential paper Robert K. White surveys much research on the development of behaviours in animals and humans, focusing on the processes of learning to interact effectively with the individual animal's or person's environment, and on that basis advances the proposition that *competence* may be a universal motivational tendency in human beings. 'Man's huge cortical association areas might have been a suicidal piece of specialization if they had come without a steady, persistent inclination toward interacting with the environment.' See his 'Motivation Reconsidered: The Concept of Competence', *Psychological Review*, Vol.66, 1959, pp.297-333; see particularly pp.305, 329, and 330.

be rendered virtually meaningless by the weight of false or misleading information, if the net result is to render most people incapable of voting in their own best interest. If the fraud could work smoothly enough, the psychological need could still be met, for a sense of freedom unaccompanied by concern with power and competence. But over the long run contradictions in any fraudulent political system (one in which pretended priorities and real priorities are wide apart) are likely to undermine this kind of need-satisfaction, with the result that 'freedom' soon becomes a manipulative slogan[22] for festive occasions, while daily lives of deprivation and political impotence contradict, whether implicitly or explicitly, the claims of freedom.

Even if neither much of a sense of power nor of competence has been achieved by most voters in the modern liberal so-called democracies (let alone in the so-called socialist states), as I suspect is the case, the formal right to vote may still serve important belongingness needs and self-esteem needs. It should be defended and preserved, also because formal democratic institutions, however empty of substance today, may become more real some time in the future. And they may perhaps provide *some* constraints on corporate greed and exploitation, even today.

Such observations underscore the necessity of distinguishing perceived personal power from perceived political power. There is no *need* for the latter, persumably; some of us may *want* both; but what I assume that every human being will need, in Maslow's sense, once he or she has had the more basic biological, security, and belongingness needs met, is a sense of being, in de Charms' words, an *origin* rather than a *pawn*[23]: capable of influencing events in one's own life and immediate social relationships, but not necessarily aspiring to be an originator of public power.

III Some need-relevant research approaches

What follows are sketches of a few research approaches that appear particularly promising and relevant; promising as sources of former knowledge about needs, and relevant to developing an emancipatory political education.

It should be said at the outset that the bulk of political behaviour research has dealt directly with want priorities and, I assume, most of these far-ranging data have implications for our tenuous beginnings toward a knowledge of need priorities as well, beginnings which must await more suitable

---

22 See my ' "Freedom" as a Tool of Oppression', in *The Case for Participatory Democracy*, eds. C. George Benello and Dimitrios Roussopoulos, Grossman, New York, 1971, pp.250-69.

23 *op.cit.*, pp.273-4 and *passim*.

concepts and theorising, and more imaginative research approaches. Simple counting or scale-measurement studies of opinions, attitudes, beliefs, and voting behaviour will not help much toward understanding basic needs. Against conventional behavioural research it may be said that it has served the illusion of democracy well.

And by reducing all the political activity within its compass to reactive behaviour, to the exclusion of authentic action, it has on at least two additional levels served political domination: in the obvious sense of measuring degrees of dissatisfaction, from one issue context and situation to another, so as to help determine the efficacy and limits of manipulation; and in the subtler, more pervasive sense of stereotyping human political behaviour as essentially passive and reactive, and above all predictable, thus inducing us to discount, or not even to register, authentic action and the possibilities of escaping from the usual patterns of socialised or programmed behaviour.[24]

At the same time, however, the accumulating behavioural research literature is an invaluable source of necessary, though of course not sufficient, varieties of data for a further understanding of how our system of domination works. Wants, attitudes, and other manifest behaviours reflect, in varying proportions, both the influence of the political and commercial mechanisms of manipulation *and* the more elusive, underlying need predispositions. There are no shortcuts toward disentangling this complex web. I shall consider only a few of the most imaginative approaches.

I begin with the work of Milton Rokeach, who is himself indebted to the authors of *The Authoritarian Personality* and ultimately, of course, to Freud. Rokeach speaks of belief and disbelief *systems*, composed of central, intermediate, and peripheral regions of beliefs (and disbeliefs).[25] '*A belief system* represents the total universe of a person's beliefs about the physical world, the social world, and the self . . . An attitude is one type of sub-system of beliefs, organized around an object or situation which is, in turn, embedded within a larger sub-system, and so on.'[26]

The most important part of Rokeach's work for present purposes is his recent and current work on values and value systems: '*A value* is an enduring belief that a specific mode of conduct or end-state of existence is personally or socially preferable to an opposite or converse mode of conduct or end-state of existence. A *value system* is an enduring organization of

---

24 See Charles Hampden-Turner, *Radical Man*, Schenkman, Cambridge, Massachusetts, 1970, Chapter 1, for a forceful and eloquent treatment of these issues.
25 Milton Rokeach, *The Open and Closed Mind*, Basic Books, New York, 1960.
26 See Rokeach, *Beliefs, Attitudes, and Values*, Jossey-Bass, San Francisco, 1969, p.123.

beliefs concerning preferable modes of conduct or end-states of existence along a continuum of relative importance.'[27]

What must be stressed here is that value systems are presumably *motivated* in large part by something less peripheral, within the person's total belief systems, than specific attitudes or beliefs or wants, which are all directed to and reacting to external stimuli and objects. Value systems are probably operating much more directly in the service of basic needs, because they are relatively sheltered from ideological and situational pressures, compared to attitudes and beliefs. Rokeach assumes this to be the case: 'If the immediate functions of values and value systems are to guide human action in daily situations, their more long-range functions are to give expression to basic human needs'.[28]

Rokeach considers Maslow's conception of lower-order and higher-order needs useful but deplores his tendency to use 'value' as nearly synonymous with 'need'. For in our society (and probably in every other society) there are social sanctions against freely acknowledging some of our presumed needs, notably sexual needs; 'but values need never be denied. Thus, when a person tells us about his values he is surely also telling us about his needs. But we must be cautious in how we infer needs from values because values are not isomorphic with needs. Needs are cognitively transformed into values so that a person can end up smelling himself, and being smelled by others, like a rose'.[29]

Thus, Rokeach's approach suggests that the study of values offers good prospects for ascertaining empirically relatively authentic, 'inner' aspects of the human personality, for at least two reasons: value statements, being more general and abstract than belief and attitude statements, are less likely to encounter conventional ideological sanctions (while they are not, of course, immune to ideological influence, most ideological pressures concern opinions and other overt behaviours); also, our views about our own value priorities are less likely to be distorted by shame or repression, compared to our views about our own basic need priorities. For example, it would appear easier for most people to admit to attaching a high value to 'mature love' than to admit to a preponderant need for conjugal or sexual love.

I must refer to Rokeach's cited works for a description of his 'Value Survey' methods and of his specific empirical findings, which in my judgement quite convincingly tend to support his basic theory about how value

---

27 See Rokeach, *The Nature of Human Values*, Free Press, New York, 1973, p.5.
28 *ibid.*, p.14.
29 *ibid.*, p.20.

priorities, and especially experimentally induced changes in value priorities, can reveal important and probably valid insights into the underlying and relatively enduring need priorities. Perhaps he is too quick, however, to assume that our value systems tend to serve one basic need only: to maintain and enhance our self-esteem.[30] As Rokeach's theory and data neither confirm nor disconfirm Maslow's specific need hierarchy, it would seem most plausible to expect our needs for sustenance, safety, and love, as well as self-esteem, to influence our value priorities, although to be sure in the context of political domination along with the ideology of 'free enterprise', our self-esteem needs may be particularly vulnerable and therefore salient. In any event, Rokeach's most important achievement for present purposes is to have demonstrated empirically that a need for self-esteem, apparently universal among the white Michigan State students studied, as a basic, enduring motivational principle appears to offer the best available explanation for certain statistically striking changes in behaviour relative to the Negro-white racial conflict in America; behaviour changes that endured for some time, although they were induced by amazingly gentle and short-duration external stimuli.[31]

More specifically, Rokeach associates self-esteem with a need to see one-self as competent and moral; at least within his sample of students, but probably among Americans more generally. In a sense he puts to the test a basic assumption in Gunnar Myrdal's classic study, *An American Dilemma*[32]: that there is a deep moral (or moralistic?) strain in most Americans, in favour of human brotherhood and fair play; a basic tendency that survives even in an alienating social order, under the daily onslaught of pressures to behave as if in a jungle, fighting for individual or corporate advantage with fair means and foul, taking advantage of handicaps affecting others. The relative weight of perceived competence and morality in the self-esteem needs of individuals Rokeach does not discuss; perhaps one may speculate here that morality tends to loom larger when a person's most basic sustenance and security needs have been well satisfied, while competence is felt to be most important when those needs have been only precariously met, and society seems mainly like a jungle.

Drawing on Rokeach's theory of belief systems and on Maslow's hierarchy of basic needs, Stanley A. Renshon has done a study of the origins

30 *ibid.*, especially p.216, where Rokeach approvingly cites William McDougall's naming of the sentiment of self-regard as 'the master of all sentiments' (in his *An Introduction to Social Psychology*, John W. Luce, Boston, 1926).
31 *ibid.*, Chapters 9 and 11.
32 Published by Harper and Row, New York, 1944.

of a sense of personal control and of its impact on political behaviour.[33] The very looseness of proposed concepts in this field of study should suggest caution regarding empirical claims: would a need for personal control (Renshon) be identical with a need for competence (White, Rokeach); and/or with a need for perceived freedom, proposed above? I think choices of terms and concepts must remain somewhat arbitrary at this stage; it is premature to speak of *any* empirically established needs beyond sustenance and safety. All that is claimed here is that a Maslow-type need theory can help us to make politically useful sense of research on need-relevant observable behaviours.

For my purposes, the important part of Renshon's study is his reported data on how a sense of personal control originates in the family situation, and its later impact on political participation. Some 300 students were interviewed and questionnaires were filled in by one or both of their parents. Data were sought on family structures as well as emotional quality of past parent-child relationships; and Renshon came up with findings confirming hypotheses about norm enforcement consistency, parent-child sharing in family decision-making, and emotional trust in parents being factors tending to enhance a sense of personal control. But the most important single influence, by a wide margin, was the extent to which the parents themselves had achieved a sense of personal control. Renshon found that basic belief systems about prospects for personal control and about whether other people as a rule should be trusted are much more likely to be 'inherited' than any specific political beliefs and attitudes.

Renshon's findings on the inheritance of a sense of personal control achieve added significance in the light of other empirical data. Melvin Kohn has studied social class in relation to parental orientations to child-raising in Italy as well as the United States, comparatively. In both countries it was found that lower-class parents tended to impress on their children a basic belief that one can have little control over the circumstances affecting one's life, and that the best way to get along in life is to learn to do as one is told and to keep a distance from nonconformists; while parents with higher class or socio-economic status would tend to make *their* children expect a good measure of personal control over their lives.[34]

How this dichotomy between highs and lows on a sense of personal control can affect a political behaviour is well brought out by Herbert

33 S. A. Renshon, *Psychological Needs and Political Behavior*, Free Press, New York, 1974.
34 Melvin L. Kohn, *Class and Conformity: A Study in Values*, Dorsey, Homewood, Illinois, 1969.

Kelman and Lee Lawrence in an American study of reactions to the trial and conviction of Lt. William Calley, convicted in 1971 for the My Lai massacre, and the only American ever to be found guilty of war crimes in Vietnam. In a large national sample it was found that hawks and doves on the Vietnam war were fairly evenly split in their reactions to Calley's conviction; in fact the *only* factors found significantly related to these reactions were the subjects' levels of education and socio-economic status.[35] It would seem, as the authors conclude, that among people who consider themselves as pawns in the social order, with very limited influence over the course of their own lives, there was a tendency to empathise with Calley as the perceived fall-guy, the patsy, the little fellow who had tried to follow his orders as he understood them. Respondents from more privileged strata, with higher levels of perceived freedom (or competence, or personal control), apparently felt that Calley could have and should have refused to become a butcher of Vietnamese women and children.

Psychologists rather than other social scientists have been in the forefront in the empirical study of prerequisites of resistance to abuses of power. From Asch to Crutchfield to Milgram, it has been shown how vulnerable most people are to blatant as well as ideological distortions of reality as well as of ordinary claims of morality.[36] Most recently, the fast expanding volume of work on Attribution behaviour suggests that our belief systems, including our self-perceptions, to a disturbingly high degree are influenced by our own behaviours, which after all are often merely reactive to outside stimuli.[37] The impact of this literature is to underscore the ubiquity of social and political domination and how easily we tend to let ourselves be dominated, not only by a tendency to behave according to manipulative cues but then subsequently having our self-perceptions subtly influenced by our induced changes of behaviour.

---

35 Herbert C. Kelman and Lee H. Lawrence, 'Assignment of Responsibility in the Case of Lt. Calley: Preliminary Report on a National Survey', *Journal of Social Issues*, Vol.28, 1972, pp.177-212.

36 Solomon E. Asch, *Social Psychology*, Prentice-Hall, New York, 1952; Richard S. Crutchfield, 'Conformity and Character', *American Psychologist*, Vol.10, 1955, pp.191-8; Stanley Milgram, *Obedience to Authority: An Experimental View*, Harper and Row, New York, 1974.

37 Fritz Heider, *The Psychology of Interpersonal Relations*, John Wiley, New York, 1958; Julian B. Rotter, 'Generalized Expectancies for Internal Versus External Control of Reinforcement', *Psychological Monographs*, Vol.80, 1966, pp.1-28; Harold H. Kelley, 'Attribution: Theory in Social Psychology 2, *Nebraska Symposium on Motivation*, Vol.15, 1967; *Attribution: Perceiving the Causes of Behavior*, eds. Edward E. Jones *et. al.*, General Learning Press, Morristown, New Jersey, 1972; Kelly G. Shaver, *An Introduction to Attribution Processes*, Winthrop, Cambridge, Massachusetts, 1975.

This increases, of course, the size of the challenge of developing a viable approach to political education as a struggle for individual and collective liberation. One particular finding that seems to emerge quite clearly, in this literature, is that it is crucial to defend and maintain the *perception* of being free, however dubious the reality of freedom may appear to be, either ontologically or for reasons of political domination in our social order. In at least two recent papers of considerable importance, while freedom as a reality, in the sense of personal causation, is questioned, a wealth of reseach data surveyed suggests the vital importance of *at least* an illusion of freedom.

Ivan D. Steiner takes the more moderate position on the ontological issue: 'Perhaps perceived freedom is an illusion, but it is at least an illusion with antecedents and consequences that deserve attention'; and he concludes: 'Research reviewed in this chapter suggests that individuals' evaluations of their own or other people's freedoms influence the attribution process, the use of ingratiation techniques, the exercise of power, compliance with the demands of associates, and effective reactions to harmful and helpful deeds ... Moreover, there is tangential evidence that perceived freedom is one of many factors determining whether people will mount a riot, commit suicide, or apathetically resign themselves to their fate'.[38]

Herbert M. Lefcourt takes the more radical ontological position, that 'freedom and control are both illusions, inventions of man to make sense of his experience', but emphasises that they have consequences, which must be studied. Lefcourt's survey of research indicates to him, without much doubt, that in general 'the sense of control, the illusion that one can exercise personal choice, has a definite and a positive role in sustaining life'. Indeed, he concludes, the alleged illusion 'may be the bedrock on which life flourishes'.[39]

IV Political education toward liberation
If an empirical case can be made for an 'illusion of freedom' being the 'bedrock on which life flourishes', in animals as well as humans, then I think it may also be said that the life of corporate and bureaucratic organisations will flourish on the basis of an opposite 'illusion': that there is no individual freedom possible. Now, wanting to sidestep the ontological problem of the reality of freedom, I will rephrase this last statement: a

38 Ivan D. Steiner, 'Perceived Freedom', *Advances in Experimental Social Psychology*, Vol.5, 1971, pp.187-248, at pp.188 and 240.
39 Herbert M. Lefcourt, 'The Function of the Illusions of Control and Freedom', *American Psychologist*, Vol.28, 1973, pp.417-26.

sense of individual powerlessness as an inescapable fact of life works like a self-fulfilling prophecy; it produces docile, reactive behaviour, it forestalls critical self-assertion and it rules out political action.

Conceivably Lefcourt (and Skinner) may be right in thinking of personal freedom as an invention of man 'to make sense of his experience'; we cannot be sure. But we do know that people in history have acted forcefully at times, even have staged massive revolutions, under the evident impression that choice and action were possible. This kind of an impression, as Lefcourt (in apparent disagreement with Skinner) affirms, needs to be sustained and imported to more people, if historical domination is to be resisted with some prospect of success. My basic value assumption remains, of course, that we must learn how to become more effective in demanding, establishing, and enforcing a steady governmental commitment to serve human life at the expense of corporate and bureaucratic interests, instead of the other way round. More precisely, the aim must be to bring about public policies that serve, first, to safeguard the environmental requirements for humankind's collective survival, in health and freedom to the fullest possible extent; and, secondly, policies that serve to meet human needs according to priorities among needs, not priorities dictated either by vested interests or by allegedly democratic majorities.

What means can be made available? In the First World, in which large parts of the populations have come to enjoy what Marcuse has called 'repressive affluence'[40], prospects for revolutionary change by way of large-scale violent uprisings have become virtually nil, unless preceded by devastating wars or eco-catastrophes. A further postulate in this paper is that revolutionary changes must be sought by means that do not, whatever their merits otherwise, or in other places or times, contribute to the likelihood of world wars, thermonuclear confrontations in any part of the world, or eco-catastrophes.

In my view this leaves political education as virtually the only viable avenue toward a liberating revolutionary development in the First World; while in the Third World, as Cuba and as Portugal's formerly colonialised peoples in Africa have shown, Marxist-inspired political and military organising may well be a viable alternative. In fact, it may in much of the Third World be the *only* alternative, which is paradoxical in view of what I shall argue in a moment: that the most important innovative work in the recent theory and practice of political education has emerged in work with

---

40 See his 'Liberation from the Affluent Society', in *The Dialectics of Liberation*, ed. David Cooper, Penguin, Harmondsworth, 1968, pp.175-92.

impoverished peasant populations in Brasil and elsewhere in South America. But on that continent few practical-political results have been achieved so far, from the work and sacrifice of Paulo Freire and his followers; for brutal police states have been established in most of South America, as elsewhere in the Third World. While high-prestige, internationally visible university populations sometimes are left relatively free to engage in political dissent, any serious efforts to liberate the minds of the masses, even far short of inciting to violent defiance, in most of the Third World provokes severe repression, including torture and executions.

In the First World, on the other hand, where, in virtually every state the right to political dissent is secure within wide limits, because the right to free speech serves as a crucial basis in the claims to legitimacy advanced by all these regimes; there are now wide open opportunities for accomplishing much that Freire and his collaborators tried but failed to achieve in South America.

Very briefly, I shall here try to paraphrase and draw on a few crucial aspects of Paulo Freire's insight and experience, rather than attempt any representative exposition of his thought.[41] In what follows I freely include inferences that are mine and not necessarily his.

The most immediate objective of a liberating political education must be to escape from and to learn to counter with one's own words the language of the oppressors. The poverty culture is mute; domination depends on a language that reflects the culture of domination, one that emphasises words like duty and obligation and God's will and meekness and the necessity of this world being a vale of tears. Truth, for Freire, is not a matter of facts but a matter of praxis. Truth is not a domain for accumulating, storing and retrieving factual knowledge, a domain with special prerogatives for scientists and experts. Truth is relative to the person, the class, and the historical situation; truth is the type of insight that can set us free, free to develop our own political consciousness: 'to speak a true word is to transform the world'.[42]

The first truth about the political world is that it is oppressive, for it severely restricts the satisfaction of basic human needs. One has to be an academic, I suspect, in order to question the substance of Maslow's premise that the most basic human needs are for physical sustenance and safety (though some may prefer another terminology). Perhaps a need for a sense

41 Paulo Freire, *Pedagogy of the Oppressed*, Seabury Press, New York, 1970; also see his *Education for Critical Consciousness*, Seabury Press, New York, 1973.
42 *Pedagogy of the Oppressed*, op.cit., p.75.

of belongingness and solidarity is not far behind. But Freire assumes this to be an empirical question, which will be resolved in practice, provided a genuine dialogue takes place: and *that*, in turn, requires that the educator comes as an equal and will be there to learn as much as to teach. And among the Third World's poor he has worked with, Freire has determined that the system of poverty, once the poor have found their voice in dialogue, is named as oppressive, on account of the physical deprivation caused by the system, but also on account of its violation of the person's right to dignity, to be somebody, to be entitled to have a mind of one's own [43]

Political education must be problem-posing: it must begin with identifying and then asking questions about the realities of domination. And these realities are different in the First World, compared to the Third. For one thing, people who have escaped physical deprivation, and who have even achieved a measure of affluence in their access to commodities, may at first balk at seeing themselves as in any way oppressed. Liberal practices of political socialisation have worked wonders in much of the 'Free World'; as Rousseau wrote, there is 'no subjection so complete as that which preserves the forms of freedom; it is thus that the will itself is taken captive'. [44]

This common orientation in our kind of society magnifies but in no way defeats the challenge of developing an effective, Freire-inspired approach to political education in the First World. As with Christianity, according to Shaw, I think the main trouble with an emancipatory political education, as distinct from socialisation or conformity-training, is that it has never been tried, not on any significant scale in the First World.

Unlike Christianity, the radical political education of the dialogue cannot readily be packaged and preached from high pulpits down to ordinary folk, along with admonitions to absorb and not to question. Unlike revolutionary conspiracies, radical political education is in most of the First World unlikely to lead to bloodshed. And unlike ordinary schooling, as well as professional training for regular jobs, radical political education is very low-cost, and can be delivered free of charge even to advanced students. Finally, the dialogue of political education can be practised on as wide a scale as the influence of radical educators can achieve, inside and outside the conventional school systems; for a liberal regime can erect few barriers,

---

43 John R. Seeley, 'Progress from Poverty', in his *The Americanization of the Unconscious*, J.B. Lippincott, Philadelphia, 1967. Also see my 'The Triple Insult of Poverty', *Sociological Inquiry*, Vol. 46, Nos. 3-4, 1976.

44 Jean Jacques Rousseau, *Emile*, Everyman's Library, Dutton, New York, 1911 (first published 1762), p.84.

if any, against mutualist, informal teaching and learning processes, however revolutionary their messages and potential effects may be. While conventional teaching has become professionalised, no academic degrees are required or even relevant to the practice of the political education of the dialogue. All it requires is a persistent commitment to the service of human needs, a belief in the possibility of personal freedom, and a craving to learn as well as teach.

Our formal school systems, unless or until enough individual teachers are motivated to practice political education in the spirit of the dialogue, will in every country continue to serve as instrumentalities of domination. In the First, Second, and Third Worlds alike, schools serve to siphon off the intelligent and politically docile for future careers of influence and privilege, and strive to convince the rest of their students that their minds are less than capable of creative achievement; implicitly or explicitly, they try to induce these lesser breeds of youngsters to limit their aspirations to menial occupations, to deaden their cultural and political imagination, and to imbue them with a sense of powerlessness.[45] Students at all levels are trained, equipped with appropriate skills, molded to become ideal future employees, competent servants of the established corporate and bureaucratic interests — intelligent, adaptable, and politically accepting.

Even at the university level, formal educational institutions are everywhere authoritarian in their structures, with increasingly professionalised staffs who see it as their prerogative to determine the curricula, and to lay down the questions to be asked and the answers to be expected, with pupils and students to be taught respect and appreciation for the words of established wisdom. The young are everywhere expected to behave in response to the requirements of the system, not to act as directed by their own needs and need-directed wants.

In the 1960s there were to be sure some encouraging signs that many students were coming politically alive in a number of countries, from the United States in the West to Czechoslovakia in the East. It seemed then that the university system, and even the occasional high school, could be subverted from within, by students and teachers who believed in political equality and could practice the democracy of the dialogue. But after Vietnam and Watergate, after the fall of de Gaulle and of Dubcek, all is now

---

45 Ivan Illich, *Celebration of Awareness,* Doubleday, Garden City (New York), 1971; and his *Deschooling Society,* Harper and Row, New York, 1971. How this weeding-out process may work in practice is well described in Burton R. Clark, *The Open Door College: A Case Study,* McGraw-Hill, New York, 1960.

relatively quiet in most academic institutions; and more quiescent still in the rest of the school systems and elsewhere in most of the leading First World countries; while in the Second World there is hardly a ripple to be observed. For how long?

'What we need to discover in the social realm is the moral equivalent of war', wrote William James at the beginning of our century.[46] Revolutionary Marxists know well that either harsh exploitation or devastating wars can create a radical consciousness in large populations; and the aftermaths of both World Wars provide ample evidence to support this observation. In the spirit of James it may be said today that we urgently need to discover educational equivalents to calamities like fascism and war, if we are to hope to move forward without a terrible cost in lives destroyed. Perhaps Freire's approach is part of the answer. But what, more precisely, should the priorities in the 'curriculum' of political education be?

Freire warns against 'cultural invasion': both in the first instance and in the last, the people whom we wish to reach, our partners in dialogue, must proceed by way of determining *their* priorities; they must uncover, articulate, and come to grips with what they come to see as *their* 'limit-situations' within *their* contextual reality.[47] Yet Freire assumes that, as the dialogue gradually sets men's and women's needs free, a unifying, 'generative theme' will emerge: 'I consider the fundamental theme of our epoch to be that of *domination* – which implies its opposite, the theme of *liberation*, as the objective to be achieved'.[48] This is as valid a proposition in the First World as in the Third, I have argued; while in the First World it may take longer to pierce through the ideological defenses within the relatively affluent classes, to say nothing of the Archie Bunker-type outlooks found in some parts of the blue-collar working class, the potential power of protest in mainly urban and literate civilisations should exceed the political resource potentials in mainly rural societies, especially in areas where people even physically have been weakened by long traditions of poverty, with inadequate nutrition and health care services.

While political liberation undoubtedly is more badly *needed* to offset the deeper human misery in much of the Third World, an effective *demand* for liberation through the dialogue, to be followed by political action, seems more attainable soon in the First World. And since the economic and military power of the First World has been preserving the international system

---

46 William James, *The Varieties of Religious Experience*, Collier, New York, 1961, p.290.
47 *Pedagogy of the Oppressed, op.cit.*, pp.89, 95, and Chapter 3.
48 *ibid.*, p.93. His italics.

that has kept much of the Third World in economic misery and political impotence, it may be said that the struggle to expose and bring down the profoundly illegitimate First World regimes is a struggle in the interest of Third World peoples as well; they would at long last be left free to bring their own Allendes or Ho Chi-minhs or Lumumbas or Arbenzes to power with impunity.

If political educators in the First World are to go to work with a radical dialogue as their approach, rather than as ideologists promoting given strategies of political or parliamentary organisation and action, we must come with questions to be asked, not with doctrines to promote. We must come with open minds, committed only (1) to seeking a *critical* political dialogue in the spirit of human solidarity, (2) for the purpose of learning as well as teaching, (3) with the ultimate aim of seeking a fuller emancipation, along with a deeper commitment to human solidarity, for ourselves no less than for our partners in the dialogue.

This is not to rule out a role for disciplined, even secretive, paramilitary organisations in preparation for a violent revolution, even in the First World. Indeed, *nothing* can be ruled out of discussion in the radical political education of the dialogue, as it is understood in this paper; nothing except lack of concern for individual human lives and for collective human survival. If people are to be expected to kill and to give their own lives in a revolutionary cause, I think they should first be given an opportunity to make such a choice as free persons. To recruit revolutionary soldiers without a real dialogue is to reduce persons to blind instruments. I concede that in some Third World countries this may be the only hope, nonetheless, for eventual emancipation, or for an end to unbearable, even genocidal miseries.

In the First World, on the other hand, where a radical dialogue is feasible, it must come first. Perhaps it will lead to a violent revolution eventually; perhaps it will lead nowhere at all; or again, perhaps it will gradually emancipate enough persons to bring about a powerful, yet largely nonviolent revolution, led by activists who will not tolerate domination over their own or anybody else's lives, either now or after the revolution.

The fact that basic human need priorities are as yet inadequately established as empirical facts ought not to keep us from acting on what we believe to be true, on the basis of such researches and argument as have been surveyed. I hope to have shown in this paper that a liberating political education must draw on empirical research and on a radical critique of society; and that in our time a properly developed political education of the dialogue may be our most valuable untapped resource, particularly in the First World context.

Needs and Wants: an Ontological or Historical Problem? *

C.B. Macpherson

Any attempt to work out a humanistic political theory sooner or later runs into the question, what are the human needs and wants which ought to be satisfied? The theorist may try to answer this by making a distinction between genuine or natural wants and artificial ones, with the former being good and the latter not so good, or actively bad. Or he may deny any distinction and say, echoing Hobbes' view of commutative justice, that all wants are equal since they are simply what people want. Or he may make a distinction between gross and refined wants, or between animal needs and fully human needs, or between wants originating in the desires of autonomous individuals and wants created in them by forces outside them. Or he may set out a hierarchy or rank order of human needs and wants, ranging from those which must be satisfied first, for the mere maintenance of life, through those the satisfaction of which is not essential for mere life though essential for a fully human life.

All of these ways of considering needs and wants are ontological: they all go back to some concept of human essence. I see nothing wrong in that. Any political theory has to have some concept of human essence.

* A revised version of a paper given at a conference of the Caucus for a New Political Science, Brown University, Providence, Rhode Island, November 9, 1975.

But that is not enough. For the essence may be seen as *change* or development, as it was by thinkers as different as Rousseau, the German Idealists, and Marx. And in that case the problem becomes a historical one as well.

I want to suggest that the problem of needs and wants is both an ontological and a historical problem, and that to neglect either dimension is likely to be self-defeating. And I want to consider whether any attempt to work out a hierarchy of needs and wants, or to distinguish between natural and artificial wants, is a blind alley. To do this I want to look at the different views of needs and wants in several modern traditions of political theory. There are at least four discernibly different positions, which may be looked at in turn: (1) Rousseau; (2) the liberal individualism of the classical political economists and Benthamist Utilitarians (which has strong echoes in twentieth century economic and political theory); (3) the ethical liberalism of John Stuart Mill, T.H. Green, and their successors; (4) Marx.

It would be convenient if each of these positions could be described in terms of some distinction they made between needs and wants. That would fit them all neatly into the categories of the common current English usage: needs are for the things absolutely necessary to sustain human life, wants are for things gratifying but not necessary: at one extreme, food and air; at the other, yachts and champagne. On this apparently sensible continuum, the line between needs and wants may be drawn almost anywhere, depending on one's view of the relative importance of various sensory and psychic gratifications. Everything seems to be taken care of.

But this way of classifying needs and wants will not do. It is both insular and ideological. It is insular in that neither the French nor German languages use different words for needs and wants: in French, both are 'besoins'; in German, 'Bedürfnisse'. English translators of French and German texts commonly use 'wants' or 'needs' as seems to them appropriate in the context. This is proper enough, but the reader of English translations of, for example, Rousseau and Marx should not assume that the author made the distinction the translator makes.

The needs/wants distinction is seen to be ideological when one notices that, of the various modern traditions of political theory, only the liberal tradition makes or comes close to making that distinction. Others, as different as Rousseau and Marx, tried to get deeper by starting with some different distinction. Rousseau's was between 'natural' and 'artificial' needs, Marx's between 'animal' and 'truly human' needs; and both came out with something very different from the liberal needs/wants continuum. When this ideological factor is added to the insularity factor, the risk of misunderstanding English translations of Rousseau and Marx is compounded, since translators who are themselves in the liberal tradition are apt unconsciously to impose it on the texts.

With these cautions, we may now proceed to look at the four abovementioned modern positions about needs and wants.

1 **Rousseau** Rousseau's well-known contrast between early man and civilised man hinges on the increase over time in wants and needs, and the change in their quality defined by their relation to 'natural' man. Rousseau's distinction is not between needs and wants but between natural and artificial *besoins*.

In his view, the very first humans had only simple physical wants: 'ses désirs ne passent pas ses besoins physiques' − food, sex, and repose.[1] Then, savage men, having only very limited needs, and so having lots of leisure, began to procure many sorts of conveniences unknown to their fathers. These conveniences then came to lose almost all their pleasantness, through habit, and were 'dégénérées en de vrai besoins': true needs in the sense that it was more painful to be without them than pleasant to have them.[2] The multitude of new needs subjected man to all of nature and especially to his fellow men.[3] The effort to satisfy these new needs led to a Hobbesian state of war, and finally to civil society with all its inequality and oppression. There, wants are infinite, and the less they are natural and pressing, the more the passions increase.[4] The ruling passion becomes an intense desire to get ahead of others, a desire which does not arise from genuine need: 'Enfin . . . l'ardeur d'élever sa fortune relative, moins par un véritable besoin que pour se mettre au dessus des autres, inspire à tous les hommes un noir penchant à se nuire mutuellement'.[5]

Thus Rousseau found the rot setting in when the artificial needs displaced the natural ones in importance as determinants of men's behaviour. Men's doom was sealed when these artificial *besoins*, which we should probably call wants rather than needs, 'degenerated into true needs'. Natural wants are good; artificial wants, when they degenerate into real needs, are bad, because they enslave everyone. Rousseau has almost reversed our usual ranking of needs and wants: natural wants or needs (*besoins naturels*) are

---

1 J.J. Rousseau, *Discourse on the Origin and Foundations of Inequality among Men*, in *The First and Second Discourses*, ed. Roger D. Masters, St. Martin's, New York, 1964, p.37.
2 *ibid.*, pp.71-2
3 *ibid.*, p.81.
4 *ibid.*, p.117.
5 *ibid.*, p.81.

good; artificial wants are bad when they become real needs.

The increase in the quantity of wants, interacting reciprocally with the acquisition of new techniques (wants and techniques producing each other), is the motor of the long transition from natural to civilised man. It is at the same time a change in their predominant quality — *from* natural wants, that are consistent with equality and freedom, *to* artificial ones, that bring inequality and unfreedom. Not only were the natural wants *consistent* with equality and freedom: in Rousseau's contrast between the values of savage and civilised man he is asserting that the savage holds equality and freedom as the ultimate values, and Rousseau leaves no doubt that that is also his view of the human essence.

So we may say that Rousseau's treatment of wants and needs is both historical and ontological. The change in wants and needs over time is a change from the needs of natural man to the needs of alienated man.

2 **Liberal Individualism**   I use this term to describe the full-blown individualism of the classical political economists and the utilitarians — Hume, Adam Smith, Bentham, and, in their wake, most of the twentieth century economic theorists, and many of the twentieth century political scientists. The essential postulate of this liberal individualism is that every individual's wants naturally increase without limit.

Hume says that what distinguishes man from other animals is his 'numberless wants and necessities' along with his natural inability to satisfy them without the assistance of others. Only in society, by joint labour, can he satisfy them. In society, 'his wants multiply every moment upon him' but his abilities multiply still faster, so he is better off.[6] Desire is insatiable. 'This avidity alone, of acquiring goods and possessions for ourselves and our nearest friends, is insatiable, perpetual, universal . . .'[7]

Bentham has every individual by nature seeking to maximise his pleasure without limit. Desire is infinite. Each want satisfied produces a new want.

> Wants, enjoyments, those universal agents of society, having begun with gathering the first sheaf of corn, proceed little by little, to build magazines of abundance, always increasing but never filled. Desires extend with means. The horizon elevates itself as we advance; and each new want, attended on the one hand by pain, on the other by pleasure, becomes a new principle of action.[8]

---

6 D. Hume, *Treatise on Human Nature*, ed. Green and Grose, Longmans Green, London, 1882, Book III, Part II, Section 2, Vol.II, p.258.

7 *ibid.*, Vol.II, p.264.

8 J. Bentham, *Principles of the Civil Code*, Part First, Chapter 5, in *The Theory of Legislation*, ed. C.K. Ogden, Harcourt Brace, New York, 1931, p.101.

There is, in Bentham's scheme of needs and wants, some similarity with current usage. It is 'need, armed with pains of all kinds, even death itself', that induces people to labour to produce subsistence: it is the hope of 'enjoyments' (which is without limit) that induces the extra effort which produces abundance.[9] And it is the hope of enjoyments (wants, over and above needs) that is relied on to produce an endless increase of wealth and therefore happiness.

Classical political economy and neo-classical economics are built on the same postulate: the infinity of wants provides the incentive that propels the market economy. And twentieth century pluralist political science has strong traces of the same postulate, insofar as it treats the democratic political system as a market in political goods.[10]

This classical liberal individualism holds that this endless increase of wants is *good* _ just the opposite of Rousseau. And this theory is unlike Rousseau's in another way: it is totally *unhistorical*. Individuals are by nature, at all times, creatures of unlimited wants. This unhistorical quality of the Hume-to-Bentham concept of wants cripples it morally: it would confine mankind forever in a predatory market society.

And perhaps because it is so unhistorical, this liberal theory, and liberal-democratic theory insofar as it accepts the capitalist market society, makes no distinction between wants: every want is as good as every other. So there is no place in the liberal theory for a distinction between 'needs' as more essential and 'wants' as less essential. Nor does it admit a distinction between natural and artificial wants, that is, between wants supposedly inherent in man's nature and those created by the capitalist relations of production and the operation of the market. No such distinction *can* be made if one postulates universal innate *emulation*, for on that postulate whatever new thing one man gets, another will therefore want, and this want will flow from his innate nature just as much as his apparently more basic or natural wants.

If one rejects the postulate of innate emulation, it is possible to distinguish between natural and artificial wants. But to do this one must also reject the Utilitarian postulate that every utility, every want-satisfaction, and therefore every want, is as good as every other; at least you must do so if you are saying that natural wants are somehow better than artificial ones. I am quite happy to reject those Utilitarian postulates. But I am

---

9 *ibid.*, Chapters 4 and 5, pp.100-1.
10 Cf. Essay X 'Market Concepts in Political Theory' in my *Democratic Theory: Essays in Retrieval*, Clarendon, Oxford, 1973.

not sure how much farther that takes us.

To assume that natural wants are more valuable, should be given more weight, than wants created by the system of production, may seem to throw us back to an extreme individualism: the criterion of a natural want seems to be that it is original in each self-sufficient individual, quite apart from society. But it need not do so. For the distinction natural/artificial is not necessarily the same as the distinction physiological/culturally determined. We may recognise that most wants and needs are culturally determined − or even that all of them are, since the need, for example, for food is for culturally determined kinds and amounts − and still make a distinction between (a) wants that develop out of new possibilities opened up by cultural and technological advance and (b) wants inculcated by the controllers of a system of production for their advantage. The (a) wants could be considered natural, the (b) wants artificial.

This is clearly a step ahead of the straight Benthamist position. But the advance, I think, lies not in its using the natural/artificial distinction, but in its emphasis on the cultural determination of wants, and its distinction between wants that people may freely develop and those in effect imposed on them by a predatory culture. And that distinction could be made without using the natural/artificial distinction at all.

3 **Ethical Liberalism**   By this I mean the liberalism of John Stuart Mill, T.H. Green, L.T. Hobhouse, and a host of twentieth century followers in the neo-idealist and modified Utilitarian traditions, such as A.D. Lindsay, Ernest Barker, John Dewey, and R.M. MacIver. Their crucial break from classical liberalism was their rejection of the postulate that every want was as good as every other. For them, the *quality* of want-satisfaction, and therefore of wants, was as important as the quantity. Mill's ideal, and that of his followers, was not man as infinite consumer, but man as exerter and developer of all his capacities. The full development of human capacities would generate a new and higher range of wants. Wants might and should change in quality, away from material desires and the desire to have more than the next man, to intellectual, moral and aesthetic wants.

Mill rejected with scorn attempts such as Rousseau's to equate 'natural' with 'good'. In his essay 'Nature'[11] he ridiculed the idea that men's 'natural' proclivities were morally better than their socially acquired ones. He showed, with example after example, that all that was most valued in human beings was not natural but artificial. So he did not share Rousseau's concept

---

11 In *Three Essays on Religion* from *Collected Works*, Vol.X., University of Toronto Press, Toronto, and Routledge, London, 1969.

of natural needs and wants as better. But though his standard of good and bad wants was different, he did share Rousseau's disgust with the needs and wants they both found prevalent in the class-divided societies of their own time.

Mill's is a more pleasing vision of man than Bentham's. And it is more realistic, in that it sees the cultural determination of wants, and the possibility of wants changing qualitatively. But it fails as a satisfying account of wants and needs, though it does not fail as badly as Bentham's. It fails because, although it sees the possibility (and desirability) of wants changing for the better in the future, it pays little attention to how they have developed up to the present. It does not see that the present want-schedules, which it deplores, are the product and inevitable concomitant of the capitalist market society, which it accepts. Thus even the ethical or developmental liberalism of Mill and Green and their successors is not historical enough to provide a morally acceptable account of human wants and needs.[12] Rousseau, for all his faults, was ahead of them in this. So was Marx.

4 **Marx**   With Marx — both the early Marx of the *Economic-Philosophic MSS* and the later Marx of the *Critique of the Gotha Programme* and of the *Grundrisse* and *Capital* — we find a rejection both of Rousseau's concept of natural wants, and of his distinction natural/artificial.

Speaking of 'crude communism" Marx says it is a 'regression to the unnatural simplicity of the poor and undemanding man'.[13] Rousseau's simple natural man was for Marx *un*natural, just because he had hardly any needs. It is in *increasing* his wants and needs that man becomes fully human. In the final stage of communism,

> in place of the *wealth* and *poverty* of political economy come the *rich human being* and rich *human* need. The *rich* human being is simultaneously the human being *in need of* a totality of human life-activities — the man in whom his own realization exists as an inner necessity, as *need*.[14]

This increase of needs and wants is of course very different from the Benthamist and classical economists' concept. Marx did not conceal his scorn for that, though he agreed that that was an accurate portrayal of what human wants are reduced to in capitalist society (or any society based on private property), that is, of the wants of alienated man. In alienated

---

12 Cf. Essay IX, 'Post-liberal-Democracy?' in my *Democratic Theory: Essays in Retrieval, op.cit.*

13 *Economic and Philosophic Manuscripts of 1844*, Martin Milligan, Foreign Languages Publishing House, Moscow, 1959, p.100.

14 *ibid.*, pp.111-12.

society all the senses have been reduced to the sense of having, of possessing. Thus wants are reduced to what gratifies the sense of having.

And the system of private property creates divisive and predatory wants: everyone speculates on creating a new need in another in order to force him to a new sacrifice, to place him in a new dependence, and to seduce him into a new mode of gratification and therefore economic ruin.

> Each tries to establish over the other an *alien* power, so as thereby to find satisfaction of his own selfish need.
> ... The need for money is therefore the true need produced by the modern economic system, and it is the only need which the latter produces ... *Excess* and *intemperance* come to be its true norm ... the extension of products and needs falls into *contriving* and *ever-calculating* subservience to inhuman, refined, unnatural and *imaginary* appetites. Private property does not know how to change crude need (rohe Bedürfnis) into *human* need (*menschlichen Bedürfnis*).[15]

At the same time as capitalism whips up desires, it reduces the workers to a level of needs lower than the savage's:

> Light, air, etc. — the simplest animal cleanliness — ceases to be a need for man ... It is not only that man has no human needs — even his animal needs are ceasing to exist ... The savage and the animal have at least the need to hunt, to roam, etc. — the need of companionship.[16]

But the political economist (reflecting, as always, the capitalist) reduces the worker's need to the barest subsistence while reducing his activity to mechanical movements:

> Hence, he [the political economist] says, Man has no other need either of activity or of enjoyment. For he calls *even* this life *human* life and existence.
> ... he changes the worker into an insensible being lacking all needs, just as he changes his activity into a pure abstraction from all activity ... Self-denial, the denial of all human needs, is its [political economy's] cardinal doctrine ... The worker may only have enough for him to want to live, and may only want to live in order to have [enough].[17]

Reverting to the point that capitalism speculates on the refinement of needs, Marx writes:

> Just as industry speculates on the refinement of needs, so also it speculates upon their *crudeness,* and upon their artificially produced crudeness whose spirit therefore is *self-stupefaction,* the *illusory* satisfaction of needs, a civilization *within* the crude barbarism of need. The English gin-shops ...[18]

---

15 *ibid.*, pp.115-16.
16 *ibid.*, p.117.
17 *ibid.*, pp.118-19.
18 *ibid.*, p.122.

What, then, was Marx's concept of fully human needs and wants? What would needs and wants be in an unalienated society? On this Marx was not very specific. His critics fasten on this vagueness, and even his followers are apt to feel that an apology is needed for it (where they don't merely brush it aside or skate around it). But no apology is needed. For Marx's whole point about the future good society was that it would be a realm of *freedom* — freedom for people to develop their own needs and wants in whatever ways they liked. It would have been perfectly inconsistent for him to say in advance what they would be.

However, one point is clear. Just as alienated labour was the root of all evil in societies based on private property, unalienated labour would be the chief characteristic of the fully communist society. Unalienated labour, but still labour. Labour in the broadest sense — creative transformation of nature and of oneself and one's relations with one's fellows. This, Marx held, was *the* truly human *need*.

He makes this point repeatedly, and most notably in his mature writings. Thus in the *Grundrisse*, taking Adam Smith to task for his view of labour, Marx writes that in alienated society work is indeed a curse, as Adam Smith thought it was absolutely. But, Marx says, Smith failed to see that work — cessation from rest, overcoming of natural obstacles — is a normal human *need* (which will emerge with the end of alienation).[19] Again, the historic destiny of capital

> is fulfilled as soon as, on one side, there has been such a development of needs that surplus labour above and beyond necessity has itself become a general need arising out of individual needs themselves — and, on the other side, when the severe discipline of capital, acting on succeeding generations, has developed general industriousness as the general property of the new species . . .[20]

Finally we may recall the well-known passage in the *Critique of the Gotha Programme* describing the 'higher phase of communist society' as a time in which 'labour has become not merely a means to live but is itself the first necessity of living' [*'sondern selbst das erste Lebensbedürfnis geworden'*].[21]

This seems to me a great advance over any of the other analyses of needs and wants. It is both ontological and historical, and its strength lies in that combination. It makes no use of the natural/artificial distinction. Nor does it set up a rank order or hierarchy of needs and wants.

---

19 *Grundrisse*, tr. Martin Nicolaus, Penguin, 1973, p.611.
20 *ibid.*, p.325.
21 *Critique of the Gotha Programme*, International Publishers, New York, 1933, p.31.

I cannot help wondering, in the light of this, whether modern attempts by behaviouralists, psychiatrists and psychologists to set up a rank order of needs and wants are well advised. For they do seem to fall back into some of the positions and assumptions that were superseded by Marx. They go to the individual psyche. And they seem to speak of an unchanging human nature: the rank order is postulated universally. They seem caught up in that same unhistorical concept of needs and wants on which both Hume-to-Bentham, and, in a lesser degree, Mill and his liberal-democratic followers, foundered.

I mention here only one such attempt, perhaps the most attractive — the scheme of wants and needs proposed by Abraham Maslow in 1943, on which Christian Bay built in his 1968 article 'Needs, Wants, and Political Legitimacy'.[22] Maslow's order of needs may be summarised as:

1 Physical (biological) needs: the need to stay alive
2 Safety needs, or 'security' — that is, assurance that levels of need-satisfaction achieved will be continued
3 Affection or belongingness needs
4 Self-esteem needs
5 Self-realisation or self-development needs.

How far does this take us? How far can it take us?

(1) is I suppose incontrovertible. Yet it is unfortunately reminiscent of what Marx objected to in the political economists: the workers must be kept alive and reproduced, and their needs can be reduced to that.

(2) doesn't make that any better.

(3), (4) and (5) do rise above that, but (3) and (4) at least don't rise above the class differentiation that can be read into (1) and (2).

(5) is much more promising, for it can be stretched to cover the sort of development that both Mill and Marx were thinking of. But it seems to me to lack the solidity of Marx's view.

Christian Bay argued that one might well build on Maslow's 1943 rank order model, at least 'until ... a more useful alternative model [is] provided'.[23] I wonder whether a more useful model than Maslow's was not provided 99 years earlier by Marx.

---

22 *Canadian Journal of Political Science,* Vol.I, No.3, Sept. 1968.
23 *ibid.,* p.247.

Abraham Maslow's Hierarchy of Needs — An Exposition and Evaluation

Ross Fitzgerald

There are at least five sets of goals, which may be called basic needs ... These are briefly physiological, safety, love, esteem and self-actualisation ... These basic goals are related to each other, being arranged in a hierarchy of prepotency. This means that the most prepotent goal will monopolise consciousness and will tend of itself to organise the recruitment of the various capacities of the organism. The less prepotent needs are minimised, even forgotten or denied. But when a need is fairly well satisfied, the next prepotent ('higher') need emerges, in turn to dominate the conscious life and to serve as the centre of organisation of behavior, since gratified needs are not active motivators.*

The most common feature of contemporary need theorists in relation to politics is that they utilise, if not base their work on, the late Abraham Maslow's theory of a hierarchy of universal human needs. This applies most notably to the work of James C. Davies, Jeanne N. Knutson, Stanley A. Renshon, and especially Christian Bay.[1]

---

* A.H. Maslow, 'A Theory of Human Motivation', *Psychological Review*, Vol.50, 1943, p.394.

1 See Selected Bibliography. Also see entries under D. McGregor, J.V. Clark, W.J. Dickson, F.J. Roethlisberger, J. Aronoff, E.L. Simpson, J. Zinker, G.M. Erickson and D.D. Van Fleet.

'Throughout this argument,' says Bay in his major work *The Structure of Freedom, 'I presuppose the probable validity of some such theory as Maslow's on the hierarchy of human motives.* New and "higher" motives are born only as more basic and essential motives receive satisfaction, and the individual comes to take their satisfaction for granted.'[2] Bay is hopeful that increasingly sophisticated behavioural theory and research techniques will increase our ability to distinguish between *genuine* and *manufactured* human needs, wishes and desires.[3] There are, he suggests, several avenues of promise in this direction. Most notable is 'the avenue of psychological theorising and research associated ... especially with the names of (Erich) Fromm and (Abraham) Maslow'.[4] In fact, while Bay uses many of Fromm's ideas, he bases his theory of needs on Maslow's hierarchy.

Maslow lists five categories of needs in the order of their assumed priority:

1 Physical (biological) needs — air, water, food, sex etc.
2 Safety needs — assurance of survival and of continuing satisfaction of basic needs
3 Affection or belongingness needs
4 Esteem needs — by self and others
5 Self-actualisation or self-development needs.[5]

This list represents a hierarchy and Maslow regards these needs as both instinctoid and universal. He does not say that these are *all* the needs we have, but that all men potentially have all these needs. Thus 'higher' needs may not become activated unless the 'lower' needs are, or at least have been, reasonably well met at some time in a person's life. However, whenever in the course of a human life the 'higher' needs have become activated,

---

2 *The Structure of Freedom,* Stanford University Press, Stanford, 1970 (first published 1958), p.372. My emphasis. 'In the extreme state of nature,' Bay argues, 'there are few needs beyond biological essentials common to all men. At an extremely high level of cultural development, on the other hand, one may assume that all or most men, regardless of their particular strain of culture, will experience an actual need for free speech if not also more specialised needs such as artistic experience.' (*ibid.*) He goes on to say that 'We may all have creative, intellectual and artistic powers deeply embedded in our nature, which may become needs for expression in a society capable of satisfying our more pressing needs'. (p.372n.)

3 *ibid.,* p.327. The emphasis is Bay's.

4 *ibid.*

5 While this paper refers to five 'basic needs', it is important to realise, as Knutson points out, that Maslow's need hierarchy is based on five 'need areas' (so that the physiological level, for example, refers to a variety of specific needs such as sex, sleep, thirst, hunger, etc.) and does *not* rest on a simplistic assumption that man's motivational patterns could be defined in terms of five single needs. *The Human Basis of the Polity: A Psychological Study of Political Men,* Aldine-Atherton, Chicago, 1972, p.23. Knutson's emphasis.

they are not necessarily extinguished as a result of later deprivation of 'lower' or more basic needs. For example, some individuals, provided they have once known satisfaction of physiological and safety needs, will sacrifice the former for love, for self-esteem or for truth. Thus a man such as Ghandi may deny himself food because 'higher' needs have become more important but, according to Maslow, a person who has never had enough to eat could not activate or articulate his 'higher' needs.[6]

In his key article 'A Theory of Human Motivation', on which all of his later need theory rests, Maslow states quite clearly that human needs arrange themselves in hierarchies of prepotency. That is to say, the appearance of one need usually rests on the prior satisfaction of another, more prepotent need. Undoubtedly to Maslow the *physiological needs* are the most prepotent of all needs. Thus a person who is lacking food, safety, love and esteem would probably hunger for food more strongly than for anything else. But if the physiological needs are relatively well gratified, then there emerges a new set of needs, which may be roughly categorised as the *safety needs*. If both physiological and safety needs are fairly well gratified, then there will emerge the *affection or belongingness needs*. If these in turn are gratified the *esteem needs* emerge (i.e. for self-respect, or self-esteem, and for the esteem of others) which if in turn are met give rise to the *need for self-actualisation* although the specific form that all these needs take will vary greatly from person to person. The clear emergence of the need for self-actualisation rests upon prior satisfaction of the physiological, safety, love and esteem needs. In this sense the latter are deficiency needs. The 'good' or 'healthy' society, Maslow says in a footnote, would be defined as one that permitted man's highest purposes to emerge by satisfying all his prepotent basic needs. Significantly, when Maslow talks about the pre-conditions for basic need satisfactions he argues that danger to these is reacted to almost as if it were a direct danger to the satisfaction of the basic needs themselves. Such conditions as freedom to speak, freedom to do what one wishes so long as no harm is done to others, freedom to express one's self, freedom to investigate and seek information are examples of such pre-conditions for basic need satisfactions. Thwarting

---

6 See, for example, Maslow, 'Conflict, frustration and the theory of threat', *Journal of Abnormal and Social Psychology*, Vol.38, 1943, pp.81-6; ' "Higher" and "lower" needs', *Journal of Psychology*, Vol.25, 1948, pp.433-6; 'Some theoretical consequences of basic need-gratification', *Journal of Personality*, Vol.16, 1948, pp.402-16; 'The instinctoid nature of basic needs', *Journal of Personality*, Vol.22, 1954, pp.326-47 and 'Criteria for Judging Needs to be Instinctoid' in *Human Motivation: A Symposium*, ed. M.R. Jones, University of Nebraska Press, Lincoln, 1965, pp.33-47.

of these freedoms will be reacted to with a threat or an emergency response. These conditions are not ends in themselves but they are almost so since they are so closely related to the basic needs, which are apparently the only ends in themselves. These conditions are defended because without them the basic satisfactions are quite impossible, or at the very least, severely endangered.[7]

Maslow also mentions *cognitive and aesthetic needs* such as the needs to know and to understand. Indeed his later work was intimately concerned with the discussion of other needs which arise when the level of self-actualisation is reached. These needs (which he variously called 'B-values' or 'meta-needs') involve such dimensions as curiosity, knowledge, understanding, beauty, meaning, symmetry and growth.[8]

The mystical Maslow of meta-needs, 'B-values' and 'the farther reaches of human nature' is especially vulnerable to attack.[9] However it is his theory of five basic needs as outlined in his 1943 article 'A Theory of Human Motivation' and his 1954 book *Motivation and Personality*, that contemporary need theorists in the West use to base their work.

It is important to realise that Maslow does not, for example, clearly differentiate between the concepts 'needs', 'wants', 'drives', 'motives', 'wishes', 'desires' or 'propensities'. Because Maslow tends to assume that the notion 'need' is not only essentially trouble-free but uses it as though it were non-normative we are obliged to ask to what extent is Maslow's concept of needs an empirical notion and to examine criticisms of this theory.

In fact, many severe criticisms have been made of Maslow's theory of needs, especially by academic and professional psychologists. The mechanistic school, and especially those influenced by B.F. Skinner's stimulus-response-reinforcement model, have tended to reject Maslow's work out of hand. But even more motivationally oriented psychologists have criticised his need-concept as metaphysical and ambiguous; have denied his claim that basic needs are instinctoid and universal and have rejected his notion of a hierarchy of needs. Moreover, many have argued that Maslow's theory is both vitalist and teleological; this they assert is especially true of his notion of self-actualisation. Further, they maintain

---

7 This is my own summary of 'A Theory of Human Motivation', *op.cit.*, pp.370-96. Emphasis mine. Cf. especially Maslow's 'Higher Needs and Personality', *Dialectica*, Vol.5, 1951, pp.257-65 and *Motivation and Personality*, Harper and Row, New York, 1954.

8 See, for example, 'The Need to Know and the Fear of Knowing', *The Journal of General Psychology*, Vol.68, 1963, pp.111-25 and 'The Farther Reaches of Human Nature', *The Journal of Transpersonal Psychology*, Vol.2, No.1, Spring 1969, pp.1-9.

9 See M. Brewster Smith's and Neil McInnes' contribution to this collection.

that his 'evidence' for 'higher' needs is, at best, impressionistic and anecdotal. Thus they conclude that Maslow is not an empiricist at all and that his work (and especially his theory of needs) is thoroughly value-laden.[10] This type of criticism, it should be noted, is not solely directed at Maslow but equally at other 'need theorists' and humanistic psychologists as well — notably Murray, Allport, Rogers, Horney and Erich Fromm.[11]

Maslow himself clearly indicates that a teleology is implied in his theory and accepts that his work *is* value-laden. Especially in the decade prior to his death Maslow argued that 'is' and 'ought' often are inseparable and often ought to be. He further argued that his subject matter (and especially his concern with growth-motivation, self-actualisation and 'peak experiences') of necessity involved a fusion of fact and value.[12]

In a similar vein, the British psychologist C.A. Mace, who also accepted a hierarchy of 'lower' and 'higher' needs, unashamedly admitted that 'needs talk' is teleological and that it is clearly evaluative. Thus Mace defined 'need' as a goal-directed process of behaviour — in his view toward the end of dynamic homeostasis. Mace, too, confronted the fact/value problem and argued that 'the gulf (between fact and value) is reduced to the extent to which the good for man is defined in terms of the fulfilling of his needs'.[13] In connection with teleology we should draw attention to Charles Taylor's defence of explanation by purpose, goal or end as opposed to explanation on mechanistic principles. The latter, to Taylor, is exemplified by behaviourist psychology and especially by Skinner and the stimulus-response-reinforcement theorists. In particular Taylor attacks the view that

---

10 See, for example, C.N. Cofer, and M.H. Appley, *Motivation: Theory and Research,* Wiley, New York, 1964, especially Chapter 13, 'Self-Actualization and Related Concepts'. For a criticism of 'higher' needs and a hierarchy of needs see pp.675-9 and 684-5 and for a criticism of Maslow's notion of self-actualisation see pp.668-73 and 683-4. See also R.S. Peters, *The Concept of Motivation,* Routledge and Kegan Paul, London, 1958, especially pp.17-18, 122-9 and 153.

11 See entries in Selected Bibliography.

12 See notably Maslow, 'Fusions of Facts and Values', The Eleventh Annual Karen Horney Memorial Lecture, in *American Journal of Psychoanalysis,* Vol.23, No.2, 1963, pp.117-31; 'Some fundamental questions that face the normative social psychologist', *Journal of Humanistic Psychology,* Vol.8, 1968, pp.143-54; 'Self-actualisation and beyond', in *Challenges of Humanistic Psychology,* ed. J.F.T. Bugental, McGraw-Hill, New York, 1967, pp.279-86; 'The farther reaches of human nature', *op.cit.,* pp.1-9, and 'Lessons from the Peak-Experience', *Journal of Humanistic Psychology,* Vol.2, 1962, pp.9-18. See also *New Knowledge in Human Values,* ed. A.H. Maslow, Harper, New York, 1959; *Toward a Psychology of Being,* Van Nostrand, Princeton, New Jersey, 1962, and *Religions, Values and Peak-Experiences,* Ohio State University Press, Columbus, Ohio, 1964.

13 See C.A., Mace, 'Homeostasis, Needs and Values', Presidential Address to the British Psychological Society, *British Journal of Psychology,* Vol.44, No.3, August 1953, pp.200-10, especially pp.201 and 209.

teleological explanations are non-empirical or pejoratively 'metaphysical'. He, too, argues that a 'need' implies a goal for which it is needed.[14] Taylor's defence, and advocacy, of teleological explanation has aroused considerable controversy and his thesis has been severely criticised.[15] It is, however, unnecessary to buy into this debate here. As we shall see, even to grant that teleological explanation is a valid form of explanation can neither aid nor save a conception of 'needs', such as Maslow's, which is related to a notion of human health or excellence. This is because the fundamental problem remains: how does one determine the end or goal or model of health or excellence to which man's 'needs' are relative?

Especially in his later work, it is clear that Maslow was involved in fusing fact and value. Thus he argued with regard to 'peak-experiences' and 'self-actualising people' that '*Is* becomes the same as *ought. Fact* becomes the same as *value.* The world which is the case, which is described and perceived, becomes the same as the world which is valued and wished for. The world which *is* becomes the world which *ought* to be. That which ought to be has come to pass; in other words, facts have here fused with values'.[16] Moreover, to Maslow, 'oughtness' is found and achieved via 'isness' and facticity. 'Peak-experiences' and 'self-actualisation' are, to him, prime examples of bridging the alleged dichotomy between fact and value.[17]

There are striking and significant similarities between Maslow's work and the focus of contemporary need theorists. This is especially so

---

14 *The Explanation of Behavior,* Routledge and Kegan Paul, London, 1964, especially pp.219-69, and his 'Explaining Action', *Inquiry,* Vol. 13, 1970, pp.54-89, which is a restatement of Part 1 of this book. Also see B.F. Skinner, *Science and Human Behavior,* Knopf, New York, 1971.

15 See, for example, Denis Noble's technical philosophical attack, 'Charles Taylor on Teleological Explanation', *Analysis,* Vol.27, No.3, January 1967, pp.96-103 and Taylor's rejoinder, 'Teleological Explanation — a Reply to Denis Noble', *Analysis,* Vol.27, No.4, 1967, pp.141-3. For more general comments see D.W. Hamlyn's lengthy critical notice in *Mind,* Vol.LXXVI, January 1967, pp.127-36, and E. Nagel, *The Structure of Science: Problems in the Logic of Scientific Explanation,* Routledge and Kegan Paul, London, 1961, especially Chapter 12, Part 1, 'The Structure of Teleological Explanation', pp.401-28.

16 'Fusions of Facts and Values', *op.cit.,* p.120. All emphases are Maslow's. This is what Michael Oakeshott argued with respect to 'practical experience' which subsumed the world of politics. See *Experience and Its Modes,* Cambridge University Press, Cambridge, 1966, pp.288-95.

17 'Fusions of Facts and Values', *op.cit.,* pp.121-2 and 126. Cf. Maslow's 'Deficiency Motivation and Growth Motivation', in *Nebraska Symposium on Motivation,* ed. M.R. Jones, University of Nebraska Press, Lincoln, 1955, pp.1-30. In terms of Maslow's scheme the first four needs in his hierarchy are 'D' or Deficiency needs (characterised by deficiency motivation) while self-actualisation, incorporating 'B' or Being needs, is characterised by a different kind of motivation, that is, *growth* motivation.

given Maslow's attempt (and in his case, stated imperative) to bridge fact and value and his optimistic view of human nature. This conception of man and its consequent stress on the inherently 'good' potentialities and capacities of human beings is true also of Allport, Rogers, Murray, Horney and Erich Fromm.

Maslow summarises his position by saying:

> What I am doing, in effect, is striking blows at one of the root conceptions upon which classical science is based, namely, its supposed value-free nature, its belief that it can study only neutral facts, and that the world of facts is totally different from the world of values. Since this kind of science has nothing whatsoever to do with values, everything and anything to do with values in any sense at all is 'unscientific', and is turned over to non-scientists (religionists, poets, humanists, philosophers and other unfortunates). The two worlds are thereby split off from each other, with the consequence that both are pathologised . . .

He concludes that 'We must seriously consider the likelihood that science not only can deal with values, but also that it can discover them'.[18] Maslow is clearly mistaken in asserting that the kind of science he allegedly describes 'has got nothing to do with values', and that any concern with values is 'unscientific'. For even an allegedly value-neutral social science does study values, but as facts.[19] Indeed this applies to the whole area of political socialisation and political culture literature. Studying values, attitudes and opinions as facts is a major enterprise in contemporary social science.

Predictably, there has been no sustained effort, on the part of academic psychologists, to follow up and develop Maslow's theoretical leads. In fact, except perhaps among the 'humanistic psychologists', there has, in recent years, been little interest shown in Maslow-type theories of universal needs and their priorities.[20] Thus Cofer and Appley point out that the 'higher needs' such as belongingness, love and self-esteem have seldom been stud-

---

18 'Fusions of Facts and Values', *op.cit.*, p.130. Cf. Maslow's 'Comments on Skinner's Attitude Toward Science', *Daedalus*, Vol.90, 1961, pp.572-3, and 'The scientific study of values', *Proceedings 7th Congress of Inter-American Society of Psychology*, Mexico, 1963.

19 An apposite example is A.D. Lindsay's 'operative ideals'. It is only by maintaining a *distinction* between fact and value that 'operative ideals' can become an object of empirical study. See Lindsay, *The Modern Democratic State*, Oxford University Press, New York, 1962 (first published 1943), especially Chapter 1, 'Political Theory and Operative Ideals', pp.27-51.

20 One should note that the 'humanistic psychologists' regard themselves as 'the third force' in psychology as opposed to the positivistic and the dynamic schools. See notably J.F.T. Bugental and Rollo May — both deeply influenced by Maslow and Rogers. References in Selected Bibliography.

ied.[21] Moreover the few specific attempts to spell out psychological theories of needs have almost exclusively stressed culturally defined and learnt rather than universal and innate needs. This is especially the case with D.C. McClelland's influential work on a pragmatic taxonomy of motives.[22]

Certainly there has been little serious study of hierarchies of needs as elaborated by Maslow, and attempts by psychologists to connect need theory to conduct have been, at best, of dubious quality.[23] Furthermore, psychological research has primarily focused on physiological drives, that is, needs as the result of bodily deficits.[24]

Admittedly in John Bowlby's recent and important book, attachment behaviour is presented as a distinct and fundamental form of instinctive behaviour and one that though most evident during childhood, nonetheless persists through life. Its function is postulated as protection from predators, a function as important for survival as nutrition and reproduction but one hitherto much neglected.[25] However, in general, Bowlby does not find 'need' a satisfactory term because it involves a vitalist notion. A legitimate usage of the term 'need' is, he argues, to restrict it to refer to the *requirements of species survival*. If the species is to survive, an animal can be said to need food, warmth, a nesting site, a mate and so on'.[26] This, though it could be accommodated to 'fit' the 'need' for belongingness, would exclude talk in terms of Maslow's other 'higher' needs. In any case Bowlby's vocabulary of 'attachment behaviour' is both more neutral and more exact that Maslow's 'belongingness'.

It is clear that empirical validation of Maslow's 'higher' needs is non-

21 *Motivation: Theory and Research, op.cit.,* p.685.
22 McClelland, *The Achievement Motive,* Appleton-Century-Crofts, New York, 1953 and *The Achieving Society,* Free Press, New York, 1961. See also Chapter 2 in *Motives in Fantasy, Action and Society,* ed. J.W. Atkinson, Van Nostrand, Princeton, 1958. McClelland deals with the 'needs' for affiliation, for power and for achievement and specifically centres on the latter.
23 One possible exception is Justin Aronfreed's *Conduct and Conscience: The Socialisation of Internalised Control over Behavior,* Academic Press, New York, 1966. However in his excellent book Aronfreed offers an *empirical explanation* of moral development and moral behaviour and does not attempt to connect need theory to imperatives. See review by P.H. Mussen in *Contemporary Psychology,* Vol.15, No.13, 1970, pp.176-9.
24 See Richard de Charms, *Personal Causation: The Internal Affective Determinants of Behavior,* Academic Press, New York, 1968, especially pp.65-91 and 192-200. de Charms, a pupil of McClelland is, however, strongly opposed to the behaviourism that treats the person as a physical object. He does, moreover, talk in terms of intentions and motives.
25 *Attachment,* Vol.1 of *Attachment and Loss,* Hogarth Press, London, 1970, *infra.*
26 *ibid.,* pp.136-8. Bowlby's emphasis.

existent. In fact evidence bearing on innate needs in Maslow's sense is very scarce. Assuming, for the sake of argument, that 'need' is a trouble-free and non-normative notion (which as I have demonstrated elsewhere it is not[27]), one kind of 'evidence' could be seen to be provided by experiments indicating that the body is capable of considerable self-regulation in the interests of homeostasis. Another indicates that dietary self-selection, in both children and animals provides, within limits, a satisfactory variety and quantity of food. D.M. Davis' study of self-selection of diet by two-year old children, designed to show 'the rationality of the body', is a case in point. Davis found that infant self-selection corresponded, over the period of study, with nutritive requirements.[28] These data can be taken to indicate that organisms can 'know' their needs and, left alone, can act appropriately in response to them. Such work may be used as evidence for the existence of need-based drives. However, it would seem to bear only slightly on need-theory as expressed by Maslow.

Maslow's formulation that needs or drives are arranged in a hierarchy of prepotency does receive at least partial support. That the support is partial is because the evidence almost exclusively concerns the needs at the two lower levels of his hierarchy, that is, the physiological and security 'needs'.[29] The dominating effects of severe hunger, cold, heat, thirst and fear on animals and men have been well documented. C.J. Warden's obstruction-box study of the albino rat, designed to show the relative intensity and persistence of innate drives, found that they corresponded to a hierarchy of importance.[30] Of far greater significance in terms of Maslow's theory is the account provided by the Minnesota Deprivation Studies. Here Ancel Keys *et al* carried out semi-starvation experiments with conscientious objectors. Their subjects, after a time, were dominated by the thought of food and all 'higher motives' succumbed to the hunger drive.[31] It has been

---

27 See my paper, 'The Ambiguity and Rhetoric of "Need" ', this collection, p.195.
28 D.M. Davis, 'Self-Selection of Diet by Newly-Weaned Infants', *American Journal of Diseases of the Child*, Vol.30, 1928, pp.651-72.
29 For a detailed review of the literature see Knutson, *The Human Basis of the Polity*, op.cit., especially pp.19-35.
30 See Warden, 'The Relative Strength and Persistence of the Normal Drives in the White Rat', in his *Animal Motivation: Experimental Studies on the Albino Rat*, Columbia University Press, New York, 1931, pp.372-98. Also see W.A. Russell, *Milestones in Motivation: Contributions to the Psychology of Drive and Purpose*, Appleton-Century-Crofts, New York, 1970, Chapter 24.
31 A. Keys *et al*, *The Biology of Human Starvation*, 2 Vols., University of Minnesota Press, Minneapolis, 1950. Also see 'The Effect of Different Intensities of the Hunger Drive on Thematic Apperception' in *Motives in Fantasy, Action and Society*, ed. J.W. Atkinson, *op.cit.*, Chapter 2.

repeatedly demonstrated that in situations characterised by the deprivation of all needs (such as occurred in the concentration camps) physiological needs become of prime importance.[32] These studies may be taken as supplying evidence for the prepotency of needs. Furthermore, Hadley Cantril's detailed report on the famous Orson Welles American Halloween broadcast illustrates the value of understanding the dominating effect of security motivation in a population characterised by large-scale satisfaction of physiological needs.[33] Cofer and Appley conclude that, to this extent, Maslow's notion of a hierarchy of 'needs' does receive support. However, they hasten to point out that 'while there is some evidence that intense physiological and safety needs can dominate behaviour, evidence for the hierarchy relationship of other needs is wanting'.[34] As we have seen, needs lying above the safety ones have seldom been studied.[35]

Apart from Bowlby's study of attachment behaviour, additional 'evidence' for the existence of a 'need' for affection and belongingness and of the damaging effects of its lack of fulfilment in early life can also be found in the work of Harry Harlow and Rene Spitz. As Knutson indicates, Harlow's work with monkeys shows on analogy that deprivation of mothering and 'contact comfort' in the young leads to a variety of neurotic symptoms, among which are the inability to give love and join in meaningful relationships with others. Spitz's studies of children raised in an institutional setting where physical needs are well provided and emotional needs ignored illustrates both the emotional and the physical damage which lack of love and affection can cause.[36] The stunting of emotional growth when

---

32 Knutson, op.cit., p.26. See J.E. Nardini, 'Survival Factors in American Prisoners of War of the Japanese', American Journal of Psychiatry, Vol.109, No.4, October 1952, pp.241-8 and J.C. Davies, Human Nature in Politics, Wiley, New York, 1962, pp.11-15. Maslow, however, does not argue that deprivation of 'lower' needs of necessity extinguishes 'higher' needs. In fact he maintains that the former can be sacrificed for the latter as long as there has been substantial and relatively durable satisfaction of the basic needs at some time in a person's life.

33 The Invasion from Mars, Harper & Row, New York, 1940, quoted in Knutson, op.cit., p.29.

34 Cofer and Appley, op.cit., p.691.

35 For a study of dubious conceptual quality using content analysis and a very small sample (N = 37) see W.K. Graham and J. Balloun 'An Empirical Test of Maslow's Need Hierarchy', Journal of Humanistic Psychology, Vol.13, No.1, Winter 1973, pp.97-108. Also see Hall and Nougaim, and Alderfer, in Selected Bibliography, p.261.

36 See H.F. Harlow, 'Development of affection in primates' in Roots of Behavior, ed. E.L. Bliss, Harper, New York, 1962; 'The Nature of Love', The American Psychologist, Vol.13, No.12, December 1958, pp.673-85; 'Love in Infant Monkeys', Scientific American, Vol.200, No.6, June 1959; and 'Deprivation in Monkeys', Scientific American, Vol.207, November 1962, pp.136-46 and R.A. Spitz, 'Hospitalism', The Psychoanalytic Study of the Child, Vol.1, 1945, pp.53-74 and 'Anaclitic Depression', The Psychoanalytic Study of the Child, Vol.11, 1946, pp.313-42, quoted in Knutson, The Human Basis of the Polity, op.cit., p.38.

human beings are denied warmth and contact during their formative years has been well documented.[37]

Despite this, the conclusion to be drawn is that there has been no unequivocally empirical verification of the existence of Maslow's 'higher' needs. We should note that these 'higher needs' are the distinctly *human* needs. And even if there is no evidence of falsification, which may say more about the ambiguous nature of Maslow's conceptual structure than its soundness, one can question the inferences drawn from this research. Most psychologists regard the purely empirical study and validation of a hierarchy of needs in Maslow's sense as presenting immense and (perhaps) insurmountable problems. It can be abstracted from this ambiguous amalgam, Maslow's theory of human needs has not been empirically established to any significant extent.

*   *   *

A major difficulty with this theory is that Maslow, like Fromm, does not speak of the potentialities of human beings as diverse individuals, but of humanity in general, and this involves him in making statements about universal human needs. Moreover those theorists using Maslow's scheme, most notably Christian Bay, make a fundamental value judgement that all human beings have certain basic needs which must be met before the less basic needs of any others ought to be satisfied. The problem here is at least twofold. First, can one discover basic needs which are common to all men despite differences in human behaviour; that is, in their ways of satisfying or promoting needs? Second, even if one can identify universal needs, there is the further problem of why ought human beings, let alone governments, feel obliged to satisfy such needs — especially in the order of their priority even if such a ranking could be established?

It is the identification of universal human *needs* which presents the stumbling block. This is not to say that universal propositions about human beings, which have a family relationship to propositions about needs, cannot be supported. Similarly, I do not see 'cultural relativity' itself as a major impediment to a general theory. People may express themselves with whatever they happen to have at hand but these variations may all be reducible to a common goal. Despite cultural variations in human behaviour, there

---

37 See for example Kingsley Davis, 'Extreme Social Isolation of a Child', *American Journal of Sociology*, Vol.XLV, No.4, January 1940, pp.554-65 and 'Final Note on a Case of Extreme Isolation', *American Journal of Sociology*, Vol.52, No.5, 1947, pp.432-7. Also see S.A. Renshon, *Psychological Needs and Political Behavior*, Free Press, New York, 1974, p.67.

do appear to be certain basic propensities, other than bodily ones, which all or most men share.[38] The point to emphasise is that the problem is not that of making universal statements about human propensities as such. Rather the problem is the *selection* of some of these propensities, on the basis of some criterion of goodness or health or human excellence, and the labelling of them as 'needs'. If 'need' is merely a concept referring to certain physiological and psychological processes and nothing else, there is no way of regarding these processes as desirable or undesirable, good or bad, without introducing some normative premise or some notion of human excellence. Disagreement on these normative premises or notions will lead to the development of a different set of 'needs'.

To attribute *needs* to people presupposes certain standards or norms as to which among human propensities or characteristics it is desirable to foster. This selection will be culture-bound and dependent on different ethical preferences. As R.F. Dearden puts it:

> If you say that in my emaciated condition I need food, I may refuse to attach any importance to the norms of health that you are presupposing, pointing out that I am engaged in a religious exercise; if you say that children need love, I may refuse to attach any importance to the ideal of a co-operative, affectionate and trusting character you presuppose, pointing out that we of the Mundagumor admire a different sort of character . . .[39]

An even greater problem than universality itself is precisely how to operationalise empirically such a theory of human needs and in so doing how validly to distinguish needs from wants. Then there is the further problem of clarifying the relationship between needs and wants on one hand and values and ideals on the other.

One of the many things Maslow has not done is to distinguish between human needs (the needs of humans as humans) and personal needs (the individual needs of particular persons). Likewise he has not come to grips in any depth with the problem of conflicting needs and values (conflicts within the person, or between competing persons, or competing groups). Nor has he dealt with the possible tension between individual and social needs. The Grand Inquisitor example is apposite here because clearly not all 'goods' or 'values' are compatible with each other. It seems part of

---

38 See *Contemporary Political Theory*, ed. Anthony de Crespigny and Alan Wertheimer, Atherton Press, New York, 1970, Introduction, pp.2-3. These authors use the term 'need' here in the way that I have used 'propensities'.

39 ' "Needs" in Education', in *Education and the Development of Reason*, eds. R.F. Dearden, P.H. Hirst and R.S. Peters, Routledge and Kegan Paul, London, 1973, p.55.

the human condition for human beings to oppose one tendency to another and, as a consequence, to be torn between competing predispositions. Thus even if one could establish a catalogue of basic human needs, one would still be left with the problem of conflicting and competing needs.

In terms of the specific needs that Maslow postulates many criticisms may be, or have been, made. Following John Anderson, one could argue that even if the 'need' for security can be established empirically, the demand for social security, and especially for the state to secure such freedoms, is itself a servile notion. This is because it involves human beings giving up responsibility for themselves.[40] It can, perhaps, be maintained that all that this type of criticism establishes is that the rhetoric of political language is double-edged in that it can be used to exploit contrary connotations — in this case 'servility' as opposed to 'security'. But, balanced against this, it seems clear that the work of Fromm and Reisman has demonstrated modern man's desire to 'escape from freedom' through conformity to 'other-direction'.[41]

It may be possible to make the 'need for affection' empirical in terms of Bowlby's notion of attachment behaviour, but then there is the problem of how this need is related to government; that is to say, how can, and why ought, governments promote attachment behaviour. It can be denied that the 'need for self-esteem' can be made empirical or universalised. It is also clear in individual cases that a predominance of self-disgust over self-esteem has been highly productive.[42] Personal neurosis has provided a fertile breeding ground for artistic creation and there may possibly, in some cases at least, be a positive connection between creative self-realisation and personal neurosis. Put more strongly, a feeling of insecurity and psychic deprivation may sometimes provide pre-conditions for creativity. Artistic creation is often the product of a critical ambivalence in consciousness between self-regard and self-disgust. Certainly there is no way one can secure artistic creation by political or psychological means. Despite all of this, it would be difficult to deny, for most human beings, the desirability of at least sufficient ego-strength to cope with their internal and social environment. The problem arises precisely when theorists talk about a

---

40 See 'The Servile State', 1943, in *John Anderson: Studies in Empirical Philosophy,* Angus and Robertson, Sydney, 1962, pp.328-39.

41 See Fromm, *Escape from Freedom,* Holt, Rinehart and Winston, New York, 1961, and D. Reisman, with N. Glazer and R. Denney, *The Lonely Crowd,* Yale University Press, New Haven, 1950.

42 Evelyn Waugh is an excellent example. See Christopher Sykes' biography, *Evelyn Waugh,* Collins, London, 1975.

'need' for self-esteem. Here, as elsewhere, 'need' substitutes for what is valuable or desirable.

It is the notion of a 'need for self-actualisation' which most clearly highlights the problems confronting Maslow. Such talk demonstrates that his theory of needs is tied to a normative notion of human excellence.

It is impossible to make such a metaphysical notion as the 'need for self-actualisation' empirical at all. Human selves have many potentialities. Thus, apart from the difficulty of determining what we mean by 'self', there are the problems of which selves and potentialities are to be realised. Here the answers must be normative. It is clear that to the questions 'What is the self to be realised?' and 'What are the potentialities to be developed or expressed?' the respective answers are 'A good self' and 'Good potentialities'. Similarly the answer to the often unasked question 'What are the needs that ought to be satisfied, fulfilled or promoted?' is 'Good needs'. This is why Bay, Marcuse and Nielsen for example, are compelled to distinguish between 'real' and 'false' needs.[43] It hardly has to be pointed out that 'real needs' in effect come to equal 'good needs'.

If by 'self-actualisation' is meant *whatever* the individual can be motivated to act out or express, it provides us with no standard whatsoever for distinguishing between desirable (or appropriate) forms of self-expression and undesirable (or inappropriate) forms. This, of course, Maslow and those theorists using his scheme do not intend. Manifestly the murderer, sadist, fascist, rapist, incendiarist or machete man do not fit in with Maslow's notion of a person developing his potentialities or expressing 'what he has in him', even though there may well be harmony between basic motives and overt behaviour. (The same applies to the accountant, soldier, stockbroker, surfer, or priest if one disapproves of these types of activities). 'Self-actualisation' cannot be rendered empirical. Maslow must, and by implication does, set up standards of what the individual in his freedom ought to become or express, and what he ought not to become or express.

To speak of a 'need' for 'self-actualisation' is either tautological or unequivocally normative. Any action of a human being is part of a pattern of actions that actualises the self of that particular human being. Thus even the most inconsequential or destructive forms of human action can be seen as part of the process of self-actualisation, unless one specifies

---

43 See Bay, Selected Bibliography. See Marcuse, especially *One-Dimensional Man*, Routledge and Kegan Paul, London, 1964, Chapter 1, especially pp.5-6 and 245, and Nielsen, this collection, Chapter 8. Cf. J.K. Galbraith, *The Affluent Society*, Houghton Mifflin, Boston, 1969 (second edition revised), who also distinguishes between 'real' and 'artificial' needs.

only certain forms of activity as properly actualising the self and conse-quently excludes other forms of action as not properly pertaining to self-actualisation. The criteria used to specify which sort of self is to be realised must be thoroughly value-laden and notions of the 'self' to be 'actualised' will vary according to different estimates of things that are worth doing and propensities that are worth developing. Thus R.S. Peters regards talk of self-actualisation or self-realisation as being about 'a new sort of omnibus end state' of what is good for man.[44] 'Self-actualisation' is merely another way of referring to what one ought to do and what one ought to be or become.

The answer to the question 'What sort of self does Maslow want express-ed and actualised?' is simple. It is 'a good self'. The self-actualised person equals in effect the good or healthy human being. Again we are back with a normative model of human excellence. This is because some notion of 'goodness' or 'health' is necessary as a criterion of selection among the potentialities to be realised.

All of this makes it abundantly clear that Maslow is resurrecting notions of human excellence and of man in his perfection. It further demonstrates that his theory of needs is inextricably related to a notion of human ends or purposes — in his case of the good man, and by way of related prescrip-tions, of the good (or healthy) polity. As Arnold S. Kaufman argues, the concept of needs is clearly tied to prospects for living 'a good life' and to notions of 'a truly human existence'. This, he maintains, is especially true of the distinction between 'human' and 'false' needs. Satisfaction of a person's human needs are at least generally indispensable for, and his having false needs generally incompatible with, his living a good life. It follows that different theories of the good life will generate different cata-logues of human and false needs.[45]

* * *

It *would* be difficult to deny, at least in our society, that physical susten-ance, safety, affection, self-esteem, and self-development are not extremely desirable aspects of human welfare. This, of course, is precisely why a framework such as Maslow's, when phrased in terms of 'needs', seems so plausible. Whether such a framework can be rendered 'empirical' is, in this sense, beside the point. Further, this approach throws more light on

---

44 *The Concept of Motivation, op.cit.,* p.131.
45 Arnold S. Kaufman, 'Wants, Needs and Liberalism', *Inquiry,* Vol.14, No.3, Autumn 1971, pp.191-212, especially p.194.

the use of rhetorical language and argument than on the validity of Maslow's hierarchy.

Christian Bay, for example, along with Davies, Knutson and Renshon, suggests that, up to now, Maslow's hierarchical system provides the most fruitful point of departure for theorising about human needs in relation to politics and human problems.[46] In Bay's judgement, Maslow's theory ought to serve as a basis for discussion and research until a more plausible and useful theory is available. He argues that while there is, as yet, insufficient evidence for validating Maslow's system, there is no evidence that suggests the superiority of an alternate theory of human needs. Nor has one so far been provided. With this last statement I would agree. However it may well be that it is the nature of the conceptual framework of need theory that no empirical progress *can* be made.

---

46 Bay, 'Needs, Wants and Political Legitimacy', *op.cit.*, pp.247-51.

Human Needs and Political Analysis:
An Examination of a Framework

Stanley Allen Renshon

Studies of political behaviour which seek to go beyond description become involved, of necessity, with questions of human motivation. Yet, motivational analysis occupies an ambivalent position in political examination. On one hand many examinations of political phenomena rely, either implicitly or explicitly on assumptions about human motives. These range from concepts of the politically ideal from Aristotle to Wolin, to assumptions of maximisation and utility in mathematical decision-making models. Yet the role of psychological explanation in general, and personality theories in particular, remain controversial and not infrequently neglected.

Given the ubiquity of psychological assumptions in political explanation more focused attention might have been expected; but then what's assumed, is rarely examined. The purpose of this paper is to explicate and analyse one set of psychological explanations, those dealing with 'human needs'. In doing so, we will examine the assumptive basis of need theory as it relates to analysis in political psychology. More specifically, we will examine need theories as one class of motive explanations, their dynamics, and their implications for social and political life.

It would be naive to assume that need theories, or any other models of personality functioning, will facilitate solutions to all, or even most of the problems which concern political analysts. But to the extent that politics is conceptualised as a human undertaking and deals with the behaviour of persons, these models will be a necessary (though not sufficient) component for any adequate explanation.

To raise questions about the 'why' of human behaviour is to plunge into an area of ambiguity and controversy, fuelled by linguistic[1] and conceptual uncertainties. Into this area one enters with extreme caution. Yet, because of the importance of motivation in political analysis the concept of human needs as one class of motive explanation merits detailed consideration. For purposes of expository convenience, the analysis which follows will focus on four related areas: (1) needs as a class of motive explanations; (2) the assessment of human needs; (3) the dynamics of need satisfaction; (4) the impact of human needs on political behaviour.

Needs as a Class of Motive Explanations

According to Peters, 'motives ... are a particular class of reasons, which are distinguished by certain logical properties'.[2] Among the most important for present purposes, is that they are reasons of a directed sort; 'if (a person) has a motive he must have a goal of some sort, however weak its influence ...'[3] Peters goes on to distinguish four types of motive explanations: (1) 'his reason'; (2) 'the reason'; (3) causal; (4) end-state explanations.

Need theories are one type of end-state explanations of human behaviour. The latter explain human behaviour by reference to requirements of the organism which serve to organise and motivate behaviour. Henry Murray's definition is illustrative in this regard and worth quoting at some length.

A need is a construct (a convenient fiction or hypothetical concept) which stands for a force (the physico-chemical nature of which is unknown) in the brain region, a force which organizes perception, apperception, intellection, conation, and action in such a way as to transform in a certain direction an existing, unsatisfying situation. A need is sometimes invoked by internal processes of a certain kind (viscerogenic, endocrinogenic, thalamicogenic) arising in the course of vital sequences, but, more frequently (when in a state of readiness) by the occurrence of a few commonly effective press* (or by anticipatory images

---

1 Useful guides to the philosophical and linguistic difficulties include Stephen Toulmin, 'Concepts and the Explanation of Human Behavior', in *Human Action*, ed. Theodore Mischel, Academic Press, New York, 1969, pp.71-104; and Donald T. Campbell, 'A Phenomenology of the Other One: Corrigible, Hypothetical and Critical', in *Human Action, op.cit.*, pp.41-66.

2 Richard Peters, *The Concept of Motivation*, Routledge and Kegan Paul, London, 1958, pp.27-8.

3 *ibid.*, p.32.

* A *press* is defined by Murray as a stimulus property of an aspect of the environment perceived by the organism in terms of its threat of harm or promise of benefit.

of such press). Thus it manifests itself by leading the organism to search for, or avoid encountering, or, when encountered, to attend to and respond to certain kinds of press ... Each need is characteristically accompanied by a particular feeling or emotion ... it may be weak or intense, momentary or enduring. But usually it persists and gives rise to a certain course of overt behavior (or fantasy) which (if the organism is competent and external opposition not insurmountable) changes the initiating circumstances in such a way as to bring about an end situation which stills (appeases or satisfies) the organism.[4]

Murray's definition suggests the crucial nature of needs for the individual, since they have substantial impacts on the perception and organisation of 'reality' as well as behavioural activities within it. Yet it is important to emphasise that 'needs' are constructs which are proposed, 'to account for certain objective and subjective facts'.[5] As a convenient fiction, they are useful to the extent that they help us to explain variations in human activities and outcomes, and are by themselves neither 'true' or 'false'. Yet because 'needs' are hypothetical processes, it is important to have empirical indicators of their existence and impact.

Murray's definition points to several possible criteria. The first is the typical direction of attempted effect. That is, the organism will attempt to transform the situations in a way which either facilitates the satisfaction of the need or minimises or postpones deprivations associated with it. The second is a typical mode or action pattern with regard to any transformation attempts. These may be thought of as routinised procedures for dealing with certain need-press situations, which develop into personal styles. The third indication concerns the person's relation(s) to particular aspects of the environment, and not others. This will involve 'the search for, avoidance or selection of, attention and response to one of a few types of press (cathected objects of a certain class)'.[6] The fourth is the exhibition of a particular type of affect connected with a particular need-press situation. Thus, when a need has become activated we would generally (but not always) expect some feeling experienced and defined by the person as discomfiture. Last, the existence of a need can be inferred by the state of the organism given a particular need-press-activity outcome. Presumably the 'satisfaction' of a need should lead to behavioural and emotional expressions classifiable as 'positive' and the failure to do so will result in dissatisfaction.

---

4 Henry Murray et al., *Explorations in Personality*, Oxford University Press, New York, 1938, pp.123-4.

5 *ibid.*, p.54

6 *ibid.*, p.124.

There is, of course, an additional criterion, which is potentially powerful, yet highly controversial. This is the examination of the continued deprivation of a need in terms of its consequences to the somatic and psychological integrity of the individual. Here the logic of the analysis begins with the 'normal' or 'required' state of the organism, and proceeds to infer the 'preferable'. It is assumed that there are certain ranges of human functioning, which, in the absence of long-term and periodic need satisfaction, will result in various pathologies.

This criterion is proposed by some as the *sine qua non* of inferential reliability in establishing the existence (and political relevance) of needs. Thus Bay, in examining the relationship between human needs and political legitimacy begins by defining a need as, 'any behavior tendency whose continued denial or frustration leads to pathological responses'.[7] Arguing along similar lines, Maslow suggests, 'a man who is thwarted in any of his basic needs may fairly be envisioned simply as a sick or at least less than fully human'.[8] The difficulty is that defined in this way the concept of need is pointedly normative. As Peters notes, 'it usually functions as a diagnostic term with remedial implications'.[9] While this may provide an important evaluative tool for the comparison of societies and political systems, its immediate and direct utilisation in that capacity is compromised at present by a number of assessment difficulties.

The Assessment of Human Needs: Some Considerations

While Murray's definition of need dynamics appears to present useful (preliminary) empirical guidelines for need assessment, they are not without difficulty. McClelland asks for example, 'Are needs to be thought of primarily in terms of the characteristic *mode of response* used to gratify them or in terms of the goal of behavior of any sort?'[10] If the former approach is selected one is immediately faced with the difficulty of discerning whether multiple behaviours are in the service of the same or different needs. Thus, for example, 'a person may show abasive, affiliative or achievement behavioral trends, all in the attempt to satisfy his N achievement'.[11] This point is further illustrated in a political context by Lasswell's 'political man', 'whose principal value is the pursuit of power'.[12] But accord-

---

7 Christian Bay, 'Needs, Wants and Political Legitimacy', *Canadian Journal of Political Science*, Vol.1, No.3, 1968, p.242.
8 Abraham Maslow, *Motivation and Personality*, Harper, New York, 1954, p.57.
9 Peters, *op.cit.*, p.17.
10 D. McClelland, *Personality*, Dryden, New York, 1951, p.406.
11 *ibid.*, p.407.
12 Harold D. Lasswell, *Psychopathology and Politics*, Viking, New York, 1930, p.50.

ing to Lasswell, the search for power is not to be understood as arising from any need for power as Adler would have hypothesised,[13] but rather, because, 'power is expected to overcome low estimates of the self'.[14] In this case the political actor would engage in behaviour whose motive was not related to its ostensible purpose, the control of others.

According to McClelland, 'It would simplify matters if Murray's needs were always conceived of in terms of inferred goals of behavior rather than in terms of the behavioral trends usually characterizing the means of obtaining them'.[15] McClelland reserves the concept of trait for the latter, but the difficulties of inferring the goal from the behaviour remain. Clearly one cannot use the behaviour itself, since this would be analogous to inferring the existence of a need by the behaviour routines that are developed in order to satisfy it. As Murray notes, 'an operational definition of a need in terms of actones* is out of the question'.[16]

There are further reasons why the direct assessment of the existence and operation of needs from overt behaviour, while plausible, must remain provisional. Viewing individuals from the perspective of multiple need areas, rather than single discrete needs represents a conceptual advance but still requires specification of need content. Early attempts to specify human need areas proceeded on the assumption that behind every behaviour one could find a corresponding drive.[17] Perhaps the high point of *reductio ad absurdum* was reached in 1924 when Luther Bernard, a sociologist, 'reviewed the various ideas of many instinct theorists and found that the

---

13 See, for example, A. Adler, 'The Psychology of Power', 1928, *Journal of Individual Psychology*, Vol.22, 1966, pp.166-72.

14 Harold D. Lasswell, *Power and Personality*, Viking, New York, 1948, p.39.

15 McClelland, *op.cit.*, p.407.

* An actone is 'an action pattern qua action pattern' according to Murray.

16 Murray, *op.cit.*, p.245.

17 Holt's early criticism of such attempts remains instructive. He notes that
   ... man is impelled to action it is said, by his instincts. If he goes by his fellows, it is 'herd instinct' which activates him; if he walks alone, it is the 'anti-social' instinct; if he fights it is the 'pugnacity instinct'; if he defers to another it is the instinct of 'self-abasement'; if he twiddles his thumbs, it is the thumb-twiddling instinct; if he does not twiddle his thumbs it is the thumb, not twiddling instinct. Thus everything is explained by the facility of magic-word magic.
   These attempts lead Brown to suggest that 'we might advance more rapidly if we started afresh and deny at the outset that each and every object and situation for which an organism has learned to strive must be accompanied by a characteristic drive for that object'. Although both points are made with reference to instinct theory, they are still of importance for its progeny, (human) need theory. See E.B. Holt, *Animal Drive and the Learning Process*, Holt, New York, 1931, and J.S. Brown, 'Problems Presented by the Concept of Acquired Drive' in *Current Research in Motivation*, ed. M.R. Jones, University of Nebraska, Lincoln, Nebraska, 1953.

list of so-called instincts included nearly 6,000 activities, ranging from generalized urges such as "social behaviour" to specific ones such as "instinct to avoid eating apples in one's own orchard" '.[18] Nor has the number difficulty been solved to date. Freud's dualistic theory of human needs offers attractive simplicity, but suffers as a concrete guide for empirical political and social inquiry because of its high level of conceptual abstraction. This is one reason why some contemporary psychoanalytically oriented political biographies have bypassed direct use of 'eros' and 'thanatos' altogether.[19] At the other end of this continuum, Henry Murray's work on human needs, while offering comprehensiveness (twenty manifest and eight latent needs[20]), presents difficulties of operationalisation and data gathering to empirically minded political psychologists of either a nomothetic or ideographic persuasion.

The problem is to conceptualise the complexity and diversity of human motives in a way that permits empirical inquiry. James Davies' early observation that, 'knowledge of human motivation is not yet adequate to establish the psychological equivalent of a periodic table of elements'[21] remains an astute observation, but advances have been made. Illustrative is Maslow's theory of a need hierarchy which includes five basic need areas.[22] While not without difficulties, such a theory offers an attractive compromise between the requirement to fully specify the widest variety of human motives, and the practical theoretical necessity to have a useful framework for political analysis. Another alternative is presented by Robert Lane, who suggests ten needs that are important for understanding human motivations in political life.[23]

---

18 Quoted in D.T. Graffam, 'Brief Historical Introduction to Motivation' in *Understanding Human Motivation*, eds. C.L. Stacey and M.F. DeMartino, Howard Allen, Cleveland, 1963, p.5.
19 See, for example, Bruce Mazlish, *James and John Stuart Mill: Father and Son in the Nineteenth Century*, Basic Books, New York, 1975. For an extended analysis of Mazlish's book within the context of assessing the adequacy of present models in political psychology, see Stanley Allen Renshon, 'Fathers and Sons Psychohistorical Perspective: Socialization, Character Development and Political Theory in the Nineteenth Century', *History of Childhood Quarterly*, Vol.2, 1976.
20 Murray *et al.*, *op.cit.*, pp.144-5.
21 James C. Davies, *Human Nature and Politics*, Wiley, New York, 1963, p.7.
22 These are (1) physiological, (2) safety, (3) love, (4) self-esteem, (5) self-actualisation. The basic statement of this approach may be found in Maslow, *op.cit.*
23 These are (1) cognitive needs (curiosity, learning, understanding), (2) consistency needs (emotional, logical and veridical), (3) social needs (affiliation, being linked), (4) moral needs, (5) esteem needs, (6) personality integration and identity needs, (7) aggression expression needs, (8) autonomy needs, (9) self-actualisation needs, and (10) the need for instrumental guides to reality, object appraisal and attainment. The list and an explication is found in Robert E. Lane, *Political Thinking and Consciousness*, Markham, Chicago, 1969, pp.31-47.

Leaving aside momentarily the extent of such advances, one must still consider another difficulty. If persons are conceptualised as being motivated in most social contexts by multiple, rather than single needs, then not only may the same need be expressed in multiple behaviours, but the same single behaviour may be linked to multiple needs. For example, a recent analysis of former President Richard Nixon, suggested that much of his behaviour could convincingly be understood in terms of a need for personal control, as well as the desire for self-esteem.[24]

These considerations decrease the confidence that one may have in inferring the existence of needs from any particular behaviour. Nonetheless, the analyst does have a number of alternatives, not all of which must or should be pursued independently. Clearly close attention to behaviour will be necessary to establish the existence and dynamics of human needs in social contexts. Yet the analyst still has a number of other assessment possibilities including the very powerful phenomenological tool, the clinically informed personal interview. Here as elsewhere, a strategy of multiple operationalism has much to recommend it.

Needs and Satisfactions

To have a need is to require satisfaction yet the linkages between the two are far from direct. The difficulty is that even if one accepts the idea that human needs are innate and part of the biologically transmitted framework within which personality develops, one must still confront the complicating effects of social learning on need satisfaction.

The first difficulty to be confronted is the assumption that a particular need infers a particular satisfaction. The assumption, were it accurate would provide social analysts with an important analytical and evaluative tool, but it is unfortunately not the case. It is true that instinctual drives in some species are part of a 'package' of biological equipment which points to specific and appropriate satisfaction objects. For example, males of the moth species are attracted to the sex pheromones emitted by the females of their species, and while they are sometimes (but rarely) 'fooled' by the pheromones of other closely related species, it never reaches the stage of attempted copulation.[25] As the focus of attention moves on to more complex animal forms the specificity of messages concerning appropriate satisfaction

---

24 Stanley Allen Renshon, 'Psychological Analysis and Presidential Personality: The Case of Richard Nixon', *History of Childhood Quarterly*, Vol.3, 1975, pp.415-50. A similar point is developed by Murray who refers to the process as 'fusion of needs', *op.cit.*, p.86.

25 This illustration is taken from Edward O. Wilson, *Sociobiology: The New Synthesis*, Harvard University Press, Cambridge, 1975, p.26.

objects decreases, with a corresponding increase in object variability and the important of social learning.[26]

The starting point of any assessment of satisfactions and human needs is the variability and range of potentially appropriate objects. At best particular needs may imply a certain class of satisfiers, but within that range there are wide variations. These are influenced as much by cultural and historical considerations as by any unique inherent capacity to satisfy. Freud, for example, recognised the variability of instinctual satisfactions. More specifically, he noted that:

> The object . . . of an instinct is the thing in regard to which or through which the instinct is able to achieve its aim. It is what is most variable about an instinct, and is not originally connected with it, but becomes assigned to it only in consequence of being particularly fitted to make satisfaction possible.[27]

In other words, needs (or instincts[28]) while all having a particular aim (for example, discharge) did not begin with any conception of appropriate discharge objects. Although Freud's drives operated according to the 'pleasure principle', the necessity to secure satisfaction from the external world gave rise almost immediately to rudimentary ego processes operating according to the 'reality principle'.

A similar point of departure for considering the linkages between needs, satisfactions and motives is advanced by McClelland and his associates. A motive according to McClelland is, 'a strong effective association based on an anticipatory goal response reaction and based on certain cues of pleasure or pain'.[29] These cues of pleasure and pain refer to the organism's tendency to maximise the small discrepancies between expectations and actualities and to minimise any large discrepancies.

In most personality theories the central, core motivating concept is thought sufficient to act as an end-state goal for the organism at the level of overt behaviour. This is certainly one assumption of many need theories, but McClelland is suggesting something quite different. This becomes clear when we focus on his discussion of biological needs:

> most psychologists have become accustomed to thinking of biological need states as the primary sources of motivation . . . in terms of our theory food deprivation *does not produce a motive the first time it occurs*. The lack of food

26 *ibid.*, pp. 151-2.
27 Sigmund Freud, 'Instincts and Their Vicissitudes', 1915, in *Sigmund Freud: Collected Papers*, ed. Ernst Jones, Vol. 4, Basic Books, New York, 1959, p. 65.
28 Freud thought the concepts of need and instinct synonymous. In one place he notes that 'A better term for a stimulus of instinctual origin is a "need" '. See *ibid.*, p. 62.
29 McClelland, *op.cit.*, p. 466.

will undoubtedly result in diffuse bodily changes . . . but these do not constitute a motive until they are paired with a subsequent change in affect. More specifically; if the organism is to survive, the cues subsequent to food deprivation must always be associated with eating, and eating results in two types of affective change — pleasurable taste sensations and relief from internal visceral tensions. Thus, internal (or external) cues resulting from food deprivation are associated very early and very regularly with positive affective change with great dependability.[30]

The implication of both Freud and McClelland's analysis is that needs are not directly translated into human motives but rather acquire motive status through social learning. This flexibility is at once a source of great advantage, but at the same time must be held at least partially responsible for the continued confusion in political theory as well as social life between needs and wants. On one hand the wide range of objects which can supply satisfaction for 'human needs' creates additional possibilities for human fulfilment; but it is also possible that socially learned 'satisfactions' (and the desires that give rise to the search for them) are a product of social inculcation rather than biological necessity.

Even at the level of biological needs, variability seems to be the rule rather than the exception. Illustrative are Murray's viscerogenic and Maslow's physiological needs. Both include in this category needs for food, air, and water and large variations in satisfiers are neither expected nor found. Air is perhaps the best example, yet small variations in oxygen content can be withstood. Water appears to be another satisfier with little variability, yet one can survive on other forms of moisture with chemical properties other than H_2O. Yet perhaps the best illustration of variability at the level of basic physiological needs concerns food. If the reader were invited to a friend's home for dinner, he would be quite surprised to find himself served a plate of tree-bark. Yet among certain cultural groups, in the South Pacific (and elsewhere) such a diet provides at least minimum subsistence. The wide variations in response to such culturally accepted satisfiers as beef, pork, and sweetbread (calves' brains) not to mention the less acceptable but nonetheless satisfying food value of our fellow men, cautions against neglecting the implications of societal impacts on the definition of and search for 'need satisfactions'.

If the range of need satisfactions contains some variability at the level of physiological needs, then it may reasonably be suggested that this variability increases as one moves up to 'higher' level needs. Take, for example,

---

30 David McClelland *et al.*, *The Achievement Motive*, Appleton-Century-Crofts, New York, 1953, pp.81-4, emphasis added.

the need for self-esteem which is posited as a basic human need by Murray, Maslow, Lane and others. Societies will clearly differ regarding the linkages they attempt to instil between estimations of self-worth and particular cultural activities. In societies which emphasise cognitive skills (for example, knowing, controlling), certain occupational pursuits (for example, managerial roles, whether governmental or industrial) will be seen as more desirable, and greater tangible and symbolic rewards will accrue to those who pursue such occupations successfully. The link between occupations and self-esteem is important but insufficiently examined and it is only illustrative of the ways in which macro (and micro) social values influence both the range and possibilities of need gratification.

In general then, one might hypothesise that as one moves from 'lower' to 'higher' needs to use Maslow's model[31], the variability in satisfaction alternatives should increase. The hypothetical end-state of that process may be seen in the concept of self-actualisation as a basic human need (one also postulated by Murray, Maslow, Lane and others), in which satisfaction becomes largely an idiosyncratic set of linkages between the skill capabilities of the individual, the freer utilisation of unblocked (by conflict) energy,

---

31 The assumption of Maslow's model is that needs are organised in a rough hierarchy in which the unmet needs are prepotent, at least until satisfied. Empirical tests of the need hierarchy model have provided mixed, but generally positive support for the idea of need satisfaction leading to activation of 'higher needs'. Hall and Nougaim analysed 49 managers in terms of Maslow's need hierarchy. Relations between need satisfaction and desire did not support the concept of need progression. In that study higher order needs seemed to be related to age and role, rather than degree of satisfaction of lower needs.

   However, Alderfer empirically testing the ordering of three needs (Existence, Relatedness, and Growth) in two separate and larger samples ($N = 300$, $N = 110$) found a tendency for a desire for one need to be negatively correlated with the degree of satisfaction with that need and the others. While the correlations were generally in the predicted direction, several were near zero and statistically insignificant. Moreover, this is more a test of the need hierarchy model, rather than Maslow's theory in particular. Still, the results do support the concept. Finally, Graham and Balloun examined Maslow's need hierarchy model with a small sample ($N = 37$) and found that the pattern of expressed concern with particular needs fits the model developed by Maslow. The small unrepresentative samples should give pause, but these studies do provide some empirical support for the concept of need hierarchies. The above studies include; D.T. Hall and K.E. Nougaim, 'An Examination of Maslow's Need Hierarchy in an Organizational Setting', *Organizational Behavior and Human Performance*, Vol.3, 1968, pp.12-35; C.P. Alderfer, 'Convergent and Discriminant Validation of Satisfaction and Desire Measures by Interviews and Questionnaires', *Journal of Applied Psychology*, Vol.51, 1967, pp.509-20; C.P. Alderfer, 'An Empirical Test of a New Theory of Human Needs', *Organizational Behavior and Human Performance*, Vol.4, 1969, pp.142-75; and W.K. Graham and J. Balloun, 'An Empirical Test of Maslow's Need Hierarchy', *Journal of Humanistic Psychology*, Vol.13, 1973, pp.97-108.

and their association with a wide range of culturally provided or tolerated opportunities.

In theory, the ability of culturally transmitted learning to forge links between needs, satisfactions and motives should increase the possibilities for general levels of need satisfaction within particular societal contexts. Yet, there are complicating factors. One of these concerns the unconscious nature of needs as motivating forces. Both Maslow and Murray note that needs may neither be conscious or unconscious, but the former goes on to note that:

> On the whole, however, in the average person, they are more often unconscious than conscious. It is not necessary at this point to overhaul the tremendous mass of evidence that indicates the crucial importance of unconscious motivation. What we have called the basic needs are often largely unconscious . . .[32]

One of the implications of conceiving of needs as unconscious processes is the possibility that satisfactions will not be pursued, not for lack of necessity, but for knowledge. As Murray notes, 'To put it metaphorically, a need may have no inkling of what it needs'.[33] This may be accurate in three ways. First, the individual may not have any conscious knowledge of the existence of need; second, he might not have knowledge of the appropriate satisfiers; and third, even given the first two, he might not necessarily be successful. Thus, for example, Lane, while examining political thoughts, found that self-insight into personal needs was present, but by no means prevalent; nor did self-insight into needs necessarily result in more successful need gratification.[34] A person with scurvy will not necessarily want Vitamin C in the absence of medical knowledge, and a person deficient in self-esteem will not necessarily discern the appropriate objects or develop the capacity to obtain them.

The above considerations point to the difficulty of separating needs and wants. Bay confronts the difficulty by suggesting that want 'refers to a perceived or felt need which may or may not overlap with a real need'.[35] Meyer, in an analysis of human needs and political philosophy, attempts to differentiate between wants and needs by suggesting:

> The identification of a want is strictly empirical, for to say 'I want' is merely to state that it is a fact that 'I want' and one's overt expressions are sufficient

32 Maslow, *op.cit.*, p.54.
33 Murray, *op.cit.*, p.68.
34 Lane, *op.cit.*, pp.61-6, and *passim*.
35 Bay, *op.cit.*, p.242.

to establish in a positive way what one wants. To the extent that wants become the subject of judgment, evaluation and purposeful change, we can begin to speak of needs.[36]

For Meyer, wants are to be distinguished from needs by rational contemplation, but this leaves unresolved the role of unconscious or otherwise unknown organism requirements. Another point of departure is suggested by Maslow's observation that, 'Everyday conscious desires are to be taken as symptoms, *as surface indications of more basic needs'*.[37] Yet, for each of these need theorists the question still remains, given the important role of social learning, of how one can differentiate between a need that is basic to the organism and one which is socially learned, rationally held, and produces indications of deprivations when frustrated?

One idea is put forward by Meyer who suggests, 'the pragmatic recommendation in that the determination of needs should be understood to involve the experimental testing of the consequences to which the pursuit of the supposed "need" leads us'.[38] In short, it is within the context of man's experiences and felt (as well as expressed) satisfaction that one can assess to what extent wants and needs are synonymous. But, as Maslow points out, 'If we are to take these superficial desires at their face value, we would find ourselves in a state of complete confusion that could never be resolved, since we would be dealing with symptoms rather than with what lay behind the symptoms'.[39] Maslow goes on to propose that 'the thwarting of unimportant desires produces no pathological results, thwarting of basically important needs does produce such results'.[40] This is not to say that the deprivations of human wants do not produce conflict, only that such conflicts do not under normal circumstances result in pathologies. We will examine the normative political implications of this position in a subsequent section.

If need deprivation of basic needs results in pathology then questions regarding the amount of gratification necessary become important. Most of the discussion in this area has focused on the concept of need potency, or motive strength. For example, in discussing the estimation of manifest need strength Murray suggests four criteria; frequency, duration, intensity and readiness. Each or all may then be considered in the context of the four general need indicators previously noted, (for example, behavioural

---

36 William Meyer, 'Democracy: Needs over Wants', *Political Theory*, Vol.2, 1974, p.203.
37 Maslow, *op.cit.*, p.56.
38 Meyer, *op.cit.*, p.204.
39 Maslow, *op.cit.*, pp.56-7.
40 *ibid.*, p.57.

trends, kind of object cathected, initiating emotion, and outcome affect). Frequency and duration can be operationalised by counting the number of acts and their temporal duration, but intensity presents more difficult empirical problems.

Murray suggests eight operational possibilities.[41] These include: tempo of action, speed of learning, strength of actional potency utilised, amount of consummatory activity, strength of action, number and magnitude of obstacles overcome, and last, the number and strength of negative needs inhibited and positive needs sacrificed. For the last criterion, readiness, Murray proposes four empirical indicators: speed of response, threshold level, appropriateness of object (lack of suitable objects under conditions of high need should result in search for similar objects even if ultimately unsuitable) and level of aspiration.

The importance of these indicators is that they give some promise of being empirically useful as a guide to research. Their exact form in any particular study will vary with the methodological tools selected. At minimum they suggest at least a preliminary operational framework within which to systematically assess the impact of human needs in political life. By themselves, however, they only point to one side of the picture, for in addition we require knowledge of the satisfaction values of particular outcomes. In particular, it would be useful to know the need satisfaction value of symbolic and tangible rewards (both comparatively and with different kinds of needs) in political life. It would then be possible to begin estimating the range of need satisfaction typically required for need gratification. As it currently stands, knowledge in this important area is exceedingly fragmentary and speculative.

In the absence of such an empirical base, the specific linkages between human needs and individual and social outcomes will remain a matter of conjecture. To the extent that this happens the evaluative implications of need theory as it relates either to assessing democratic character development or as a method by which to evaluate particular socio-political arrangements, will remain a promise rather than an actuality.

Human Needs and Political Behaviour

Following Murray's delineation of need dynamics we would expect their impact to be felt in political life in the following related areas: (1) the perception of political reality; (2) the processes of organising and interpreting political events and experiences; (3) affective evaluations of political

---

41 The points which follow are discussed by Murray in *op.cit.*, pp.254-5.

phenomena; (4) motives for participation in political life; (5) the direction of political activity. Additionally, to the extent that the long term implications of need deprivations or satisfactions can be related to the somatic and psychic integrity of the person, an empirically based dimension of normative political evaluations will have been established. Last, one must not overlook the importance of socio-political institutions in the creation and satisfaction of human needs.

Examination of the impact of human needs on social perception is well established in psychological research. In a series of early studies, Postman and his associates sought to demonstrate that anxiety producing stimuli would, given the psychic needs of the individual, result in 'perceptual defense'.[42] Experiments involved flashing words on a tachistoscope and measuring recognition times. While early experiments demonstrated differences, it was not until McGinnies[43] flashed taboo words such as 'whore', 'Kotex', etc. that the results become dramatic. As expected such words required greatly increased recognition time. In addition, physiological measurement supported the existence of high anxiety levels.

While needs may occasionally result in 'screening out' of some stimuli, they more frequently result in perceptual distortion in the socio-political sphere. Anxiety over tension or conflict producing information will have unfortunate consequences for political decision-making. Janis[44], in his study of group decision-making process during political crisis found that the tendency to discount information discordant with the dominant group assumptions led to ill-advised and unsuccessful policy recommendations. A more recent study of Israeli 'surprise' during the Yom Kippur War points to the important role of inaccurate assessments of Arab capacities, based in part on rejecting information at variance with Israeli self-images and assumptions.[45]

If need deprivation distorts political (and social) perception what may be expected under conditions of need satisfaction? Although systematic re-

42 J.S. Bruner and L. Postman, 'Emotional Selectivity in Perception and Reaction', *Journal of Personality*, Vol.16, 1947, pp.69-77; L. Postman, J.S. Bruner and E. McGinnies, 'Personal Values as Selective Factors in Perception', *Journal of Abnormal and Social Psychology*, Vol.43, 1948, pp.142-54. For a later summary see C.W. Erikson, 'Perception and Personality', in *Concepts of Personality*, eds. J.W. Wepman and R.W. Heine, Aldine-Atherton, Chicago, 1963.
43 E. McGinnies, 'Emotionality and Perceptual Defense', *Psychological Review*, Vol.56, 1949, pp.244-51.
44 Irving L. Janis, *Victims of Groupthink*, Houghton Mifflin, Boston, 1972.
45 Avi Shlaim, 'Failures in National Intelligence Estimates: The Case of the Yom Kippur War', *World Politics*, Vol.28, 1976, pp.381-95.

search remains to be done, a suggestion comes from Maslow's informal study of potential self-actualisers in a college community. Discussing their acuity of perception he notes, 'an unusual ability to detect the spurious, fake, and the dishonest; . . . In art and music, in things of the intellect, in scientific matters in politics and public affairs, they seemed to be able to see concealed or confused realities . . .'[46] One cannot help but note in passing the implications of these very tentative findings for the perennial discussions regarding voter 'competence' among American citizens. If Maslow is correct, the need-satisfied person approximates the character-istics of the democratic citizen put forward by classical political theorists.

The second area of need impact concerns the organisation and intepreta-tion of political events and experiences. The individual assumptive frame-works which perform these dual functions are belief systems. Robert Lane notes, 'As necessity is the mother of invention, so more generally, human needs are the parents of social thought; the effort to gratify these needs or reduce their urgency stimulates and shapes thinking'.[47] Thus DeVita, one of Lane's twenty-four college age subjects, builds a political philosophy because:

> Liberalism gives me a pattern by which to understand the political world. I can understanding it because I create it. My drives to know, understand, and control are satisfied.[48]

In another approach to the impact of needs on belief organisation I have suggested[49] that in the attempt to satisfy human needs the individual develops certain basic assumptions about the nature of social reality. These include beliefs about (1) physical reality (time, space, etc.); (2) the potential for individual action; (3) evaluations of the world one inhabits; (4) evalu-ation of others; (5) assumptions about one's self. While this model suggests a way in which patterns of need gratification may give rise to politically relevant beliefs, it does not provide a direct linkage between basic beliefs and political beliefs. One possible linkage is suggested by the work of Nathan Leites and more recently Alexander George on 'operational codes'.[50]

---

46 Maslow, *op.cit.*, p.153; also 203-28.
47 Lane, *op.cit.*, p.24.
48 *ibid.*, p.12.
49 S.A. Renshon, *Psychological Needs and Political Behavior*, Free Press, New York, 1974.
50 Nathan Leites, *The Operational Code of the Politburo*, McGraw-Hill, New York, 1951, and *A Study of Bolshevism*, Free Press, Glencoe, Illinois, 1953. More recent attention has been redirected towards this conceptual framework by Alexander George, 'The Oper-ational Code: A Neglected Approach to the Study of Political Leaders and Decision Mak-ing', *International Studies Quarterly*, Vol.13, 1969, pp.190-222.

Of direct interest are the philosophical dimensions of the operational code which are, in large part, basic assumptive beliefs about the nature of politics. These include such questions as, 'what is the essential nature of political life?' and 'what is the role of chance in human affairs?' The apparent congruency between these political 'operational codes' and the basic beliefs touched upon above, can only be posited. Their empirical specification remains a matter of future research.

A third area of need impact concerns affect towards political institutions, procedures, and personnel. We would expect that general feelings towards these political objects would be at least a partial function of an individual's gratification history. Thus, for example, I found that individuals who had sufficiently satisfied their needs for personal control in political life were more likely to have feelings of confidence in their government, were less politically alienated, and were more likely to view the government as effective.[51] In short, need satisfaction appears to be linked with positive evaluations and supportive orientations.

Need satisfaction or deprivation will result in direct affective linkages to politics only to the extent that linkages are forged between individual requirements and governmental responsibilities. To the extent that government is viewed as incapable (but not unwilling), or not required to provide need satisfaction, the relationships between rewards and political affect will be attenuated. The important boundary setting functions of political socialisation should not be overlooked in this regard. Nor should the impact of general socio-political dislocation on collective citizen affect (public moods) be overlooked. Barber, for example, has suggested at least three under the rubric of 'climate of expectations', including public needs for reassurance, sense of progress and action, and legitimacy.[52]

The next area of need impact concerns political motives, whose strength will be a partial function of the history of need gratification or deprivation. Neither must be viewed in absolute terms.[53] For example, Lasswell's compensation hypothesis suggests political man seeks power to compensate for

---

51 Renshon, op.cit., pp.153-76. Yet, it must be added that the respondents were generally from advantaged backgrounds, attending a prestige university during a time of great student activism.

52 James David Barber, *The Presidential Character*, Prentice-Hall, Englewood Cliffs, New Jersey, 1972, p.9.

53 One of the few discussions of the issue notes:
    If one need is satisfied, then another emerges. This statement might give the false impression that a need must be satisfied 100 per cent before the next need emerges ... A more realistic description of the hierarchy would be in terms of the decreasing

low self-esteem. Yet Lasswell goes on to note that, 'compensation is favored when the deprivation is not overwhelming'.[54]

If for purposes of illustration we assign three outcomes to need deprivation, (overwhelming or severe, moderate and slight), it seems plausible the last two and not the first will be more likely to operate as political motives. Moreover if we order human needs in a rough hierarchy à la Maslow, it can be suggested that even moderate deprivations of physiological needs will cause political withdrawal. Even the highly politicised conscientious objectors who took part during World War II in food deprivation experiments ceased to be politically concerned when put on a semi-starvation diet.[55] For the 'higher' needs, however, moderate deprivation would not seem to be a bar to political activity. On the contrary, in the absence of strong environmental constraints, they would be expected to propel not retard motive activation. Yet many questions remain about the impact of mixed gratifications and its effects on political motivations. Maslow's self-actualisers did not necessarily spend large amounts of time in the public arena, yet, Knutson found that when they did their pattern of behaviour differed markedly from those who were need deprived.[56]

This brings us to the fourth area of impact, political behaviour. The range of impact here is exceedingly wide and well illustrated by other chapters in this volume. First, we may expect that needs will influence the frequency of participation. Paradoxically, high need satisfaction may have the same impact as severe deprivation, namely withdrawal from political contention, one difference being that in the former case this withdrawal would be temporary (but periodic). It seems that moderate satisfaction would have the most effect on increasing frequency of political acts. Second, needs can be theorised to affect the intensity of political activity. To the

---

percentages of satisfaction as we go up the hierarchy of prepotency. As for the concept of the emergence of a new need after satisfaction ... it is not a sudden, salutary phenomenon, but rather a gradual emergence from nothingness. For instance if a prepotent need A is satisfied only 10 per cent, then need B may not be visible at all. However, as this need A becomes satisfied 25 per cent, need B may emerge 5 per cent, as need A becomes satisfied 75 per cent, need B may emerge 50 per cent, and so on.
See Maslow, op.cit., p.54. Obviously these hypothetical figures are inadequate substitutes for the detailed empirical exploration this concept merits.

54 Lasswell, *Power and Personality*, op.cit., p.40.
55 Davies, op.cit., pp.12-13.
56 Jeanne N. Knutson, *The Human Basis of the Polity*, Aldine-Atherton, Chicago, 1972; and also Jeanne N. Knutson, 'The Political Relevance of Self-Actualization' in *Public Opinion and Political Attitudes*, ed. A. Wilcox, Wiley, New York, 1973.

extent that need deprivations decrease activity and affect levels one could expect less sustained behavioural commitment. Yet, the experience of political success (and the resultant need satisfaction) coupled with high ambitions for further and subsequent need gratification can produce an intensity of behavioural commitment that can occasionally carry persons to the higher levels of political power. Third, needs can be theorised to effect the types of political behaviour selected. In the most extreme cases past, continuing, and expected deprivations especially of higher level needs, may lead to the selection of politically violent behaviours. These deprivations may justify such actions, or may simply result in sufficient felt discomfort to impel them.

One must caution however against the too easy linkage of need deprivation with violence. In enumerating a number of testable propositions about self-actualising persons, Maslow includes the following characteristics[57]; delight in bringing about justice; delight in stopping cruelty and exploitation; their fighting is not an excuse for hostility but for setting things right; they hope that society will be improved and believe that it can be and they believe every person should have an opportunity to develop to his highest potential. Elsewhere in discussing some problems of such people he notes they

> are occasionally capable of extraordinary and unexpected ruthlessness. It must be remembered that they are very strong people. This makes it possible for them to display a surgical coldness when it is called for, beyond the power of the average man.[58]

These remarks are interesting for they would appear to fit many dedicated revolutionaries. The difficulty, of course, is that Maslow has proposed so many characteristics of self-actualising persons (based on very limited empirical data) that there are others that would not fit (some would also be irrelevant). Still the origins of many revolutionaries are not the most deprived societal strata, but rather the more gratified. A similar possibility is taken up by Lasswell, in his discussion of the aggressive tendencies in otherwise 'democratic characters'. He notes that:

> It is apparent that the destructive energies may be directed against enemies of the democratic community. Indeed, any other behaviour would betray the

---

57 A.H. Maslow, 'A Theory of Metamotivation', *Journal of Humanistic Psychology*, Vol.7, 1967, p.98. Some further 'imperfections among self-actualizers' are discussed in Maslow, 'Some Dangers of Being-Cognition', *Journal of Individual Psychology*, Vol.15, 1959, pp.24-32.

58 Maslow, *Motivation and Personality, op.cit.*, p.175.

opportunities and responsibilities of democratic citizenship.[59]

Human needs do not, of course, always result in expected behaviour or, in some cases, any behaviours. In addition to the difficulties pointed out in previous sections, several other points merit brief attention. First, needs may be in conflict with each other. Thus King (one of Lane's respondents):

> a politically minded young man, needs to think to himself as independent and autonomous of group pressures at the same time that he needs evidence of his popularity and acceptance. A liberal Democrat, he nevertheless joins the Conservative Party . . . and then worries about his conformity. He denies that he is a conformist and differentiates himself politically in minor ways, but he becomes self-contradictory in the process.[60]

A second point along these lines regards the multiplicity and confluence of character factors for any particular political behaviour. In part, this is a problem of linkages and the adequacy of our models of personality. Biological factors (intelligence, temperament) personal style, belief structures, defense strategies, and individual skills, while related to needs are not isomorphic with them, nor in many cases immediately derivative. Moreover, it is clear that much political behaviour can be adequately explained by wants rather than needs. The 'revolution of rising expectations' especially to the extent that it involves desire for more luxury or consumer goods provides one illustration. It follows then, that future attempts to integrate need theory into political analysis might profitably move beyond the need → behaviour model to a more fully configurative analysis. This will certainly include attention to the situation in terms of both 'objective' and actor definitions.

Clearly, some political contexts are more supportive of need expression than others. The acting out of aggression in American politics for example, is highly regulated by custom and context, and direct public displays of temper and hostility are acceptable only in unusual circumstances. Similarly, the direct expression of some needs is more socially acceptable during some periods than in others. Achievement needs, especially defined in terms of accumulating wealth and status were certainly more acceptable in the 1800s than during the 'socially conscious' late 1960s.

59 Harold D. Lasswell, *The Political Writings of Harold D. Lasswell*, Free Press, Glencoe, Illinois, 1951, p.507.
60 Lane, *op.cit.*, p.67.

A Note on the Normative Political Implications of Need Theory

It has been argued that the study of politics is intimately concerned with 'the necessary or sufficient conditions for obtaining ends, which are deemed ... good or desirable'.[61] To the extent that this contention is accepted, an empirically based theory of human needs would have enormous normative implications. Here, as elsewhere in this essay, space limitations preclude exhaustive treatment of these important areas, yet some general points appear to merit note.

Theorists have not been insensitive to the remedial implications of need theory. Maslow, for example, has frequently noted the importance of society in structuring, creating and satisfying human needs. To the extent that human needs require satisfactions available only in a social context, 'then the good or healthy society would be defined as one that permitted man's highest purposes to emerge by satisfying all his basic needs'.[62] The difficulty of course is that the social definitions of need satisfaction suggest that there are many routes to the same end. Thus, while it is true that public debate is frequently focused on whether one or another public need (or want) is a legitimate responsibility of government, one should not overlook the equally important disagreements on procedure.

What role can Political Science play in resolving these difficulties? Bay has forcefully argued for a political science more concerned with human needs than with explaining variance.[63] Yet, not only are these two approaches not mutually exclusive (as Bay recognises); each cannot profitably proceed without the other. The problem is not one of the relative moral superiority of one or another position. Nor is it a question of 'value-free' research. Rather as Harold Lasswell pointed out some time ago, it is a question of putting 'objectivity ... where it belongs, in the service of goal values'.[64]

As this essay has suggested, the path to an empirically based need theory will not be easy. Nonetheless, the potential rewards of establishing linkages are immense. As Bay has correctly pointed out, 'As the horizons of behavior research expand to encompass latent need behavior as well as manifest want behavior; our political science will not only produce a new order of intellectual challenge, it may also become a potent instrument for pro-

61 Sheldon Wolin, *Politics and Vision*, Little Brown, Boston, 1970, p.13.
62 Maslow, *op.cit.*, p.58. See also *The Farthest Reaches of Human Nature*, Viking, New York, 1971, pp.199-249.
63 Christian Bay, 'Politics and Pseudopolitics: A Critical Evaluation of Some Behavioral Literature', *American Political Science Review*, Vol.59, 1965.
64 Lasswell, *Power and Personality*, *op.cit.*, p.122.

moting political development in the service of human development'.[65]

Postscript-Models of 'Human Nature' in Social Life

As models which attempt to understand and explain human character development and dynamics, 'need theories' are but one of several extant models. Each begins with certain assumptions about 'human nature' and proceeds to erect a theoretical superstructure. Yet, it is these very assumptions which, rather than being the basis of theory, should be the starting point of empirical research and specification. Broad generalities such as 'is man essentially good or evil?' are widely recognised as useless theoretical guides and the specifications of the conditions under which one or another character outcome is more likely have proven far more productive. The outcome of continued research into the assumptive frameworks of these models is likely to result in a series of conditional character models, continually undergoing revision in the light of changing historical and societal circumstance. Thus the search for *the* definitive model of 'human nature' like that mounted for the Holy Grail is likely to prove unproductive. Yet, these models and the assumptions that underlie them have social importance beyond their ability to explain variance.

Politics can be characterised by a set of assumptions about the nature of people, government, and their relations which are, however imperfectly, integrated into their major social institutions. From this it follows that individuals can be characterised as being more or less in consonance with these dominant assumptions. For example, if totalitarian regimes operate under the assumption that leaders' interpretations of political reality and necessity have *a priori* precedence over collective citizen interpretations, a citizen who had the characteristic of ego strength (defined as the ability to pursue one's motives in the face of adversity) would be less valued than one who did not.

Similarly, the institutions and processes of democratic politics also operate under a set of assumptions about people, leaders, and their interactions. As Gordon Allport has pointed out:

> ... the theory of democracy requires man also possess a measure of rationality, a portion of freedom, a generic conscience, appropriate ideals, and unique value. *We cannot defend the ballot box, or liberal education, nor advocate free discussion and democratic institutions, unless* man has the potential capacity to profit therefrom [emphasis added].[66]

---

65 Bay, 'Politics and Pseudopolitics', *op.cit.*, p.51.
66 Gordon Allport, *Becoming: Basic Considerations for a Psychology of Personality*, Yale University Press, New Haven, 1955, p.100.

These considerations suggest the possibility that models of human nature operate as ideals for both the individual and society. At the individual level, such models present an image of our 'ideal selves' and a possible goal or standard of comparison for self and others. At societal level, such models also operate as 'cultural ideals' as portrayed in such mass media as movies, novels, aphorisms, popular music, and other implements of everyday life. In short, these models function in part *to set boundaries of the possible* or probable. They indicate not only what we do, but equally important, what we think we can do. The ability of these models to influence conceptions of political possibilities is only one side of the coin, for as Robert Young remarks, 'it is just as likely to be the case that political and ideological perspectives set definitions to the limits of human nature'.[67]

This last consideration returns us to the necessity to probe and not assume the dynamics of human motivation. That no one model is likely to be accurate under widely varied circumstances diminishes neither the value nor the importance of the undertaking. Every prescription for social intervention from 'scientific socialism' to the 'policy sciences' assumes some knowledge of individual (and societal) processes and advances in collective and individual possibilities are unlikely to proceed very far without it.

---

67 Robert Young, 'The Human Limits of Nature', in *The Limits of Human Nature*, ed. J. Berthall, Dutton, New York, 1974, p.242.

The Development of Individuals and the Development of Polities

James Chowning Davies

All political theory is based on some idea about what human beings are like — some idea of human nature. Some theory may merely imply or even attempt to ignore the human aspect of its equations. It may then proceed to discuss political institutions as though they were structures designed for some purpose other than their use by the people who inhabit them. Some theory may argue that the end, the purpose, of the state is to glorify a particular race, a god, 'the masses', humanity, or some other abstraction. Whatever the intent of such argument or the specified purpose of the polity, the effect has been to justify the establishment or maintenance in power of some particular ruling elite. So justified, rulers see themselves as dedicated servants of some perfect idea and not in practice servants of the real-life, imperfect human beings in a polity, the people whom the rulers may help to become better — or worse.

But whether a theory declares itself justified on some higher moral principle or some totally inclusive principle and whether it explicitly justifies or condemns the rule of one particular kind of ruling elite or another (Plato's guardians, Calvin's saints, and Marx's proletarian vanguard), it cannot escape human beings as an active ingredient, a determining element in the political equation. People are there: they ineradicably exist and act. Even if they are seen as instruments of some higher purpose, they affect the ways governments function and are justified. The basic question here considered is whether indeed human beings do not provide the ultimate justification for government and whether human nature is not the ultimate basis for judging political institutions.

I will here argue that the ultimate criterion for judging the empirical, practical suitability and the moral rightness of various political systems is indeed human nature. I will further argue that the kind of political system which is appropriate to human beings depends on the general stage of mental development that prevails among a particular people at a particular point in their historic progress from uncivilised anarchy to more advanced stages. This is not to say, as Marx did, that the human essence is altogether a product of its social conditions. Rather it is to say that human nature is a constant, with some innate predispositions becoming manifest while others remain latent. Successive stages of the emergence of human nature depend on an appropriate interaction between what humans want at a particular stage of their development and what the environment provides at that particular stage.

The psychological basis for this political theory states that human beings want different things at different times, in the innate, organic process of moving from infancy to maturity. If the environment meets these demands when they are activated, then human beings will move on to demand other things. The potential demand is innate but its activation depends on the timely intersection of its natural emergence from within the organism and a response from without, in the form of favourable environmental circumstances. This is the manner, I am suggesting, in which individuals and polities emerge and evolve. The appropriateness and the rightness of political institutions are to be judged by the kinds of human needs that predominate at a particular stage in the development of people.

The Stages of Individual Development
Abraham Maslow is the first psychologist that I know of who systematically argued, in 1943, that innate human needs affect observable actions *in a hierarchical order*. My view of human needs stems directly from Maslow's but modifies it in a couple of crucial ways. And it emphasises that the hierarchy functions not only as needs first emerge in *sequence*, in human development from birth to adulthood[1], but also as they re-emerge in *priority*. A newborn infant's first demands are for satisfaction of its physical needs for food and warmth, then affection. This emergence phenomenon

---

1 James C. Davies, *Human Nature in Politics,* John Wiley, New York, 1963, Chapters 1 and 2.

we may call sequence. A mature adult who is altogether absorbed in his or her career will stop work when he or she gets tired or hungry — that is, when the physical needs become active again. This re-emergence we may call priority.

Some theory of sequence and priority is, as Maslow[2] first made clear, most helpful in explaining the behaviour of individuals. But such a theory has far broader implications and is a necessary part of any fundamental theory of social and political development. It is necessary if we are to understand more than superficially the development of large aggregates of individuals — of peoples, nations, and indeed the human race from its social beginnings. And it is necessary to explain the behaviour of developed peoples when they experience crisis which makes them become pre-occupied again with physical survival after having previously become accustomed to it.

The sequence of needs as I see them first emerging and their priority as they re-emerge in individuals is the following:

1 The physical needs for food, clothing, shelter, health, and safety from bodily harm
2 The social-affectional needs for getting, being, and staying together with other individual humans
3 The self-esteem or dignity needs for being recognised as an individual of unique worth in the eyes of self and others
4 The self-actualisation needs for engaging in that kind of activity that is uniquely appropriate to each individual's particular gifts — activity so inherently satisfying to the individual that he or she easily gets almost totally 'lost' in it, so totally identified with that activity that the individual loses the boundaries that otherwise distinguish him or her from that creative kind of interaction with some particular aspects of the environment.

The following Figure 1 shows the sequence in which needs emerge and the priority with which they re-emerge.

The *sequence* of emergence of these four needs is as indicated. The new-born infant with its partially developed and almost unconditioned brain, is at first little more than (to him or her) an ill-defined, undistinguished part of total reality. This reality consists almost entirely of eating, sleeping, staying warm and dry, etc. Then — no later than a few weeks after birth — the infant becomes very vaguely conscious of the distinction between

---

2 A.H. Maslow, 'A Theory of Human Motivation', *Psychological Review*, Vol.50, 1943, pp.370-96.

Figure 1
Mental Preoccupations in the Course of a "Normal" Lifetime, using Maslow's Hierarchy

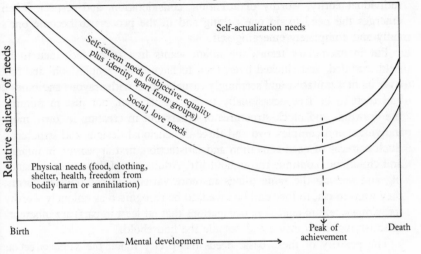

Mental Preoccupations in the Course of a Lifetime Interrupted by Deprivation

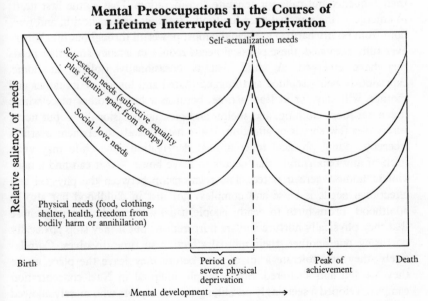

From J. C. Davies, *Human Nature in Politics*, (1963). Used by permission of the publisher, John Wiley and Sons, Inc.

self and other. At this time the desire begins to emerge to be with others (typically but not at first necessarily mother) and to enjoy the comfort of others' closeness. Then emerges the third need, to be recognised as an individual entity, worthy of attention, consideration, and respect. Then emerges the need to do one's thing and in the process to become one's fully and completely emerging self.

Put in exemplary terms, the infant wants first to be fed; then to be held, cuddled, and clucked over; then to have other people 'ooh' and 'ah' over its first imitative and seemingly casual efforts with crayons and blocks; and then to be free occasionally to act on its own, not just in miming the drawings and block-structures of others but in creating its own, more individual and complex two and three-dimensional designs and structures. Such patterns of need activation and satisfaction, first appearing in infancy and childhood, continue throughout life. Adults spend their lives demanding and seeking the same things in more varied and complicated forms: they want to eat, to love and be loved, to be recognised as uniquely worthy individuals, and to engage in occupations that (at least in part) are inherently satisfying, both inside and outside the household.

The priority of these basic needs has pretty much the same effect as their sequence but calls for separate consideration. That is, the first needs to emerge — the physical ones for food, clothing, shelter, health, and freedom from bodily harm — are also the most powerful throughout life. Whenever fully activated, these physical needs reduce to latency any other needs that have emerged. A child that is occasionally isolated at home, capriciously being scolded and hugged (hated and loved) by its father and mother, will stay for at least a time, because it has no other place where it can get food, clothing, and shelter and pick up occasionally — but never surely — a few shreds of affection. If the hatred leads to frequent beatings (thereby adding physical to emotional deprivation), the child may avail itself of any opportunity that occurs to leave home — *if* it can find a non-violent home where it is fed. The relationship between the physical and affectional needs is close and complex, not just in childhood but also in adulthood. From birth to death, people usually live and sleep with those that they physically nurture and are nurtured by; but if they stop physically nurturing one another, their mutual affection in time dissolves. Correlatively, they will tolerate a lot of hate before they leave the place where they are fed and sheltered. Some people interned in Nazi concentration camps developed a seemingly odd liking for the captors who merely allowed them to live.

The posited relationship between the need for self-esteem or dignity and the usually stronger need for affection is similarly one of priority. In order to avoid separation, abandonment, and solitude, people will accept many indignities. Spouses take occasional, even frequent, humiliation from spouses who are faithful and generally love them. In order to demand dignity, they must first have become at least minimally secure in the satisfaction of their higher priority needs for affection and for food. Correlatively, in order to eat and in order not to become physically or emotionally isolated from others, people will accept many indignities, many frustrations of esteem in their own eyes and the eyes of others. Correlatively, divorces seem more common among those who have been degraded by their spouses but have come not to depend on them for either affection or sustenance.

The need to self-actualise is generally the last to emerge and the first to go latent when needs of higher priority move from latency to activation. A person who would be an artist or a farmer or an athlete will abandon such activity as a career if he or she is not recognised as being good at either occupation, if he or she suffers too much isolation from others in the process of being an artist, farmer or athlete, or if he or she cannot thereby support family and self. Such immortals as Beethoven in music, Picasso in art, and Hemingway in writing all needed to create and could not live without doing so. But they very likely could not have created without public recognition, without the usual presence of friends or family, or when their health failed.

One additional factor merits mention because it often appears to affect both the sequence and the priority of needs, as they emerge and re-emerge in a developing individual. That factor is the effect of a prolonged earlier inability to be secure in finding satisfaction of any one particular need. The effect is a mental fixation, an occasionally neurotic and continued preoccupation with seeking satisfaction of a particular need that for a crucial period was not securely fulfillable.

Some examples will help explain the security phenomenon. Many people who survived the Nazi concentration camps of the 1930s and 1940s remained preoccupied with food after they got out: many of them became fat after having been little more than ambulatory skeletons for months or even years in the camps. A similar eating neurosis developed among subjects in a human starvation experiment under controlled laboratory circumstances.[3] An example among the affectional needs is the lifelong — even addictive, as it has been called — preoccupation of some people with

---

3 See A. Keys *et al.*, *The Biology of Human Starvation*, Vol.2, University of Minnesota Press, Minneapolis, 1950.

being loved, because they never got a sufficient or a predictable supply of it as children. An example among the self-esteem needs is the lifelong preoccupation with social status among people who have just made it from a socially degraded class to one that represents success and receives deference. There is a preoccupation with the prerequisites of status among such upwardly mobile people and then a bafflement at the offhand, casual rejection of status by their children who have been raised with intense concern for their physical and emotional security – and indeed their dignity as they are sent off to one of the most prestigious colleges to be finished off. The children, secure in being provided for, cared for, and socially deferred to, take these satisfactions for granted and are preoccupied with self-fulfilment.

The preoccupation with the present satisfaction of a need that is now readily fulfilled because it was in an earlier time not securely fulfilled may be called mental lag, developmental dissonance, or baser-need fixation. In Marxian terms, it's a contradiction. And it is, as we shall see, of enormous portent for the rate and the ease with which vast groups of individuals (socio-economic classes, ethnic groupings, and even nations themselves) are able to progress, to develop. This baser-need fixation – the contradiction between objectively secure progress and persistent insecure preoccupation with it – slows down and at times helps to block the process by which human development beyond physical subsistence becomes a real possibility for more than a minority of the members of a society. That is, it helps block the long road to total fulfilment for the great majority of human beings.

The Stages of Political Development
The basic stages of political development as I see them are these:
1 *Primitive anarchy* In it the rules governing the making of decisions that affect everyone are firmly established and 'immutable', having developed over centuries and having become authoritative – that is, well accepted and internalised by everyone.
2 *Anomic anarchy* In it traditional rules are cast aside and people are reduced to a war of each against all, and the only law is individual and family survival.
3 *Oligarchy* In it the authority of timeless tradition and the law of survival are replaced by the power of a living elite, an oligarchy that is mainly accountable to itself or some small group or some principle or god but not to the citizenry, for and against which it makes and administers public policy.

4 *Democracy*   In it the rules for making such decisions establish principles and practices that make the governing elite accountable periodically to the general public.

5 *Civilised anarchy*   It shares with primitive anarchy the internalisation of conformity to rules but differs from primitive anarchy in at least two ways. It is highly complex, involving widespread specialisation of occupation and function among a people integrated in polities that may number even billions of citizens; and what is internalised is not timeless tradition but a system of values and practices whose history is known and critically approved or modified. Values and practices are based on empirical knowledge and moral acceptance of human nature, which becomes (as it is increasingly understood) the criterion for judging the appropriateness of economic, social, and political practices.

Let me indicate the social and economic circumstances that characterise life in these five successive stages of political development. It might indeed be more accurate to say that there are only three stages, because the first stage (primitive anarchy) is prepolitical and the fifth (civilised anarchy) is postpolitical. In the first stage the social unit is tribal, manorial, or small communal, and virtually all the basic policies have become established by immemorial tradition. In the fifth stage the social unit is vast, and all the basic policies have become established by a process in which broad interpersonal identification — the awareness of each individual's identity as a human being with every other individual — has largely replaced earlier sources of authority. Primitive and civilised anarchy are alike in that the basic rules governing people's interactions — governing society — are internalised within individuals.

Primitive anarchy is the stage that prevails in a static society whose nearly total preoccupation is with survival and in which there is little recognition of individuality and indeed little flowering of what we regard as culture. Tradition, having developed over centuries, in a milieu where few people are literate, controls day-to-day decision-making. Individuals conform to tradition because conditions change little, people change little, and so the basic policies (which pertain to the maintenance of a stable and simple society) are adequate to the survival-oriented demands of people. Tradition dominates the mode of hunting and gathering of food and its cultivation, in more or less communal (that is, extended-family) plots. Tradition dominates the relationships between parents and children, husbands and wives, brothers and sisters, and cousins and those outside the sharply demarcated community. Population levels are typically rather static in such static societies, a condition that reflects the near-total preoccupation with self- and species-preservation.

Life in the survival economy and society that produce primitive anarchy may not be, to paraphrase Hobbes, solitary, but it very likely is poor, nasty, brutish, and short. It is poor, nasty, and brutish in that people lack material and other means of interesting themselves in activity unrelated to food, shelter, and sex. If there is material abundance of food, shelter, and sex, people may live lives that seem serene. On closer examination, however, they are most of the time boring, gossipy, and niggling. There may be too much or too little to do, in order to survive, but that is about all there is to do.

I am referring not only to the primitive circumstances that prevail among pre-literate tribal villages, whether in Afghanistan, Bantustan, or Samoa. I am including all pre-modern cultures: most of the human race in Europe in the late Middle Ages and in Russia until the late nineteenth century, and I am including most people even in the late twentieth century in Central and South America, in most of the Middle East and Far East – except for Japan and parts of China and South-East Asia. These pre-modern cultures, descended from vast imperial polities (Roman, Islamic, Buddhist, Confucian, Roman or Greek-Orthodox Christian, or Latin Christian), became decentralised and fragmented to tribe-, manor-, and commune-sized groups governed primarily by tradition and the exigencies of survival.

In earlier epochs, Greco-Roman, Mayan, Aztec, Incan, Chinese, and Islamic civilisations had produced high levels of culture (based on serfdom or slavery); and not all people in them were totally governed by the prescriptions of tradition and the exigencies of survival. These cultures were relatively integrated and centralised, and they supported large cities. Life for the elite was full and exciting. And for reasons ill-understood, they gradually disintegrated, leaving virtually everyone to a stabilised struggle merely to survive. There is too much evidence that civilisations can decline and fall, reducing their inhabitants to the simple and isolated life, to make it appropriate to consider as primitive only those cultures that have no great past.

What causes the beginning of development, environmentally speaking, is the introduction of new material and social technology, which begins to free the inhabitants of their nearly total concern with staying alive, and with propitiating the past and the gods of nature. The process, particularly in its economic aspects, has been classically analysed by W.W. Rostow.[4]

---

4 W.W. Rostow, *The Stages of Economic Growth*, Cambridge University Press, Cambridge, 1960.

People begin to see that they may have a little control over their own destinies, that there is no total inevitability as to what nature 'wishes', and that traditional rules do not work in new circumstances. Examples of new technology are these: the beginnings of trade with another culture; the development of a medium of economic exchange; the introduction of new methods of growing crops and livestock; and (among those societies that have only in the twentieth century begun to develop) the introduction of health measures that manifestly reduce the seeming omnipotence of nature and nature's gods to take human life at will. Figure II (page 84) shows the successive stages of political development.

The social and political effect of the beginning of development is the first bursting of the age-old and very high dams that have constricted human behaviour and blocked human development. Individuals now begin to see — *and to see for themselves* — that there can be much more to life than survival: now they can control their own destinies — a little, but to an incredible extent — because they no longer have to propitiate timeless forces of tradition and nature, in order merely to survive. And so they do not need to stay where they were born, live as their ancestors always lived, and they do not need to obey their elders, the living bearers of the dead ikons of the past. Primitive, all-enveloping anarchy is now shucked off like the shell of a newborn bird.

A wild and omnipotent anomic anarchy replaces primitive anarchy. The new kind knows no law; no consideration of causes and consequences of individual action; no past; and only an excitingly bright, totally manipulable future. This process has been classically analysed by Emile Durkheim.[5]

What causes the beginning of development and anomic anarchy, *non*-environmentally speaking, are the innate needs, notably those beyond survival. These are the demands for which the potential exists genetically in the human organism. They are now released by a more dependably nurturant environment that enables the organism to develop beyond mere self- and species-preservation. Individuals no longer are totally preoccupied with just their physical and rudimentary social needs. They migrate to the city or to another country. They get jobs in warehouses, mines, or factories. They even have a little money left over after eating and buying some clothes and paying the room rent. They can seek sex partners who are not selected for them by their elders and, perhaps after some experience in buying the commodity of sex, may even fall in love.

---

5 Emile Durkheim, *The Division of Labor in Society*, (1893), The Free Press, Glencoe, Illinois, 1947.

Figure 2.
Stages of Political Development

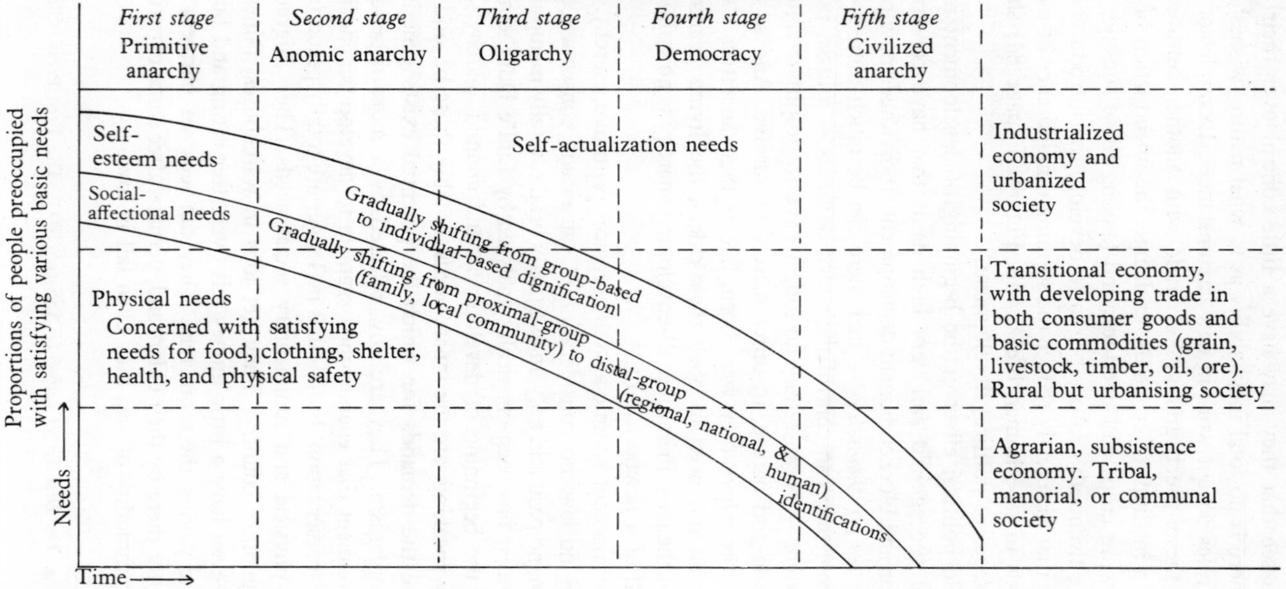

The times that various peoples use to go through successive stages of (national) development are very variable, and so the time scale is not fixed or fixable. Only the *sequence* of stages is here regarded as invariable. That is, it is not deemed possible for any people to avoid the disorder of transition from primitive anarchy to oligarchy; nor is it deemed possible for any people en route to civilised anarchy to avoid experiencing either capitalist elitism or its socialist alternative, the dictatorship of the proletariat's vanguard. It is also deemed impossible for capitalist or socialist oligarchy to outlive its utility for very long.

They can establish some kind of identity, some individuality, and — at least for the time being — can begin to fulfil themselves in activity that they never dreamed of: changing jobs, advancing from a job of lesser to one of greater skill, going to movies, sightseeing. And they don't go home again, at least not for longer than a visit that starts with fond greetings, continues into boredom, and ends with eager anticipation of return to the new world of the city.

However, the past of the village or the farm is not yet dead in the minds of those commencing development. They imagine that they are quite free of tradition and the whims of nature, but not even the struggle to survive is altogether ended. It now includes, more than rarely, trying to avoid physical violence, whether at the hands of others who share the same raw, new circumstances in the port cities or mines or factories or at the hands of the police who occasionally (and perhaps as capriciously as nature with its floods and droughts) crack heads, imprison, torture, and kill.

The new anomic anarchy, quite lacking the internalisation of primitive anarchy, soon becomes insufferable. Being unable for long to endure a war of each against all — whether as Hobbes described it in *Leviathan* in 1651 or as Marx angrily denounced its systemic causes in *Capital* two centuries later — newcomers to the complex life of the city begin to conform to a new authority, the governing elite and its long arm in the form of the armed policeman. The forces that make newcomers begin to obey are both external and internal. They have to obey the cop to avoid being beaten and jailed — that is, to avoid physical deprivation. And they have to obey inner coercive forces: they need some kind of inner control in order not only to enjoy the city's excitement but also to survive. The newcomers begin to develop a respect for a new authority; they begin to develop a concern not only for self but also for others, because each cannot survive alone. They have emigrated from the oppressive, boring life and authority of their primitive community. But they do not for long abandon authority. Circumstances demand it and their own innate needs for security in gaining a living, in getting friends, and in establishing some kind of new identity also demand it.

Nevertheless, the authority is most of the time, in most new situations, imposed. It is far more external than it is internal. And newcomers are compelled to obey an elite who make and administer rules because the only alternatives — occasional injury and constant fear of death, or return to the village and the past — are neither possible nor desirable.

A newly developing society that produces and maintains in power an oligarchy responsible actually to itself only and not to the general public is extremely self-centred. It may intensify egocentricity among both members of the tiny segments of the population who command and the vast majority who obey. It is the egoistic society in the sense that Adam Smith described it – a century after Hobbes had observed it in urbanising, modernising England and said that it required absolute surrender of power to the government. In the late twentieth century, it is the egoistic society of the Soviet Union and its satellites and of military dictatorships in Latin America.

But the ruling oligarchy in such a society, as it continues to develop and integrate, becomes increasingly oppressive, so people become more urbanised, more cohesive, and more civilised. New forces emerge within the human organism. These forces help to produce a demand for the public recognition of the communality of misery that attends transition and of the public, political responsibility for relieving it. Underlying this demand is the recognition, among once anomic individuals, of the need to band together against the hitherto necessary – and therefore acceptable and therefore authoritative – control of government by the oligarchy.

There is a growing sense of broad solidarity in major segments of the general public, which comes to realise that it has the ability to constrain the total power of the elite. Industrial strikes develop and become effective, as the interest of the group of workers becomes at once their self- and group-interest. It becomes gradually less and less possible for the government, typically working in its own and the economic elite's self-interest, to break strikes either by force or by getting workers who are outside the workers' organisation to do the jobs that are necessary but which the strikers refuse to perform.

In addition to recognising their own economic interest in *more* – in a larger portion of the ever-expanding national product – workers now demand the recognition and respect that were the trade-mark of the middle class. And they demand the right to a good life. If the opportunity to fulfil themselves once involved coming into the city to find excitement unavailable in the rural setting, that is no longer enough. Workers now demand opportunities for less than all-consuming labour, so that they can enjoy themselves in ways far removed from the once challenging but now stultifying life of feeding machines in the factory and of fighting to stay alive in the slum.

It is at such points in the development of integrated societies that oligarchy becomes insufferable and democracy becomes possible. As each successive group that has endured hunger, ill health, isolation, degradation, and discrimination gains recognition and power, the governing elite becomes at first reluctantly and then eagerly responsive and responsible to these newly potent groups. Rulers who once only served industrial and other entrepreneurs now seek the votes of workers, ethnic minorities, and women. Political institutions that may have been democratic only in principle become increasingly democratic in practice.

This process of making an initially unresponsive, even irresponsible political elite increasingly responsive to ever more self-conscious groups within the society is the one that the most advanced nations are in at the moment. Political elites in nations in the earliest stages of economic and social integration on an industrial basis typically are responsible only to themselves or at most to the first new group to become self-conscious and politically effectual: the economic elite. In capitalist societies like England, France, Germany, the United States, and Scandinavia until at least the early twentieth century, the economic elite were not formally part of the political elite but they dominated it. In the Soviet Union and its satellites, in India and in most socialist nations in the Middle East, Africa, and East Asia, the economic elite is within the government. Whether the economic system is called capitalist or socialist, neither the economic elite nor the political elite is truly responsible in any significant degree to the general public. The dominance of the elite — the rule by oligarchy — is not a consequence of ideology but of the early stage of development.

As integration and interdependence increase, economic and social groups that once were violently in conflict become interest groups that bargain non-violently for their demands. At this point, restiveness at governmental control increases and spreads from established economic to established social groups. All groups want the government to support them and to control all other groups. Industrialists want trade unions regulated more totally; unions want industry regulated more totally; workers who have just become middle class want government to control groups that are less advanced and more anomic but do not want government to force their schools to include the children of the poor; ethnic minorities want laws that will give them the right to equal opportunity, to equality in all ways but not enforcement of laws against violence unless they are the victims; and women want the same as ethnic minorities. But industrialists want to be free to run their businesses as they see fit; unions resist laws giving individuals the right not to join unions; blacks want a minimum but not a maximum quota of jobs for blacks; and women want the right not to have children. And all groups, whether poor or rich, continue to want government welfare — for their own group only.

This condition of political bargaining for equal dignification, for equal rights of groups as groups, is about where we are now in the process of political development. The principles on the basis of which such bargaining takes place are universalist: all men (and as an afterthought women) are created equal and are entitled to equal rights, to equal dignity. But at this stage each group asserts its equality with other groups. Two things are still lacking: first, a significant recognition of the equality, the equal dignity, of all individuals who share common interests as citizens of a nation rather than as group members and second, a significant recognition of all individuals as individuals. That which is uniquely individual, even that which is within each individual and is uniquely valuable to the community, only slowly emerges, even though he or she is the moral entity in whose name equality has been extended and gradually becomes available — to more groups rather than to more individuals. In short, the unique value of each elite member of society — of each publicly distinguished person — is generally recognised but not the unique value of undistinguished individuals, who remain hidden behind the shield of their group status.

But as larger numbers of individuals gain more kinds and amounts of political influence, the society itself becomes more individual oriented. The diversification and individuation begin with the reaction that develops out of the monotony and uncertainty of preoccupation with survival, with the collective division of labour, and with the individual specialisation of function. That is, in the very process by which individuals become individually specialised, they see the possibility of becoming more specially individual. This was envisioned by Saint-Simon and Marx in the nineteenth century; society can become increasingly individual at the same time that it becomes increasingly integrated. Individuals begin to sense their individuality as individual human beings also rather than only as members of a particular group, in the factory or in the slum neighbourhood. Without losing their identity in terms of their origins as members of a class or other group, including a nation, people increase their concern with fulfilling that portion of their needs and expectations that relates to their individuality.

When the opportunities for individuation have become generally available — that is, to a large majority of the public — and when the ruling elite is truly and routinely responsible to all individuals as citizens and not as group members — a society has become democratic. That is, all people have equal opportunity to acquire material wealth, equal dignity, and equal participation in the establishment of public policy. Only then is a society ready to start to move into the next stage: civilised anarchy. This can occur only when economic and social development have advanced to the point when virtually everyone has become secure in the availability of labour that pays well and does not bore one to death and has become sufficiently identified with other individuals and with groups to be able to afford to establish his or her separate identity, his or her own unique individuality. In the most advanced industrial nations, this point has been reached for large minorities of the total population and soon may be available to large majorities. In societies just beginning to industrialise, the point has been reached for only very small minorities. This is the stark reality, whether industrialisation has taken place under capitalist or socialist ideology.

The Interaction between Individual Development and Institutions
The relationship between the development of individuals and of socio-economic and political institutions is highly dynamic and continuously interactive. As successive kinds of organic, innate needs — from the physical to social to dignity to self-actualisation needs — emerge within individuals, those institutions and practices that were appropriate to a prevailing earlier stage become inadequate, and individuals collectively put pressure on the institutions to change. As the institutions become more appropriate to a particular prevailing stage of development of individuals in any particular society, the institutions become facilitators and thereby make it possible for individuals to advance an additional stage — and then quite naturally commence to demand further changes to institutions.

While it is impossible to establish which came first — new demands of individuals for their own further development or change in institutions — it is evident that neither can develop or even begin to develop without the other. A totally unsupportive environment would never have provided the conditions for life itself. A human organism that made the demands on the environment that an amoeba makes, or even a tree or a flatworm or a kangaroo, would never have led to the establishment of any such 'unnatural' structures in the world as socio-economic or political institutions.

Individuals whom circumstances compel to spend their entire lives in a struggle to survive cannot even form an elementary community. As Colin Turnbull has made clear in his *Mountain People*[6], even an established primitive hunting and gathering community and even husband-wife and parent-child solidarity are destroyed when hunger becomes extreme.

Individuals — when circumstances permit them to concern themselves with things other than survival — begin to establish solidary groups, from the family to the local community or the tribe or the socio-economic class.

---

6 C. Turnbull, *The Mountain People*, Simon and Schuster, New York, 1972.

And they thereby establish the social base for making demands for recognition, for dignification as equals, on whoever have power in their community.

And when institutions have been established to meet this level of demand, individuals begin to demand freedom from their government, so that they may become individuals. The development of individuals is thus reciprocal with the development of institutions. The pressure for environmental changes comes from within individuals, from their nature. But individual development requires an environment supportive of one kind of organic need before another can emerge.

The Implications for Political Morality

The empirical basis for political morality lies in the nature of human beings, but this nature requires institutions (social, economic and political) to facilitate its emergence. The interaction and interdependence between the demands of individuals that are innate and may therefore be called human nature and the functions of institutions has not been well recognised. Ideological advances of particular socio-economic and political institutions speak of them sometimes in some kind of timeless, context-free way, as though any particular set of institutions — whether private capitalist or socialist and oligarchic or democratic — were appropriate to all times, places, and circumstances. But it is apparent that all institutions cannot be rationally judged or morally justified without observing their appropriateness to the successive stages of development of the great majority of individuals within a community.

Advocates of either private capitalism or state socialism take it for granted that everyone involved — whether as capitalist entrepreneur or socialist factory manager or labourer — is getting or even has the equal opportunity to get the same things out of capitalism or socialism. The assumption is empirically false and morally obtuse. Entrepreneur, manager, and worker do make more money out of their interaction than they would if entrepreneurs and managers did not organise or if workers refused to work in them. But individuals who are members of the capitalist and socialist elite get far more. To the capitalist entrepreneur or the socialist manager, the manufacture of a product that enriches him, his customer, and society gives great release to his desire not just for material welfare but also for recognition, for dignification, and for self-fulfilment as an individual. To the factory worker, the benefits may be limited to material welfare and to more solidary ties to family and to other workers. In other respects the factory system — even the socialist factory system — often has degraded workers in the starkest terms. It has made them anonymous nurturers of machinery, forcing them to adapt as slaves to machines and to a set of institutions (including assembly lines) that deify machinery and efficiency. Workers live in homes that are not air-conditioned but work in factories that are. The superior adaptability of the human organism is exploited and subordinated to the benefit of machinery that cannot adapt. And when workers return home from tending machines, they are usually compelled to live in either filthy slums or starkly monotonous and impersonal highrise apartments. Whether in capitalist or socialist systems, these unsanitary or sanitary slums afford no more sexual privacy than a primitive tribal village and they lack the village's warmth. In short, in a variety of ways workers within either system are deprived of social warmth, of dignity, of any inherent worth that is distinct from their worth to the system, and of any initiative that is relatable to their discovering their own unique individuality.

It is easy for those with a private capitalist ideology to argue the virtues of industrialisation because they benefit in so many fundamental ways — material and non-material — from it. It may be even easier for those with a socialist ideology to argue the virtues of industrialisation — and truly for just the same reasons that work among their capitalist entrepreneurial brethren — because the socialist elite benefit in so many fundamental material and non-material ways from it. It may be easier because socialists, unlike the most primitive anarchic economic egocentrists, have the advantage of being able to hide their own high personal benefits by mentioning only their service as instruments for establishing justice for the 'masses'. They can assert the formal reality that the economic institutions belong to the 'masses' and work solely for the benefit of the 'masses'. They can ignore the stark reality that workers have the right neither to control enterprises nor even to withold their labour by strikes. Where the division of labour is accompanied by a division of power, with bosses having all of it and workers none, the elimination of the dehumanising aspects of industrialisation becomes an impossible and false hope.

Socio-economic systems and political institutions are morally justifiable only as they are more appropriate or less appropriate, as means to human ends. When this means-end relationship is lost, it becomes reversed. The ends become the perpetual maintenance of systems or institutions or of an established elite, and ordinary people become means to those ends.

To reiterate, the appropriateness of institutions has to be judged in accordance with the prevailing stage of development of the great majority of people within a society. It is absurd to regard either oligarchy or democracy as the appropriate political form of government for all people in all times, places, and circumstances. During the enormous disorder of development beyond mere survival, society is typically fragmented in a war of each against all. Society is then a struggling, anomic agglomerate, not a conglomerate. Each individual, trying, first of all, to survive, is continually threatened with hunger, injury, or death. He has been desocialised by his new circumstances and cannot yet act very civilised or even humanised.

In this stage of development of large populations, oligarchy is the dominant mode. It prevails simply because most people in a newly developing society do not have the time, the energy, or the self-assurance to establish restraints on government. They are physically and mentally exhausted by the labour and stress of their new life. They accept, even welcome for a time, the rule of an oligarchy that can establish order and thus reduce the stress. In this stage the criterion for saying whether a capitalist or a socialist economic system is more appropriate is its efficiency in creating abundance of goods, *not* who controls the system. In either case, the system will be controlled by an elite that is not institutionally responsible to the public it professes to serve. Oligarchy, in short, seems to be inevitable in societies that are commencing intensive economic development and broad social integration.

Some of the societies that have gone through this stage under a capitalist system have done so at enormous cost in terms of the exploitation of the inmigrants from the countryside or immigrants from abroad. These people went eagerly into the mines, mills, and factories − and bore the cost of capital accumulation. The capitalists filled their coffers and fulfilled their individuality. Some of the societies that are undergoing this early stage under a socialist system seem truly to have paid much more attention to the health and the job security of people who work with their hands, but the workers have borne the mental cost of the struggle to survive and the material cost of capital accumulation. The factory managers have filled their coffers and fulfilled their individuality.

The Marxist ideology of the new societies has done as effective a job of blinding the socialist elites to their own superordinate role and therefore to the degradation of ordinary people as did the Christian Protestant ideology in blinding capitalists to what they were actually doing. If anything, capitalist development has provided speedier transition to real popular control of the elite. The first popularly based effort to limit the entrenching tendencies of the American revolutionary (and capitalist) elite came in the election of Jefferson in 1800, a quarter of a century after the revolution began. the first such effort to limit the entrenched power of the Russian revolutionary (and socialist) elite had not yet come by 1976, more than half a century after the revolution began.

However late in coming, democracy is the inevitable next step after oligarchy outlives its functions. Democracy is very unlikely to develop until a substantial majority have become secure in the provision of their physical needs and have formed a voluntarily cooperative and therefore solidary society — solidary first within groups and then among individuals. When such a majority begins to form, the process commences of making political institutions responsible to that majority. At the stage where developed and industrialised societies now are, the process is still continuing and is not yet anywhere really completed.

The democratising process lays the groundwork for moving to new, post-democratic institutions which will provide for *generally* available means whereby *all* individuals (and not just an elite) can become individuals, can fully become themselves. Such a new society will inevitably be more social-ised and less freely private capitalist or state socialist. To the extent that the purposes and demands of ordinary citizens become freely expressed through their government, they limit the freedom of action of private entrepreneurs and state enterprise managers when their action conflicts with those of the general public, with the non-elite. But the label socialist or the label capitalist tells little about the actual functioning of the system and institutions, including large labour unions. Trade union leaders share with capitalist entrepreneurs and with socialist factory managers a re-markable tendency to perpetuate themselves in power and to exploit workers.

In a post-democratic society, restraints will develop not only on the elites but also within them and within ordinary citizens. Civilised anarchy will gradually come into existence, as each individual increasingly identifies with all other individuals and internalises those limits on each individual's action that are necessary for people to live, work, and develop together. There develops an obedience to a newly internalised set of rules that gradu-ally makes government in any fundamental policy-making sense unnecess-ary. Without this new internalisation, civilised anarchy is impossible. With it, even democracy becomes oppressive.

But there is no big society that I know of, anywhere in the world, that has even yet achieved adequate democratisation of its socio-economic and political systems. And so there is no society ready to move toward a gradual withering away of the state. Neither elites in the (capitalist or socialist) economy and polity nor general publics in any societies have shown the measure of self-restraint and broad identification with all other members of the society that are necessary before there can be a sure movement toward civilised anarchy.

There can be no withering away of the state until each individual in some critical way regards every other individual as equal in value to him or herself and until each individual regards all others as having a unique potential for self-development. This has already begun to happen in the most integrated advanced societies, so the general direction is clear, even if progress has been minimal. Within the integrated factory, individual workers usually tend enormously complex and expensive machinery with the skilful care that they would show it if it belonged to them as individuals rather than to the corporation or (in state-capitalist countries) the trust. Occasionally people in public places give help to others whom they have never seen before and will never see again. Automobile traffic in cities and on superhighways sometimes moves in obedience to traffic rules, evidently not just because the rules exist but because they are recognised as serving a common public purpose. Young people living in the transitory community life of university students do so in nonprotest times with an easy mutual regard and acceptance of individuality that requires incredibly small forces of law and order, of campus police. University communities number anywhere from ten to forty thousand students, most of whom never knew each other before they came and few of whom will know each other after they leave. Their sense of community has to have preceded their entry into the university. And some people of enormous wealth do not violate tax laws but pay what the collectivity has, through its law-makers, decided wealthy people should pay. So there are indeed portents of the human ability to internalise those identifications and those prescriptions that must be internalised before civilised anarchy can come into being.

What then are the scientific implications of relating stages of individual development to stages of political development? It is clear psychologically that the behaviour of individuals is continually responsive to various basic, innate drives that are arranged in sequence and priority. That is, the physical needs for food, clothing, shelter, health, and freedom from bodily harm are active at birth and dominate all other needs when the physical ones become strongly reactivated, at *any* time during an individual's lifetime. And so on through the other needs up to self-actualisation, each need having lower priority throughout life than those that originally emerged earlier in the sequence of activation.

It is now possible to use this need system, first generated by Maslow, to explain scientifically the stage of development through which polities pass, from the most primitive to the most advanced. Marx made a radical indictment of the exploitation of ordinary people, as a society becomes integrated and industrialised, and he made the first grand, majestic statement on the evolution of socio-economic systems. But he did not systematically set forth a scientific basis for the passage of a society from economic exploitation to cooperation and beyond that to dignification and individuation. It is now possible to escape the circular Marxian analysis, whereby individuals are altogether determined by their environment and are never themselves determinants of socio-economic and political change. This process does indeed appear to be inevitable, for reasons that are scientific, but change is rooted not just in the development of systems but also in the innate development of human beings. The theoretical scientific movement beyond Marx therefore derives from discovering the dynamics of a process in which socio-economic and political systems do not magically change themselves but are changed by the human beings whose development is the result of the interaction between powerful organic and environmental forces.

What then are the moral implications of relating individual stages of development to political systems? The first basic implication is that the criterion for judging appropriateness to systems and institutions remains, not humanity or the masses, but the human individual. And the individual has to be viewed, as Kant said it, as an end withal and not as a means only. The second basic implication is that the appropriateness of systems and institutions depends on the stage of individual development of the general public considered as a total group. When the large majority is moving beyond survival, then oligarchy is for a time not only seemingly inevitable but also justifiable. Physically and emotionally deprived people cannot at first be their own providers or their own therapists. And when the large majority has established a sufficient sense of identity of their common interests, not merely as oppressing or oppressed minorities or majorities, then a mature and extensive democracy is not only seemingly inevitable but also justifiable. Healthy people with broad identifications can collectively rule each other.

If the large majority has succeeded in ruling its elite and itself, then it is ready for the next stage. It can internalise these rules so that each person governs him or herself, nobody governs anyone else, and everybody is free to find and express fully his or her own individuality. The problem up to the present has been that each person, from the time he is a child or lives in primitive anarchy, believes that he is capable of self-rule and that everybody else is not (particularly the shes, the females). In fact, whether male or female, nobody is. Yet.

Human Needs Constraining Political Activity*

Jeanne N. Knutson

The analysis of political activity has been approached from many directions. Opportunity structures, social background factors, institutional constraints and differential power bases have proven to be valuable avenues for the exploration of this phenomenon. Another turn of the kaleidoscope and the same reality assumes a different perspective: that of the psychic resonance between the activity itself and the intrapsychic needs of individuals so unusually involved in politics. The thesis underlying all these approaches to the study of political activity counters the democratic myth by asserting (and repetitiously confirming) that every citizen is *not* equally likely to become a political leader.

The different perspectives through which political activity has been studied are best seen as complementary, rather than exclusive views of reality. Although the present state of recruitment analysis does not permit a high degree of sophistication, it is apparent that the most powerful model must be inclusive in approach and multivariate in nature. Thus our concern here with psychological factors is an admittedly narrow focusing on one major aspect of the recruitment process.

* I would like to express appreciation to Professors James MacGregor Burns, Daniel Katz and Alexander L. George for their reviews of an earlier version of this paper. It represents a portion of a longer, more theoretically focused paper issued by The Wright Institute under the title of 'Psychological Variables in Political Recruitment: An Analysis of Party Activists', Berkeley, 1974.

That a kind of 'psychological selectivity' interacts with the selectivity of social, cultural and political factors to determine both who becomes a political activist and who is likely to function successfully in such a role does not, we should initially stress, place our discussion in the realm of abnormal psychology. Instead, we assume that the same psychological processes which operate in the mass of citizenry also constrain the behaviour of those citizens who become political leaders. Further, (agreeing with Lasswell, 1968[1]), we assume that those psychological processes which critically affect political recruitment also operate in the recruitment of *non*-political leaders. The major issue in the analysis of psychological factors in the recruitment process is that of the *ratio* of certain intrapsychic constraints which operate at various levels of leadership activity and at various points along the ideological continuum compared to the ratio found within (a) human nature, as theoretically understood, and (b) any defined citizenry, as empirically investigated.

In this chapter, we explore some of the psychological constraints affecting political activity through examination of data from a non-random sample of activists ($N = 107$), ranging ideologically from the Communist Party to the American National Socialist White People's (Nazi) Party. While the six parties sampled have greatly disproportionate influence on politics in the United States, the comparative analysis of their members here facilitates awareness of psychological factors contributing to disparate ideological stances. In analysing the psychological factors which influence their political activity, we define personality as the organised, stable internal predispositions which each person brings to a situation, which serve to orient his behaviour and which vary among individuals (Knutson, 1973d, p.30).

Political office can serve a variety of human needs — and satisfy several simultaneously. In studying the ways in which personality shapes political behaviour, it is necessary to be sensitive to those aspects of personality which both shape the content of political belief as well as those which determine the style in which political beliefs are expressed (which includes the type of activity selected to actualise beliefs).

An Examination of Some Party Activists

In political psychology, random samples are usually unavailable if one is concerned with studying leadership — particularly if one wished to probe the sensitive relationship between the intrapsychic and political. Such sam-

---

[1]All references in this chapter can be found in Selected Bibliography p.261. [Ed.]

ple limitation undoubtedly biases the results in unknown ways so that our acceptance of findings must remain tentative until replicate studies convince us that a stable pattern of relationships exists. This caveat applies to the present study as well, which is based on data collected from 107 members of the governing bodies in Los Angeles County of the following political parties: Communist, Peace and Freedom, Democratic, Republican, American Independent, and Nazi. These data were collected to assess the pull ideology exerts on personality in constraining political activity.

In order to enlist the cooperation of the central committees of the four registered parties and of the major leaders of the Communist and Nazi parties, and to preserve the anonymity of the people who were willing to participate, the questionnaires were given out by the leaders of each organisation and then returned directly by the respondent, through the mail, if the person wished to participate. As closely as can be ascertained, approximately 325 questionnaires were actually given out to possible subjects, with the return as follows:

Table 1
Leadership Sample

	Questionnaires Distributed	Questionnaires Returned
Communist Party	60	11
Peace and Freedom Party	50	40
Democratic Party	63	21
Republican Party	72	11
American Independent Party	30	11
Nazi Party	50	13
	325	107

In view of the minute percentages of the American population who hold any political office, the respondents in this southern California sample would necessarily be considered 'activists', 'influentials' or 'leaders'. Certainly, this sample is distinguished by an unusual degree of interest and participation in politics (Robinson, 1952). Thus, as our introductory remarks suggest, some facets of their personality traits should be indicative of those characteristics typical of political activists as a whole. On the other hand, it is also important to affirm the view that subtypes of political leaders may vary considerably. Certainly the growing literature on the differences between amateur and professional leaders (Czudnowski, 1974) would suggest that our data are more likely to be predictive of characteristics of party activists than of other types of political leaders.

Because of the considerable time required to complete the total questionnaire and the politically and personally sensitive nature of the questions (factors which undoubtedly influenced the respondent's willingness to participate), this activist sample cannot be considered representative. The results are best seen as an attempt to replicate and enlarge present knowledge concerning the psychic foundations of various ideologies. The political data provide an unique opportunity to compare a wide spectrum of political ideologies through a standardised instrument which focuses on the intrapsychic characteristics of those espousing disparate political beliefs. Further, analysis of the data indicates that if a person chose to complete the questionnaire, he did so carefully, completely, and in line with his political and personal convictions.

The Research Instrument

In attempting to differentiate party members on the basis of personality characteristics, past research has indicated that a number of measures are likely to be discriminating. The keystone of our research design are scales measuring personality need level which were developed to assess the assumptions of Maslow's (1954) personality theory. In addition to the political distinctions which these scales might uncover, we are thus also interested in a further assessment of the psychologically and politically predictive validity of Maslow's need hierarchy. (See Knutson, 1972; 1973c for large-scale efforts in this validation process.) Brief scales (having only face validity as judged by Maslow and by the present author) measuring Maslow's deprivation needs (physiological, safety, affiliation and both social and self-esteem) proved discriminating in two studies of political relevance (Knutson, 1967, 1972) and, as revised and expanded, in a third study (Simpson, 1971). These initial scales were then considerably expanded for use in the present study (after a thorough literature review of work related to Maslow's personality theory).

The present Index of Psychic Deprivation includes 17 physiological, 23 safety, 19 affection, 21 social esteem and 19 self-esteem items. Self-actualisation needs (Maslow's definition of psychic competence) were not assessed directly. However, in addition to measuring the five deprivational needs directly, scores on these five scales were summed to form a Continuum of Unmet Needs, with the subjects' rank ordered in terms of their total need scores. In this Continuum, as in the individual need scores, a high score indicates lack of psychic competence, thus providing a measure of the subject's psychic growth or self-actualisation.

Although the distinction between personality and politically relevant measures is inexact, for purposes of presentation the other measures employed are roughly divided as follows:

Personality Measures: (1) *Anomia:* a scale developed by Srole (1956) to measure a sense of profound alienation from self and others (See Yinger, 1973). A high score indicates an anomic perspective. (2) *Faith-in-People:* a general measure of distrust and misanthropy developed by Rosenberg (1956) and used in revised form here. A high score indicates a misanthropic response. (3) *Manifest Anxiety:* a scale derived from the clinically validated MMPI by Taylor (1953) to assess somatic indicators of anxiety. A high score indicates anxiety. (4) *Dogmatism:* a well-known measure of cognitive functioning devised by Rokeach (1960) which has been variously shown (Rokeach, 1956; Parrott & Brown, 1972) to have low, positive correlations with conservative beliefs. High scores indicate dogmatism. (5) *Threat Orientation:* a scale developed by Martin and Westie (1959; Martin, 1961) measuring a (nonclinical) paranoid perspective and shown previously to be correlated with basic need deprivation (Knutson, 1972). A high score indicates a threatened orientation. (6) *Intolerance of Ambiguity:* measured by Budner's (1962) scale and previously related to basic need deprivation (Knutson, 1972). A high score indicates intolerance of ambiguity. (7) *Authoritarianism:* measured by the well-known F-scale (Adorno, Frenkel-Brunswik, Levinson & Sanford, 1950; Sanford, 1973) and also shown to relate to Right political ideology (Rokeach, 1960). A high score indicates an authoritarian response. (8) *Internality-Externality:* a measure developed by Rotter (1966; Lefcourt, 1966) which indicates a person's view of the locus of control in his world, with the internality end of the continuum variously shown to relate to psychic competence. Rotter's measure is composed of paired, forced-choice items. In the present study, the measure was revised and 15 pairs which appeared clearly unrelated to other dimensions being measured were included in the form of 30 items, randomised throughout the questionnaire and scored in a Likert form. A high score indicates perception of external control. (9) *Empathy:* because of the clinically observed relationship between empathy and psychic competence, a 39 item scale developed by Mehrabian (1972) was included. A high score indicates lack of empathy.

Political Measures: (1) *Citizen Duty:* a measure developed at the University of Michigan's Survey Research Center (Campbell, Converse, Miller & Stokes, 1960) indicating the degree of political socialisation in the area of accepting citizen responsibility. A high score indicates lack of belief in citizen duty. (2) *Alienation from System:* Four original items were included. The items (with scoring to indicate alienation) are:

1 The way our political system is heading, there is no opportunity for a good life in this country. (+)
2 It will take some drastic political action before this country can have a good future. (+)
3 The political system in America has no room for people with my beliefs and values. (+)
4 America may not be perfect, but the American Way has brought us about as close as human beings can ever get to a perfect society. (−)

A high score indicates alienation. (3) *Political Efficacy:* measured by a scale also developed by SRC (Campbell, Converse, Miller & Stokes, 1960) which was related in past studies to political activism as well as being a good subjective measure of a sense of political competence. A high score indicates a lack of efficacy. (4) *Radicalism-Conservatism Index:* To prepare the questionnaire used in this study, the questions employed in the past two years by the Field polling organisation in California were studied; eight issues were selected as typical of current political concerns in California:

1 Students who challenge and defy university and college authorities should be kicked out to make room for those who are willing to obey the rules. (+)
2 The state university and college system should accept many more black students than it does now, even if many of them do not meet regular scholastic entrance requirements. (−)
4 The tax-paying public should have more say about how the state university and college system is being run. (+)
5 The death sentence should be kept in California as a punishment for serious crimes. (+)
6 Marijuana is a drug and people who use it should be punished. (+)
7 Prohibitions on the sale of guns through the mails deprive citizens of a basic right. (+)
8 Sex education courses should be offered in the public schools. (−)

In Likert form, these eight items were included in the questionnaire to provide a validation and anchoring point for the political positions adhered to by the respondents. A high score on this index indicates conservatism. (5) *Continuum of Parties:* In addition to the Radicalism-Conservatism Index, it was possible, of course, to determine the subject's political affiliation from the political party to which he belonged, with the parties aligned as follows: Communist, Peace and Freedom, Democratic, Republican, American Independent, and Nazi (with a high score indicating conservatism). While the choice of group placement is in part subjective, the reader should note the correlation of .84 between the two measures of ideological direction. (6) *Political Issue Outcome:* Each respondent was asked 'What to you is the most burning political issue today?' and then asked to discuss the means which he would like to use to solve this political problem and to state the likely political outcome of this issue. By comparing the stated issue and the likely outcome, it was possible to score each subject as optimistic, pessimistic or indeterminate. (7) *Political Candidate Outcome:* Each subject was also asked to list his choice for President in 1972 and then to state whom he thought was likely to be elected. Like the previous measure, this comparison also allowed the respondent to be scored as optimistic, pessimistic or indeterminate.

Social-Economic Status Index: Our final measure to be reported is an index composed of equally weighted measures of total family income (Low = below $8,000; Medium = $8,000 to $20,000; High = $20,000 and over); education (Low = some or completed high school; Medium = some or completed college; High = Graduate School and/or higher degree) and occupation (Low = blue collar; Medium = White collar office, sales, etc. positions; High = professional).

Results

In analysing our data, we will be concerned primarily with indications that certain personality characteristics are predictive of political ideology (and thus likely to underlay recruitment into a particular party organisation), as well as with evidence that our Indices of Psychic Deprivation

Table 2
Education and SES by Political Party

A. Educational Level	Low	Medium	High
Communist	27.3%	27.3%	45.4%
Peace and Freedom	-0-	30.0%	70.0%
Democrat	14.3%	14.3%	71.4%
Republican	18.2%	9.1%	72.7%
American Independent	-0-	63.6%	36.4%
Nazi	53.8%	46.2%	-0-
Total Sample	41.2%	46.6%	12.2%

B. Social Economic Status Index	Low	Medium	High
Communist	72.7%	27.3%	-0-
Peace and Freedom	45.0%	45.0%	10.0%
Democrat	23.8%	61.9%	14.3%
Republican	-0-	36.4%	63.6%
American Independent	36.4%	54.5%	9.1%
Nazi	76.9%	23.1%	-0-
Total Sample	42.1%	43.9%	14.0%

are valid measures of general levels of psychic competence. It is important first to ground our discussion in an understanding of the social character-istics of our respondents. As Table 2 indicates, the generally younger Nazis have a low level of education, compared to the respondents from other parties.

Further, while both the Communists and then the AIP members have more education than the Nazis, these two groups have relatively less edu-cation than the respondents from the remaining three parties. This accords with the findings of Elden (1968) that PFP leaders in Southern California are firmly middle class. (Elden's data indicate that, compared to the two centre parties, PFP leaders have a somewhat higher education level.) When education is combined with income and occupation to form a general index of SES (Table 2, B), the demographic differences between respondents are even more apparent. Both the Nazis and the Communists are predominantly lower class; in terms of SES, they cannot be distinguished. The AIP, PFP and Democratic party respondents are generally middle class — with the Democrats having a slightly higher level of social economic status. Significantly different from these two demographic groups are the Republicans, the majority of whom are upper class and none of whom fall into the lower class column.

A second method of presenting our findings in perspective is to examine Table 3, which records the degree of political optimism expressed by our respondents.

Table 3
Political Optimism — Pessimism by Party

A. Political Issue Outcome	Optimistic	Pessimistic	Indeterminate
Communist	54.5%	9.1%	36.4%
Peace and Freedom	42.5%	30.0%	27.5%
Democrat	52.4%	-0-	47.6%
Republican	18.2%	36.4%	45.4%
American Independent	27.3%	54.5%	18.2%
Nazi	46.2%	30.7%	23.1%
Total Sample	42.1%	25.2%	32.7%

B. Political Candidate Outcome	Optimistic	Pessimistic	Indeterminate
Communist	9.1%	-0-	90.9%
Peace and Freedom	12.5%	45.0%	42.5%
Democrat	42.8%	28.6%	28.6%
Republican	72.7%	9.1%	18.2%
American Independent	36.3%	36.4%	27.3%
Nazi	-0-	79.9%	23.1%
Total Sample	25.3%	36.4%	38.3%

Looking first at Issue Outcome — a measure which reflects the respondent's belief that the major tenet of his political ideology will eventually be actualised, we note that the Republicans and the AIP are the least optimistic, whereas the Communists and the Democrats, followed by the PFP and the Nazis, are more optimistic. Clearly, as other observers have noted, there is more optimism on the Left in terms of long-range goals. In terms of immediate success, however, the Candidate Outcome measure (Table 3, B) suggests that the Republicans, followed by the Democrats and the AIP, feel more sanguine about their chances for electoral success, than do other parties. How does long range optimism or pessimism — with its various combinations of immediate electoral success or failure — reflect the scores of our respondents on other political measures? Let us turn to Table 4, where those analyses of variance which yielded a significant F were further analysed by the Newman-Keuls test (Winer, 1962, pp.81-5) for significant differences between individual means and to Table 5, where means of variables with significant F tests were analysed, through t-tests, by political Left, Centre and Right.

1   *Alienation from System:* Looking first at variable 12, we note that the Republicans are significantly less alienated than all other political groups *except* for the other centrist party, the Democrats. Further, the Democrats are significantly less alienated than all other political groups, again except for the Republicans. Finally, AIP members are significantly less alienated than members of all other groups, except for the centrist parties. This finding is confirmed on Table 5, where the centrist parties are (by t-tests for significant differences between means) less alienated than the Left or Right parties.

2   *Citizen Duty:* Turning next to variable 11, we see that the Nazis are significantly more likely to deny that a citizen's duty is to vote and support the existing system than all other political groups. On Table 5, we see rather that it is the centrist parties that are least lacking in perception of citizen duty, and that (because of the low Nazi mean and the high Communist mean), the Left parties are more likely to affirm the duty of participation than the Right.

3   *Political Efficacy:* Looking at variable 13, the developing picture of the centrist parties as essentially politically positive is confirmed. We note that the Republicans possess more political efficacy than the Nazis or the AIP to the right or the PFP to the Left and that the Democrats are more efficacious than the Nazis or the PFP, and finally, that the Communists are more efficacious than the Nazis. Indeed, as Table 5 confirms, the Centrist party members are more efficacious than either the Left or the Right.

Table 4
Mean Differences on Major Variables

Group Order: 1 = Communist, 2 = Peace & Freedom, 3 = Democrat, 4 = Republican, 5 = American Independent, 6 = Nazi

Variable & F Value	Group Order and Group Means						Significant Differences Between Means (Newman – Keuls Test)
1 Anomia $F = 8.64**$	6 4.45	2 3.86	5 3.76	1 3.05	3 2.86	4 2.40	4 < 6**, 2**, 5** 3 < 6**, 2*, 5* 1 < 6**
2 Physiological Needs $F = 2.53*$	6 3.06	1 2.91	2 2.87	3 2.52	5 2.51	4 2.38	4 < 6*
3 Safety Needs $F = 5.51**$	6 3.55	5 3.35	4 2.89	3 2.85	2 2.83	1 2.82	6 > 1**, 2**, 3**, 4**
4 Affiliative Needs $F = 1.52$	2 3.31	6 3.31	1 3.06	3 3.00	5 2.94	4 2.86	NS
5 Social Esteem Needs $F = 2.98*$	6 3.22	5 2.67	4 2.64	2 2.58	3 2.52	1 2.31	6 > 1**, 3*, 2*, 5*
6 Self-Esteem Needs $F = 1.04$	1 2.74	6 2.73	3 2.69	2 2.67	5 2.65	4 2.27	NS
7 Faith-in-People $F = 16.79**$	6 4.20	5 3.24	4 2.69	3 2.60	2 2.60	1 1.89	6 > 1**, 3**, 2**, 4**, 5** 5 > 1**, 3** 4 > 1* 2 > 1*

Table 4
Mean Differences on Major Variables (continued)

Group Order: 1 = Communist, 2 = Peace & Freedom, 3 = Democrat, 4 = Republican, 5 = American Independent, 6 = Nazi

Variable & F Value	Group Order and Group Means						Significant Differences Between Means (Newman – Keuls Test)
8 Manifest Anxiety F = 0.76	6 3.33	3 3.28	2 3.16	5 3.02	1 3.01	4 2.83	NS
9 Dogmatism F = 15.45**	6 5.07	5 4.02	4 3.65	1 3.56	2 3.48	3 3.08	6 > 3**, 2**, 1**, 4**, 5** 5 > 3**
10 Threat Orientation F = 38.58**	6 4.97	5 4.75	4 3.93	3 2.95	2 2.81	1 2.46	6 > 1**, 2**, 3**, 4** 5 > 1**, 2**, 3**, 4** 4 > 1**, 2**, 3**
11 Citizen Duty F = 13.62	6 4.21	2 2.38	5 1.82	4 1.82	3 1.67	1 1.39	6 > 1**, 3**, 4**, 5**
12 Alienation from System F = 34.45**	6 6.06	1 5.70	2 5.23	5 3.66	3 2.87	4 2.32	4 < 6**, 1**, 2**, 5** 3 < 6**, 1**, 2**, 5* 5 < 6**, 1**, 2**
13 Political Efficacy F = 7.07**	6 3.83	2 3.57	5 3.34	1 2.84	3 2.51	4 2.07	4 < 6**, 2**, 5** 3 < 6**, 2* 1 < 6*

Table 4
Mean Differences on Major Variables (continued)

								Comparisons
14	Intolerance of Ambiguity $F = 6.81**$	6 3.69	5 3.63	4 3.18	1 3.02	3 2.83	2 2.78	$6 > 2**, 3**, 1*$ $5 > 2**, 3**, 1*$
15	Authoritarianism $F = 56.72**$	6 4.76	5 4.29	4 3.23	3 1.99	2 1.62	1 1.49	$6 > 1**, 2**, 3**, 4**$ $5 > 1**, 2**, 3**, 4**$ $4 > 1**, 2**, 3**$
16	Internality-Externality $F = 2.93*$	2 3.66	6 3.39	3 3.39	4 3.29	5 3.10	1 2.94	$1 < 2*$
17	Empathy $F = 5.58**$	5 3.73	6 3.67	3 3.40	4 3.15	1 3.11	2 2.99	$5 > 3**, 2*, 1*$ $6 > 3**, 2*, 1*$
18	Radicalism-Conservatism $F = 130.08**$	5 5.84	6 5.52	4 5.09	3 2.23	2 1.95	1 1.61	$5 > 1**, 2**, 3**, 4**$ $6 > 1**, 2**, 3**$ $4 > 1**, 2**, 3**$ $3 > 1*$
19	SES $F = 8.67**$	4 2.43	3 2.13	2 2.02	5 1.70	1 1.49	6 1.23	$4 > 6**, 1**, 5**$ $3 > 6**, 1*$ $2 > 6**, 1*$
20	Continuum of Unmet Needs $F = 2.60$	6 15.85	2 14.75	5 14.10	1 13.85	3 13.55	4 13.05	$4 < 6*$

$* = .05$ $** = .01$ or beyond

Table 5

Mean Differences by Ideological Divisions

Left: Communist,
  Peace & Freedom
Center: Democrat,
  Republican
Right: AIP, Nazi

	Variable	Means and Standard Deviations			*Direction of Significance (T − tests)*
		Left	*Center*	*Right*	
1	Anomia	3.69	2.57	4.13	C < L***
		1.02	.86	1.41	C < R***
2	Physiological Needs	2.88	2.47	2.81	C < L***
		.63	.68	.67	
3	Safety Needs	2.83	2.86	3.46	L < R***
		.50	.44	.61	C < R***
4	Affiliative Needs	3.26	2.96	3.15	C < L*
		.68	.59	.71	
5	Social Esteem Needs	2.52	2.56	2.97	R > L**
		.65	.51	.78	R > C*
6	Self-Esteem Needs	2.77	2.54	2.69	NS
		.62	.58	.57	
7	Faith-in-People	2.45	2.37	3.76	L < R***
		.73	.74	.98	C < R***
8	Manifest Anxiety	3.13	3.12	3.19	NS
		.71	.70	.10	
9	Dogmatism	3.50	3.27	4.59	L < R***
		.66	.65	.96	C < R***
10	Threat Orientation	2.74	3.28	4.87	L < C**
		.63	.91	.54	L < R***
					C < R***
11	Citizen Duty	2.17	1.72	3.11	C < R***
		1.11	.73	1.74	L < R**
12	Alienation from System	5.33	2.68	4.96	C < L***
		1.06	1.11	1.51	C < R

Table 5 (Continued)

Mean Differences by Ideological Divisions

Left: Communist,   *Center:* Democrat,   *Right:* AIP, Nazi
Peace & Freedom   Republican

		Means and Standard Deviations			Direction of Significance
Variable		Left	Center	Right	(T — tests)
13	Political	3.42	2.36	3.60	C < L***
	Efficacy	1.01	.97	1.14	C < R***
14	Intolerance	2.83	2.95	3.66	L < R***
	of Ambiguity	.60	.64	.66	C < R***
15	Authoritarianism	1.59	2.42	4.55	L < R***
		.52	.91	1.12	L < C***
					C < R***
16	Internality-	3.51	3.35	3.26	NS
	Externality	.62	.76	.70	
17	Empathy	3.11	3.13	3.70	L < R***
		.47	.54	.61	C < R***
18	Radicalism-	1.82	3.18	5.67	R > C***
	Conservatism	.61	1.40	.58	R > L***
					C > R***
19	SES	1.90	2.23	1.44	C > L*
		.64	.55	.45	L > R**
20	Continuum of	14.17	13.40	15.07	C > R**
	Unmet Needs	2.21	1.81	2.48	

N's: Left = 51, Center = 32, Right = 24

4   *Radicalism-Conservatism Index:* In terms of the means associated with variable 18, the reader should note the highly significant confirmation of the alignment of political parties which we are employing here. (The reversal of AIP and Nazi parties is nonsignificant.)

From an analysis of the political measures, we see that the Left and Right respondents are generally alienated from the political system and feel themselves to be politically inefficacious. In part, one might propose, such scores reflect the political realities of America today and are thus a confirmation of the obvious. To what extent, however, does this alienation reflect underlying personality characteristics? Let us next turn to the measure of psychological characteristics for evidence of an intrapsychic basis for the process of ideological adherence which extends beyond short-term political realities.

1 *Anomia:* This variable (1) is most likely to reflect — on an intrapsychic level — the dimension of alienation. Indeed, we see that there is a clear congruence between the two measures, with the Republicans and Democrats, both together and singly, significantly less anomic than the parties on the Right and the PFP on the Left. (The Centrist respondents are *not* significantly different from the Communist respondents on this dimension.) While our research design does not allow an assessment of causality, a causal imputation from anomic (self to other alienation) feelings to political alienation is psychologically justified. Further, while anomic respondents do not uniformly possess that low SES and marginal social status which has frequently been associated with (and suggested as causing) an anomic viewpoint (Meier and Bell, 1959; McClosky & Schaar, 1965), low SES is clearly related to anomia in this study.

2 *Faith-in-People:* It is important to note that a sense of alienation has a significant, but politically uneven, relationship to misanthropy (variable 7). All three Right groups are significantly higher in misanthropy than those parties to the Left. Indeed, the Communists are distinguished by their high trust in others. Both the Left and the Centre are significantly more trusting in others than are the parties on the Right — a finding which supports the typical view of the Right orientation as negativistic, if not clinically paranoid (Hofstadter, 1965). This finding is borne out by the correlation of .58 between conservatism and lack of faith-in-people (Table 7).

3 *Manifest Anxiety:* This measure (variable 8) did not significantly differentiate any political group.

4 *Dogmatism:* In a number of studies (DiRenzo, 1967; Rokeach, 1956, 1960; Parrott & Brown, 1972), dogmatism has been associated with a Right ideology. These studies were based on samples which either did not encompass the political spectrum or were not composed of people actively involved in politics. In our more ideologically comprehensive sample, it is important to note that the findings are consistent with those reported: it is the Nazi and AIP respondents who are distinguished by their significantly higher dogmatism scores. As Table 5 illustrates, both the Left and the Centre parties are significantly less dogmatic than the Right parties. This relationship is supported by the correlation of .50 (Table 7) between dogmatism and conservatism. Finally, as a whole (see Table 8), this group

of political activists had a lower group mean (3.68) than did a large undifferentiated group of common citizens (N = 495) whose mean was 4.53
(Knutson, 1972, p.243).

5 *Threat Orientation:* In terms of variable 10, we see that threat orientation is clearly a perception of the political Right. The Nazis are significantly more threatened than all parties, except the AIP, with the AIP
significantly more threatened than all the parties to their Left, and the
Republicans significantly more threatened than the parties on their Left.
Indeed, as Table 4 and 5 indicate, there is a perfect linear ordering (with
a correlation of .79 on Table 7) between a threatened orientation and the
political spectrum, with threat related to the Right end of the spectrum.

6 *Intolerance of Ambiguity:* Supporting the correlation between Dogmatism and the political Right, we note that a similar measure, intolerance
of ambiguity (variable 14) is also associated with the Right. Both the Nazi
and the AIP respondents are significantly more intolerant of ambiguity
than the parties on the Left half of the political spectrum, a finding borne
out by both Tables 5 and 7.

7 *Authoritarianism:* This variable (15), even more than dogmatism, has
been considered a classic indicator of the political Right. On Table 4, we
see that this relationship is supported in our data. In a perfect, linear relationship, the Nazi, AIP and Republican parties are *each* more authoritarian than all the parties to their political left. This finding is illustrated
again on Table 5 and by the highly significant correlation between authoritarianism (.83) and conservatism (Table 7). It is also of considerable interest
that the group mean of 2.50 in this study is considerably lower than that
from the 'common man' study; the mean there was 3.49 (Knutson, 1972,
p.243).

8 *Internality-Externality:* On variable 16 (with high scores indicating
externality), we find that there is only one significant difference: the Communist respondents are significantly more likely to perceive the locus of
control as internal than are the PFP respondents.

9 *Empathy:* Looking next at variable 17, we see that both the Nazi and
AIP respondents are significantly more likely to lack empathy than are
the parties to their Left, with the Republicans falling midway between.
On Table 5, both the Left and Centre are more empathic than the Right
and there is a significant correlation between lack of Empathy and Conservatism (.39 on Table 7).

Finally, let us examine the relationships between political ideology and
basic personality needs, remembering that theoretically it is personality
needs which determine the emergence of certain personality characteristics,

as well as — within the interaction of social and situational factors — shape their actualisation behaviour.

1   *Physiological Needs:* Looking first at variable 2, we see that only one significant relationship emerges: the Republicans are significantly lower than the Left parties.

2   *Safety Needs:* On variable 3, the Nazis are significantly higher than all other political parties, with the exception of the ideologically nearby AIP. On Table 5, both the Left and Center parties are lower than the Right parties and (on Table 7) there is a significant relationship (.42) between conservatism and Safety Needs. We must assume that there is a psychological similarity between Safety Needs and a Threatened Orientation which accounts for the similarly strong correlations on both of these measures. While not all the mean differences are significant, the reader should also note the perfect political ordering on this variable (Table 4).

3   *Affiliative Needs:* There are no significant differences between group means on this variable (4), although when pooled, Centrist parties are significantly lower in Affiliative Needs than are the Left parties.

4   *Social Esteem Needs:* On variable 5, we see that the Nazis are significantly higher on this variable than all other parties. Indeed, while all the mean differences are not significant, there is a general linearity between Social Esteem Needs and the political spectrum, borne out by the significant correlation (.30 on Table 7) between Social Esteem and Conservatism.

5   *Self-Esteem Needs:* On variable 5, we see that there is no relationship between this personality measure and political ideology.

6   *Continuum of Unmet Needs:* On this Continuum, which combines the scores of the respondents on all five lower needs measuring forms of psychic deprivation, we find only one significant difference: the Nazi respondents have more unmet needs than do the Republicans. When the means are combined, we see that the Centrist parties exhibit significantly more psychic competence than the parties to their Right. While Tables 6 and 7 underline the importance of differential need analysis, they also indicate that psychic competence, in holistic terms, is not significantly predictive of the direction of political ideology.

Finally, we need to briefly examine the relationships between our scales measuring Psychic Deprivation, and other measures which we have employed. As Cronbach and Meehl (1955) have noted, it is the 'nomological net' built of theoretically predictable interrelationships between various measures which is necessary to validate new psychological constructs. Looking first at Table 6, we note that all the lower needs are predictive of a lack of political efficacy and that Physiological Needs are correlated

Table 6

Intercorrelations of Basic Needs and Political Measures

		2	3	4	5	6	7	8	9	10	11
1	Physiological Needs	.39***	.41***	.37***	.40***	.74***	.17	.30**	.26**	-.07	-.05
2	Safety Needs	---	.43***	.44***	.19	.68***	.25*	.08	.26**	.41***	.42***
3	Affiliative Needs	---	---	.48***	.28**	.75***	.14	.15	.34***	-.08	-.05
4	Social Esteem Needs	---	---	---	.25*	.73***	.17	.05	.29**	.28**	.30**
5	Self-Esteem Needs	---	---	---	---	.59***	-.05	.14	.19	-.06	-.04
6	Con. of Unmet Needs	---	---	---	---	---	.19	.21*	.38***	.13	.19
7	Citizen Duty	---	---	---	---	---	---	.35***	.32***	.22*	.36***
8	Alienation from System	---	---	---	---	---	---	---	.40***	-.16	-.14
9	Political Efficacy	---	---	---	---	---	---	---	---	.04	.05
10	Radicalism-Conservatism	---	---	---	---	---	---	---	---	---	.84***
11	Continuum of Parties	---	---	---	---	---	---	---	---	---	---

$* = .05$ $** = .05 - .01$ $*** = .01 - .001$ or beyond

Table 7

Intercorrelations of Basic Needs and other Psychological Measures

	7	8	9	10	11	12	13	14	15	16
1 Physiological Needs	.19*	.16	.48***	.37***	.01	.12	.10	.22*	.00	-.05
2 Safety Needs	.29**	.46***	.41***	.55***	.50***	.59***	.57***	.16	.20*	.42***
3 Affiliative Needs	.24*	.17	.56***	.39***	.11	.20*	.05	.35***	-.15	-.05
4 Social Esteem Needs	.12	.31**	.45***	.59***	.29**	.31**	.43***	.23*	.19*	.30**
5 Self-Esteem Needs	.14	.18	.50***	.25**	.10	.10	.01	.41***	-.17	-.04
6 Con. of Unmet Needs	.28**	.36***	.69***	.62***	.28**	.37***	.32***	.39***	.02	.19
7 Anomia	--	.50***	.18	.41***	.24*	.13	.09	.23*	.08	.13
8 Faith-in-People	--	--	.17	.57***	.63***	.41***	.55***	.17	.33***	.58***
9 Manifest Anxiety	--	--	--	.39***	.17	.14	.07	.41***	-.41***	.03
10 Dogmatism	--	--	--	--	.60***	.38***	.64***	.12	.21*	.50***
11 Threat Orientation	--	--	--	--	--	.54***	.80***	.10	.30**	.79***
12 Intol. of Ambiguity	--	--	--	--	--	--	.61***	.03	.22*	.44***
13 Authoritarianism	--	--	--	--	--	--	--	-.13	.43***	.83***
14 Inter.-Externality	--	--	--	--	--	--	--	--	-.23*	.08
15 Empathy	--	--	--	--	--	--	--	--	--	--
16 Continuum of Parties	--	--	--	--	--	--	--	--	--	--

* = .05   ** = .05 - .01   *** = .01 - .001 or beyond

with Alienation from the System (as is lack of Citizen Duty). As noted above, both Safety and Social Esteem Needs are related to Right ideology, but the other basic needs are not correlated with the direction of political belief. Looking at the correlations between basic needs and other psychological variables (Table 7), we find that — with the exception of Empathy, the composite measure of basic deprivation — the Continuum of Unmet Needs — is significantly related, in a predictable direction, to other measures of psychic competence and that the majority of individual need correlations are likewise significant. While the value of individual need analysis is based on the differential importance of these needs in predicting other personality characteristics and aspects of political behaviour, it is important to note that — as a whole — these combined needs are clearly measures of what are generally conceptualised as dimensions of psychic deprivation.

Psychological Underpinnings of Political Ideology

For what reasons does a person become active in a particular political party? What factors determine his selection of one ideological perspective over all the others? Clearly, demographic factors are important, as our data again confirms. The social and economic status of a person obviously makes certain ideological choices more congenial than others. Further — in support of previous studies — additional demographic data from the lengthy questionnaires employed herein illustrate that many respondents have selected the party of their parents.

Above and beyond these demographic influences, however, it is apparent that psychological factors also interact to determine a person's political beliefs. In our data analysis, several main trends emerged which deserve further comment. First of all, the Centrist party respondents are clearly the most system supportive, as would be predicted. On the three political measures (Alienation from System, Citizen Duty and Political Efficacy), the Republicans and Democrats clearly and comparatively identify with the political system of which they are such a major part. Further, the scores on the Anomia Scale indicate that the political relatedness felt by Centrist party members is combined with a sense of self-to-others relatedness. Whether there is a causal relationship between these forms of relatedness is beyond the scope of this essay. However, we must also note that the Centrist party respondents are not distinguished by the significant presence of any of the lower need motivations: rather — by comparison — they generally appear to be self-actualising or at least minimally growth oriented. We are reminded here of the well-known DiPalma and McClosky (1970) study in which conformance with basic political orientations was clearly associated with psychological competence.

Second, it is noteworthy that the Right party respondents are *highly* characterised by a misanthropic, intolerant, dogmatic, threatened viewpoint. Significant correlations between party ideology and these variables hold up when party means are examined separately and, generally, when they are combined into ideological direction. Such correlations give major support to the consistent findings which view the political Right as misanthropic, nonempathic, dogmatic, intolerant and threatened (Schoenberger, 1969; Knutson, 1973c). Our data thus underline the view that the political Right is an ideological stance which gains support from those who are punitive and hostile in their views toward others and live in a world which they perceive to be profoundly threatening and insecure.

It further appears that such personality characteristics are related to underlying needs for Safety and for Social Esteem. A recent study comparing conservative and progressive students in the Netherlands on Maslow's need hierarchy (Liebrand, 1974) replicates our results: only safety and esteem needs differentiated the two ideological groups, with deficiency needs significantly correlated with conservative ideology. As the measures of need fulfilment here differed wholly from those employed in our Southern California Study, Liebrand's data provide important substantiation of our results here.

Such unusually high intercorrelations suggest a basic psychological insecurity which is far more generalised and profound than the insecurity which is realistically determined by membership in a Right party in America today or which corresponds with the objective degree of optimism with which such respondents may view their political future. Rather, it appears (as postulated by Tompkins, 1966) that for many on the political Right it is a subjective, existential state of threatened insecurity which finds resonance in a political viewpoint which urges the dominance of values of law and order. For the typical respondent at the Right end of the political continuum, it appears that inner insecurity is projected outward and political controls are urged to deal with the ensuing tensions.

At this point, the reader is undoubtedly reminded of McClosky's (1958) well-known study of conservatism which found, as we have done, that a wide battery of measures of neuroticism were correlated with a conservative view of political ideology. Our study offers needed confirmation of McClosky's results, for a major criticism of this study (Kendall, 1958; Knutson, 1972) has been that the Conservatism Scale employed by McClosky enlisted the acceptance of only those conservatives who could be defined as feeling threatened and insecure. The present Leadership Study, however, has taken great care to define 'Radical' and 'Conservative' in a manner which is independent of both subjective interpretation and of possible bias on the part of the researcher. Thus two determining measures were employed: the subject's total score on a group of commonly used political issues recently employed by the Field Polling Service and the person's active membership (usually officership) in a political group. In the case of each of these highly intercorrelated measures, there is a very significant correlation between what could perhaps be described as a threatened, Darwinian view of the world and Conservative, Right orientations in politics.

Third, we must note briefly the obverse of the preceding remarks: the political Left respondents can be consistently characterised as cognitively open, tolerant of ambiguity and of others, empathic, unthreatened and trusting. Further, as Lane earlier noted (1965), our study also suggests that Affiliative needs may provide the psychological foundations of liberalism. As noted in another study (Knutson, 1973c), it appears that — despite all efforts to make psychological measures 'ideology free' — there are certain personality needs which consistently differentiate Left and Right respondents and which may be considered valid psychological underpinnings of these ideological directions, rather than measurement artifacts.

Fourth, the importance of a major area of non-significant relationships must be underlined. Considered holistically, psychic competence does not predict the acceptance of any one political ideology. Nor are all the five deprivational needs equally related to ideological direction or to other measures of neuroticism. Rather, the idiosyncratic performance of each need suggests that the 'flavour' of the deprivation does indeed shape the manner in which an individual behaves politically, as well as the psychic strengths with which he acts. Impressionistically and empirically, no one political ideology has an 'exclusive' on mental health. What is important here is the selective influence of different personality needs. Thus, while persons who are motivated by Affiliative Needs may tend toward a Left orientation, those motivated by Safety and Esteem needs appear to seek compensation through the furtherance of Right political beliefs.

Fifth, we must ask what our data illustrate about the personality characteristics of the political leader, species party activist, in relation to the mass citizenry from whom these leaders are selected. Few comparisons are possible: except for three scales, my Common Man sample (Knutson, 1972) unfortunately did not employ comparable measures. From these three measures, however, some interesting comparisons can be derived. The

group mean here for Dogmatism is 3.68, considerably lower than the mean
(4.53) for the Common Man sample and lower than the mean of the most
self-actualising group of ordinary citizens in that comparative sample. The
mean for Intolerance of Ambiguity in the present study (3.05) is again
considerably lower than that of the Common Man study (4.32). Finally,
the mean achieved here by party activists on the measure of authoritarianism (2.50) is significantly lower than that of the Common Man mean
(4.08) *and* than that of any other group which I have found reported in

Table 8
Group Means for Party Activists*

		Mean	*Standard Deviation*
1	Anomia	3.45	1.23
2	Physiological Needs	2.74	.67
3	Safety Needs	2.98	.56
4	Affiliative Needs	3.14	.67
5	Social Esteem Needs	2.63	.66
6	Self-Esteem Needs	2.64	.59
7	Faith-in-People	2.72	.97
8	Manifest Anxiety	3.14	.77
9	Dogmatism	3.68	.88
10	Threat Orientation	3.38	1.09
11	Citizen Duty	2.25	1.28
12	Alienation from System	4.46	1.66
13	Political Efficacy	3.14	1.15
14	Intolerance of Ambiguity	3.05	.70
15	Authoritarianism	2.50	1.41
16	Internality-Externality	3.41	.68
17	Empathy	3.25	.57
18	Radicalism-Conservatism	4.87	1.79
19	SES	6.10	.64
20	Continuum of Unmet Needs	25.86	2.23

* Based on an N of 107 and 7 point Likert scales.

the literature. While Table 8 will hopefully provide the basis for future
comparisons between leaders and led, our initial analysis suggests that our
party activists (who may or may not be representative of political leaders
generally) are significantly more psychically competent than the aggregate
of the citzenry whom they choose to lead, a conclusion which Stouffer
(1955) suggested over 20 years ago.

What, then, is the value of studying the personality correlates of political
ideology and behaviour as an integral component of political activity? I

would suggest that its utility is twofold. In the first place, the performance of each of the need groups on a wide variety of personality measures suggests vitally different degrees of psychic competence available for basic political tasks such as persuading, utilising resources (human and informational), possessing the efficacy by which action and decision are possible, and a host of other functions in which a vast differential in performance can – through incremental or monumental acts – truly make history, as the political process enables different individuals to achieve political power.

Of equal importance to political analysis is the phenomenological view, the *Weltanschauung* or personalised philosophy through which a person mediates his world. A person may establish his agreement with a political ideology in many ways, such as joining a particular political group or by assenting or disagreeing with proposed solutions to a number of current issues. What matters in the long run, however (and politics is the long run) is whether the person does so with a tolerance for those who establish a different political stance, with a belief that he *can* shape his political destiny because cooperative political action *is* possible, with an understanding that ambiguity is the essence of politics (and of life) and thus 'final solutions' are profoundly unpolitical or – on the other extreme – whether he sees his existential state as precarious and profoundly threatening in an environment in which human mutuality is obviated by the inherent antagonisms of human nature and thus is impelled by a simplistic imperative because the uncertainties of politics are perceived as both frightening and frustrating.

In sum, personality is indeed of considerable importance in both understanding and predicting the content and form of behaviour made possible through the political process. It is important to understand the influence of a person's politicisation, his attained social status, occupation and education. But deeper understanding also requires an analysis of the individual in terms of the inner needs which interact with outer constraints to produce ideologically disparate forms of political behaviour.

Appendix A
Indices of Psychic Deprivation

Physiological Needs
1 Having enough food to really satisfy me worries me at times. (+)
2 I'd much rather live in a hot climate than in a cold climate where I had to worry about keeping warm. (+)

3 When I was young, in general I always got enough sleep. (−)
4 When I was a child, keeping clean was a big problem in our family. (+)
5 Most people don't realize what a luxury it is to have enough living space in their houses. (+)
6 The most important thing about a job is a chance to earn enough for necessities. (+)
7 When I was a child, I was beaten frequently. (+)
8 Having enough health and strength have never been problems for me. (−)
9 Being always tired and having little energy have never been problems for me. (−)
10 Some people are always worried about diets, but I feel better with a little "extra" weight. (+)
11 When I was little, I didn't think I would live to grow up. (+)
12 It's useless to save money; you can't ever get ahead enough to make any real difference. (+)
13 I never worry about having enough money for the necessities of life. (−)
14 I have always had enough clothing so that I could be warm and dry. (−)
15 Many times I order more food than I feel comfortable eating. (+)
16 Just staying alive is not easy for me. (+)
17 When I was a child, I never had enough clothes to wear to school. (+)

Safety Needs

1 When I was young, I never knew when I was going to be punished. (+)
2 There are lots of nights when I expect some disaster to strike the house before I wake up. (+)
3 A good boss lets his men know exactly what he wants. (+)
4 There is no need for strong leaders today to guide us. (−)
5 I'd be very happy in life if I could always count on enough money for food, clothes, house payments, etc. − "the basics". (+)
6 It is better to buy what you can get of the good things in life than to put money away in the bank. (−)
7 When I see a car coming toward me, I am usually afraid it won't stop in time. (+)
8 I often feel the need to buy more things than I need. (+)

9 I would rather keep a house that I can easily afford than try to support the costs of a better one. (+)

10 I sometimes worry about how you can't ever tell what is going to happen to you next. (+)

11 It would be great if you could take a job when you got out of school and know that you could keep it until you retire. (+)

12 A person who leads an even, regular life in which few surprises or unexpected happenings occur, really has a lot to be grateful for. (+)

13 The biggest cause of happiness is being able to *know* what you are going to be doing next month, next year and in ten years. (+)

14 I like to work for someone who will tell me just how he wants things done. (+)

15 To me, a job with a good retirement program is much more important than one that provides more advancement. (+)

16 It frightens me to drive on busy streets or highways because it is so easy for an accident to happen. (+)

17 When I was a child, I lost my father through death or divorce. (+)

18 Religion is important in bringing rules into a person's life. (+)

19 When I am in an elevator, I am always afraid that it won't work properly. (+)

20 It is better to have good friends than money in the bank. (−)

21 The most important thing about a good marriage is having someone who will take care of you. (+)

22 In my experience, change is always for the worse. (+)

23 I always seem to expect the worst to happen. (+)

Affiliation Needs

1 I often daydream about belonging to someone. (+)

2 Even if I was as good-looking as a movie star, nobody would really love me. (+)

3 The kind of friend that I would choose is someone who likes me. (+)

4 I have always been sure of my mother's love for me. (−)

5 The most important thing about a job is having friends that you really like. (+)

6 I wish I had more friends than I do. (+)

7 It is very difficult to make good friends. (+)

8 Compared to other people, I really have no close friends. (+)

9 I am lucky to have had good companionship in my life. (−)

10 I don't need to be close to people. (−)

11 I often feel that I am missing a lot of the fun that friends have together. (+)

12 It is possible to be very happy in love. (−)

13 When I was a child, I lost my mother through death or divorce. (+)

14 I worry that I may go through life without ever knowing real love. (+)

15 One nice thing about a family is feeling that you are all part of a close group. (+)

16 The worst thing that could happen to me is to go through life feeling alone. (+)

17 I like the idea of belonging to groups where everyone knows each other really well. (+)

18 Even when I am with a lot of people, I have a feeling of loneliness. (+)

19 I'd rather be liked than respected. (+)

Social Esteem Needs

1 I am often self-conscious about being in front of others. (+)

2 I don't think I'm a very worthwhile person, and I don't see much reason for anyone else to think I am. (+)

3 It is important to me that others accept my viewpoints. (+)

4 I feel that I have gotten enough recognition for the things I have done in my life. (−)

5 Other people don't pay much attention to me — and given what I know and feel about myself, I can't say that I blame them. (+)

6 It really makes me angry how you never get any appreciation for a job well done. (+)

7 I feel my parents were always really ashamed of me. (+)

8 People seldom pay any attention to my opinions. (+)

9 Among those who know me well, I feel I'm respected. (−)

10 I feel a need to have others approve of what I do. (+)

11 I'm never sure I've done a good job until somebody else says so. (+)

12 I'm just as smart as other people, but I never seem to get any respect for it. (+)

13 I know by the words of others that I am good at the work I do. (−)

14 You can judge what a person is really worth by how many people look up to him. (+)

15 Whatever I do with other people, my efforts are never really appreciated. (+)

16 The most important thing to me about a job is having a position of authority so that the other workers will respect me. (+)

17 I am seldom treated right. (+)

18 The kind of person I like to be with is someone whom others look up to. (+)

19 The most important satisfaction in life is being able to do something so well that everyone looks up to you. (+)

20 I like to be in control of other people. (+)

21 I like to be an important person in every group I belong to. (+)

Self-Esteem Needs

1 Most of the things that I really want in life I probably can never attain. (+)

2 I think I can usually get what I want if I work at it. (−)

3 I've just about given up hope that I'll do anything important or worthwhile. (+)

4 I need to feel that I am living for some big purpose. (+)

5 It is important to me to be able to do something very well. (+)

6 There are some things I'm not good at, but a lot of things I can do very well. (−)

7 I don't expect much from myself, either now or in the future. (+)

8 My ideas are just as good as the next person's. (−)

9 I can't do many of the things I'd like to do or do them the way I think they should be done. (+)

10 I'm not sure I have much to offer any employer. (+)

11 I wish that I had done something else with my life. (+)

12 I feel satisfied with what I've achieved in my life. (−)

13 I know that I can handle almost any problem with which I am faced. (−)

14 Whatever I do for a living, I know I'll be able to do a good job. (−)

15 I am good at figuring things out. (−)

16 I'm often ashamed of the things I do. (+)

17 I can learn just about anything I put my mind to. (−)

18 Compared to the opinions of other people, I feel that I have some good opinions about public affairs. (−)

19 I'm proud of a lot of things I do. (−)

Metapsychology, Politics, and Human Needs *

M. Brewster Smith

Can the study and criticism of politics be based on psychology? Or, in important respects, ought we to look at the relationship from the other end of the tube? My intent in contributing this somewhat fragmentary essay is to help to clarify our thinking about this perennial arena of controversy, as it is focused on questions of human motivation. The present symposium is only one more round of discussion of the topic felicitously named by Graham Wallas in the first decade of the century in his book, *Human Nature and Politics*, a title resurrected (with a minor variation) by Davies about a decade ago.[1] What has happened recently in the intellectual development of our disciplines to change the terms of discussion? *Have* there been developments that warrant reconsideration?

As a social psychologist, I am keenly aware of two major developments from the outside that affect my field, each of which requires, I think, a fundamental reorientation of its agenda. I am still very much caught up myself in the attempt to digest them; many of my colleagues seem to remain blissfully unaware of the changed context. Both call for a reformulation of our questions about human needs and politics. One is the decline of

---

* Written during my tenure of a senior fellowship from the National Endowment for the Humanities.
1 G. Wallas, *Human Nature and Politics*, Houghton Mifflin, Boston, 1909; J.C. Davies, *Human Nature in Politics*, Wiley, New York, 1963.

positivism as a prescriptive, even dogmatic philosophy of science. The other is the opening of radically new perspectives on the emergence of human nature in the biology of evolution – now a 'sociobiology'.[2] The first development, a liberating one, is abstract and metatheoretical; the second, also liberating to the imagination, is empirical though still highly speculative. It has taken me much working through to realise, partly, the far-reaching implications of each of these developments; I can only begin to suggest their implications for our present topic. The substantial task of making the implications explicit, and elaborating them in relation to evidence and to critical thought, is for the future.

First, very briefly, about the collapse of positivism as a consensual, prescriptive frame for the human sciences. This shift in basic assumptions has been so widely heralded and so often discussed that I can best help the reader who seeks to catch up by calling attention to four representative recent works that among them cite the relevant theoretical and critical literature in its bearing upon psychology from somewhat different perspectives: an article by Buss[3] that summarises the attack on positivism in psychology in very short compass; a book edited by Israel and Tajfel[4] critical of modern social psychology from European perspectives, especially those influenced by Marxism; another by Harré and Secord[5] reflecting for social psychology the British tradition of analytic philosophy that stemmed from Wittgenstein; and the widely read synthesis by Berger and Luckmann[6] of ideas from the European phenomenological tradition and the American symbolic interactionist one.

A generation ago, when I shared in launching the political behaviour movement in political science, positivism – especially in its Vienna variety – was the regnant assumptive framework in the social and behavioural sciences. But it was a peculiar feature of positivism that it *denied* that it was an assumptive framework at all – let alone one among many conceivable and potentially legitimate ones. Cleaving to the model of the physical sciences as they understood it, the positivists thought to eliminate metaphysics as 'meaningless', and to pursue questions of human behaviour

2 E.O. Wilson, *Sociobiology: The New Synthesis*, Belknap, Harvard, 1975.
3 A.R. Buss, 'The emerging field of the sociology of psychological knowledge', *American Psychologist*, Vol.30, 1975, pp.988-1002.
4 *The Context of Social Psychology: A Critical Assessment*, eds. J. Israel and H. Tajfel, Academic Press, New York, 1972.
5 R. Harré and P.F. Secord, *The Explanation of Social Behaviour*, Blackwell, Oxford, 1972.
6 P.L. Berger and T. Luckmann, *The Social Construction of Reality*, Doubleday, Garden City, New York, 1966.

in the spirit of the physical sciences, with an apparatus of operational definitions and the so-called hypothetico-deductive method.

We have since learned that the positivist interpretation of physics was essentially mythical, and that there is no avoiding prior assumptions or stipulations of one kind or another (including, possibly, positivist ones) if we are to formulate scientific questions, constitute scientific data, and establish criteria according to which we let our data help us answer our questions. To recognise the arbitrariness of positivism's dogmatic exclusions is especially liberating to our treatment of such inherently human topics as politics. If we wish the advantages of quasi-cumulativeness and corrigibility that science often has to offer, of course, we are not liberated from evidence (as some neo-humanists in psychology would have it). We are alerted, however, to the importance of our assumptions in determining what we will regard as evidence, as data. We are alerted to the importance of metatheory. After introducing the new evolutionary perspective on human nature, I will return to examine how 'needs' and related motivational concepts are entangled in our metatheoretical commitments.

The new perspective on human evolution radically undercuts the previous sharp distinction between Nature and Culture that social scientific theory shared with mythic thought,[7] and requires of us a novel, essentially dialectic view of the nature of human nature. I am thinking, of course, of the great expansion of the time-span of human evolution, as we now understand it, to as much as three million years when our small weakminded forebears arose on two feet and began to find rocks useful to help them get their livelihood. I am thinking especially of the prevailing interpretation that it was *because* using rocks (and presumably more perishable sticks) as tools made having a bigger, brighter brain pay off – there were now clever, useful things to be done with it – proto-people evolved rapidly to become the big-brained, behaviourally complex creatures that we know today. Proto-humanity's capacities and performances as tool-users (and thus as bearers of culture) entered into the constitution of biological human nature.

So much seems reasonably firm. More speculatively (here I find Geertz's reinterpretation[8] helpful), it seems plausible that along with tool use, people's symbolic capacities and performances were also evolving in parallel powered by a similar selective advantage. But the relics that remain for us to observe are stones and bones and fire hearths, not indicators of sym-

---

7 C. Levi-Strauss, *The Savage Mind,* University of Chicago Press, Chicago, 1966.
8 C. Geertz, *The Interpretation of Cultures,* Basic Books, New York, 1973.

bols and beliefs and rituals – until just the day before yesterday, some 50,000 years ago, when late Neanderthal burial sites show persuasive evidence of belief in an after-life.[9] Along with symbolism and, specifically, language evolved self-conscious awareness and, presumably, the complexities of selfhood-in-community. My point is that our standing as a social, even a political animal is as much part of our distinctive animal nature as it is of our human nature. We have evolved as organisms over the eons because emergent culture helped shape our biological human nature. One used to have to be a Lamarckian or a mystic to believe such things; now such speculation seems called for by the findings of hard science, and is made the more plausible by the great expansion of our time scale. People have participated in the creation of their biological human nature in a dialectical process of spiralling interaction with their worlds.

The distinction between Nature and Culture remains useful as a polarity, if not as a dichotomy. In the course of the biological evolution catalysed by Culture, people's biology came ever increasingly to depend upon cultural learning to fill in the content provided for by biological templates. A good example is the case of language, in which, after Chomsky and his successors, we seem to have to think of each human toddler in every known society as predisposed to *invent* a language for him or herself constructed on a limited set of universal organising principles, resembling in its specifics the features prevalent in the language community in which the child is immersed. Again a melding of Nature and Culture, presumably the result of long evolution. But the structural propensity, the reaching out to develop childish language and to use it creatively, has become part of our Nature, whereas the particular variant symbol system each child acquires is a matter of Culture.

What do these considerations, philosophically abstract or phylogenetically remote, have to do with our topic of human needs and politics? I think they affect the very terms of our discussion. Let us begin with a look at the concept of human needs, where clean semantics are hampered by the accretions of long and loose employment in psychology.

If we try to keep the word 'need' close to its everyday meanings, we use it to refer to *requirements* of the person as a biological and human system – for substances or relationships or states of affairs in the absence

---

9 Since writing this, I have encountered Marshak's useful review article, which summarises the relevant evidence, provides the key references, and, incidentally, makes a strong case for abstract symbolism and, probably, language in Mousterian-Neanderthal times. See A. Marshak, 'Implications of the paleolithic symbolic evidence for the origin of language', *American Scientist*, Vol.64, 1976, pp.136-45.

of which the person fails to develop or to function normally and may even falter or die. Developmental psychologists do speak of the needs of children in this vein; Harlow[10] taught us about the monkey need for contact comfort, the absence of which leads to specifiably defective development.

Note that this narrow and I think proper use falls naturally in a causal-functional, 'objective', natural science context, and that, further, the reference is not inherently 'motivational'; it does not necessarily have to do with the organisation and direction of action. I can need things that I do not want: thus particular vitamins; I can want and seek things I do not need: thus, the sweetness of saccharine or maybe the highs of a psychedelic drug. Over a considerable range — just how big a range is important, moot, and a matter for empirical clarification — needs *are* linked to motives, as a result of long stabilities in the context of biological evolution. In regard to most of the familiar biological essentials that require effective directed behaviour if the species is to survive and thrive, we have come to be creatures that for the most part want what we need. Otherwise we wouldn't be here. But it is dangerous to extrapolate uncritically to the 'farther reaches' of human motivation that touch on politics. Perhaps it may help to remind ourselves of Fromm's equally simplistic though provocative conception under the rubric of 'social character': we are also creatures that, in some other respects, have come to want what 'society' needs.[11]

Henry Murray's familiar and useful catalogue of human needs[12] on which I cut my eye teeth as a psychologist — *n* Achievement, *n* Sentience, *n* Sex, *n* Aggression, *n* Dominance, *n* Succorance, and the rest — does not use the word in the foregoing strict sense. He offered rather a general taxonomy of classes of human *motives*, similar to McDougall's[13] on whose doctrine of instincts he drew, but more differentiated and with the biological claim explicit in the term 'instinct' now disavowed. In the present context, Murray's choice of the term 'need' seems purely coincidental. As with 'needs' in the strict sense, however, Murray's list of motives is to be understood for the most part in a causal-functional, potentially positivistic framework. He wanted a chemistry of human action that amounted to a causal analysis. But he also wanted to assimilate Jung and Freud, and was an artist in psychological *interpretation*. As a confirmed holist who emphasised the proactive rather than the reactive aspects of human

---

10 H. Harlow, 'Development of affection in primates', in *Roots of Behavior*, ed. E.L. Bliss, Harper, New York, 1962.

11 E. Fromm, *Escape From Freedom*, Farrar and Rinehart, New York, 1941.

12 H.A. Murray, *Explanations in Personality*, Oxford, New York, 1938.

13 W. McDougall, *Introduction to Social Psychology*, Methuen, London, 1908.

nature, he fought positivism valiantly, and it would be grossly unfair thus to pigeon-hole his motivational concepts.

In contrast with objective need is subjective wish, desire, or want, all of which are motivational terms that find their home in a metapsychological framework of meaningful human action. They assume the peculiar human property of *intentionality* that May[14] has emphasised in interpreting the European existential tradition to American psychology. They are terms from everyday language that many of us want also to use in our more formal psychological theorising because they seem to provide a natural phrasing for the self-direction of action among the thoughtful yet passionate symbolising creatures that we have in fact become. But how are such terms to be employed in the causal-functional framework that many of us wish also to retain even after the passing of its monopolistic predominance with the era of positivism? The philosophical and psychological puzzles here are far from resolved; they are just beginning to be clarified.

We now see, thanks particularly to Loevinger[15] and Holt[16], that Freud was thoroughly confused and ambivalent on this matter. Throughout his long intellectual career, he appears to have been torn between clinical formulations in terms of wish and meaningful conflict (to which his addition of an unconscious dimension was invaluable) and 'metapsychological' formulations cast in mechanistic metaphors drawn from the first and second laws of thermodynamics, with which he became enamoured in his early physiological training in the anti-vitalist school of Helmholz and Du Bois-Reymond. The mechanistic and humanistic sides of Freud do not fit comfortably with one another.

In the light of modern information science and of developments in physics, the nineteenth century view of mechanism on which Freud drew is definitely outmoded and no longer useful even for metaphorical psychological purposes (the concept of psychic 'energy' is a snare). So we need to give some care to sorting out Freud's important clinical contributions to the interpretation of meaningful action if we are to reconstruct a psychoanalytic psychology that is useful in the study of politics. Freud's concept of instinct (*Trieb*) was an unanalysed amalgam of mechanism and meaning. We may still be struggling to bring these two frames together;

---

14 R. May, *The Meaning of Anxiety*, Ronald, New York, 1950.
15 J. Loevinger, 'Three principles for a psychoanalytic psychology', *Journal Abnormal Psychology*, Vol.71, 1966, pp.432-43, and Loevinger, *Ego Development: Conceptions and Theories*, Jossey-Bass, San Francisco, 1976.
16 R.R. Holt, 'Freud's mechanistic and humanistic images of man', *Psychoanalysis and Contemporary Science*, Vol.1, 1972.

Freudian metapsychology does not give us a solution.

To review the terminological spectrum in metatheoretical perspective, human needs in the strict sense are a matter for empirical determination that is objective in principle but difficult in fact. The version of need theory that has seemed most attractive for application to politics is that of Maslow[17], whose concept merges the notion of motive with that of requirement. The patron saint of humanistic psychology, Maslow was no positivist, but he was quite confused about how to relate the biological and the human action aspects of his thinking. We will return to his views later on. The term 'drive' has been customarily used for biologically given motives like those involved in hunger, thirst, and elimination, but drives so conceived and emphasised as fundamental by positivists lie far from the realm of politics.

Politics as its practice is understood by participants, and as it has been formulated and criticised in normative political theory since Plato and Aristotle — politics as political relations and political action, not just 'political behaviour' — requires primary reference to human wants, desires, and wishes, and their conflict and/or mutual adjustment in the context of man-made, culturally transmitted but humanly modifiable institutions. Politics as a significant component of human history, and political theory as a major perspective on it, make sense only within an assumptive view of human action that has room for intentions and meanings. The positivist assumptions tended to reduce politics to mere power and manipulation, a cynical view that can be self-confirming. Our liberation from positivist dogmatism gives us the freedom to take other possibilities seriously, and perhaps to encourage their development in social life.

But I am a psychologist, not a philosopher or professionally a political advocate. Causal and functional analysis are my stock in trade, not interpretation or 'hermeneutics' (a term I encountered more recently than I like to admit). I see the primary context for political analysis as falling toward the latter pole: first and foremost, politics is to be regarded as meaningful historical action. So for me the great puzzle is the one on which Freud stumbled, and as I will argue, Maslow too: how to link causal and functional analysis in psychology (to which the term 'need' belongs) with a view of people as potentially responsible political actors. Elsewhere[18], I have dealt with parts of the problem more concretely, less self-consciously and

---

17 A.H. Maslow, *Motivation and Personality,* Harper, New York, 1954.
18 M.B. Smith, 'Political attitudes', in *Handbook of Political Psychology,* ed. J.N. Knutson, Jossey-Bass, San Francisco, 1973, pp.57-82.

owlishly. Here I must admit to persisting puzzlement. The challenge is to find a metatheoretical stance that meets the pragmatic test of putting our thoughts and findings in some defensibly consistent order and allows us to bring evidence to bear on understanding and in humanising politics.

Let me venture a provisional attempt at linkage in midstream, which will also serve to re-introduce the evolutionary perspective that as I asserted is a second reason for fundamental revision in our thinking. When we inquire about need, we are adopting an *extrinsic* perspective on the human actor. The actor may be pushed by drives or pulled by wishes and wants; naively he or she does not *know* about needs, although individual or cultural conceptions of need may have a part in the formation and in the justification of wants. The technical concept of need belongs to the biological or social scientist, not to the motivated person.

There are two ways in which needs *sensu strictu* can educate wants. One is the slow, enduring way of biological evolution: the feedback process that governs genetic selection. Creatures that go on wanting things that interfere with fulfilling their needs or do not come to want the things they need are likely in the very long run to have their genes dropped from the genetic pool of the species. The other is the much more rapid and flexible joint process of individual learning and collective cultural change that became possible on a grand scale when protopeople crossed the divide to become selves linked in shared systems of symbolisation. It is hard to imagine how any human needs that did not remain constant over the long eons of eolithic and possibly paleolithic time – the Pleistocene – could have got translated into drives of wants embedded in the genetic code: people ceased living as dispersed bands of hunters and gatherers so recently, and biological evolution is so slow. Most needs that have characterised human beings distinctively as peasants for some ten millennia and as citizens or subjects in historic times must be mediated by culture and only indirectly by biology (insofar as our biology now requires for our survival that we remain culture-bearing animals).

Entirely new needs (system requirements for human survival) are emerging that as yet have very little psychological representation as motive, wish, or want. Given unprecedented and absolute new powers of mutual destruction, we *need* to learn to live more peaceably with one another than ever before in the course of human history – but we have not sufficiently learned to want to. Now that our technological culture has given our species equally unprecedented short-run biological success in populating the earth (the pre-programmed objective of every species), we need to discover ways of calling a halt before we spoil everything for ourselves and many other species with which we are interdependent; we also need to learn to live within the limited means of our planet. But for the most part, the motives, the wants, even the knowledge required remain to be developed. Because we are not just biologically programmed behavers but rather, thanks to the special cultural biology of human evolution, we are conscious actors, there remains the possibility, the *hope* (a legitimate word, even in social science, when we are talking about people) that we can develop the knowledge, wishes, and intentions that might save us, and find ways of carrying them into effective collective action.

Of course, this becomes a matter of politics. The human needs are there, but it will take politics and luck for them to be translated into motives, knowledge, and action. Because we are symbolising, sometimes thoughtful creatures, and because, collectively, we have so recently invented the cultural mutation of science, of systematically collaborative evidential thought, we have a chance of meeting our novel and urgent needs. We have a chance denied to our forebears of using the immediate and powerful informational feedback that is now available to us. That is what the polymath John Platt was talking about in a powerful polemic.[19]

There is a much-bandied Marxist concept that has always bothered me by its presumption: 'false consciousness'. What Marx had in mind, of course, is the situation that has made Marxist prophecies go so far awry. The proletariat do not know their own *needs*. They do not recognise their 'objective' class interests, at least as Marx and Engels had diagnosed them. Marcuse[20] has carried this idea much farther in his portrayal of the extent to which contemporary American society has seduced and co-opted people to participate in their own alienation.

I am ambivalent about 'false consciousness' in two respects. First, it presupposes a 'correct' diagnosis of need and interest, which is likely to be a dogmatic diagnosis. Even with the best scientific input, the diagnosis of need is bound to be approximate, fallible, and debatable. Democratic process recognises this, and gives priority to people's own wishes and wants, while leaving channels open for persuasion and the infusion of evidence to bring wishes and wants more in tune with needs. Marxist societies mostly do not.

And, second, some manner or degree of 'false consciousness' would seem to be the normal human condition. Freud taught us that much of our reasoning is also, or maybe only, rationalisation. We know that for eons

19 J. Platt, *The Step to Man*, Wiley, New York, 1966.
20 H. Marcuse, *One-Dimensional Man*, Beacon Press, Boston, Massachusetts, 1964.

people lived in culturally evolved worlds of myth and magic that comforted them in and lent meaning to their predicament as mortals become vulnerably aware of their mortality.[21] 'False consciousness?' There was a very real emergent human need for comfort and meaning, which the lost magical world supplied. I do not think that our privileged scientific world view is just one myth on all fours with others, but it has its mythic aspects. The term 'false consciousness' suggests a 'true consciousness' as the norm. It is rather a shifting ideal, a moving target, to which we can aspire. If we think we have reached it — we have fallen into the trap of becoming True Believers.

The evolutionary perspective leads us to a cross-cultural one, since the cultural evolution that first parallelled biological evolution, then largely (because of its much greater flexibility) superseded it occurred in separated groups of people who were in little interchange with one another. Can we talk sensibly — cross-historically as well as cross-culturally — about panhuman needs? We should try, but clearly there are limits. We have already seen one source of limits: needs arise as much from the historical situation of people as from their biological nature. We can see new human needs emerging today. Needs once valid have lost their relevance. For example, the Plains Indian culture that flowered between the arrival of the horse with the Spaniards and the arrival of the locomotive with the Yankees depended on the numberless buffalo herds. The herds once gone (in Murray's language, n Buffalo?), all the needs intrinsic to this heroic way of life collapsed, with the setting in which it was possible to meet them for a while. The culture, and the needs of people in *that* culture, can never be resurrected.

Cross-cultural immersal led the great humanistic anthropologist Dorothy Lee (to whom I here pay tribute after her death a year ago as I write) to raise in a classic paper the question, 'Are basic needs ultimate?'.[22] Her quarrel was with functional anthropologists who followed Malinowski in seeing culture as an answer to a list of needs — a controversy quite akin to issues underlying the present volume. She did not admire the borrowings of anthropologists from psychology, especially of the behaviourist variety then prevalent, and her complaint took the form of challenging two assumptions that she found prevalent when she wrote in 1948: '(1) the premise that action occurs in answer to a need or a lack; and (2) the premise that

---

21 E. Becker, *The Denial of Death*, Free Press, New York, 1973.
22 D.D. Lee, 'Are basic needs ultimate?', reprinted in D.D. Lee, *Freedom and Culture*, Prentice-Hall, Englewood Cliffs, New Jersey, 1959, pp.70-7.

there is a list' [of basic needs to replace the old lists of instincts].[23]

We have already encountered grounds for both objections: the loose or absent linkage between need, want, and action (and the different assumptive frames in which these terms are most at home), and the dubious stability of human needs across historical settings. Her proposed alternative introduces a concept that is new to our discussion: that of diverse cultural *values* pursued for their own sake with no sense of lack, as orienting features of an intact way of life. Cultural — and personal — values pose an alternative to 'need' that, like other intentional terms such as want and wish, fit with a pro-active, humanistic interpretation of human life as meaningful. At least in Lee's writing, value more than wish or want connotes commitment to a desirable, not merely desired, order of things that seems entirely objective to the participants in an intact culture.

Like many anthropologists, Lee valued as good in itself the diversity of value realised among human cultures. She embraced cultural relativism as a kind of absolute: one should admire and cherish each culture on its own terms, not analyse or criticise it in terms of external standards. Aesthetically, that is an admirable stance. Ethically, it doesn't quite work: in the test case for the last generation, we cannot bring ourselves to appreciate Nazi Germany on *its* own terms. And conceptually or pragmatically, there are also problems. Think once more of the Sioux, or of the other vanishing unlettered peoples from among whom she draws her own examples. In a Platonic eternity, these cultures remain admirable as each expressing one variant of human potentiality. In the real, conditional, historical world, some of these variants remain viable, others have become obsolete, while new possibilities for human valuing are emerging.

In a dialectical view of emerging human nature, we can accept the critical message of relativism (to be cautious about the blinders entailed in our own ethnocentrism), but note that real limits on the range of conceivable human values which can be realised by actual human groups are set by historical contingency, by human genetics, and by the particular interactive historical process by which each culture-bearing group has arrived at its pattern for living. Values conceived in Lee's terms are both intentional and motivational concepts, whereas needs are not. As Rokeach[24] has particularly emphasised, values can be a unifying concept in the social sciences, playing, I think, a role much more central than that of needs.

I bring our discussion to a more concrete focus by looking briefly at

---

23 *ibid.,* p.70.
24 M. Rokeach, *The Nature of Human Values,* Free Press — MacMillan, New York, 1973.

two recent conceptualisations of human needs that have been applied in political analysis: Maslow's proposed hierarchy of needs[25], which has been brought to bear on political theory and data by Knutson[26] among others, and the need for personal control, which Renshon[27] has recently related to political efficacy and participation. The first uses a broad brush to sketch a general framework for human motivation; the second treats a more limited topic of direct political relevance, one that draws upon an active area of research interest in contemporary psychology. Both are representative of contemporary need theory as it is being applied to politics.

Maslow's theory is very widely known and cited, often loosely applied, and almost never tested. This is a frustrating state of affairs. His conception makes explicit his view of the linkage between need, intended in the strict sense, and motivation. When needs are satisfied, they are not motivating. Only when they are unfulfilled do they become motives. Since needs are human biological requirements, moreover, their satisfaction is essential for normal psychological development and mental health. A further specification is distinctive of his theory: needs fall into a natural hierarchy of pre-emptiveness, such that only when needs more basic in the hierarchy are met does or can the person attend to higher needs; only then do the higher needs become motivating.

The need hierarchy is composed of five ordered categories: physiological needs, safety or security needs, needs for affection and belongingness, needs for esteem, and needs for self-actualisation. The first four groups Maslow regards as 'deficiency needs'. The person driven by lacks in these areas is short of full humanity or mental health; he or she *is* driven. When a person's deficiency needs are satisfied, a variety of further potentialities for self-actualisation open out, which emerge in what Maslow calls B-motives (for Being) in contrast with D-motives (for Deficiency). It is his elaboration on these 'farther reaches of human nature'[28] that has made Maslow the patron saint of the humanistic movement in psychology.

The scheme has the attractiveness of plausibility. Maslow's classification of human requirements and motives makes intuitive sense, though the fact that a need for personal control does not fit neatly anywhere in the scheme should give one pause. And the idea of hierarchy must have some factual basis. People struggling desperately for subsistence are not likely to devote

25 Maslow, *Motivation and Personality*, op.cit.
26 J.N. Knutson, *The Human Basis of the Polity*, Aldine-Atherton, Chicago, 1972.
27 S.A. Renshon, *Psychological Needs and Political Behavior: A Theory of Personality and Political Efficacy*, Free Press — MacMillan, New York, 1974.
28 A.H. Maslow, *The Farther Reaches of Human Nature*, Viking, New York, 1971.

themselves very much to the refined arts that appeal to a self-actualising leisure class. (But they may produce a high art, nonetheless, in the service of ritual.) All the same, Maslow's classification of needs is loose, and the claim for any strict heirarchy lacks support. It is easy to imagine circumstances in which a need for safety takes priority over physiological needs, at least in the short run; or instances in which needs for affection or for esteem become modes of 'self-actualisation' and at the same time may eclipse physiological and safety needs. Maslow's proposal has the appeal of satisfying simplicity, but facts of human motivation are surely less orderly.

Elsewhere[29], I have discussed in some detail why I cannot accept Maslow's interpretation of self-actualisation. Here I will note some of the main difficulties, putting my criticism more explictly in the context of a view of his entire need hierarchy and also of my now clearer view of the evolutionary perspective. My objections centre on the conviction that Maslow's metapsychology is too biological, or at any rate, inappropriately biological, and that it is also too individualistic, too much a captive of the present moment in our own culture in this respect.

Too biological. Consider the following passage: 'Man demonstrates *in his own nature* a pressure toward fuller and fuller *Being,* more and more perfect actualisation of his humanness in exactly the same naturalistic, scientific sense that an acorn may be said to be 'pressing toward' being an oak tree, or that a tiger can be observed to 'push toward' being tigerish, or a horse toward being equine ... The environment does not give him potentialities or capacities; he *has* them in inchoate or embryonic form, just as he has embryonic arms and legs'.[30] Putting aside the traps that lie in Maslow's metaphorical portrayal of the interactive process of epigenesis (no modern biologist could write like that), we cannot accept as plausible the suggestion that people's guiding commitments to engage with their historical, cultural worlds of work, play, religion, art, politics, and, generally, their relations with themselves and one another can be usefully conceived as unfolding from some preformed biological potential, except from the multipotential for feeling and symbolic thought.

The situation is worse, because Maslow has definite ideas about the direction towards which biologically-rooted self-actualisation points. In an extremely informal 'study'[31] that he asks to bear much more weight than

29 M.B. Smith, 'On self-actualization', in M.B. Smith, *Humanizing Social Psychology,* Jossey-Bass, San Francisco, 1974.
30 A.H. Maslow, *Toward a Psychology of Being,* Van Nostrand, Princeton, New Jersey, 1968 (second edition), p.160. The emphases are Maslow's.
31 Maslow, *Motivation and Personality, op.cit.,* pp.199-234.

it can possibly support, Maslow looked at what seemed to be the common and distinguishing characteristics of notable people whom he regarded as self-actualising. These were, of course, people whom he saw as exemplifying *his* values: humanitarians, artists, and saints, not generals, rogues, or captains of industry. For the most part, Maslow's heroes happen also to be mine. But I cannot accept his surreptitious attempt to find bogus support for one set among the conceivably infinite directions in which human potentialities can be realised. His faith in a fictitious biology blinds him to the human drama of consequential choice among alternatives; to the perennial problem of good and evil; to the human context in which politics is significant; to the potential for tragedy and the grounds for comedy in the human condition. This 'humanistic psychologist' is not sufficiently humanistic.

Too individualistic. Maslow's individualistic assumptions are evident even at the level of his Deficiency needs. Take, for example, parental care and love, or 'altruistic' concern for the safety of one's family, band, or in-group, not represented by Maslow's theory. Modern primatology gives good grounds for regarding such social motives as pre-existing human culture, and modern evolutionary theory[32] suggests selective mechanisms by which they probably gained a firm genetic foothold in human biology. Mother love and paternal aggressive defense of family may get integrated into motivational elaborations that are in some sense self-actualising, but to place such fundamentals at a rarified level of the hierarchy seems dead wrong. When these needs are activated, as by a child in danger or distress, they have the driven quality of the most urgent D-motives — and may lead to the sacrifice, not the 'actualisation' of self. They are missing from Maslow's scheme.

At the level of 'B-motives', Maslow's doctrines of self-actualisation have fitted comfortably into the ideological platform of the counter-culture.[33] 'Hippies' talked of 'doing your own thing', and idealised a kind of 'careless love' that somehow evades the effort demanded by caring love among mutually responsible persons. They combined extreme individualism with shallow communion and communalism, and ignored or despised humankind's historical discoveries about the necessity for ethics and politics and the important consequences of different political forms — mostly with chaotic, anti-human results.

Maslovian theory, as it was developing around the time of his death

---

32 Wilson, *Sociobiology: The New Synthesis, op.cit.*
33 See a brilliant discussion of Maslow's theory from this perspective by Adrienne Aron-Schaar, 'Maslow's other child', *Journal of Humanistic Psychology,* scheduled for Vol.17, No.2, Spring 1977.

in 1970, has the same defects, which make it peculiarly irrelevant to politics. Self-actualisation as an ethical goal is individualism writ large, with a pseudo-biological sanction. It is a glorification of 'doing one's own thing', even though Maslow did note that the 'own thing' of his hand-picked sample of self-actualising people was mostly altruistic. In the humanistic psychology movement, interest has substantially shifted to a so-called 'transpersonal psychology', the emergence of which had Maslow's sponsorship. Transpersonal psychology is mystical and religious in emphasis. It is the latest attempt to balance the excesses of Western individualism by borrowings from the Wisdom of the East, whether Hindu, Tao, Zen, Sufi, or some grand ragout of them all (as in Areca). It provides a haven for True Believers in which rational appraisal of evidence is frowned upon, and *ESP, est,* and tales of flying saucers are welcome. Maslow himself cannot be held personally responsible for all this foolishness, but the wholly individualistic cast of his conception of human needs does seem to call for a magical counterpoise. What is missing, of course, is any psychological base for politics, for the management both of conflicts and of common interests among complex, partly responsible people in the real world.

If our discussion of Maslow's theory has involved us in mind-boggling issues of *Weltanschauung,* current interest among psychologists and political scientists in the need for personal control and allied concepts is much more down to earth and, at least for the moment, more relevant and useful. Renshon[34] has recently provided political science with a competent summary and integration of relevant research and theory in both disciplines, along with some suggestive data of his own. But interest in the topic goes back at least two decades, during most of which its political relevance was apparent. In Renshon's phrasing, people have 'a basic need to gain control over [their] physical and psychological life-space. A person's life space can be as varied as human experience, but generally refers to those aspects of the environment that are perceived by the individual to be important in the on-going pursuit of his goals, values, and needs. Very often this will include neither politics nor the political system . . . When politics is perceived to be a control-relevant aspect of the individual's psychological life-space, the link is forged between psychological needs and political life'.[35]

The background for this interdisciplinary agenda goes back to an important theoretical paper by Robert White on the concept of competence[36],

---

34 See Renshon, *Psychological Needs and Political Behaviour, op.cit.*
35 *ibid.,* pp.1-2.
36 R.W. White, 'Motivation reconsidered: The concept of competence', *Psychological Review,* Vol.66, 1959, pp.297-333.

which was mainly concerned with marshalling evidence and arguments against the view, then predominant in psychology, that motivation can be understood fully in terms of lacks, drives, and 'tension reduction' (also, remember, of concern to Dorothy Lee and to Maslow). White drew evidence from many sources that people share with other mammals an intrinsic motive to produce intended effects on their environments, and that the sense of competence in one's ability to produce such effects is intrinsically gratifying. A little later, Rotter[37] showed that people — well, college students — differ from one another in the degree to which they attribute the outcomes of their endeavours, their successes and failures, to their own abilities and skills (Internal Control) or to fate and chance (External Control). Others were not slow to point out that Blacks' feelings of impotence in the face of The Man, and alienated youths' similar feelings vis à vis The System, were also instances of external control. The motivation for personal control or competence then became a *variable* of individual differences to be explored in its correlations, not just an assumption about human nature.

de Charms[38] gave a slightly different phrasing to the variable in his distinction between Origins and Pawns. Origins are people who feel themselves to be the source of their actions, whereas Pawns are those who feel constrained or manipulated from without. Whether one is more an Origin or a Pawn makes a difference in the extent, in actual life, that one exercises initiative in shaping one's world, or merely reacts as a 'patient', not an agent. (A self-fulfilling prophecy is activated, when concepts or theories of the self are involved.) Nearly a decade ago, I discussed this developing perspective on the empirics of human autonomy or 'free will'[39], including notice of its relation to the concept of 'civic competence' featured by Almond and Verba in their classic comparative study of political systems.[40]

By now, what began as simple has become more complicated. Conceptualisation and measurement, both of the motive for personal control and of the sense of efficacy (personal *or* political), turn out to be difficult and controversial. And the ready availability of Rotter's original and now badly

---

37 J.B. Rotter, 'Generalized expectancies for internal versus external control of reinforcement', *Psychological Monographs*, Vol.80, 1966.

38 R. de Charms, *Personal Causation: The Internal Affective Determinants of Behavior*, Academic Press, New York, 1969.

39 M.B. Smith, 'Competence and Socialization', in M.B. Smith, *Social Psychology and Human Values*, Aldine-Atherton, Chicago, 1969, pp.210-50.

40 G.A. Almond and S. Verba, *The Civic Culture: Political Attitudes and Democracy in Five Nations*, Princeton University Press, Princeton, New Jersey, 1963.

antiquated instrument, along with a parcel of others[41], has led to the pro-liferation of fashionable but mindless research that has muddied the waters more than it has clarified them. All the same, as in the case of the spate of research on authoritarianism two decades ago, I think it is clear that we are dealing with an area of psychological dispositions that is genuinely relevant to politics.

The relevance is clearer than in the case of Maslow, because the am-bitions of all concerned have been more modest. True enough, White and others have tried rather persuasively to legitimise the need for competence or control through some kind of general mammalian charter. But research has been concerned mainly with personal control and the sense of efficacy among real people today, living under democratic political systems or in modernising ones that provide a reasonable foil for comparison. Further, no claim is made that personal control is *the* primary human motive: only that it is an important one, in terms of which people now vary, and one that has transparent relevance to the workings of politics. After all, 'personal control' is only a slight variant, with different conceptual associations and connotations, of Hobbes' old concept of power as a rational prerequisite for the satisfaction of the whole range of other human appetites.

And the relevance in this case involves a two-way street. As a sometime student of alienation and protest among American youth[42], I have been impressed with the extent to which young people's sense of hopeless powerlessness in relation to a national politics of which they disapprove may feed back to leave them feeling like pawns in their personal lives. The badly eroded capacity of the young to *hope* in regard to national issues of war and peace, justice, and planetary survival surely has much to do with the spread of privatism among them and with their vulnerability to irrational and occultist messages that seem to offer avenues of escape. We may need to improve our politics before our psychology regains its morale.

This may be a good note to end on. Traditionally, theorists have looked to doctrines of human needs for a sound psychological base on which to build a theory of politics. The available doctrines, beginning with instinct theories, tended — wrongly — to conceive of human nature as independent of political life but setting its terms. From the perspective that I have been illustrating, human nature has emerged in political life; the relationship

---

41 A.P. MacDonald, 'Measures of external-internal control', in J.P. Robinson and P.R. Shaver, *Measures of Social Psychological Attitudes*, Institute for Social Research, Univer-sity of Michigan, Ann Arbor, 1973 (revised edition).

42 M.B. Smith, 'Activism and apathy in contemporary adolescents', in M.B. Smith, *Humanizing Social Psychology*, Jossey-Bass, San Francisco, 1974, pp.57-94.

is reciprocal or interactive. Psychologists ought not to look mainly to rats and pigeons but to the records of political history and thought (along with art and literature) for the phenomena of human nature that it is their task to formulate systematically. Psychological views of human nature should meet the test of whether they can give an intelligible account of human triumphs and failures in polities; social scientists are in no position to cast doubt, as some have, upon the possibility of democracy because its prerequisites appear not to correspond to their impoverished assumptions about human nature.

Human nature, including human needs, values, motives, and wishes, is an emergent — the self-transforming product of an interactive, dialectical process in which human actions on the world, first in evolution, then in history, have created conditions that keep bringing new needs, values, motives, and wishes into being. *Of course* social psychology and the other human sciences are historical, as Gergen[43] has recently been arguing to the shocked response of many of his colleagues. It should be a source of strength, not an admission of weakness, to grasp this understanding. Let social psychology and the social sciences also point forward to an open, not a closed future.

---

43 K.J. Gergen, 'Social psychology as history', *Journal of Personality and Social Psychology,* Vol.26, 1973, pp.309-20.

True Needs, Rationality and Emancipation

Kai Nielsen

I

It is natural that there should be a reluctance on the part of a tolerably chastened philosopher to speak of 'true needs' and 'false needs'. It is natural to suspect that these are little more than rhetorically disguised partisan notions introduced by ill-disguised persuasive definitions. 'True needs', like 'true art', 'true democracy' or 'true champions', is what W.B. Gallie has characterised as an essentially contested concept and indeed — since concepts can be more or less essentially contested — a very relativised one at that.[1] In such a linguistic environment, 'true' functions persuasively and emotively to recommend certain needs or laud certain needs beyond what is carried by the normally normative force of 'needs' itself; moreover, reflective and informed people do not agree on criteria for what is to count as 'true needs' any more than they do for what counts as 'true art', 'true religion' or 'genuine democracy'. 'True needs' and thereby 'false needs' do little more than function as partisan instruments in ideological debates

---

1 W.B. Gallie, 'Essentially Contested Concepts', in *The Importance of Language*, ed. Max Black, Prentice-Hall, Englewood Cliffs, New Jersey, 1968; W.B. Gallie, *Philosophy and Historical Understanding*, Shocken Books, New York, 1968, Chapter 8; Alasdair MacIntyre, 'The Essential Contestability of Some Social Concepts', *Ethics*, Vol.84, No.1, October 1973, pp.1-9; William E. Connolly, *The Terms of Political Discourse*, Heath, Lexington, Massachusetts, 1974, Chapter I.

and thus they should not be a part of a conscientious social theorist's or social critic's lexicon.

I am sometimes tempted to say such things but I am tempted as well to say that these vague notions, which have been part of historically important social analyses, can be given a reading which reveals their importance and shows that it would be incorrect simply to regard them as I have done above. In this essay I want to set out and partially justify something of the rationale for giving in to the latter temptation. Its argument shall be that essentially contested and often partisan as such concepts are, their essential contestedness is not so deep or so intractable that true and objectively verifiable or warrantable claims cannot be made about what are and what are not true needs. I shall further suggest, but not fully argue, that these claims can in turn be seen to play a useful role in a social theory which can withstand close critical scrutiny.

There are a number of avenues that might be taken in arguing for the above, including, of course, an attempt perspicuously to display the way talk of 'true needs' and 'false needs' functions in reflective social criticism and analysis. I shall not attempt to assemble reminders for such a purpose, but shall instead take the more indirect route of showing how talk of needs, including talk of 'true needs', is to be seen as an integral part of a conception of what it is to be a thoroughly rational person or a fully reasonable human being. Adapting and developing some remarks of Jürgen Habermas', I shall relate and in a way tie the notions I have just mentioned to the concepts of emancipation and enlightenment.[2] These notions, of course, generate suspicions not unlike those generated by 'true needs'. I shall try to allay or at least reduce these suspicions and to establish that an understanding of needs and an understanding of rationality reciprocally require each other. Thus when we see what this understanding involves, we will come to acknowledge that while the concepts of emancipation and enlightenment and the related concept of needs are in some measure essentially contested, we will also come to acknowledge that they are not so essentially contested that straight-forwardly true and humanly important claims cannot be made about (a) what emancipation and enlightenment and thereby human ration-

---

2 Jürgen Habermas, *Toward a Rational Society*, tr. Jeremy J. Shapiro, Beacon Press, Boston, 1970; Jürgen Habermas, *Theorie und Praxis*, Suhrkamp Verlag, Frankfurt am Main, Germany, 1971 (fourth edition); Jürgen Habermas, *Erkenntis und Interesse*, Suhrkamp Verlag, Frankfurt am Main, Germany, 1968; Jürgen Habermas, *Philosophischpolitische Profile*, Suhrkamp Verlag, Frankfurt am Main, Germany, 1971. See also his 'Summation and Response', *Continum*, Vol.8, No.I, Spring-Summer 1970, pp.123-33, and his 'A Postscript to Knowledge and Human Interest', *Philosophy of the Social Sciences*, Vol.3, No.2, June 1973, pp.157-89.

ality (as distinct from irrationality) consist in and (b) what answers to the needs of human beings. If we can come to understand the role and place of needs in such a conceptualisation, we will come to see something of what talk of true needs or genuine needs consists in.

There are two preliminaries I should dispatch. I should briefly say something about what an essentially contested concept is and I should indicate something – a rather minimal something – of what we are talking about when we speak of 'true needs' or 'genuine needs'.

In speaking of essentially contested concepts, I am speaking of concepts which are in part appraisive with complex criteria over which strong but persistently conflicting claims are made concerning which criteria give what it really is to be a such and such. Furthermore, for the fully essentially contested concepts, there is no prospect of general agreement concerning how we could in a non-arbitrary manner establish the core criteria which define the contours of the concepts such that we could say quite objectively and unproblematically what such concepts really signify. When we examine the different uses of the terms expressive of essentially contested concepts and 'the characteristic arguments in which they figure, we soon see that there is no one clearly definable use of any of them which can be set up as the correct or standard use'.[3] Yet these appraisive terms are such that the users of these terms, with their varied ideologies and normative commitments, will for through and through essentially contested concepts continue to maintain, without any basis of proof, that their particular reading most adequately, among the competing readings, captures the really crucial sense of the term. Think here of the members of the various Christian sects disputing over 'a Christian life' or 'true Christian doctrine' or of the participants in the various religions and genuinely informed atheist theologians, for example Feuerbach, Hagerstrom, Hedenius or MacIntyre, disputing over 'true religion'. Or, for a purely secular application, think of contemporary Marxists disputing over 'genuine Marxism' or 'the Marxist tradition'.

I turn now to my second preliminary. 'Needs' in many of its characteristic employments is a normative conception, though it is not – as if we understood what that means – 'a purely normative conception'.[4] But in those contexts, which indeed are quite standard contexts, and where the needs in question are also 'true needs' or 'genuine needs', we are speaking (though

---

3 Gallie, 'Essentially Contested Concepts', in *The Importance of Language, op.cit.*, p.122.
4 Kai Nielsen, 'Morality and Needs', in *The Business of Reason*, eds. J.J. MacIntosh and S.C. Coval, Routledge and Kegan Paul, London, 1969.

perhaps not exclusively) of needs which answer to the pervasive interests of human beings. True needs answer to such interests, false needs do not; rather false needs are those things that people come to want and feel they must have as a result of social stimulation and ideological indoctrination and would not otherwise feel such, or typically even any, attachment to or concern about. Most obviously they are many of the needs created by advertising but more generally — and often more subtly — they are needs created by the consciousness industry. Such social stimulation induces people to want and feel they must have things which they would not continue compulsively to want or typically want at all let alone feel they must have if they were having the desires that thoroughly emancipated and enlightened, and thereby fully rational, people would have when they were being tolerably well informed and in situations where communication was not distorted. What answers to the pervasive and enduring interests of human beings and what are the things they truly need is an unexpungeable part of what such people in situations of undistorted communication and full information would desire and believe it was crucial for them to have. What people truly need in such circumstances is what we are talking about when we speak of their true needs or genuine needs.

For this conceptualisation to get off the ground, it is crucial that the concepts of emancipation and enlightenment and thereby the concept of a rational person be given a reading such that they are themselves not seen as partisan ideological instruments so deeply and essentially contested that they cannot be truth-bearing. It is to this task that I shall turn. It is a crucial part of my case for the objectivity and importance of a conception of true or genuine needs.

II

A key element in Habermas' conception of rationality is the claim that a fully rational person will be an emancipated, enlightened human being. Such people will have critical insight and an enlightened consciousness, that is, a coherent total consciousness. But what are the criteria of enlightenment and emancipation and are they essentially contested concepts? And what is this 'coherent total consciousness'?

Let us start by trying to get a purchase on what it is to be an enlightened and emancipated human being. Such person will have a reasonable self-understanding as well as a good understanding of other human beings. The requisite understanding is not a very clearly delineated notion. What it is, in particular, to acquire self-understanding is not very evident. But it surely involves a good understanding of the motivating forces operative on one and a knowledge of the probable effects of acting on them. It also involves an ability to assess one's motives and the attaining of what Lucien Goldmann calls an historical consciousness, namely an understanding of the type of society one is in and the social forces operating on one and the historical possibilities of altering them. The having of such a historical consciousness plus an ability to act in the light of it is indeed a very finely honed degree of self-understanding. But to attain any self-understanding at all, one would at least have to have understanding of one's motives. One would have to be able to assess their significance and the effects of acting on them as well as to understand the import of one's feelings, deceits and masks. That is to say, one must be good at catching oneself in acts of self-deception and at understanding their crazy rationale. But to have this self-understanding we must have an understanding of others.

We know from the history of philosophical analysis that conceptions such as 'motives', 'motivating forces', 'self-identity', 'self-understanding' and 'self-deception' have proved very troubling indeed. We can, to take one example, easily get ourselves into the state of being thoroughly perplexed over *how* self-deception is even possible while knowing full well there is such a phenomenon. With the possible exception of self-identity, there are clear cases of what it is we are talking about when we use such conceptions. In that important way their reality and objectivity is indisputable.

It will also be the case that an emancipated person will have a good understanding of others. He will understand their motives, their anxieties and aspirations and he will be able to assess their significance. With this knowledge, and with a firm sense of self-identity, he will be able to act resolutely. No matter what difficulties we may have with the concept of a person, if it makes any sense at all to speak of an 'emancipated person', part of what we would be talking about in using this vocabulary would be to speak of people with a firm sense of self-identity who, while remaining flexible and open to the influence of others and changing events, remain self-controlled and autonomous human beings.

There are, of course, further characteristics of emancipation or enlightenment. An emancipated person will be a person capable of fairness, objectivity and impartiality. Perhaps he will not always be fair but he will have that capability and he must be a person capable of calm and impartial judgment. He will also be an informed person knowledgeable about his world and most particularly about his social world. The having of such knowledge will evidently involve a knowledge of the technically correct strategies available to such a person and, while this knowledge will not be sufficient to dictate his actions, he will take careful cognizance of it in his actions. While knowledge of the social world is not limited to this, what more is actually involved is not fully evident. What is it to know what our society is really like and how do we make sense together? What is it to be held captive to a myth or an ideology and who is it who is held captive to social myths and is gripped by a distorting ideology and how do we decide? These are plainly not easy questions to answer. An emancipated person is a person who can see through the ideology of his society and class and the ideologies of others as well. But ideologies are things the other chap has. We do not see the mote in our own eyes. But to more than ritualistically claim knowledge of the social world — at least the full kind of knowledge that emancipation and enlightenment, if they are to be attained, require — we would need in some objective way to be able to identify ideologies and myths and the various illusions to which mankind is prone. (Is religion the opiate of the people?) But we appear at least to have very little cross-cultural agreement about that or very little understanding of what would constitute a rational basis for resolving such issues. We are all in the abstract inclined to admit that we are prone to deceits, but we are rather short on techniques for locating them. There would not be a terribly wide general agreement concerning a list of the major deceits or illusions of humankind. Is belief in a socialist future — a genuinely classless society — or the objectivity of some aesthetic norms among these illusions?

An emancipated or enlightened human being would understand human needs, including his own, and understand their relative importance (their schedule of priorities vis-à-vis each other) and in the light of that understanding he would understand his desires and aims and know which ones to control and sublimate and which to seek to satisfy and when. But again there is room for scepticism or at least there are rather deep-going perplexities. It is doubtful that we would agree on a list of needs, let alone agree about their relative importance and a scheduling of priorities for the satisfaction of needs. We can move to talking of the *true* needs or *genuine* needs of humankind, but then what work is 'true' and 'genuine' doing here? Are they not veiling the fact that implicit *persuasive* definitions are at work in such contexts introducing in effect a selective and controversial list of needs as those which are distinctive of and/or essential for *homo sapiens*?

Yet isn't it also possible to exaggerate these difficulties? Human beings need love, companionship, security, protection, a sense of community, meaningful work and a sense of involvement in what they are doing, adequate sustenance, shelter, sexual gratification, amusement, rest, recreation, recognition, respect of person and the like. I am not trying to catch all the needs there would be widespread agreement about, but I think I have caught at least some of the central elements that would be on any thoughtful list of basic human needs. Such needs are true needs.

Some of these needs indeed have rather sharply different contextual applications. Meaningful work surely will not be the same thing in all cultures and all periods of history, though this is not to say it will not have identical or at least closely similar deep structures. Similar things obtain for respect for person, recognition, recreation, amusement, shelter, involvement, a sense of community, love and companionship. There will, as well, be cultural and indeed other variants concerning even such biologically rooted things as adequate sustenance, sexual gratification and rest. A capitalist might take adequate sustenance to be sustenance sufficient for the workers to work with productivity and to reproduce themselves. Perhaps the new synthetically based 'food' made from re-cycled paper being considered for experiment on the Chilean workers will do? It might enable them to reproduce themselves and to keep the production lines going. Need we, as far as adequate sustenance is concerned, ask for anything more? But others with different ends in view will have different conceptions of what would count as 'adequate sustenance'. But while there will be an important cultural overlay there will, as well, be biologically determinate limits about malnutrition. Similar things should be said about rest and perhaps even sex.

On our short list of needs, we indeed have conceptions which are in one way or another problematic ('meaningful work', 'community'), or vague ('love', 'involvement'), and at least almost all of them are subject to differing contextual and cultural applications and readings, though the former need not betoken a relativism or 'a social determination of truth'.[5] But do these differences point toward such a hodge-podge that we are warranted in claiming that 'true human needs', 'genuine human needs' and 'basic human needs' are so essentially contested that we are as at sea concerning them as we are concerning 'true art', 'true champions', 'true religion' or perhaps even 'genuine democracy'.

In response to this charge of essential contestedness, we should begin by asking whether in spite of our very real differences it is not evident that basic needs are being more adequately met in Sweden and China than

---

5 For comments about the so-called social determination of truth see Stephen Lukes, 'On the social determination of truth', in *Modes of Thought*, eds. Robin Horton and Ruth Finnegan, Faber and Faber, London, 1973, and Kai Nielsen, 'On the Diversity of Moral Beliefs', *Cultural Hermeneutics*, Vol.2, No.3, November 1974.

in Bolivia and Bangladesh. Is there any doubt about that at all — and while there might be dispute about a comparison of Zaire and South Africa or China and the United States do our differences here result from the essential contestedness of the concept of 'genuine human needs' or do they result from a lack of information on our part and a failure, over these specific problems, to reason through in a careful fashion to the attainment of an informed position about what is to be said concerning such comparisons? Perhaps what is actually involved is some blend. Something might, at a given time, be more or less essentially contested. But what should be evident is that we are hardly in a position to lay it all at the door of 'essentially contested concepts'.

Whatever we want to say here, we need to recognise that sometimes these needs conflict and that in some circumstances at least they cannot all be simultaneously satisfied or as fully satisfied as might otherwise be desired. The problem of their scheduling is a very real one. Judgments about their relative importance, particularly when they are not clearly conceptualised, are not easy to resolve. What weight we give to involvement and community is not independent of the reading we give these terms. But even with identical or similar readings of the key terms on our list of human needs, there appears at least to be wide disagreement about and confusion concerning their relative importance. Here we may have something which is essentially contested. Yet we should be cautious in making such a judgment for these problems have not yet been carefully and analytically probed by people with the requisite information. What we can say, generally and probably unhelpfully, is this; enlightened and emancipated people will have an understanding of human needs and while this understanding is in various ways indefinite, it is at least not so indefinite that material truth claims cannot be confirmed or disconfirmed concerning them.

III

Enlightened and emancipated people will also have an understanding of human aspirations and an understanding of what human good — a distinctive human flourishing — would consist in and some understanding of the possibilities of its attainment. (This, of course, is not unrelated to their understanding of human needs.) They would likewise have an acute understanding of the evils of the world and of those features of the world contributing to human alienation. Here, even more evidently than in our discussion of needs, we have concepts which have repeatedly been the source of philosophical perplexity. Do we really know what human good or human flourishing consists in or do we, even if we know that, really have anything like an adequate conception of the social conditions for its attainment, or, if in turn we know that, do we know how to bring those social conditions into being? And do we agree on the lists of human evils?

There are two postures here which are natural, not infrequently struck, and — or so it seems to me — plainly mistaken. One is to say that, apart from confused and confusing philosophical perplexities, we in actual life have a sufficient understanding of these things. We, so the claim runs, understand in their essentials human good and evil. If this is taken to mean that we know what the *summum bonum* is or even the correct set or cluster of objective moral principles, then what needs to be said is that at least to this date such a claim has not been sustained by an impartial study of the history of morals or moral philosophy. Disagreement has been and continues to be deep and endemic and there is little agreement even about how we would resolve these issues. The reception of Kurt Baier's *The Moral Point of View* and John Rawls' *A Theory of Justice* shows this very well. Both are systematic, elaborately worked out, sustained and powerful statements of a system of putatively objective principles of morality and both have not only provoked criticism but the most varied sort of critical rejection of the very foundations of their work. It isn't as if all the criticisms or most of the criticisms cut in the one direction, indicating where we might alternatively go in setting out the rational foundations of a system of morals. Rather the criticisms are radically diverse, indicating very little agreement concerning either the foundations of morals or what would count as a rational consensus concerning the principles of ethics. In what Habermas would call 'the public sphere' or what Kant thought of as the legitimate domain of the public use of reason, we have not attained a consensus over such matters. So I think it is little more than an ignorant or a foolish boast to claim we have knowledge of the highest good or of the principles of human flourishing or knowledge of a determinate system of moral principles set out with some acceptable lexicality which will guide our lives and provide us with the grounds for a critique of the social order. But a recognition of this need not, and by itself should not, drive us to moral scepticism or a Westermarkian subjectivism.

The other pervasive error — the other side of the same coin — is to deny that we have any knowledge or grounded understanding of good and evil at all. But that is plainly wrong. We at the very least know that starvation, malnutrition, torture, exploitation, denial of all chance to develop one's potential, a total lack of freedom and respect for one's person are all evils. We can describe concretely and in detail, circumstances of life in which what happens is plainly an evil. Most capitalists, for example, would not deny that the industrial workers surrounding San Paulo are being exploited and that the conditions under which they live are very bad indeed. They would only try to defend it as a necessary evil during a stage of industrialisation and modernisation without which, they claim, poverty in Brazil could not be overcome. This claim of theirs is a very arguable proposition indeed, but my point in alluding to it is to illustrate how there is extensive agreement about what is evil and, to a lesser extent, about what is good even in the absence of agreement about the *summum bonum* or *a system* of moral knowledge. The capitalist and the class conscious proletarian do indeed disagree morally, as well as factually; their disagreements cannot be reduced simply to disagreement about the most efficient means to attain commonly agreed on and commonly conceived ends. Their conceptions of moral priorities, their attitudes toward human beings and their beliefs about community and social justice and the possibilities and importance of human cooperation will significantly diverge. But there will also be an extensive common acceptance of certain plain evils and plain goods.

If my arguments are in the main correct, it is a mistake to say that the concepts of enlightenment and emancipation are without objective import because even reflective and informed people do not have an understanding of what human good or human flourishing consists in or even a rudimentary understanding of how to attain these things. There is *some* understanding of and agreement about human aspirations toward an achievement of more humane conditions of life and there is some understanding of and agreement about the steps to be taken toward its achievement. Moreover, there is a somewhat better understanding of some of the *evils* to be avoided, of some of the things not to be done and some of the things to be undone. We have this understanding even though we do not have rational agreement concerning the foundations of morals or on what constitutes an adequate systematic normative ethic. Surely there is a greater and a lesser understanding of human aspirations and a greater and lesser understanding of what would constitute a truly human society on the part of different people. Enlightenment and emancipation, like neurosis and ambivalence, admit of degrees. But there is some common understanding as well.

With such an understanding, we have some grasp of the conditions of alienation and the overcoming of alienation and with that we must also, to attain enlightenment and emancipation, have an understanding of what divides people and classes and of the relative importance of these divisions. With this understanding, an emancipated person has some understanding of what human freedom, that is, liberation, consists in and of the conditions for its attainment. Even in adverse circumstances – the circumstances most of us live in – we, to the extent that liberation is partly an attitude of mind, must in that 'inner way' be free in order to be liberated and indeed we can, in a way, be liberated if we have that mental set and an understanding and control of ourselves. But we will, of course, recognise the necessity for struggle to attain as well an outward and manifest liberation, where we have reasonable grounds for the hope that there are prospects that such a struggle will have such a liberating effect.

Between the Marxs and the Mills, on the one hand, and the Schopenhauers and the Kierkegaards on the other, there will be a clash about the prospects for the attainment, sustaining and enlargement of such liberation. Depending on where one thinks it is reasonable to come down on such an issue (even as a matter of reasonable hope), one will, to a greater or lesser extent, stress the exclusiveness of 'inner liberation'. If, like Schopenhauer, we believe that our prospects for throwing off the external bonds of servitude are slight, we will stress the value of the 'inner side' of liberation. Alternatively, to the extent that we think, as does Marx, that the shackling conditions are principally socio-economic and specific to certain historical epochs, we will think it a swindle, implicitly protective of the *status quo*, to settle for such 'inner liberation'. Yet between such people there need not be any vast difference concerning what in optimum conditions liberation would consist in. The key difference turns around beliefs concerning the achievability of these optimum conditions. It need not be the case that the young Horkheimer and the old Horkheimer had radically different conceptions of morality and enlightenment. Rather the old Horkheimer ceased to hold the more optimistic factual beliefs and conceptions of human nature of his youth and middle age.

The concepts of freedom, liberation, integration and alienation notoriously have their problematic side, but we understand them well enough to understand something of their material truth conditions. Life for most people in New York city hardly makes for integration and non-divisiveness or for escape from isolation and atomisation, while exactly the opposite is true in Peking. Life in Zaire or Saudi Arabia hardly makes for human liberation in the way it does in Sweden or the way it did in Chile under the Allende government.

With such a stress on human liberation as a feature of emancipation and enlightenment, we should also, once again, allude to the fact that the attainment of emancipation involves the conscious development of one's powers — I do not speak of a drive for power — or, if you will, the recognition of the value of self-realisation. Self-realisation understandably is an old bugaboo in moral philosophy. We have no very clear understanding of what we must do to realise ourselves. But though this is a far from pellucid notion, it is plainly conceptually linked with human liberation and the development of our powers. We will be at odds with each other about what our essential powers are, but we are not totally at sea here. We know a very schizoid or paranoid person is very far from the realisation of his powers and while those labels are not without their conceptual difficulties, they are also not totally devoid of intelligible application.

There is a further cluster of characteristics of emancipation and enlightenment which are rather more straightforwardly intellectualistic. An enlightened person and indeed an emancipated person as well is a person with a developed sense of relevance and pertinence concerning evidential and argumentative matters. Like any rational person he will not ignore evidence and he will act in its light. But he will as well have a more acute sense of what evidence is relevant and what is not or what is of a diminished relevance to the various matters with which he needs to concern himself. He will recognise where arguments are relevant, where they will have force and when and with whom they are rather beside the point. He cannot, where genuinely enlightened, but be a perceptive human being.

A thoroughly enlightened human being will combine many of the rather disparate virtues of a Hume, Kierkegaard, Peirce and Wittgenstein. Such a person will be acutely aware of the limits of intersubjectively valid knowledge and he will have a good nose for incoherent pseudoprofundities, while remaining wary of doctrinaire and unsupportable employments of philosophical terms of art such as 'pseudo-questions' or 'category mistakes'. But over such matters, at least, he will be a fallibilist. He will take his various beliefs and at least most of his commitments to be open to critical examination and possible revision. He will — and here we need some of the virtues of Marx and Nietzsche as well — be a person who can extricate himself from the distorting influences of the historically and culturally given conceptions he has been socialised into accepting and he will, as we have noted, be a person who can create new and more adequate conceptions or at least revise and de-mythologise his culturally received conceptions in such a way that he comes to see the world rightly.

These 'intellectual' characteristics of enlightenment and emancipation are

not, of course, sufficient to fix the concepts of emancipation and enlightenment and exhibit how they are central elements of rationality. In addition
to those broadly 'moral' characteristics of these concepts which we have
already noted there is as well the very fundamental 'moral' feature that
an emancipated human being will be self-reflective about his ends and will
for the important areas of his life choose what he chooses after a cogent
and objective examination of his alternatives, with a knowledge of his
preferences, the causal conditions of these preferences, and the probable
consequences of the various alternative policies embodying those
preferences should they be adopted. Enlightenment, and indeed human
rationality as well, are in part — and essentially — constituted by controlled
and dialectically ramified reflection on the ends of life. The upshot of
this might be to conclude that reflection on the ends of life is a fruitless
enterprise, but even this sceptical conclusion, to meet the conditions of
rationality and emancipation, would have to be reached and sustained
reflectively.

IV

To say what substantive rationality is we would at least have to say what
it is to be emancipated and enlightened and to flesh that out — to overcome
the difficulties generated by the problematic and essentially contested conceptions used in its articulation — we would have to be able to solve or
dissolve a fair number of the most central and intractable classical
philosophical problems. Yet is is also plain enough that the conception
of substantive rationality is not a confused metaphysical construction but
is a conception of rationality found quite ubiquitously in the workings
of our language and in the stream of life. An acknowledgement of these
considerations should lead us to recognise the justice of MacIntyre's claim
that rationality is a most central and a most baffling philosophical
problem.[6]

That the above claim is not hyperbolic can be seen from the fact that
determining what this substantive rationality is would involve settling what
self-knowledge is and its extent, what self-identity is and its delusions,
what autonomy and liberation are and their extent, what it is, in some
depth and in a non-ideologically distorted way, to have a knowledge of
one's social world and what genuine and basic human needs are and the
order of their importance in social life. Moreover, we would as well have

---

6 Alasdair MacIntyre, 'A Perspective on Philosophy', *Social Research*, Vol.38, No.4, Winter
   1971.

to resolve such fundamental questions of moral philosophy as central questions about justice, the good (and its relations to needs), evil, self-realisation and human flourishing, and our capacity to make actual judgments or assessments of intrinsic value. We would also have to be tolerably clear about the extent and limits of knowledge or at least of warranted belief and we would have to have an understanding as well of how ideological conceptions have infiltrated knowledge claims or putative knowledge domains. That is to say, we would need to have a clear understanding of what ideology is, its extent, its force in our collective lives and the possibilities and conditions for its transcendence. We would as well need a good understanding of the relation of theory and ideology to evidence.

In fine — and zeroing in on the relation of rationality to needs — what should be said is this. There is a problematic but still viable substantive conception of rationality in our stream of life which is in part cashed in in terms of the concepts of emancipation and enlightenment. These concepts are, of course, vague with complex criteria, some of which are distressingly indeterminate. But the concepts are not so vague or the criteria so indeterminate that we can never make objective assessments of rationality or of what people truly need. However the concept of rationality is sufficiently essentially contested so that we have yet to have any promise of gaining the kind of general conception of rationality which would give us the Archimedean point we want for adjudicating many of the ideologically significant clashes over what to do or believe or over what human beings truly need. Such general assessments appear at least to be elusive. Even here caution is in order concerning such pessimism. Sometimes further knowledge — and indeed knowledge of a conceptually unproblematic sort — will cause a reversal in our assessments and while the criteria of rationality we have displayed are in many instances indeterminate and are the occasion for a variety of disagreements, including disagreements about what human beings really need, there is no *a priori* reason to believe that some of this indeterminateness cannot be reduced by careful investigation, reflection and a taking to heart of what we reflect on and investigate.

The import of this for an account of human needs should by now be evident. Talk of 'true needs' and 'false needs' need not be wanton, though sometimes it is indeterminate; still the concept of 'true needs' is not so essentially contested as to be merely an ideological instrument. We have some understanding of what it is to be a rational person and what it is to satisfy that conception fully. What answers to the permanent interests of such people, taken collectively, is also what are the true needs of humankind. What answers to such interests is what such people would, under conditions of adequate knowledge and undistorted communication, desire at least for representative people and believe that these people must (*ceteris paribus*) have. What would be so desired and taken as something that people generally and *ceteris paribus* must have, at least under normal conditions, is also something which human beings truly need. So this unpellucid conception finds a not unproblematic but still not necessarily ideological home in the conceptualisation of rationality I have teased out of, clarified and developed from some of the work of Habermas and the Frankfurt School. If my argument is near to the mark, we can quite properly speak of true needs and use such a conception in an articulation of a rational conception of a good society and of what Marx calls a truly human society.

Karl Marx on Human Needs *

Patricia Springborg

Social theory which focuses on human needs has a longer history than one might suppose from much of the current literature. An early and signal example is Seneca's ninetieth letter on Philosophy and Progress, written in the first century A.D., where he attributes all the evils of civilisation to artificial needs and praises the virtuousness of the frugal life. Ancient philosophy was very much preoccupied with the question of whether the pursuit of pleasure and the unlimited gratification of needs were compatible with the ethical life and Plato's *Philebus,* concerned with true and false pleasures, is only one of the many discussions on this subject. That it did not end debate is evident from the fact that the question is vigorously taken up by post-Platonic schools, the Stoics, Epicureans and Sceptics, who among them foreshadowed most later positions on the subject.

Human needs are only really problematic given certain assumptions. No-one can sensibly deny the satisfaction of basic subsistence needs and these would not be problematic at all were it not for the fact that subsistence

* I wish to express my warmest thanks to Professor Leszek Kolakowski, who first drew my attention to the problem of needs in Marxist thought. Without his generous help this essay would not have been written. I am also very grateful to Agnes Heller, Lukacs' former student in Budapest, with whom I have corresponded and whose book, *La Teoria dei bisogn in Marx,* Feltrinelli, Milan, 1974, has recently been published in translation by Allison and Busby, London, 1976.

needs always takes a specific form. People want this food and not that, these clothes and not those, this style of shelter and not that, their sex objects to take this form and not that. Just any food, shelter, clothing and sex will not do and men will demonstrate their independence by going without rather than accepting the satisfaction of their needs in a form that has been foisted upon them. This creates the practical difficulty that it is impossible to say from the point of view of an individual what is a need and what is not, apart from what he himself feels about it — a classic case of what is perceived as real being real in the eye of the perceiver. The insights of psychology have reinforced this point and if one takes account of such needs as the need for security, the need for self-esteem and so on, there is no conceivable limit to what might genuinely constitute a need in a given case. Why do people try to set limits then? Because the needs of some will infringe the rights of others. This turns out to be the perennial problem of ethics and politics.

The debate over needs and wants in English linguistic philosophy has sought an easy way out of this problem in the meaning of words and has thus obscured the issues of substance involved. Pareto said of Marx's words that they are like bats, one can see in them both birds and mice, but this at least forces us to consider the substance of his arguments.[1] The concept of needs historically belonged within a wider constellation of ideas, from which in current discussion it has largely been divorced; as such, needs were synonymous with wants, desires, appetites, interests, demands and propensities. The needs/wants debate artificaly limits the question to a verbal distinction which is not readily found in other languages and which excludes the issues around which discussion has historically revolved.

The first of these is the question of human motivation and its relation to economic and cultural forms of life. A second is the question of social justice, or the relative merits of conflicting demands for a share of society's resources. The question of human needs as a motivating force arose dramatically in the context of economic and technological expansion in the early modern period. What could account for the enormous impetus given to world exploration and the scientific development of nature but the increasing demand for commodities, in other words, the proliferation of needs?

Interestingly enough, almost all dominant political thinkers — Plato, Aristotle, Machiavelli, Hobbes, Rousseau — addressed themselves from time to time to the question of the morality of political expansion and

---

1 Quoted by B. Ollman, *Alienation*, Cambridge University Press, Cambridge, 1971, p.3.

economic growth and, with the exception of Machiavelli, their judgment was negative. By the eighteenth century such an attitude was seriously called into question by social realities: the gap between the rich and the poor had increased so dramatically that, at the very least, it seemed that economic expansion had a moral application in the amelioration of the condition of the poor.

Discussion of human needs has always thrived in an atmosphere of scepticism and inquiry. So, for instance, during the Middle Ages needs were very little discussed for the reason that Christian dogma demanded abstemiousness and unequivocally ruled out the gratification of wants and the expansion of needs as hedonism and capitulation to the world, the flesh and the devil. In this respect too, under the great systems of Plato and Aristotle, there had been far less room for an open-ended discussion of needs than there was among their successors, once their universal philosophic systems were called into question. It is small surprise, therefore, that the next historical period in which a discussion of human needs is revived should be the Enlightenment, the age of the new sceptics and the birth of modern science and modern social theory.

Karl Marx was uncannily aware of the relation between social context and the form of philosophic problems, and he expressly attributed his early interest in the Stoics, Sceptics and Epicureans to the fact that he, like them, followed in the wake of a great systematiser whose world view was now called into question – in his case it was that of Hegel.[2] In addition, Marx noted that in such cases philosophers were forced back from the 'rich intellectual forms' and the 'universal range' of the great systems to the simpler and more elemental questions of man's relation to nature and the practical relation of philosophy to reality. In this context the question of needs could be reopened.

Of course it already had been, and out of the plethora of attitudes on the question of human needs which abounded in the Enlightenment period, Utilitarian, Stoic and so on, two themes began to emerge which involve a hidden antinomy. The first is the doctrine of true and false needs which may be traced back to the Stoics and was revived by Enlightenment thinkers. The second is summarised by the old socialist slogan 'to each according to his needs', and represents the belief that it is possible to engineer social conditions in such a way that all needs can be satisfied, so that the requirements of individual self-realisation and social justice will be

---

2 Marx's Doctoral Dissertation, *Marx-Engels Collected Works*, Vol.1, Lawrence and Wishart, London, 1975, pp.35 and 491.

simultaneously met.[3]

It was almost commonplace in socialist thought up to 1848 to attribute the evils of civilisation, and particularly social inequality, to 'artificial' needs, which modern society was seen to inculcate and from which, in turn, it gained its momentum. From Meslier, Morelly and Mably, Helvétius, Diderot and Rousseau, to Babeuf, Buonarroti, Fourier, Saint-Simon, Comte, Cabet and Owen, the 'scientific' analysis of society constituted a debate over the relation between 'nature' and 'culture'.[4] How far were the problems of secular society attributable to human nature *per se*, and to what degree were they systemic and eliminable under a different form of social organisation? To what extent were the effects of civilisation the responsibility of moral individuals, and therefore open to correction through education and self-discipline, and how far had they exceeded the individual level and become institutional and social problems?

---

3 Of the vast literature on Marx, those works which have been especially useful include: H. Arendt, *The Human Condition*, Doubleday, New York, 1959; H. Caton, 'Marx's Sublation of Philosophy into Praxis', *Review of Metaphysics*, Vol.26, 1972, pp.233-59; A. Cunningham, 'Objectivity and Human Needs in Marxism', *New Blackfriars*, Vol.55, 1974, pp.112-23; R.V. Daniels, 'Fate and Will in the Marxian Philosophy of History', *Journal of the History of Ideas*, Vol.21, 1960, pp.538-52; I. Fetscher, 'Karl Marx on Human Nature', *Social Research*, Vol.40, 1973, pp.443-67; E. Fromm, 'Marx's Contribution to the Knowledge of Man', from his *The Crisis of Psychoanalysis*, Cape, London, 1971, pp.62-76; A. Heller, 'Theory and Practice: Their Relation to Human Needs', *Social Praxis*, Vol.1, 1974, pp.359-73; L. Kolakowski, 'Responsibility and History', and 'Determinism and Responsibility', from his *Marxism and Beyond*, Paladin, London, 1971, pp.105-61 and 206-27; N. Livergood, *Activity in Marx's Philosophy*, Nijhoff, The Hague, 1967; N. Lobkowicz, 'Karl Marx and Max Stirner', in F.J. Edelman, *Demythologizing Marxism*, Nijhoff, The Hague, 1969, pp.64-95; N. Lobkowicz, *Theory and Practice: History of a Concept from Aristotle to Marx*, Notre Dame Press, Indiana, 1967; S. Moore, 'Marx and the Origin of Dialectical Materialism', *Inquiry*, Vol.14, pp.420-9; S. Moore, 'The Metaphysical Element in Marx's Labour Theory of Value', *L'ISEA, Cahiers*, Vol.7, pp.73-95; A. Nasser, 'Marx's Ethical Anthropology', *Philosophy and Phenomenological Research*, Vol.35, 1975, pp.484-500; J.J. O'Malley, 'History and Man's "Nature" in Marx', *Review of Politics*, Vol.28, 1966, pp.508-27; A. Schmidt, *The Concept of Nature in Marx*, N.L.B. London, 1971; A.W. Wood, 'Marx's Critical Anthropology', *Review of Metaphysics*, Vol.26, 1972, pp.118-39.

4 Works on Enlightenment and early socialist thought where these themes are treated include: G.M. Bravo, *Les socialistes avant Marx*, 3 Vols., Maspero, Paris, 1970; L.G. Crocker, *An Age of Crisis, Man and World in Eighteenth Century French Thought*, John's Hopkins Press, Balitmore, 1959; L.G. Crocker, *Nature and Culture, Ethical Thought in the French Enlightenment*, John's Hopkins Press, Baltimore, 1963; P. Gay, *The Enlightenment, An Interpretation*, Vol.1 *The Rise of Modern Paganism*, Vol.2 *The Science of Freedom*, Knopf, New York, 1966 and 1969; M. Leroy, *Histoire des idées sociales en France*, Vol.2 *De Babeuf à Tocqueville*, Gallimard, Paris, 1950; A. Lichtenberger, *Le socialisme au xviiie siècle*, Paris, 1895, Kelley reprint, New York, 1967; G. Lichtheim, *The Origins of Socialism*, Weidenfeld and Nicolson, London, 1972.

Those theorists who arrived at socialism as an answer to these questions tended to come down on the side of 'culture', concluding that social problems were indeed systemic, that human nature was itself a social product, and that human reason could devise a form of social organisation under which human needs and their 'normal' satisfaction would be in equilibrium.

Both of these themes play a role in the thought of Marx but in a formulation much more complex than his predecessors devised. To begin with the concept of needs is more central to Marx's theory of human nature because it brings together different areas in his thought: his ontology, his anthropology, his psychology, his economics and his theory of justice.

Under the influence of Hegel and Feuerbach he was already committed to a theory of needs in his account of the human essence and the actualisation of man's dormant powers in characteristically human activity. In the *1844 Manuscripts* he emphasised the ontological significance of human powers conceived in this way, as potentialities actualised through 'sensuous' needs, whose form and mode of gratification depend on specific historical conditions.[5] Needs here play a role of meditation between Man as Subject and Nature as Object and Marx introduces the concept of nature as man's 'inorganic body' which he develops in the *Grundrisse* and *Capital*.[6] (His pantheism is also reminiscent of Enlightenment thinkers and has its roots in Stoic and Epicurean thought with which we know he was familiar.) Moreover, needs, as an instrument of actualisation constitute a psychological mechanism, as well as providing criteria to distinguish between human activity proper and mere animal or alienated activity. The consideration of needs in the *1844 Manuscripts* is cast in Feuerbachian materialist terms and, as I shall try to show, Marx never succeeded in ridding himself entirely of these Left-Hegelian ontological presuppositions.

However, certain influences – his association with the socialist movement, his reading in political economy and, most importantly, the devastating criticisms of Max Stirner – came to bear in such a way that in *The German Ideology* of 1845, Marx publically rejects the idealist elements in Feuerbach's philosophy and turns from an ontological to an anthropological account of human nature and a more tough-minded form of materialism. Marx's anthropology, much like that which Rousseau outlined in the

---

5 'Economic and Philosophic Manuscripts of 1844', *Collected Works*, Vol.3, p.322. By an ontological conception of human needs, I mean that Marx derived needs as a philosophical category from his concept of the human essence, rather than as a fact of empirical anthropology.

6 *ibid.*, p.275; *Grundrisse*, Penguin, London, 1973, pp.409-10; *Capital*, Vol.1, Progress, Moscow, 1971, pp.173 and 476.

Second Discourse, traces man's development from his condition as a quasi-instinctual animal to the point where he determines his own nature, socially, as the history of the progressive expansion of human needs and forms of production designed to satisfy them.

This line of departure was already indicated in *The Holy Family*, where Marx criticised the Left-Hegelians and a number of early socialists as old-style moralists who still believed in individual solutions to social problems and failed to see the significance of socialism as the conclusion to materialist premises about man's susceptibility to his environment.

In *The German Ideology* he spells out these premises: man's material needs, the forces of production that he develops to satisfy them and the social relations to which productive activity gives rise.[7] That this materialist anthropology is dynamic is due to the constant proliferation of needs and the corresponding expansion of man's powers as developing technology is applied to meet them. This in turn permits a disjunction between the forces of production — the resources man can command through his augmented powers — and the relations of production — the forms of social organisation which govern the exercise of these powers and control of the resources. The anthropological account thus turns into an economic one.

How do true and false needs feature in Marx's theory? In the *1844 Manuscripts* much is made of the alienating effects of artificial needs such as the need for money, propagated by the rule of private property.[8] It is interesting to note that Marx means by artificial needs something quite different from the 'superfluous wants' and 'luxury demands' of his predecessors, Seneca, Diderot and Rousseau. (Marx had nothing against the benefits of 'civilisation' and criticised 'crude communism' for negating them. By the *Grundrisse* he had come to see wealth as 'the universality of needs, capacities, pleasures, productive forces ... the full development of human mastery over the forces of nature ... the absolute working out of [man's] creative potentialities'.[9])

True to the Hegelian formula for dichotomies, false needs are those in which appearances substitute for reality. Needs which are false pose as their opposite, and thereby displace true needs: for example money, which pretends to mediate between man and his needs, but actually places their satisfaction further out of reach of those who sell their labour to have it. With Marx, for the first time, 'true' or 'false' needs are to be understood

---

7 *The German Ideology*, Progress, Moscow, 1964, pp.31, 39-40, 86-95.
8 'Economic and Philosophic Manuscripts of 1844' *op.cit.*, pp.270-82, 293-316, 322-6.
9 *Grundrisse, op.cit.*, p.488.

literally. This means that needs, like other features of the real world, are susceptible of truth and falsity and the distinction between reality and appearance. True needs are claimed to be objective in the sense that they represent real processes, where for earlier thinkers, with perhaps the exception of Plato and his doctrine of true and false pleasures in the *Philebus*, true meant 'good' or morally efficacious, and false meant 'bad' or morally harmful. (Marx makes much of the distinction between subjectivity and objectivity, maintaining that the false needs of his predecessors were arrived at from a subjective standpoint by considering their moral consequences in the individual. His concern was not with the effects of false needs at the 'subjective', individual level, but with the 'objective' falsity of alienated social relations from which they arise. It follows from this that alienation is to be eliminated not at the level of the symptoms, the individual level, but at the level of the cause, the level of objective social relations.)

In *The German Ideology*, the emphasis on true and false needs has also shifted and, as a corollary of his anthropology, Marx develops a materialist psychology which distinguishes between essential needs, those found in all social formations, whose expression merely changes, and artificial needs, those which are the product of a specific mode of production. Those universal needs, 'which only change their form and direction under different social conditions', will, under socialism, be permitted 'to develop normally'; but those false needs which are entirely the creation of a social system will be 'totally deprived of their conditions of existence'.[10]

In *The Holy Family*, Marx had already indicated that man is the product of his environment to such an extent that if you wish to change men you must first change it.[11] The doctrine of needs which he develops in *The German Ideology* is consistent with this view: only socialism can solve the problems to which false needs give rise because it is predicated on their elimination. But socialists do not begin with individual needs, they begin with society, and once they have achieved the appropriate organisation of the forces of production they find that false needs have already disappeared and that the 'normal' satisfaction of all needs is possible, 'a satisfaction limited only by the needs themselves'.[12]

Marx's dialectic of needs substitutes both for a psychology and an ethics in the conventional sense. In his view needs constitute a motivational force which cannot be supplanted through education or moral training – which

---

10 *The German Ideology, op.cit.,* p.277.
11 'The Holy Family', *Collected Works, op.cit.,* Vol.4, pp.130-1.
12 *The German Ideology, op.cit.,* p.277.

sets him apart from the Stoics, Diderot and Rousseau. Nor can the constant expansion of needs and the concomitant development of human powers be arbitrarily halted. The movement of history is such that these newly unleashed powers await only the appropriate social relations for a balance between man's needs and their objects to be struck.

It is worth noting that this is the kind of solution in practice that Marx postulates for all social problems under capitalism: false needs, like false theories, will wither, because communism, 'the real movement' of history, will not sustain needs or theories which do not accord with its premises. Criteria to decide which needs are essential and which are not, are unnecessary, because this is achieved in practice 'by changing the real actual desires and not by making comparisons'. Only communists, realising this 'empirical connection', have abandoned the 'impotent moral injunctions of all moralists down to Stirner' and through their practice attack 'the fixity' of ideas and needs at its material base.

The theory of needs which Marx arrives at in *The German Ideology* is one with which he seems to be finally satisfied, for he expands on it in the *Grundrisse* and clearly assumes it in *Capital*. Marx develops his own version of Adam Smith's 'hidden hand' and Hegel's 'cunning of reason', constituted precisely by 'socially determined needs' and by the *Grundrisse;* he comes to see even the artificial needs of capitalism as a 'civilising influence', breaking down all barriers to the expansion of man's powers and their means of satisfaction.[13] Capital is responsible for the creation of forces of production which permit greatly increased control over the environment and the release of natural resources, for which corresponding forms of social organisation lie in the future — under socialism. Here the power of money, as an artificial need, and exchange value, as an artificial social bond, will be superfluous and wither away. Then and 'only then can the narrow horizon of bourgeois right be crossed in its entirety and society inscribe on its banners: From each according to his ability to each according to his needs!'.[14]

But has the contradiction between true and false needs and the legitimate satisfaction of all needs under socialism really been resolved? If the long term consequences of capitalism are benign and even false needs serve to augment man's powers and realise his human potential, then are those needs really false? Or, alternatively, if they are false and the expanded control

---

13 *Grundrisse, op.cit.,* pp.409-10.
14 'Critique of the Gotha Programme', *Marx-Engels Selected Works,* Vol.3, Progress, Moscow, 1969, p.19.

of nature is predicated on them, how can a change in social relations miti-
gate the effects of overdeveloped forces of production, much less eliminate
the artificial needs on which those forces are based? Why should we accept
Marx's assertion that the need for material wealth, as the driving force
of capitalism, will suddenly turn into a need for 'social wealth' under communism? And why should 'real' individuality suddenly emerge at this stage
when all along individual activity has borne an obverse relation to reality?
People learn by doing: if all social activity has exhibited tendencies of
a marked sort, it requires more than a change in material conditions to
explain a reversal in these tendencies, especially if material conditions appear to have been changing gradually as the notion 'expansion of the forces
of production' would suggest. Marx does not attempt to confront these
problems and carries over the distinction between true and false needs in
his economic theory in which use-value and exchange-value are key
concepts.[15]

What does it mean to speak of true and false needs at all? If, as Marx
admits in *Wage Labour and Capital*, deprivation is relative and a palace
built beside a house will make it look like a hut, does that not mean that
needs are relative too and ultimately subjective?[16] If needs are not objective
in the usual sense, this does not rule out normative distinctions between
need claims. The whole debate over nature and culture was only possible
once the authority of religion had been sufficiently eroded to warrant a
secular account of human nature. But one might well ask, like Stirner,
why a truly secular approach should concern itself with such questions
as whether needs are 'true' or 'false', or whether the direction society is
taking is right or wrong, since these are fundamentally eschatological questions and outside the compass of a secular ethics concerned with the actions
and judgments of individuals.

Even greater problems emerge with a materialist-based secularism: as
long as behaviour is seen as the response to the stimulus of needs it can
only be changed by changing this motivational mechanism, and what would
warrant anything so drastic so long as needs are 'the ultimate grounds
of their own satisfaction'?[17] If needs are indeed a natural reflex of material
conditions, that means changing those conditions — a Promethean undertaking! To add 'dialectical' to 'materialism' does not alter the necessarily

---

15 *Grundrisse, op.cit.*, pp.325, 408-10, 488, 540-2.
16 'Wage Labour and Capital', *Selected Works, op.cit.*, Vol.1, p.163.
17 'Introduction' to the 'Contribution to the Critique of Hegel's Philosophy of Law', *Collected Works, op.cit.*, Vol.3, p.178.

apocalyptic nature of changes in social conditions man is capable of consciously undertaking, even though it appears to permit man to determine himself historically and, by implication, gradually. These problems account for the intangible nature of Marx's distinction between the 'realm of necessity' and the 'realm of freedom'.[18]

What is the character of this much advertised end-state where society is such that it permits the satisfaction of all needs? When it comes right down to it, 'free', 'creative' and 'spontaneous' activity is not at all what we might suppose. It is 'free' in the sense that society has so determined man that self-imposed restraints are no longer necessary, since all his needs are benign; 'creative' in that his objectification through work will be his self-affirmation, because motivational responses to satisfy baser instincts such as avarice and cupidity will be long disposed of; 'spontaneous' because external and internal constraints are superfluous when man's relationship to his environment is completely harmonious.

There is latent in Marx's theory a quietism highly reminiscent of that which he condemned in the ancients, Feuerbach and Stirner, and this arises from his unitary theory of the personality. In Marx's account of human nature, like that of the Stoics, the Sceptics and a number of Enlightenment rationalists, the old distinction between 'reason' and 'the will' is collapsed and the will is merely the internalisation or individuation of Reason. This view assumes that the connection between ideas and action is a necessary one: when ideas are erroneous, needs are false and behaviour is bad; when ideas are correct, needs are true and behaviour is good. Such a view leaves no room for individual self-determination or responsibility through voluntary behaviour as, for instance, Aristotle or Kant would understand it.

A unitary theory of the personality has almost always accompanied a familiar constellation of ideas: a materialist orientation which assumes that physical processes alone have a real existence and that ideas are merely their subjective expression; a concern with cosmic order and harmony and a propensity to see the universe as a rational ordered totality, governed by uniform and ineluctable laws, whose reality principle is Reason. Freedom can only be conceived of in terms of the reconciliation of Reason and Nature. Stoic thought was an early synthesis of this philosophical position and it is significant that it, for the first time, developed a theory of true and false needs which made freedom dependent on the elimination of corruption.[19]

---

18 *Capital, op.cit.,* Vol.3, p.820.
19 See K.F. Roche, *Rousseau, Stoic and Romantic,* Methuen, London, 1974, Chapter 1, 'The

Where the Stoics saw the resolution of man's struggle with nature and himself in the social taming of the will, however, Marx sees it in the social determination of the species. Freedom is the *absence* of necessity, and that means silencing wants, an end to the ever-proliferating needs which urge men on to ever-intensified labour. Where classically, in a long line of thinkers from Plato, Aristotle, Epicurus and Seneca, to Machiavelli, Diderot, Helvétius, Rousseau and Kant, freedom was an achievement of the moral individual who learns that happiness comes from the ability to subjugate the appetites through the will, for Marx freedom is a social product which issues from the correct organisation of the realm of necessity.[20]

It is one of the peculiarities of Marx's theory of needs that it turns the phenomenon it purports to explain, characteristically human activity, into something else. For activity, as it was classically understood, assumes moral autonomy — the human capacity for self-governed behaviour or character formation through the will.[21] As such, activity was more or less synonymous with freedom. Marx's notion of 'activity', while preserving some of the classical form, dispenses with its content. Like Rousseau, he talks of human activity as distinct from the behaviour of animals because 'Man makes his life activity itself the object of his will and of his consciousness.[22] But this does not mean, as it might appear, that the individual is therefore free and responsible, a morally autonomous agent. It is the burden of all Marx's arguments to deny this 'individual', 'moral' approach, even though he holds out some hope that under socialism the grounds for freedom, as traditionally understood, will suddenly be inaugurated. However, because these grounds are actually material conditions, they completely erode the meaning of freedom, responsibility and moral autonomy which, to mean anything at all, must be universally applicable, and to which material conditions are only relevant as the middle term of a practical

---

Stoic Origins', pp.1-21; see also J.B. Gould, 'Being, the World and Appearance in Early Stoicism and other Greek Philosophies', *Review of Metaphysics*, Vol.28, 1974, pp.261-88; and Seneca Letter 90, 'Philosophy and Progress', in M. Hadas, *The Stoic Philosophy of Seneca*, Doubleday, New York, 1958; E. Bloch, *Avicenna und die Aristotelische Linke*, Suhrkamp, Berlin, 1963. Marx demonstrates quite a detailed understanding of the Stoics in his criticism of Stirner's treatment of the ancients in *The German Ideology*, *op.cit.*, pp.141-50, and in 1841 was still intending to develop the work he had begun in his doctoral dissertation into a large scale history of Epicurean, Stoic and Sceptic philosophy (*Collected Works*, *op.cit.*, Vol.1, p.29).

20 *Capital*, *op.cit.*, Vol.3, p.820.

21 The classic formulation of the concept of ethical activity is Aristotle's in the *Nicomachean Ethics*; Arendt, Kolakowski and Lobkowicz discuss Marx's theory in relation to ethical activity; Livergood, surprisingly, does not.

22 'Economic and Philosophic Manuscripts of 1844', *op.cit.*, p.276.

syllogism. If the benefits of freedom are a bonus which can only be provided once necessities are taken care of, then freedom with Marx is something other than the ability to free oneself from the domination of circumstance by adopting a rule of behaviour and following it, and freedom is certainly irrelevant to men as we know them. It awaits the 'new man' of socialism indeed, but if this new man is both its presupposition as well as its product, where does that leave us?

It is my contention that Marx's main defence for the doctrine of needs remains ontological — despite his attempt to recast it in tough-minded materialist terms. That is to say, it relates to his concept of the human essence and the way in which human potentialities are progressively actualised in history through the exertion of human powers against the forces of nature. Even at the ontological level, however, Marx's doctrine of needs leaves many of his claims unvindicated. It does not permit us to see man's powers as 'free', 'creative' or 'spontaneous' in any usual sense, nor does it lend any substance to the concept of human 'activity' in the sense in which it is claimed (and Marx does claim this) to involve 'the passions' and 'the will'.[23] If, as it turns out, the passions will be nothing but the bland articulation of socially-determined needs, and if the will means nothing better than concentration of the mind on an intensive physical task, then everything that was gained by Aristotle's concept of activity and its relation to human potentiality has been lost with Marx. As other authors have noted, Marx has substituted for the properly ontological contention of Aristotle and Kant, that man can *realise* himself through his activity, the suggestion, which Hegel first intimated, that man can *create* himself by transforming the material world: *homo faber creans seipsum*.[24] Where the original claim may be verified in the experience of particular men, the latter one depends on the development of the species. This creates a practical antinomy: if we must await the outcome of history to decide whether a particular man is true to his nature or not, or if particular ventures are humane or not, how will we ever get there? If our social selves are in any way to be our own product besides being a creation of material conditions, what, besides historical hindsight, can provide us with criteria for judging that this is so?

Max Stirner, in *The Ego and His Own*, had already found the Achilles

---

23 *ibid.*, pp.276 and 322; and *Capital, op.cit.*, Vol.1, p.174.
24 Arendt, *op.cit.*; Lobkowicz, *Theory and Practice, op.cit.*, p.139; L. Kolakowski, 'The Myth of Human Self-Identity: Unity of Civil and Political Society in Socialist Thought', in *The Socialist Idea, a Reappraisal*, eds. L. Kolakowski, and S. Hampshire, Weidenfold and Nicolson, London, 1974, pp.18-35.

heel of Hegelian theory: this failure to account satisfactorily for the moral activity of the individual. There is an inbuilt fatalism in a theory that leaves it to history to vindicate the actions of individuals. Who then is capable of happiness if, as the ancients and our experience tell us, happiness is the reward of individual effort? And who is responsible if only history can tell? This and the corresponding tendency to sublate the individual in the world-historical state, is the thrust of Hegelian theory. Under the transformation of Marxism, this tendency is intensified rather than diminished: not only are individual moral judgments not what they seem, they are categorical misconceptions, for the individual, when he judges or chooses in a certain way is merely satisfying a socially determined need under an ideological disguise. The question, as Marx poses it, is not whether a judgment is true or false, but whether a need is true or false. But to what criteria do 'true' and 'false' then apply?

As I have tried to show, their appeal is still essentially ontological and Marx's attempt to establish by an anthropology of needs that existence precedes essence ultimately fails. This is because, as Stirner's criticisms point out, materialism cannot escape its fate as a doctrine of essences, so that even in its most tough-minded form it constitutes a metaphysics. Just so long as classes of individuals, rather than individuals themselves (and here of course I do not necessarily mean social classes, for the same would hold true of classes of things), are seen as the determining mechanism, we are back in the realm of 'essences, spooks and ghosts' and Platonic ideas and scholastic universals have been reintroduced in a more mundane form.[25] This is because classes of persons, like classes of things, are arrived at by *post festum* analysis* and cannot, therefore, be postulated as causes. In the final analysis, society only enters an aetiological chain through individuals, for individuals are the ultimate agents of social activity. In light of this understanding, Stirner held the peculiarly apocalyptic view of history which sees revolution as the means to man's redemption, to be an extension of this ontological confusion.[26] Men are not redeemed by history, revolution or anything else, they must take care of themselves.

Marx in writing off the ethics of the ancients as quietist and the ethical

---

25 M. Stirner, *The Ego and His Own*, ed. J. Carroll, Cape, London, 1971, p.56.

* '*Post Festum*' literally means 'after the feast'. Marx uses the term to characterise the 'after-the-fact' nature of social theory. In the chapter on 'The Fetishism of Commodities', he declares: 'Man's reflections on the forms of social life, and consequently, also, his scientific analysis of those forms, take a course directly opposite to that of their actual historical development. He begins, post festum, with the results of the process of development ready to hand before him'. *Capital, op.cit.* p.80.

26 *The Ego and His Own*, pp.115 and 221.

theory of Stirner and Kant as petty-bourgeois apologetics, has not successfully dealt with questions which impinge very directly on his theory.
Epicurus' distinction between different kinds of desires points up, for instance, a rather simple mistake of which Marx is guilty, and that is to
generalise from man's basic physical needs, whose satisfaction is compulsory for survival, and which satisfy the double criteria that they are both
needed and wanted, to the consideration of all man's desires as 'needs'
or 'wants' of the same order.[27] This is illegitimate, for there is a uniqueness
about subsistence needs, such that they cannot ordinarily be denied. But
beyond these, other demands or wants do not have the same force and
are subject to the criteria that generally apply in moral judgments. This
does not mean that the individual is not convinced, rightly or wrongly,
that non-essential needs are necessary, but what it does point out is that
these 'needs' are the product of his judgment and will and are in no way
materially or physiologically dictated. In practice, of course, the distinction
between essential and non-essential needs is rather hard to draw, but this
implies that we should talk less, rather than more, about needs. Death
is the only test of true necessity, and even the threat of death does not
make the satisfaction of needs compulsory, as the example of those on
hunger strikes can demonstrate.

The conclusions which Marx drew from the conflation of all desires
with basic subsistence needs are desperate: man's relentless pursuit of this
and that false pleasure can only be halted by changing society so that the
conditions which nourish artificial needs will be eliminated and the needs
with them. The conjunction of materialism, sensationalist psychology and
socialist doctrines about man's nature, tells us that since man's actions draw
on the world of the senses and his experience gained in it, what has to
be done is to arrange the world differently so that what he experiences
is human. (A reversal of subject and predicate if there ever was one!) Hope
can lie only with 'new-fangled' man, the product of history and developing
material and social conditions. His is the 'shape of the shrewd spirit' of
History — and here we have a clue to the propensity of determinism to
issue in voluntarism![28]

The whole preoccupation with 'needs', which has been taken over by

---

27 See Marx's 'Notebooks on Epicurean Philosophy', *Collected Works, op.cit.*, Vol. 1, p.508,
where he quotes Cicero on Epicurus' three classes of desire. 'One kind he classified as
both natural and necessary, a second as being natural without being necessary, and a
third as neither natural nor necessary.'

28 'Speech at the Anniversary of the People's Paper', 1856, Karl Marx, *Surveys From Exile*,
Penguin, London, 1973, pp.299-300.

behaviouralists, assumes what it is required to prove, and by the self-fulfilling prophecy seems to prove what it assumes: that man is a compulsion-ridden creature. What is more, in Marxist theory it has bred a kind of Manicheism or schizophrenia, where man under present conditions is seen as impotent and incapable of happiness, entirely at the mercy of a pernicious social environment, but redeemable in the future under conditions which seem increasingly less likely.[29] Such a theory issues an open invitation for someone to stage-manage History.

There are in addition to these general problems that Marx's anthropology of needs, as a substitute for a conventional psychology and ethics, poses, the specific antinomy we have mentioned. The difficulty with his true needs/false needs distinction, especially once Marx has introduced the concept of the civilising influence of capital, is that it is redundant. His conclusion that conditions must be changed, by revolutionary means if necessary, so that false needs are deprived of their grounds of existence, is far from convincing, if in the long run, through the hidden hand of socially determined needs, capitalism serves to expand man's powers despite the hostile social environment that it creates. There is a basic equivocation here: if capitalism gives rise to socially determined needs such that a mere change in the relations of production will produce a socialist utopia, then socialism is not required to reorganise society to produce a more satisfactory need structure at all. As long as artificial needs do not prevent the ultimate triumph of social justice, why eliminate them merely to produce psychic tranquility? As Marx has long informed us, happiness is active, not passive.

And what about the objectivity of needs anyway? The light which the writings of Sigmund Freud and others has cast on the complexity of human motivation, and the very notion of the 'unconscious', makes the objectivity of needs highly questionable. Is it conceivable that under socialism men will really know what their *true* needs are? Marx's admission in *Wage Labour and Capital*, that deprivation is relative and that in a time of rising profits, even though the wages of the worker have risen and his enjoyments have increased, he feels poorer when he compares his improvement with the immeasurably greater benefits to the capitalist, suggests that needs are relative too. And at one point Marx actually does admit this, declaring: 'Our desires and pleasures spring from society; we measure them, therefore, by society and not by the objects which serve for their satisfaction. Because

---

29 For example H. Marcuse, *Eros and Civilization*, Allen Lane, London, 1969, *One Dimensional Man*, Beacon, Boston, 1964, and *Negations*, Penguin, London, 1972.

they are of a social nature, they are of a relative nature'.[30] On several occasions in his discussion of the irreducible minimum to which capitalism drives the level of wages, he admits that there is a conventional element in the determination of this minimum, which also suggests that needs are relative.[31]

To deny the objectivity of needs does not mean that people themselves cannot be trusted to know what is good for them. On the contrary: once objectivity has been put out the door, it cannot be brought back through the window. It is a mark of the peculiar ambivalence of Marx's theory that he hoped to have it both ways. On the one hand he claimed that needs which realised truly human powers were objective; on the other that malignant needs were the product of hostile social forces and not, therefore, the responsibility of individuals themselves.

Hegel had already pointed to the preposterousness of assuming that men can be ruled counter to their own interests. Social needs are a peculiar 'conjunction of immediate or natural needs with mental needs arising from ideas'.[32] 'By means of his ideas and reflections man expands his desires, which are not a closed circle like animal instinct, and carries them on to the false infinite.'[33] In this way we can hold both that men pursue their interests, subjectively understood, and that they are enticed by those who stand to profit from their constantly expanding desires.[34]

To say that needs are relative, measured by society rather than the objects which satisfy them, is to admit that needs have no natural limit, and to deny that an end-state can be postulated where all needs will be satisfied: '... it is a defect of human nature never to be satisfied', Aristotle declared in the *Politics*: 'At first (men) are content with a dole of mere two obols; then, when that is well-established, they go on asking for more and their demands become unlimited. For there is no limit to wants and most people spend their lives trying to satisfy their wants'.[35] In the same vein Machiavelli declared: 'Moreover, as human desires are insatiable, (because their nature is to have and to do everything whilst fortune limits their possessions and capacity of enjoyment,) this gives rise to a constant discontent in the human mind and a weariness of the things they possess; and it is this which makes

---

30 *Wage, Labour and Capital*, op.cit., p.163.
31 'Wages Price and Profit', *Selected Works*, op.cit., Vol.1, pp.71-2; *Capital*, op.cit., Vol.1, pp.108-9.
32 Hegel, *Philosophy of Right*, Clarendon, Oxford, 1967, p.128.
33 ibid., p.267.
34 ibid., p.269.
35 Aristotle, *Politics*, Penguin, London, 1972, Book 2, Chapter 7, p.76.

them decry the present, praise the past, and desire the future, and all this without any reasonable motive'.[36]

Classical political theory has, since Plato, postulated reciprocal needs and services as the basis of the state. This does not rule out the necessity of placing restrictions on the acquisitiveness of the powerful, but, as Aristotle observes, 'It is more necessary to equalize appetites than property and that can be done by adequate education under the laws'.[37] Although this may seem a lot to hope for, it makes nonsense of the very notion of the secular state to distinguish between true and false needs and expect the elimination of the latter and the inauguration of a utopia from conditions which are not the product of individual (moral) activity. This was Aristotle's criticism of Plato's *Republic*. Political science does not make men, it takes them as they are, hoping to optimise the virtues that they have.

---

36 Machiavelli, *Discourses*, Random House, New York, 1950, Book 2, Introduction, p.274.
37 Aristotle, *Politics, op.cit.*, p.74.

Politics and the Need for Meaning

David Holbrook

Where, in any area of politics today, is there a vision of a new future? There cannot be such a vision unless there is an adequate conception of the human needs which radical politics (or conservative politics for that matter) can serve. One outstanding conclusion in many humanistic studies today is that the primary human need is the need for meaning, but this is not yet recognised in politics.

A radically new approach to politics is evidently necessary, and this, I believe, may well be based on 'philosophical anthropology', the father of which is Edmund Husserl. In his *Crisis of European Science*[1], Husserl wrote that, armed with his kind of approach to philosophical problems, we should be able to strike through the crust of the externalised 'historical facts' of philosophical history, interrogating, exhibiting, and testing their inner meaning and hidden teleology. 'Gradually, at first unnoticed but growing more and more pressing, possibilities for a complete reorientation of view will make themselves felt, pointing to new dimensions. Questions never before asked will arise; fields of endeavour never before entered, correlations never before grasped or radically understood, will show them-

---

1 Edmund Husserl, *The Crisis of European Sciences and Transcendental Phenomenology*, tr. David Carr, Northwestern University Press, Evanston, 1970.

selves.'[2] The whole idea of philosophy, he felt, must now be revised, and its practical possibilities would be revealed through its execution. This work was published in German in 1954, and in English, by Northwestern University Press, in 1970. Over twenty years have passed since the first date: how many students in the Humanities Departments of our 'new' (or old) universities have heard of Edmund Husserl? I have no doubt that in many academic philosophy departments, Husserl would be greeted with cries of 'Ah! Non-philosophy!', not least because he asks, 'what should we, who *believe*, do in order to *be able* to believe?' It is quite clear from the prospectuses of universities that no-one should suppose they feel obliged today to offer anything to believe in. But that is part of our disease.

Husserl's studies are concerned with the problem that the one unquestioned authority in our world is 'science' — and yet this science has stripped the world of meaning. The fundamental problem in politics, as in all departments of our life today, is to have something to believe in — something that satisfies the basic need for meaning and values. Not even Marxism does this; beyond its immediate power goals: in a recent report from Moscow Philip French spoke of the way in which people in Russia are asking the Party to give a moral lead — which it cannot supply. Eventually the Party came up with a list of moral precepts which bore an uncanny resemblance to the Ten Commandments.

I begin with philosophy, because behind our present crisis in politics lies a fundamental philosophical problem. When I use the word 'philosophy' I mean attitudes to life in general, rather than the narrow application of logical analysis, of course. Our world believes in the rational application of man's thought to social, national and international issues. Now, we are faced with pressing problems of survival. Economies seem likely to collapse; the environment seems to be menaced by our barbarity and ignorance; the resources of the world may not be able to sustain man as we have traditionally supposed they might; world population may be levelling out at 15,000,000,000 — but it could still be, through a series of disasters, that the sheer numbers of human beings might outstrip the amount of water, and food, that is available to them. These grave problems are continually discussed, besides the more common ones of strife, war, subversion, hatred, and disintegration in communities. We try to believe all these problems will be solved by rational approaches: by 'science'. In the face of these difficulties, which in our time have taken on a world-wide scale,

---

2 *ibid.*, p.18.

and a doomsday quality, because we dare not think about what might happen if we can't solve them, we even still hold on to our traditional belief in 'progress', though this has suffered from a good deal of scepticism in recent decades. Of course, there still *is* progress: the triumph of man over smallpox is a clear indication that the philosophy and science of the period since the Renaissance have brought a new kind of freedom to man — by the subjugation of certain malevolent aspects of the natural world, to his will, and to his idea of the good life. And there are many areas in which we may recognise scientific and technological achievements on which no-one would wish to go back. One may hear this progress in the talk of farmers, on radio programmes; their discussions are rich with references to stages of growth, ratios between feeding stuffs and carcass weight, names of plant diseases, of pests which need control. No-one would want to relinquish the scientific approach to food supplies, or medical virology, or intensive care and surgery, or the advances in veterinary medicine, of the last hundred years. Even the mis-use of resources, in the development of an aeroplane like Concorde, belongs to a progress which astonishes by its technology, even by its amazing qualities of 'intentionality'. Man, through science and technology, can intend to land on the moon, on one exact spot; or he can travel in an air-liner, eight miles above the earth, at the speed of a bullet, in our time. Yet such achievements now seem disproportionate. So, do we still believe that our social and political problems can be solved by reason?

Here our confidence is faltering — because something is missing, in the relationship between science and man's existence. What is this 'crisis' of which Husserl speaks? The question that he raises is not the scientific character of the sciences, but what science in general has meant, or could mean, for human existence. The era to which we still belong is that of the second half of the nineteenth century, when the total world-view of modern man was almost exclusively dominated by the positivist sciences and the 'prosperity' these produced, by manipulations of the material world. This means, says Husserl, an indifferent turning away from those questions which are decisive for a genuine humanity (*Menschentum*) — the kind of questions to which Charles Dickens continually drew attention. In *Hard Times*, for example, Dickens showed the consequences of an education and a philosophy which, while serving industry and commerce, ignored the demands of the human heart and aspirations: as Husserl puts it, 'Merely fact-minded sciences make merely fact-minded people'. He refers to a detectable hostility towards science, which breaks out from time to time in our civilisation, especially among young people. They feel that in our vital need, this science which is yet that unquestioned authority, the repository of truth, has nothing to say to us.

> It excludes in principle precisely the questions which man, given over in our times to the most portentous upheavals, finds the most burning: questions of the meaning or meaninglessness of human existence. Do not these questions, universal and necessary for all men, demand universal reflections and answers based on rational insight? In the final analysis they concern man as a free self-determining being in his behaviour towards the human and extra-human surrounding world (*Umwelt*).[3]

What does science have to say about reason and unreason or about us as men as subjects of this freedom? The mere science of bodies, says Husserl, meaning science in the tradition of Newton and Galileo, clearly has nothing to say; it abstracts from everything subjective. As for the humanistic sciences,

> their rigorous scientific character requires, we are told, that the scholar carefully excludes all valuative positions, all questions of the reason or unreason of their human subject matter and its cultural configurations. Scientific, objective truth is exclusively a matter of establishing what the world, the physical as well as the spiritual world, is in fact. But can the world, and human existence in it, truthfully have a meaning if the sciences recognise as true only as what is objectively established in this fashion . . .?[4]

Can we console ourselves with that? Can we live in this world, where historical occurrence is nothing but an unending concatenation of illusory progress and bitter disappointment? The crisis of science, says Husserl, is the loss of its meaning for life.

The problem is seen by many others. As Marjorie Grene says, if the world is the world which 'objective' science sees, mere matter in motion, operating according to the laws of chance and necessity, then we do not belong in it.[5] Man becomes, in this picture, simply one more expression of the laws of matter in motion, and wholly alien to nature. The achievements of man, art, religion, legal and political institutions, science itself, *can* have no significance in this naturalistic, one-level, world, where there is nothing but particles in a four-dimensional space-time continuum. If mechanism, the theory that the universe and we in it is but a great machine driven by impersonal forces and inexorable laws, which is what the Newtonian and Galilean universe appears to be, essentially a world without

---

3 *ibid.*, p.6.
4 *ibid.*
5 Marjorie Grene, *Approaches to a Philosophical Biology*, Basic Books, New York, 1968.

life, the only appropriate philosophy would be one of absurdity or despair.

Yet it is obvious that this universe of 'science' is, in fact, in stark contradiction of the facts of our experience. Why should we resign ourselves to it? A commonsense recognition of the multifarious nature of living creatures, and not least the massive human fact of consciousness, of the inner lives we do in fact lead, reveal this world-view of the sciences as inadequate. We need to revise our ways of thinking about nature and man, evidently: but how? Even when we turn to the problem, since we feel we must turn to it in a rational way, we find that science has shown that values are 'relative' and 'culture-bound'. Science applies logic to observed facts: neither logic nor factual observations are able to say anything about ends and values, and certainly not about ultimate meanings. In a civilisation in which science is supposed to be the final arbiter, only values supported by science, many feel, would be valid goals of human endeavour. But science has left us without a guide for our aspirations.

At the same time, it has seemed to many that 'science says' that man is driven by his 'instincts', and is at the mercy of the darker and more brutal side of his nature. Freud's attempts to create a metapsychology based on nineteenth century natural science led him to postulate quantitative dynamics behind psychological processes.[6] Since (according to the Second Law of Thermodynamics) energy systems must be running down, in universal Entropy, so living energy systems sought 'equilibrium' − conceived by Freud in terms of a reduction of all forms of stimulation and excitement. It seems now that the laws of Entropy cannot be applied in this way to 'systems' like man which are characterised by an intrinsic openness, while the concept of 'equilibrium' should not be applied like that to living organisms.[7] Moreover, Freud was in any case talking about dynamics within the psychic reality, which are not to be equated with the physical realm. Yet these confusions persist in many prevalent models, not least the popular 'naked ape' dogma.

Politically, Freud's system led to extremely pessimistic conclusions. For one thing, in its impulse towards equilibrium, the psyche seemed to be dominated, ultimately, by a death instinct. And since this was called an

---

6 Harry Guntrip, *Personality Structure and Human Interaction*, Hogarth, London, 1961.
7 Viktor Frankl, 'Nothing But −', *Encounter*, Vol.XXXIII, No.5, 51, November, 1969; also see Frankl, 'Reductionism and Nihilism', in *Beyond Reductionism − New Perspectives in the Life Sciences: The Alpbach Symposium*, eds. A. Koestler and J.R. Smythies, Hutchinson, London, 1969, pp.396-416. See also Ludwig von Bertalanffy, *Problems of Life* and other works.

'instinct' rather than an impulse, it seemed ineradicable, and also ineducable. There seemed no possibility, then, of the successful socialisation of man. Whatever improved arrangements were made for man's social life, civilisation would always be inimical to personal fulfilment. The only hope was to remove the individual's inhibitions as far as was possible, while recognising the requirements of communal morality. But, essentially, by this view, man is a creature who must always be subjected to control for his own good, while his fundamental nature is beyond access of being redeemed, by any improved social arrangements. The interests of the individual and society are of necessity mutually exclusive and antagonistic, while civilisation is not the expression of all that is best in man, but rather a mechanism for controlling and policing instinctual impulses. If one accepts Freud's natural science model, a society in which people give free assent to community existence, because it is the best expression of man's sociableness, is impossible.

The effect of reductionist attitudes to man, supposedly scientific, are in effect extremely nihilistic. Viktor Frankl reports coming across a book in which man is defined as 'nothing but a complex biochemical mechanism powered by a combination system which energises computers with prodigious storage facilities for retaining encoded information'. In the *Alpbach Symposium,* he argues that this reductionist view, developed on that 'nothing but' basis, creates nihilism by devaluating and depreciating that which is human in man. Human phenomena are turned into mere epiphenomena. Love, to the reductionist, is derived from sex; it is conceived of as a sublimation of sexual instincts or, as Freud once put it, 'aim-inhibited' sexuality. Conscience is reduced to the mere super-ego. And in the background, biological evolution is the result of nothing but random mutations preserved by natural selection; mental evolution is the result of nothing but random tries preserved by reinforcements; all organisms including man are nothing but passive automata controlled by the environment, whose sole purpose in life is the reduction of tensions by adaptive responses; and the only scientific method worth the name is quantitative measurement. Therefore complex mechanisms, to be understood, must be reduced to simple elements accessible to such treatment, without undue worry about whether some specific characteristic of a complex phenomenon (for instance, man!) may be lost in the process. These principles, of positivist science, as formulated by Arthur Koestler in the same symposium, lead to a situation in the modern world in which even the educated man feels there is nothing to live for.

When we turn to society and politics, the consequence of this kind of view of man is that we feel we cannot escape from being 'functional man'. In his *The Philosophy of Existence*, Gabriel Marcel, the Christian existentialist, discusses this problem. The individual tends to appear, in this way of thinking, both to himself and others as an agglomeration of functions.

> Travelling on the Underground, I often wonder with a kind of dread what can be the inward reality of the life of this or that man employed on the railway – the man who opens the doors, for instance, or the one who punches the tickets. Surely, everything both within him and outside him conspires to identify this man with his functions – meaning not only his functions as a worker, as a trade union member, or as a voter, but with his vital functions as well. The rather horrible expression 'time table' perfectly describes his life. So many hours for each function. Sleep too is a function which must be discharged so that the other functions may be exercised in turn. The same with pleasure, with relaxation; it is logical that the weekly allowance of recreation should be determined by an expert on hygiene; recreation is a psycho-organic function which must not be neglected any more than, for instance, the function of sex.[8]

The effect of this functional view menaces man with a complete loss of meaning:

> As for death, it becomes, objectively, and functionally, the scrapping of what has ceased to be of use and must be written off as total loss.[9]

As Marcel says, this functionalised world gives us a stifling impression of sadness. But,

> besides the sadness, there is the dull, intolerable unease of the actor himself, who is reduced to living as though he were in fact submerged by his functions. This uneasiness is enough to show that there is in all this some appalling mistake, some ghastly misinterpretation, implanted in defenceless minds by an increasingly inhuman social order and an equally inhuman philosophy (for if the philosophy has prepared the way for the order, the order has also shaped the philosophy).[10]

This is why I began with philosophy: the social order in which we exist, and the philosophy of life which it embodies, go together. The 'new town' in England manifests in space on the ground both the failure of our philosophy, and the inhumanity of our system. If we compare any modern New Town with Sienna, or Venice, ancient Rome, or even an English

---

8 Gabriel Marcel, *The Philosophy of Existence*, tr. Manya Harari, Harvill Press, London, 1948, p.2.

9 *ibid.*, p.2.

10 *ibid.*, p.3.

mediaeval village or Beechworth in Australia, we can surely see what is wrong. The mediaeval or Renaissance community shaped itself around foci of *meaning:* mill, piazza, square, village green, church, forum, stadium, temple. The modern living centre consists almost solely of buildings to satisfy the functions of day to day living, the function of sleep, the function of raising children, the function of working, and the function of eating and surviving. All around will be billboards saying GO TO WORK ON AN EGG or symbolising some other aspect of functional living. Recreation is provided for, as a function, and 'pleasure' — but even that, as in sadistic or pornographic displays, tends, today, to sink to a functional level.

And then, as if in protest, there are outbursts of blasphemy. As Professor Walter Weiskopf says, because science has excluded elements of being and existence from its world view, and has derationalised the dimension of values, it has created a 'power vacuum', and the *forces of irrationality* have moved in.[11] The darker aspects of human existence will not be denied, by the reduction of existence to the 'nothing but' dimension. So in our society these burst out in strange forms of unexpected irrationality — now troubling the world in 'mindless' violence, occultism, witchcraft, religious sects of a predatory kind, gambling, suicide. Pornography is now described as a 'plague' by *Time* magazine[12], and it moves into areas of filmed murder, torture, degradation and beastliness whose influence in undermining values is feared, even by those who have supported permissiveness. Professor Robert Stoller, the psychotherapist, speaks of how sexual perversions in our culture are releasing 'rage' and hostility into our civilisation.[13] The fanatical immoralists are pouring out hate through the media, actually undermining reason. In the film *The Exorcist,* for example, subliminal techniques are used — flashed death's heads, accompanied by the sound of angry bees, people dying, *cris de joie* from sexual intercourse, and the noise of pigs being killed. Powerful electronic devices are employed to undermine reason, and people in the audiences of *The Exorcist* and other films of this kind have been taken into mental hospitals, have committed serious assaults, or have been irreparably disturbed. In the Soviet Union, drunkenness is a problem, as it is in America and Britain, where alcoholism is now a serious problem among young people. Sexual casualties, crime, violence in the family, and other manifestations of disturbance and mental

---

11 'Existence and Values', in *New Knowledge in Human Values,* ed. A. Maslow, Harper, New York, 1959.
12 *Time,* April 5, 1976.
13 Robert J. Stoller, *Perversion: the Erotic Form of Hatred,* Harvester Press, Sussex, 1976.

illness are all on the increase. In France, suicide is now the primary cause of death among young people between sixteen and twenty-five — and an organisation of social workers are asking for a national campaign, to stop youth destroying itself.

These are the forms of distress which show in the statistics. But there is a general level of dismay, indicated by the massive consumption of drugs through the health services, not least tranquillisers. In Joseph Conrad's *Under Western Eyes,* a character asks, 'Who could bear life in our country without the bottle?' In our society it would be, 'who could bear life in our country without Librium or Valium?' The underlying affliction is variously described as anomie, amorality, anhedonia, rootlessness, emptiness, and hopelessness. The functional model, insofar as it has any value, is adhered to because it helps people feel a kind of strength: if one is a Naked Ape, or sexy beast, one is at least someone. Yet underneath this posture of false meanings we often detect a dreadful emptiness. Nothing in politics suggests meanings to set against this, today, because it has attached itself to things rather than the need for meaning.

While trust in scientific progress has grown sceptical, we still go on believing that our social problems can be solved by an economy of abundance with a high productive capacity, increased efficiency and productivity. In Britain, the solution is to be found in 'North Sea Oil': in Australia, it is, or was, selling mountains of iron ore to Japan. Every hope rests on the economic principle which drives us towards an ever higher national product, with which we can raise 'the standard of life'. In Britain, at the moment, something different, reminiscent of wartime, seems to be happening, by contrast. Although every statesman who speaks on the radio or television declares that our standard of living must go down, and wages must be restrained, most people seem happier and more confident. Fear may be a factor, but people are cooperating more eagerly in social planning. Yet, all the same, the ultimate promise is that, once again, one day, our 'material standard' will increase. We have no better goal. Yet during the present crisis, there is a definite increase in morale. One small but significant indication is that whereas only a few years ago local parish councils in the countryside could not let their garden plots, today all the allotments are occupied, growing land is scarce, and every evening in the springtime men are working on their gardens which are full of crops. Here is a small indication that, under the surface of a hedonistic, materialistic life, there is a yearning for meaningful satisfactions of a simple kind of which Cobbett would approve. People are happy in this work because it tastes of self-reliance, creative achievement, and in making a future. People in general

POLITICS AND THE NEED FOR MEANING   183

enjoy being 'good' in such ways, in 'contributing in' to the community, more than selfishness.

We know, of course, that suicides decline during crises and in wartime. Evidently this is a philosophical problem, a question of people's personal 'philosophical space', their feelings that life is worth living. Indeed, I am now going to argue that the whole question of politics is a philosophical problem, in the existentialist sense. Fundamentally, it is an ontological problem, that is, a problem to be dealt with through the *science of being*. I want here to return for a moment to functional man, and the problem of death. If we reduce men to their functions, both in their life and in the predominant philosophy of their existence, they are doomed – they are, in the words of the Church service, 'confounded'. 'Let me never be confounded' is the most awful plea in the liturgy: we can translate the word into our modern terms as excommunicated, alienated, cast out, and destroyed as a being. For a man reduced to functional man, there is no possibility of finding any meaning in his life. It is to this nihilistic fate that science has brought us, and to which our economic and social arrangements have reduced us. We *are* confounded.

As Professor Wieskopff says[14], the 'economic man' is the prototype of alienated man. He is confined to conscious, deliberate action. All spontaneous, emotional, non-utilitarian behaviour is suppressed.

> Economic theory has, in spite of its lipservice to economic freedom, eliminated real freedom from its image of man by maintaining that perfect consciousness and knowledge permits only one, unequivocally determined kind of action, that is, action which leads to the maximization of material gains measured in terms of money.[15]

This has led to a disintegration of those aspects of life where the computer-like measurements of money calculation cannot be applied:

> Friendship, love, charity, creative activity, aesthetic and religious experiences cannot be calculated according to the economic principle. The goals are not unequivocally given and no calculable relationship exists between means and ends which could serve as a guide for action.[16]

The effects of the economics of our world have tended to obliterate other ways of life, and human behaviour, and the range and perspective of human potentiality have become limited to only one or two small segments, to

---

14 *New Knowledge in Human Values, op.cit.*
15 *ibid.,* p.116.
16 *ibid.*

cramped dimensions, that is, to alienation.

And there is a deeper problem, touched on by Marcel above. At the heart of the existentialist concern with man's existence is his nothingness, his death. Contemporary nihilism, says Frankl, brandishes a nothing-butness. But this is also a nothingness, since it reduces values and meanings to nothing: to 'defence mechanisms' or 'reaction formations' perhaps. But, as Frankl says, a man is not prepared to die for his defence mechanisms or reaction formations. Frankl was in the concentration camp, Auschwitz, and he should know: a man is prepared to die for his meanings, but not for 'power' or the 'release of instinct'.

So, there are two sides to the problem of nothingness. As Frankl argues, 'the true message of existentialism is not nothingness, but the no-thing-ness of man — that is to say a human being is no thing, a person is not one thing among other things'.[17] However, the nothingness of man must not be forgotten, in another sense. In the end, he is swept away by death. Then, what we have to ask is — what has he done, that is meaningful, before that nothingness overtakes him? In the especial branch of existentialism which practises therapy on this basis, called *Dasein*-analysis, the question which is pursued with the patient is this: what *Dasein* quality does his life have? In what sense can he claim to have *'been there'*, at this point in time and space, in a meaningful way? Mere materialism, acquisitiveness, hedonism, even communism and socialism, offer no answers: nor do irrationalities, 'sex', blasphemies or forms of violence.

The fundamental question in politics thus seems to me to be: what opportunities does our society provide for solutions to the *Dasein*-problem? And if not, how shall we provide these? Obviously this brings meaning, ends and values to the centre of the picture, as science never could, nor can life-sciences, like sociology, so long as these remain strictly positivist and 'objective'. But unless we solve this problem, people in our society will continue to suffer from 'existential frustration', and manifest those sicknesses of the soul to which I have referred. Material gains, acquisitiveness and an 'increased standard of living', by themselves as goals can never solve the *Dasein*-problem. Freud placed foremost in human life the 'will to pleasure' with the 'death instinct' behind it: but, says Frankl, in any therapist's experience there are many examples of people who cared little or nothing for pleasure, but *did* care about meaning. By contrast, the pursuit of pleasure in itself is self-defeating. So much for the Benthamite objectives.

17 Victor Frankl, 'Reductionism and Nihilism', in *The Alpbach Symposium, op.cit.*, p.398.

If instead of groping towards meaning, people apply themselves to the 'pursuit of happiness', declares Frankl, 'happiness falters and collapses'. Happiness, he suggests, from his psychotherapeutic work, is only ever a by-product of meaning-fulfilment. The more attention we give to the 'pursuit' of happiness, the more we make pleasure the target of our intentions, by way of what he calls hyper-intention, to the same extent we become victims of hyper-reflection.

> That is to say, the more attention we pay to happiness or pleasure, the more we block its attainment, and lose sight of the primary reason of our endeavour; happiness vanishes, because we are intending it, and pursuing it. This makes it impossible for fulfilment to ensue.[18]

The goals of the commercial promotion-man and advertiser: the politician of economic growth and prosperity, and even the Marxist kind of materialistic radical — all these can never satisfy the primary human need for meaning. Yet all our political theories still point towards such goals, because of the essentially scientific 'model' of man behind them, from which values and meaning have been excluded. What we must pursue, according to Frankl, is the 'will to meaning'. Only thus can we hope to overcome the sense of meaninglessness in life, that threatens us, and find the key — the opportunity for every man to fulfil his latent potentialities for self-transcendence.

While this impulse requires the rejection of a certain scientific tradition, it is by no means unscientific or anti-scientific. Far from it: the emphasis on man's need for meaning, and for that kind of *Aufforderungskaracter* ('demand quality') which can draw out potentialities of this kind in him, is based on disciplines in, roughly speaking, the area of the life-sciences themselves. While in the arts we seem to be plunging further and further into despair, the sense of futility, the cults of schizophrenia and suicide, and nihilism, there is a powerful revolution in the sciences, associated with philosophical anthropology, groping towards the restoration of man's wholeness, including his meaning-dimension. The father of philosophical anthropology is Edmund Husserl, himself, and that is why I began with him. What is 'philosophical anthropology'? On the map of contemporary philosophy, says Marjorie Grene, it is hard to locate. It is a philosophical study of the nature of man. It may use psychology, physical and social anthropology, sociology, and subjective disciplines requiring insight, description, and other phenomenological methods such as the interpretation

---

18 *ibid.*, p.401.

of symbols. But it entails no method of reduction, devising no abstract units of sense and not using the traditional modes of empiricism. Rather, it is concerned with experience, with 'simply everyday experience in the most ordinary and comprehensive sense' (Helmuth Plessner).

Philosophical anthropology is thus the study of man as a being-in-the-world, rather than as a natural object, and seeks the whole truth about man, in the spirit of that original *telos* of Greek philosophy, to which Edmund Husserl requires us to return. In this return man's moral dimension is restored, while those secondary qualities which Descartes rejected as unreliable become primary qualities in the investigation. Man is explored in terms of the maxim *sentio ergo sum* rather than *cogito ergo sum*. And this change, which requires attention to inwardness, transforms the picture of man in the world. If we make this change, from a universe reduced to what can be measured, to one which includes all those aspects of inner experience and reality which Descartes and Galileo relegated to a 'limbo of paradox and anomaly', then what we find as one writer puts it, 'the unseen planet that had to be there' in our universe: *meaning*. The world of value is of such a nature that mathematical and empirical methods cannot be applied to it. But this does not mean that values do not exist: it is just that we are not able to see them. Our problem so far has a simple explanation: if we confine ourselves to mathematical and empirical methods, we cannot find the dimension of meaning and values at all. The universe simply looks bleak, dead and sterile while we wear those particular spectacles. As soon as we apply the subjective disciplines, which have their own validity, we rediscover that force whose absence has created such frustration and anguish in our time. There are many social and political implications of this discovery. See, for example, Rollo May's *Power and Innocence*[19], as a psychotherapist's account of how violence and other forms of social disruption are generated as compensations for a deep lack of a sense of meaning.

It should be said at once that there are no conclusive findings in the area of philosophical anthropology, by which to work out a politics. It is simply that, as Husserl suggests, we are beginning to know where to look. As Abraham Maslow says, introducing his Symposium on Values, a symposium consisting of a group of scientists and other thinkers in the Humanities, for the first time in history it seems that a validated, usable system of human values may be possible.[20] We need this, in Husserl's sense,

---

19 Rollo May, *Power and Innocence*, Norton, New York, 1972; Souvenir, London, 1974.
20 *New Knowlege in Human Values, op.cit.*

to believe in and to devote ourselves to, *because it is true*. There need be no longer a search for a source of values outside man or outside the world, nor is it a question of being exhorted to 'have faith'. This value-system could be based squarely upon 'valid knowledge of the nature of man, his society, and of his works'.[21] Humanists, says Maslow, have been trying for years to construct a naturalistic, psychological value system, derived from man's own nature. Today it is possible to feel confident that this age-old hope may be fulfilled if we work hard enough. Moreover,

> it looks as if there were a single, ultimate value for mankind, a far goal toward which all men strive. This is called variously by different authors self-actualization, self-realization, integration, psychological health, individuation, autonomy, creativity, productivity, but they all agree that this amounts to realizing the potentialities of the person, that is to say, becoming fully human, everything that the person can become.[22]

Erich Fromm, in the same symposium, puts it in a slightly different way:

> values are rooted in the very conditions of human existence; hence ... our knowledge of these conditions, that is of the 'human situation', leads us to establishing values which have objective validity.[23]

From this discovery, we can certainly reject the Freudian political view that self and civilisation are irreconcilable. Of course, many enormous problems still arise. While healthy people choose rightly, because they enjoy being 'good' and 'contributing in', giving their gifts to society, for instance, there are those who tend to choose wrongly, or who remain in ignorance of their potentialities. While the inner striving of every individual may be self-realisation, he probably does not know it — and can easily become attached to false goals, unless he is helped to find his true path. But if genuine striving succeeds, the gratification of one need, in the search for meaning, opens the consciousness to domination to another higher need. The problem continually arises of drawing out in people devotion to their life-tasks. Maslow's importance in this kind of psychology is that he emphasises the psychological needs of ordinary healthy people — believing that psychology has drawn too many conclusions from sick individuals. These tend to lack confidence in the future, and lack the capacity to fulfil themselves. The emphasis on the new existentialism and phenomenology is on

---

21 *ibid.*, p.viii.
22 *ibid.*, p.123.
23 *ibid.*, p.151.

'intentionality', a concept from Husserl himself: the protensions in any individual towards the future.* Again, we have the recognition of a dynamic the natural science view cannot find. The human being, says Maslow, is 'simultaneously that which he is and that which he yearns to be'.[24] Another related theme of Maslow's Symposium (held in 1957) was an emphasis on the reality of altruistic love, and on love in general, as the basis of many of man's capacities – a scientific truth itself, bound up with meaning. An individual who is capable of love may find a sense of uniqueness in the other and the self, and this may be a valuable source of meaning in existence. Referring to many examples of this human truth, Professor Pitrim Sorokin declares that:

> Whereas the biology of the nineteenth century emphasized the role of the struggle for existence, the biology of our time more and more emphasizes – whether in the evolution of species or in the survival of separate species or in maintenance of health, vitality and longevity – the factor of mutual aid, cooperation, or friendship, all these terms being but different words for designating diverse aspects of the same creative unselfish love.[25]

Sorokin suggests that we deliberately foster this creative unselfish love in the human universe, pointing out that history shows that societies based on hate are short-lived, while those based on love seem much more endurable. It is a mask of the degeneration of our culture and our morale, that we should feel so uncomfortable at contemplating love and altruism as possible sources of a new radical politics.

To these observations Maslow adds the psychological observation of 'peak moments', and the need in human beings for these transcendent experiences. The search to 'become' is rewarded by the experience of 'being'. Those who have striven to create meanings, by realising the potentialities within themselves, have moments of absolute delight, perfect in themselves. Everyone is capable of such 'peak-moments', when they experience a sense of transcendence. In the realm of meaning, it is these which give us the experience of *Dasein*, of 'being there' in a meaningful way, which we can set against death and nothingness. As Maslow points out, these experiences may be everyday ones – the woman who has cooked a good meal, the lover who has found being in union with his partner, the man who has created something lasting or who has found a sense of *gestalt* in some project whether it is tuning a car or growing a row of beans – besides

---

* The notion of 'protensions' is itself drawn from Husserl [Ed.].
24 *ibid.*, p.130.
25 See Sorokin's contribution to *New Knowledge in Human Values, op.cit.*

those who have the special privileges of being able to compose, invent, or develop intellectual or cultural patterns and organisations. These are moments of 'heaven', and memories of these, says Maslow, sustain us when life becomes full of stress or pain.

On what are these conclusions based? Here we may refer to a whole series of well-established disciplines, under the general heading of 'philosophical anthropology'. There is post-Kantian philosophy, as developed by Ernst Cassirer and Susanne Langer. Cassirer argues in *An Essay on Man*[26] that the natural sciences could not give an adequate account of man, who must be seen as the *animal symbolicum*. Susanne Langer[27] declares that she believes there is a primary need in man, which is his need to symbolise — and thus to explore meanings in existence. There is the philosophy of science of Michael Polanyi[28], the distinguished chemist who turned to explore the grounds of knowing. He finds knowing rooted in 'tacit' processes, proclivities in our bodies of which we are unaware, but which yet enable us to 'indwell' in the things we observe. By his investigation of this involvement of the whole being of the scientist in his work, Polanyi came to argue, too, that reductionism and 'objectivity' were inadequate to describe reality, and were also based on false grounds. 'Objectivity' became idolised, as if there were a body of objective unquestionable knowledge, to which we needed to submit ourselves. Polanyi finds that there is never anything other than scientists knowing: nothing other than human beings trying to make sense of their lives. Thus, man's moral being is restored to the picture: even science, however objective, depends upon passion and faith, and its findings are always contingent, dependent, in being upheld, on the collaboration of individuals in deference to values and the achievement of a few great men. Polanyi's work is elaborated by Professor Marjorie Grene, who tries to demonstrate the inadequacy of the Newtonian-Galilean view, in her book *The Knower and the Known.*[29]

Marjorie Grene also admires the existentialists, and the phenomenologist Maurice Merleau-ponty. He, like Polanyi, explores the meanings of the body and our protestations towards the world, on which all our knowing is based, and he strives in *The Phenomenology of Perception,* to give an adequate whole account of being-in-the-world, as does Ludwig Binswanger

---

26 Ernst Cassirer, *An Essay on Man — An Introduction to a Philosophy of Human Culture,* Yale University Press, New Haven, 1944.
27 Suzanne Langer, *Philosophy in a New Key,* Harvard University Press, Cambridge, Massachusetts, 1942.
28 Michael Polanyi, *Personal Knowledge,* Routledge and Kegan Paul, London, 1958.
29 Faber, London, 1965.

in the book of that title. In *Approaches to a Philosophical Biology*[30], Marjorie Grene summarises the work of a number of such philosophical anthropologists, who are seeking a more adequate account of the natural world and man in it than natural science has proved able to give. Perhaps the most important observation in this book is that science itself is finding the 'centricity' of living systems – the way in which they live from their autonomous centres, through their boundaries, towards the environment. This mode of existence, obviously, cannot be examined by empirical science, by Cartesian epistemology. Once science learns to respond to these facts of living beings, it must obviously devise new approaches to the universe which restore to it the autonomy of living creatures, and especially the autonomy of man – and his transcending consciousness. With these, man's moral being is restored, too, since in all these studies loving communion, *libende Wirheit*, is seen as a primary principle of life.

This has two important effects in other related disciplines. For one thing, it enables those philosophical anthropologists, like F.J.J. Buytendijk and Helmuth Plessner, to offer a kind of existentialism which does not, like the 'old' kind (derived from Heidegger and Sartre), find relationship impossible, but rather finds it a basic reality, the basis of autonomy. It also confirms those findings in psychotherapy which make intersubjectivity a primary element in human existence, such as D.W. Winnicott's theories of how the child develops a true self through the 'creative reflection' of the mother.[31]

To take the political implications of these points: In the philosophy and politics of Sartre, man was 'abandoned' in an alien and hostile universe. He must rely on nothing outside himself, but must choose his freedom, and make himself, by moral choice and action. By such means he sought to overcome his nothingness. Yet in Sartre, there is no question of ever solving the problem of seeking authenticity and freedom. Man's striving must always end in defeat. As for love: the gaze of the 'other' always tends to make the self into an object, and love must always end in sadism, masochism, or indifference. Thus, in Sartre's politics, there can never be, in the end, a 'we': there can only be endless hostility, and, as with the man himself, a collapse into apathy and pointlessness. So, the 'old' existentialism could never yield an adequate politics. In culture itself, Sartre must bear a large burden of guilt, for the obsession of our culture at all levels

---

30 Basic Books, New York, 1968.
31 D.W. Winnicott, 'Mirror Role of the Mother', in *Playing and Reality*, Tavistock, London, 1971.

with disgust, pornography, false solutions, hate and perversion — all of which has promoted irrationality, nihilism, and disintegration, rather than any new moral state or hopefulness. Perhaps the most serious disaster of our time is the failure of radical politics to find a philosophy upon which a politics can be based. (Consider, for example, Sartre's influence on the Paris riots: or the 'Anti-university' in London which had the slogans 'madness ... revolution ... Black Power' — and quickly fizzled out.)

The work of the psychotherapists and other existentialist philosophers has overthrown this nihilistic and pessimistic position. Martin Buber, for instance, in his important essay 'Distance and Relation'[32] finds intersubjectivity as a primary principle in human existence. Man needs to be confirmed in his being by man. He differs from the animals, because he lives not in his immediate world, like a fruit in its skin, but in a life-world, a 'mansion' of consciousness, which has both past and future, and in which he can extend his vision over all the universe. But this mansion of consciousness is the product of being over against 'the other': 'it is from man to man that the heavenly bread of self-being is passed'. This basis of the capacity of man to be autonomous, and effective in the world, is confirmed by the work of psychotherapists like D.W. Winnicott with children, and of Rollo May with adults. May declares it to be an ethical principle emerging from therapeutic experience, that an individual's capacities to deal with the world are based upon his capacities to develop in relationships with others for whom he feels responsible.[33] Love, that is, in the light of these philosophical and psychological observations, is a primary principle of the universe, and the basis of man's meaningful existence.

Another important point made by Maslow and Winnicott is that the 'democratic character', the capacity to bear the burden of making decisions in community politics, itself requires a degree of maturity which is developed in good family life. Assaults on love, and on the family as the basic unit of society, as in nihilistic art and pornography, are therefore serious assaults on democracy itself, and politically tend to lead towards barbarism or neo-fascism. George Kepes, writing on the arts in Maslow's symposium, suggests that art has to do with the achievement of 'the joy of felt order': in our time, he complains, the artist has timidly reduced his vistas to 'the narrow ranges of reacting to personal hurts', and this has been a decadent withdrawal from the organising and ordering power

---

32 In *The Knowledge of Man — Selected Essays of Martin Buber*, ed. with an Introductory Essay by Maurice Friedman, Harper and Row, New York, 1966.
33 Rollo May, *Love and Will*, Norton, New York, 1969.

of creativity[34] leaving the gap to be filled by irrationalities and blasphemies.

All the disciplines represented in Maslow's book move towards the recognition of meaning, as a primary need in man. Bertalanffy says, 'Man's unique position in nature is based upon the predominance of symbols in man's life'. What is required now is:

> a new symbolic universe of values . . . or an old one reinstated . . . if mankind is to be saved from the pit of meaninglessness, suicide and atomic fire.[35]

The most urgent political need then is to satisfy psychological needs which are as real as our physiological ones. They may be considered, says Maslow, as deficiencies which must be optimally fulfilled by the environment to avoid sickness and to avoid subjective ill-being.

I have avoided here making specific references to practical means, whereby meaning can be restored to our existence. There are, however, plenty of hints in Viktor Frankl, as in his *The Doctor and the Soul*, where he discusses the meaning of work, and in the work of Maslow, who experimented with new methods in factories and other organisations to provide a sense of responsibility and purpose. The general principle is that individuals thrive best when they are faced with demands, to draw out of them capacities to fulfil a 'calling', and to draw out potentialities in them.

At the moment, we are still obsessed with rewards of a material kind as a political goal, and these may actually be destructive of meaning, and even of satisfaction. An evident example of this today is the British Health Service, where a new preoccupation with payment, differentials, status, and 'equality' rather than better care and medical science has led to a situation in which the whole system is threatening to collapse. In many such areas of our life today chaos threatens because the symbolic system threatens to collapse, even in education, even in the humanities. Bertalanffy argues in Maslow's symposium that even present economic and financial difficulties are associated with the collapse of the money system as a symbolic system. Certainly, it is not difficult to list problems in the modern world in which the symbolic element, the deficiency of meaning, is the crucial element, while meanings of all kinds are threatened with nihilism.

As Professor Weiskopf says in the same symposium, without attention to this essential question of meaning, our economy and politics become a tower of Babel which must in the end break down because of the limitless-

---

34 *New Knowledge in Human Values, op.cit.*, p.88.
35 *ibid.*, p.74.

ness of our striving for more material goods, more and bigger gadgets and the possession of things or sensations. In order to balance the economy, we have to 'integrate work with leisure, and material need satisfaction with spiritual and intellectual pursuits'. Growing technical efficiency will require a new basis for the distribution of income other than labour and work, Weiskopf suggests:

> This, in turn, will require a value orientation; intellectual, artistic, and spiritual creation will have to receive higher rewards than production of material goods and gadgets. A person will have to be rewarded rather on the basis of what he is than of what he does in the market place. This is not only an ethical postulate, but will become an economic necessity ... all this union and integration: our economic activism will have to be tempered with a 'passive', contemplative, way of life.[36]

Perhaps 'from each according to his ability, to each according to his need' needs a new twist. Erich Fromm argues that the 'male' modes of existence have become bankrupt: perhaps we need to foster female elements in ourselves more, modes of being. This may be the lesson of philosophical anthropology: but it is a measure of our deepening nihilism since 1957 that we cannot feel unembarrassed at such a suggestion. To say that politics needs to be based on love and meaning would today be likely to be greeted with a guffaw – or a bomb.

For one only has to quote Weiskopf's paragraph to realise that since 1957, the world has gone quite in the opposite direction. Under the influence of its own mythology – such as the *James Bond* myth, our society has become increasingly obsessed with acquisition, with sensuality, with 'pleasure' for its own sake, and the false strength of hate. Pseudo-maleness has triumphed, not least in women's rejection of their own femininity. In the economic realm, hedonism ('You've never had it so good' – a Conservative Party slogan in the sixties) has ended in despair, cynicism and greater existential frustration. The present economic crisis is still engaged with in terms of promises of ultimate economic growth, and a 'standard of living' in which basic requirements are a colour television set and package holidays in Spain. The possibility of promoting a more balanced life of creative leisure, greater responsibility at work, and a more meaningful life for all in the community, seems even more remote. Humanness has seriously ebbed, while education itself has been betrayed into nihilistic paths, and forms of anomie. Where, in all our new educational establishments, is the

---

36 *ibid.*, p.118.

hard Humanistic labour in thought, to which Husserl and Maslow direct us, in attempts to solve our problems, by finding a new sense of *humanitas*, being undertaken? Yet only in such a transformation of philosophical perspectives, of fundamental attitudes to man and his existence, is there any hope of avoiding the 'atomic fire'. So much now depends upon the intellectuals. They must reject the culture of decadence to which they have become addicted, dislodge themselves from a sterile 'objective' science, cease to endorse the politics of violence and hate and apply themselves to the duty of being what Husserl called 'functionaries of mankind' — so as to give a lead towards a new politics, based on man's fundamental need for meaning.

The Ambiguity and Rhetoric of 'Need'

Ross Fitzgerald

I

In common language and in much contemporary political theory the concept 'need' amalgamates and confuses normative and empirical utterance. When looked at uncritically, talk in terms of 'human needs' can appear to bridge the logical gap between 'is' and 'ought' and to overcome the 'problem' of the gulf between statements of fact and of value. But philosophers and political theorists are fundamentally mistaken if they believe that discoveries about human needs can enable us validly to move from a basis of allegedly 'empirical' statements about human needs to prescribing what human beings or governments ought to do. This is because the notion 'need' itself involves a conjunction of 'is' and 'ought'.

The very ambiguity of the concept 'need' in large part explains its plausibility in use. The notion 'need' has such currency, especially among popularisers and propagandists, and gains such persuasive force, because on one hand it involves imperatives and on the other because it appears to root them in common sense and in empirical reality. Once we have called something a 'need', in common usage it would be odd without considerable explication either to deny that it is good or that it should not be satisfied.

*   *   *

The notion 'need' clearly has meaning, and does make sense, in ordinary language. So too does the distinction between a 'need' and a 'want' and the associated distinction between 'real' or 'imagined' and 'true' or 'false' needs. Moreover 'need', as opposed to 'want' or 'desire', carries extremely persuasive connotations. It is therefore not surprising that political theorists have seized upon it.

In everyday use 'need' can often appear to be an empirical notion. But to talk in terms of 'needs' involves smuggling in a view of what ought to be under the guise of what is, or what can be, a matter of fact. Built into the word 'need' is a notion of necessity and one is unsure whether what is meant is an empirical and factual necessity, a logical and analytic necessity, or a normative necessity. R.S. Peters argues that to say 'a man needs food' implies that 'a man *must* eat'. He goes on to argue that, at a common sense level, the term 'needs' is inescapably normative. It implies that something is wrong with a person if certain conditions are absent. Thus a statement like 'Every child needs at least ten hours sleep' carries the implication that there is a state of affairs the absence of which is, or is likely to be, damaging or harmful to the individual in question. Indeed, to Peters, when we say that a person needs something we are often indicating a discrepancy between what a person ought to be doing and what in fact he is doing.[1] This is because the absence of a state of affairs does not create a 'need' unless this absence *ought not* to exist.

Similarly, Benn and Peters argue that 'needs' are not, as they sometimes appear, simple matters of fact, but rather presume norms. To attribute to anyone a 'need' is to indicate either the lack of something which it would be injurious or detrimental to the subject not to supply or alternatively, a lack which frustrates some end envisaged on his account. 'X needs food' implies that not having it is detrimental to him. But, Benn and Peters maintain, to talk of 'injury' or 'detriment' is to imply a norm or standard by which states or achievements are assessed. Thus to talk of a 'need' implies the lack of something which prevents a person reaching or maintaining some state defined by the norm. It is this, they suggest, which distinguishes 'need' from 'want'.[2]

---

1 *The Concept of Motivation,* Routledge and Kegan Paul, London, 1958. See especially pp.17-18 and 123.

2 S.I. Benn and R.S. Peters, *Social Principles and the Democratic State,* George Allen and Unwin, London, 1959, pp.141-54, especially pp.141-2. Note, however, that while in use 'need' usually presupposes a lack or deficiency, it does make sense to say 'He needs all the food he has', 'He needs the book he owns', 'He needs all the love and affection he is getting'. See Alan R. White, 'Needs and Wants', *Proceedings of the Philosophy of*

The philosophers Paul Taylor and Kai Nielsen have attempted to analyse and unravel the concept 'need' in some detail. Specifically they have attempted to describe several central uses of 'need sentences' as they occur in ordinary language and to elucidate the relations between the uses of such sentences and moral judgements.[3] While there are fundamental disagreements between Taylor and Nielsen, they clearly show the categorical ambiguity of 'need'. Taylor does, however, argue that there can sometimes be 'purely normative' need statements.[4] In this he is mistaken. As Nielsen demonstrates, 'need statements' are intelligible only against a background of certain assumed ends, goals, or purposes. Thus in asserting 'We need leaders who cannot be bribed' or 'The slums need to be replaced by good housing' we are not simply stating a fact, we are making a normative judgement as well.[5]

Taylor points out what he regards as the error of those social scientists and psychologists who claim to be able to establish a 'scientific ethics' on the basis of our knowledge of human needs. Significantly he suggests that A.H. Maslow's *Motivation and Personality* and Erich Fromm's *The Sane Society* are two cases in point.[6]

Taylor argues that this claim rests on a twofold failure. First, a failure to notice that statements about human needs may be both factual assertions which are empirically verifiable and (pure) recommendations. Second, a failure to realise that to verify statements of the first type is not *eo ipso* to establish the rational justifiability of making recommendations of the second type. For, Taylor argues, even if it can be shown empirically that man has certain basic needs in the first sense, it is neither self-contradictory nor logically odd to refrain from recommending that such needs be satisfied, or to recommend that they be not satisfied. The purposes and goals to which needs in this sense are relative may, he suggests, be morally undesirable. Moreover we may disapprove of certain human conative dispositions, however dominant they may be in some individuals or groups. Thus he concludes that whether human needs *ought* to be met must be established

---

Education Society of Great Britain, Supplementary Issue, Vol.VIII, No.2, July 1974, pp.159-80, especially p.171.

3 Paul Taylor ' "Need" Statements', *Analysis*, Vol.19, No.5, April 1959, pp.106-11 and Kai Nielsen, 'On Human Needs and Moral Appraisals', *Inquiry*, Vol.6, 1963, pp.170-83.

4 Taylor, *op.cit.*, pp.108-10.

5 Nielsen, *op.cit.*, pp.173-4, Also see Nielsen, 'Morality and Needs' in *The Business of Reason*, eds. J.J. MacIntosh and S.C. Coval, Routledge and Kegan Paul, London, 1969, pp.186-206.

6 Taylor, *op.cit.*, pp.110-11, cf. p.107.

on grounds independent of the 'need claims' themselves. This follows, he argues, from the principle that there is neither logical entailment nor contextual implication holding between any statement of the first type and any statement of the second type. And this principle, he maintains, is one of the lessons we have learned from Professor Moore's 'naturalistic fallacy'.[7]

Like Benn and Peters, Taylor suggests that the reason why arguments going from empirical assertions about human needs to recommendations that such needs be met appear so convincing is that empirical statements about needs, which belong to the first type, are so frequently used in everyday life for the purpose of making recommendations. But when social scientists and psychologists make statements of this type, they are making them not as recommendations but as confirmable statements of matters of fact. And this usage, he maintains, is only psychologically connected (by association), not logically connected (by implication), with the everyday recommendatory use of 'need' statements.[8]

Nielsen rejects much of this argument and specifically maintains that Taylor is mistaken in concluding that the fact

> that human beings have a need for love, or for freedom or for knowledge . . . is not in itself . . . even a good reason in support of the recommendation that these needs be met.[9]

Nielsen's rebuttal is that, while not unintelligible or self-contradictory, it would be 'logically odd' (a deviation from a linguistic regularity in a normal stating context) to assert, for example, (A).

A Children have a need for love and affection but they ought not to have it satisfied.

Similarly, to Nielsen, it would be 'logically odd' to assert (B).

B Man's fundamental needs ought always to be frustrated.[10]

Nielsen's notion of 'logically odd' is itself odd. Clearly (B) would not be logically odd if, for example, one held to a theory of instinctual renunciation and sublimation.

Nielsen agrees with Taylor that it is impossible to *derive* what is morally

---

7 *ibid.*, p.111. Taylor's emphasis. For reasons of simplification my classification and selection of 'need statements' does not rigidly follow Taylor or Nielsen.

8 *ibid.* Taylor's emphasis. Cf. R.S. Peters, *The Concept of Motivation, op.cit.*, especially pp.17-18 and 122-9.

9 See Taylor, *op.cit.*, p.111. Taylor however, adds, 'assuming that assertions of this kind could be empirically confirmed'. This crucial point Nielsen virtually ignores in his paper.

10 Nielsen, 'On Human Needs and Moral Appraisals', *op.cit.*, pp.175-7, cf. p.180.

good (in the widest sense of 'good') from statements asserting 'the needs of man' where such an expression is taken non-normatively.[11] He agrees that to say someone needs something is one thing; to say he ought to have it is another. Thus he accepts that we cannot derive 'Men ought to have X' from 'Men need X', for even though we may establish that X is a basic need, it is still not self-contradictory to claim that this need should not be satisfied. But, Nielsen maintains, while it is not self-contradictory to assert 'He needs it but he ought not to have it', in a normal stating context if it is said that someone needs something or that something is needed, we are entitled to infer, everything else being equal, that he ought to have it or that it should be done. Just as if a promise is given the presumption is that it must be kept, so too if human beings generally need something we are *justified* or *warranted* in the presumption that they ought to have it. Everything else being equal, if it is a fundamental need then it should be satisfied.[12] Nielsen's argument associating promise-giving and need-having gains plausibility because in both cases imperatives are implied in common usage. But while, in this sense, there are parallels between 'promising' and 'needing', Nielsen ignores an essential difference between the action of promise-giving and the state of affairs of need-having, however one may interpret having a 'need'.[13]

In Nielsen's view, given the way in which we use moral language, to say that children need love and affection is a good reason for satisfying that need, though other good reasons might, in certain circumstances, outweigh it.[14] It can, however, be seen that the plausibility of Nielsen's argument here would be gravely weakened if we substituted 'needing punishment and deprivation' for 'needing love and affection'.

It sounds inappropriate to speak of a need for punishment, of a need

---

11 *ibid.*, pp.178-9. Nielsen's emphasis.
12 *ibid.*, pp.175 and 177. Nielsen's emphasis. Cf. J.R. Searle, 'How to Derive "Ought" from "Is" ', *Philosophical Review*, Vol.LXXIII, January 1964, pp.43-58.
13 Promise-giving is itself a moral act which *only has meaning* in a moral setting in which giving a promise is associated with the prescription that 'promises ought to be kept'. Having a 'need', or being 'in need', is not an action, but a state of affairs. Even though, in use, 'needs' contains a normative aspect, it would not make the notion of 'needs' *meaningless* to deny that needs should be satisfied. We could not accuse such a person of not knowing the meaning of 'needs' or of self-contradiction or of other forms of illogicality. But if a person said that 'promises ought not to be kept' we could properly accuse him of self-contradiction in that 'promise-giving' can be a *meaningful* activity only in an environment where the morality of promise-giving is accepted. A person who rejects this should not assert 'promises ought not to be kept' but that 'promises ought not to be given'. This is a revised version of a point brought to my attention by G. Shipp.
14 Nielsen, 'On Human Needs and Moral Appraisals', *op.cit.*, pp.170-1, 175 and 182.

to be sadistic, or of a need for destroying one another precisely because the notion of a need (in common language) relates to a good, or to what is essential for *valuable* life. This highlights the problem of need theorists having, in effect, to differentiate between 'good' and 'bad' (or 'real' and 'false') needs. It hardly has to be pointed out that 'real needs' come to equal 'good needs'.

Nielsen maintains that in seeming to imply that there is a purely contingent connection between 'being a human need' and 'being good', and in giving the impression that discoveries about human needs are irrelevant to moral appraisal, Taylor has misled us.[15] He has obscured, Nielsen argues, how great the importance of discoveries about 'fundamental human needs' would be to sound appraisals, if only such discoveries could be genuine discoveries, free from conceptual confusion and well-confirmed. Here Nielsen misses a crucial point, for the construction of a trouble-free notion of need and the empirical verification of human 'needs' are precisely two of the major problems at issue. Thus he is forced to concede that there are many pitfalls even in the expression 'fundamental human needs'.[16]

Although, as we shall see, I reject Nielsen's argument that 'need statements' provide good reasons for imperatives, it is sufficient at this point that Taylor and Nielsen have demonstrated the variety of uses of the concept 'needs'. In particular this discussion illustrates that in terms of the categories of fact and value 'need', in common and theoretical usage, is almost pathologically ambiguous. Hence the enormous difficulty of separating the empirical and valuational components of the term in its many meanings and usages.

To dismiss ambiguity merely as a fault, however, leaves a great deal unsaid. It has recently been argued that political theorists have traditionally played on ambiguities plausibly to advance their arguments.[17] One form of ambiguity relevant here is when two or more distinctive strands of argument appear to coalesce. Where this happens an ambiguity emerges in so far as it is difficult to tie a given statement or concept to one strand or

---

15 *ibid.*, p.183.

16 Three issues must be kept separate: (1) as to whether the very expression 'need' can be given a clear and unambiguous meaning; (2) as to whether, even if (1) does not provide intractable difficulties, fundamental human needs can be empirically discerned or 'discovered'; and (3) as to whether, even if (1) and (2) are satisfied, any normative inferences could be derived and, if so, the nature of these inferences, for example, plausible, contingent, *ceteris paribus*, etc.

17 See C.S. Condren, 'Ambiguity in the History of Political Thought', unpublished Ph.D. dissertation, University of London, 1969, especially Chapters 5, 6, 7 and 8.

another.[18] This is manifestly the case with the political use of the concept 'need'. In general, however, it would be wrong to say that this use of the word is inconsistent; rather it is consistently ambiguous. As I have demonstrated elsewhere Christian Bay, for example, only achieves the plausibility that he does because of the ambiguity of his use of the concept need. The systematic ambiguity of 'need' is the most important motor mechanism by which Bay's whole argument is propelled.[19]

It is from its very ambiguity that 'need' gains its rhetorical strength. In common language 'need' is an imperative form of want or desire; 'need' itself implies a claim or demand. As K.R. Minogue explains, in ordinary usage 'desire (or want) may be capricious; need always claims to be taken seriously ... A need ... is something which, by definition, has a right to satisfaction'.[20] 'I want water' or 'I desire bread' involves no serious claim and imposes no serious demand on anyone. 'I need water' or 'I need bread' does involve such a claim and does impose such a demand.[21] This is so because, in common usage, we are not (as Nielsen argues) usually justified in denying human beings what they 'need'. Even the very young know this, for if the child does not get what he demands he will often switch (the claim statement) from 'I want it, I want it' to 'I need it'. Children, and adults as well, use 'need' as a persuasive and emotionally loaded term. As Minogue suggests, in common language 'need' implies a *legitimate* desire, a legitimate or morally sanctioned demand.[22] The word itself is a persuasive device and a vehicle of special pleading.

The concept of 'need' operates as a mechanism to camouflage imperatives under an empirical guise. Such a term, Minogue argues, is 'likely to attract both propagandists and philosophers (and especially those political theorists who combine both roles). Its emotional overtones are beautifully persuasive'.[23] He further argues that those philosophers and social propagan-

---

18 *ibid.*, p.173.

19 Ross Fitzgerald, 'Human Needs and Political Prescriptions: A Study of the Work of Christian Bay', unpublished Ph.D. dissertation, University of New South Wales, 1975.

20 See K.R. Minogue, *The Liberal Mind*, Methuen, London, 1963, Chapter 4, 'Moral and Political Evasions', Section 1, 'The Doctrine of Needs', pp.103ff. The quotation is from p.103. For an analysis of the imperative power of 'need', as opposed to 'want', 'prefer', or 'desire', see also David Braybrooke, 'Let Needs Diminish That Preferences May Prosper' in *Studies in Moral Philosophy*, ed. Nicholas Rescher, Blackwell, Oxford, 1968, pp.86-107. While Braybrooke is opposed to 'the dominion of needs' in ethical and moral discourse he nonetheless regards the notion itself as trouble-free.

21 Minogue, *op.cit.*, p.46.

22 *ibid.*, p.52.

23 *ibid.*, p.103. 'Need' as a term of propaganda is clearly seen in advertisements where the product to be sold is passed off as a necessity, as something which people *must* have.

dists who use it wish to establish the term 'need' as something whose relationships do not require serious examination.[24]

The term 'need' when used in politics carries with it the persuasive overtones of ordinary usage. This is reinforced by establishing 'need' in contexts where its imperative power is unlikely to be denied and then by using the term in such a way that it conjures up similar connotations. This is most obviously the case in relation to survival. Thus the statement 'Food and drink are basic human needs' (in the sense of basic to survival) does not seem to require serious examination. For if the issue is life and death then most people will agree that death ought to be prevented where possible. As Minogue demonstrates, the bedrock case of survival establishes the emotional tone of the doctrine of needs, and this tone can be carried over into its many other uses. Given the bedrock case any uneasiness about the actual concept of 'need' looks like pedantry. Further, with its imperative tone guaranteed, needs talk may move in any direction.[25]

In fact the direction in which most contemporary theorists wish to move 'needs' is towards 'individual freedom'. By using 'need' and 'freedom' in conjunction, the two terms reinforce each other and in the process elevate the imperative power of the notion of 'need'. Key emotive terms have always provided theorists with an effective means to persuade and denigrate. This particular juxtaposition and manipulation of 'need' and 'freedom' thus enables political theorists to persuasively push specific arguments and to advance and 'legitimise' their normative position. This is even more significant given the fact that talk in terms of human needs is tending to become a more urgent way of expressing human rights.[26]

The concept of needs, in common language, is connected to that of rights. Thus Arnold S. Kaufman argues that to claim that someone has an unmet human need entails at least that he is *entitled* to satisfaction of its corresponding want. But to Kaufman the important difference between a theory of human rights and a theory of human needs is this: whereas rights focus exclusively on satisfaction of wants which a person does or might have, implying nothing about which wants one ought to have, theories of human needs are centrally concerned with establishing criteria for the desirability of wants. Human needs, he maintains, imply an ideal conative pattern for those said to have those needs, whereas human rights do not. This shift in emphasis from doing what we happen to want, to doing what we *should*

---

24 *ibid.*, p.104.
25 *ibid.*, pp.105-7.
26 The work of Christian Bay is the prime contemporary example.

want is, to Kaufman, the most important factor in the shift in political preoccupation from rights to needs.[27]

Bearing in mind the rhetorical functioning of the notion of 'need' it is understandable that part of Bay's and Marcuse's endeavour is to dissociate 'needs' from 'wants' and to discount 'wants' and 'desires'.[28] It is not accidental that Bay and Marcuse manipulate the rhetoric of value-laden words. Rather than following on from an empirical theory of needs, their political prescriptions are tied to a particular notion of human excellence and of the healthy polity. Reference to 'needs' is often used as an unfalsifiable rhetorical device to make claims and demands on government and to promote their own vision of the good man and the just society.

Bay and Marcuse are trying to root 'needs' substantively by empirical reference. It is significant that Bay in particular uses a behavioural vocabulary, thus enlisting the authority of empirical science. This is because one aspect of 'need' is empirical; part of the persuasive power of the term is that it does seem to be objective.[29] By stressing the empirical and 'objective' aspect of 'need', by dissociating 'needs' from 'wants', and by giving priority to the satisfaction of the former, Bay and Marcuse are not only using 'needs' as a significant item in political language but are making a persuasive claim for its central importance in political discourse and in political theory.[30] All of this highlights the ideological effectiveness of talking in terms of 'needs' (which, rhetorically, require satisfaction) rather than in terms of 'wants' or 'desires' (which *prima facie* do not demand fulfilment).

*   *   *

Given the ambiguity and rhetorical role of the concept of 'need' one is force to confront directly the question of whether or not it is possible to construct an empirical theory of human needs and to establish necessary connections between such a theory and political 'oughts'.

---

27 'Wants, Needs and Liberalism', *Inquiry*, Vol.14, No.3, Autumn 1971, pp.191-212, especially pp.194 and 197. His emphases.
28 This is also true to a lesser extent of Charles A. Reich, Kai Nielsen and C.B. Macpherson for example.
29 See Braybrooke, *op.cit.*, pp.82-92 for the alleged 'objectivity' of needs.
30 See Marcuse, *One Dimensional Man*, Routledge and Kegan Paul, London, 1964, especially Chapter 1, and Bay, especially 'Needs, Wants and Political Legitimacy', *Canadian Journal of Political Science*, Vol.1, September 1968, pp.241-60, 'Politics and Pseudopolitics: A Critical Evaluation of Some Behavioral Literature', *American Political Science Review*, Vol.59, No.1, March 1965, pp.39-51 and 'The Cheerful Science of Dismal Politics' in *The Dissenting Academy*, ed. T. Roszak, Penguin, Middlesex, England, 1969, pp.187-205.

Because the notion 'need' combines both empirical and normative elements, one cannot produce a purely empirical theory of human needs. Talk of *human needs* must involve value judgements, and it is talk of human needs which is important to political theory. For the same reason, while a purely empirical theory is not feasible, neither is a purely normative one. It is no doubt possible to reconstruct or stipulate a usage of an ambiguous concept in such a way that its normative (or empirical) aspects are excluded. But such a concept would tell us nothing about political activity and human behaviour where, in practice, is and ought are linked. Moreover such a stipulation would completely change the character of the word 'need', and so cut off a whole area of meaning contained in common usage. It would therefore be quite irrelevant to understanding the way the term is used, the problems that have arisen from it, and also its plausibility.

The only other way out of this dilemma would be explicitly to posit or construct a normative goal in terms of a model of Man or a conception of human excellence and then to talk about 'needs' in order to achieve this goal or end. And, at least in common language, 'need' is a teleological concept in that it always presupposes some end or goal or purpose. A 'need' is always *for* something. But, apart from the possibilities of authoritarian imposition, the problem about a model of human excellence is that it is a *normative model* by definition. On one level this use of the notion does avoid some of the problems involved in the is/ought distinction. For if one accepts 'a model of Man' one can, in principle, make 'needs' empirical. Thus one can say 'Man needs X in order to achieve or become Y'. But on another level it does not overcome the fact/value distinction at all. This is because one can have several, indeed many, models of human excellence and one is still left with the normative problem of choosing between models. Need theory in politics presupposes a trouble-free notion of human excellence. Thus to Bay and Marcuse there is essentially *one* valid model of man which they somehow regard as empirically verifiable and ascertainable. In fact, contemporary experience and the history of political thought confirms the existence of many different, and conflicting, models of man. And different models of man and conceptions of human ends, goals or purposes will generate different catalogues of 'needs'. Further, all models of human excellence involve a distinction between man as he is and man as he ought to be. And 'needs', or more precisely the satisfaction of needs, is still the mechanism of getting from one to the other.

Even if the amalgam of 'is' and 'ought' contained in the notion 'need' could be separated and clarified, it is likely that the confusion over the basic catalogue of needs to be accounted for would still remain. Even lists of allegedly physiological needs are extremely varied[31] and problems of cataloguing are clearly compounded when one tries to extend the list.[32] Apart from the enormous difficulty of agreeing on a schedule of needs it would seem that all need theory, at least in relation to politics, involves something like a division between 'good' and 'bad' needs. This is often, if not always, related to differing conceptions of the nature of man and to differing notions of human excellence. One of the most obvious ways of distinguishing competing political philosophies is in terms of differing 'needs' or 'propensities' which are encouraged or discouraged. Those 'needs' that are encouraged are almost always regarded as somehow 'natural' or more 'basic'. Thus social Darwinists tend to encourage 'dominance and aggressive needs' and discourage 'dependency needs', while utopian socialists encourage 'belongingness and love needs' and discourage the 'needs for status, recognition, domination, power and aggression'.[33]

On the premise that man wants to survive, one can empirically verify the existence of physiological, safety, and possibly attachment 'needs'. But these are not the distinctly *human* needs. In terms of Abraham Maslow's need-hierarchy, the characteristically human needs cannot be validated at all without building-in an end state of human excellence such as I have described.[34] And here, of course, there are many problems. Specifically how does one arrive at such a goal? By consensus? That, to understate the case, would seem unlikely. And even if there were consensus, agreement or consensus on values (either by experts or by people at large) does *not* validate

---

31 Gardner Murphy, for example, classifies such 'needs' in terms of visceral drives (hunger, thirst, rest and sleep, oxygen drive, sex, etc.), activity drives (restlessness, preservation, rhythm, curiosity, impulse to cope with environment), sensory drives and the drive to express emergency responses (excitement, fear, rage, disgust, shame, grief, etc.). See his 'Social Motivation' in *Handbook of Social Psychology*, ed. Gardner Lindzey, Addison-Wesley, Cambridge, Massachusetts, 1954, p.609. Similarly Henry A. Murray developed a list of 27 such 'needs'. See his *Explorations in Personality*, Oxford University Press, London, 1938, pp.80-5 and 109-15.

32 David McClelland, for example, reduces all politically relevant needs to the three basic 'needs' for affiliation, for power and for achievement, while Maslow talks about five basic needs though they are not regarded as simple needs but rather five basic need areas which moreover do not claim to be exclusive. See McClelland, *The Achievement Motive*, Appleton-Century-Crofts, New York, 1953, and *The Achieving Society*, Free Press, New York, 1961, and Maslow, *Motivation and Personality*, Harper and Row, New York, 1954.

33 A similar argument is to be found in Robert Lane's *Political Thinking and Consciousness*, Markham Publishing House, Chicago, 1969, pp.24-9.

34 See my article 'Abraham Maslow's Hierarchy of Needs — An Exposition and Evaluation', this collection p.36.

judgements of value. Moreover, without the addition of an evaluative premise, even common 'needs' like breathing do not, of themselves, tell us that any particular man should be allowed to breathe.

Even assuming a theory of human needs was, or could be, empirically grounded, its prescriptive powers are limited. Disregarding the major problem of conflicting and competing 'needs', clear and unambiguous and widely accepted 'ought' statements do not follow. Thus, even if a catalogue of needs could be empirically validated, contrary and contradictory prescriptions might well emerge. This, of course, is related to the point that human beings may agree on 'facts' and yet profoundly disagree on the significance of facts and on attitudes, values and prescriptions. Factual statements even if agreed upon are not decisive. Despite the attempts of Black, Searle and Hannaford to undermine the fact/value distinction[35], one cannot logically derive 'ought' from 'is'.[36]

It is not hard to understand how theorists could believe in the possibility of bridging the gap between 'is' and 'ought' by using the concept of 'needs' as a middle term. To repeat, this is explicable given the very character of the term itself. The notion 'needs', when looked at uncritically, can give the appearance of moving from 'is' to 'ought'. In reality, of course, the concept itself encapsulates both elements without providing a logical bridge. The attempt to move from 'is' to 'ought' by way of a concept that contains and confuses both elements is therefore invalid and in violation of Hume's Law. As Antony Flew strongly emphasised

> it is, therefore, wholly wrong to do what so many people nowadays do, and to maintain that some term or theory (like that of 'needs') in which this necessary and fundamental distinction [between fact and value] is not made, when it should be made, in fact transcends it. Such terms and theories 'transcend' the distinction only through their own confusion.[37]

Granted that one cannot logically bridge 'is' and 'ought', it is often held

---

35 See Max Black, 'The Gap Between "Is" and "Should" ', *The Philosophical Review*, Vol.LXXIII, April 1964, pp.165-81; John R. Searle, 'How to Derive "Ought" from "Is" ', *op.cit.*, pp.43-58; and Robert V. Hannaford, 'You ought to derive "ought" from "is" ', *Ethics*, Vol.82, 1971-2, pp.155-62.

36 See especially Antony Flew, 'On Not Deriving "Ought" from "Is" ', *Analysis*, Vol.XXV, No.2, December 1964, pp.25-32; *The Is-Ought Question*, ed. W.D. Hudson, Macmillan, London, 1969; Roger Montague, ' "Ought" from "Is" ', *Australasian Journal of Philosophy*, Vol.XLIII, 1965, pp.144-67; Robert M. Martin, 'What Follows from "I promise . . ."?', *Canadian Journal of Philosophy*, Vol. III, No.3, March 1974, pp.381-7, and Warren J. Samuels, 'You Cannot Derive "Ought" from "Is"!', *Ethics*, Vol. 83, No.2, January 1973, pp.159-62.

37 Flew to me, August 29, 1973.

that there is a rational or reasonable connection between empirical evidence and normative utterance.[38] Specifically in terms of the focus of my enterprise it has been argued that 'need statements' constitute good reasons for action and for imperatives.[39] Forgetting for a moment the problem of empirically verifying 'higher' or distinctly human needs, one must reject the 'good reasons' argument, at least in regard to statements about human needs.

As we have seen, even if one could have indisputable factual evidence about the existence of human needs, any prescriptive statements allegedly derived from them would still depend on value premises. Thus human beings who believe that all (or certain) 'needs' ought to be renounced will draw vastly different conclusions from the same body of 'evidence' than those who hold that such needs ought to be satisfied. However the fundamental reason why I am uncomfortable when 'needs statements' are cited as good reasons for actions or imperatives is that the notion 'needs' is almost always introduced as though it were an empirical notion. But as I have shown this is not so. Any reference to 'needs' is introducing standards of evaluation or normative principles and imperatives at the start. In common language the notion of a need is already a notion of a reason for doing something.

The connections between need statements and value-judgements are, of course, plausible; so plausible in fact that theorists have mistaken them for being logical, rational, reasonable or necessary connections. All of this means that new knowledge in political psychology and personality psychology as presented by the work of Knutson, Renshon and Rokeach for example[40], does not represent development as far as political prescriptions based on a theory of needs are concerned. This is because while evidence

---

38 See especially Stephen Toulmin, *The Place of Reason in Ethics*, Cambridge University Press, Cambridge, 1961; and Kurt Baier, *The Moral Point of View: A Rational Basis of Ethics*, Cornell University Press, Ithaca, New York, 1958, especially pp. 183-201. Also see Philippa Foot, 'Moral Arguments', *Mind*, Vol.LXVII, 1958, pp.502-13; Stuart Hampshire, 'Fallacies in Moral Philosophy', *Mind*, Vol.LVIII, 1949, pp.466-82; and Charles Taylor, 'Neutrality in Political Science' in *Philosophy, Politics and Society*, Third Series, eds. Peter Laslett and W.G. Runciman, Blackwell, Oxford, 1967, pp.25-7.

39 See Kai Nielsen, 'On Human Needs and Loral Appraisals', *op.cit.*, and Charles Taylor, 'Neutrality in Political Science', *op.cit.*, especially pp.54-6. Also see Leslie Sklair, *The Sociology of Progress*, Routledge and Kegan Paul, London, 1970, especially Chapter XI, 'Needs, morals and society', pp. 189-292; Amitai Etzioni, *The Active Society*, Free Press, New York, 1968, especially 'Basic Human Needs', pp.622-32 and Etzioni's review of Sklair's book in *American Political Science Review*, Vol.67, No.3, September 1973, pp.998-9.

40 See Selected Bibliography.

about human behaviour might establish plausible connections between 'need statements' and political 'oughts' they do not establish logical or necessary ones. Or more precisely, the connection is there at the beginning because 'oughts' are already intimated and implied in the notion 'needs' itself. Certainly any attempt to ground political prescriptions on the basis of allegedly empirical statements about human needs is doomed to founder logically and could only appear to succeed by sleight of hand.

*   *   *

Having rejected the possibility, not only of a derivation of political 'oughts' from 'need statements' but also of an empirical theory of needs itself, it still remains necessary to account in more detail for the plausibility, persistence and present currency of the concept — not only in common sense and ordinary language but in political thinking and utterance as a whole. The character of the word itself, which coalesces different logical categories of utterance, in large part explains its appeal. As an emotive term in common usage 'need' has highly laudatory connotations. It is therefore not surprising that 'good' and 'right' are often taken as synonymous with 'satisfying human needs' or that the satisfaction of human needs is held to constitute *prima facie* reasons for ascriptions of 'good'. Thus Charles Taylor, to mention a theorist using this approach, concludes 'that something is conducive ... to the fulfilment of human needs ... is a *prima facie* reason for calling it good, which stands unless countered'.[41]

It *does* sound strange in ordinary language to say 'He needs it but he ought not to have it'. This is reinforced when the 'He' refers not to an individual in a specific role but to man as a human being. And it is especially the case when the notion 'need' is prefaced by 'real', 'genuine', or 'authentic' as opposed to 'false', 'alien', or 'imposed', or when it is simply replaced by 'want' or 'desire'. But while it sounds strange to say 'He genuinely needs it but he ought not to have it', it does not sound at all odd to say 'He wants it but he ought not to have it'. The differences between 'need' and 'want' here lie precisely in their rhetorical possibilities.

If used, or looked at uncritically, needs talk, and especially talk in terms of universal human needs, is a plausible and effective way of making claims and demands upon politicians and political systems. For 'needs' itself implies a claim. It is the 'strength' of this kind of rhetorical demand that 'needs' are what everyone, whether they know it or not, really want, or

---

41 'Neutrality in Political Science', *op.cit.*, p.55.

ought to demand. As Alan R. White asserts, while it is arguable that, in some sense, we always know what we want, it is not at all plausible to suppose that we always know what we need.[42] While each man is his own authority upon what he wants or desires, with needs, the case is different. People may 'need' things without knowing that they need them, and their needs may even directly contradict their wants and desires.[43] Here one can see striking similarities with Rousseau's notion of the 'General Will' — what men would will if they were fully conscious and true to their essential natures. As Minogue demonstrates 'a small set of people may establish themselves as experts in the pronouncement of what is the general will. Actual popular support is unnecessary'. The concept of needs, he argues, is a less dramatic example of the same kind of device.[44]

It is indicative that needs talk has become increasingly fashionable in regard to education. Of all human beings children are in the least authoritative position to pronounce upon what they 'want' or 'desire', or to resist the findings of 'experts'. As in other areas, talk in terms of 'educational needs' or 'the needs of the child' gains persuasive purchase by drawing on the 'bedrock case' of survival and the allegedly empirical character of 'needs'. Antony Flew points out that references to 'educational needs' suggest that even if they are not quite like the starving man's 'need' for food, which can be seen by anyone, at least they are like a patient's 'need' for thyroxin, which can be recognised and agreed upon by everyone with a modicum of medical expertise. But, he argues, this is not at all how things are with regard to the supposed 'needs' for cooperation, as opposed to competition; for unchallenged happiness, as opposed to the certain strains and possible frustrations of attempts to achieve; and, one could add, for 'spontaneity', as opposed to external and internal discipline.[45] As in all other contexts of use, to speak of 'a need' or being 'in need' presupposes a standard or norm, and different norms will create different 'needs'. In short, needs talk in education, as elsewhere, cannot exclude the normative aspect.

Flew rightly argues that R.F. Dearden's recent paper, ' "Needs" in Edu-

---

42 'Needs and Wants', op.cit., pp.171-2.
43 Minogue, op.cit., p.107. As Benn and Peters express it: 'To say that a man *wants* food is simply to describe his state of mind, to say that he *needs* food is to say that he will not measure up to an understood standard unless he gets it', *Social Principles and the Democratic State*, op.cit., p.143. Their emphasis. An important function of 'need' is that it is a way of discriminating between conflicting wants and desires.
44 Minogue, op.cit., pp.103ff. The quotation is from p.107.
45 'Philosophising about Education', *New Humanist*, Vol.88, No.12, April 1973, pp.482-3.

cation' is 'an especially fine example of how a few moments of sharp philosophical thought can fundamentally upset comfortable fashionable complacencies'.[46] Dearden attempts to explicate the logic of the concept of 'need' in a similar manner to the above. He concludes that the concept of 'need' is such an attractive one in education because

> it seems to offer an escape from arguments about value by means of a straightforward appeal to the facts empirically determined by the expert. But it is false to suppose that judgements of value can thus be escaped. Such judgements may be assumed without any awareness that assumptions are being made, but they are not escaped ... For example, curricular discussions revolving round 'children's needs' often leave it uncertain whether it is individual or social values that are being presupposed ... Yet it is extremely important to be clear about this. Value-judgements are inescapable in determining what ought to be done in education; and if, therefore, discussions are to be framed in terms of 'need', then the valuational basis of the concept, and the subservience of the relevant research findings to this, should be explicitly recognised.[47]

Flew himself goes on from where Dearden stops to urge that, in politics, references to people's needs, as opposed to their wants, are often the mark of the authoritarian. The famous slogan 'From each according to his abilities, to each according to his needs' ought, he suggests, for that reason, to make liberals and those who are committed to personal freedom shudder.[48] For who determines what individuals or the people need? Experts, the State Big Brother? Certainly not the individuals themselves. Again the reason for this appeal to needs is obvious: 'I am the only expert about what I want; but someone else may claim to know what I need (though I myself do not know this, and perhaps do actually want something quite different)'.[49]

One can also account for the apparent strength and plausibility of the concept in terms of the search for certainty. As with the notion of 'the

---

46 *ibid.*, p.482.
47 R.F. Dearden, ' "Needs" in Education' in *Education and the Development of Reason*, eds. Dearden, P.H. Hirst and R.S. Peters, Routledge and Kegan Paul, London, 1972, pp.50-64. The quotation is from pp.63-4. Also see B. Paul Komisar, ' "Need" and the Needs-Curriculum' in *Language and Concepts in Education*, eds. B. Othanel Smith and Robert H. Ennis, Rand McNally, Chicago, 1961, pp.24-42.
48 Flew to me, August 29, 1973. Flew's recent book, *Crime or Disease?*, Macmillan, London, 1973, and particularly Part 1, treats Plato's favourite image of the Guardian politician as the doctor prescribing from his expert knowledge for the needs of the citizen. Flew, like Popper, regards Plato as an arch authoritarian.
49 Flew to me, August 29, 1973. The words of Yevgeny Zamyatin seem particularly appropriate: 'I want to want for myself ... I do not want others to want for me'. *We — a novel of the future*, new trans. by Mirra Ginsberg, Viking Press, New York, 1972, p.5.

general will', prescriptions phrased in terms of 'needs' are such that they appear to be not merely the demand of one person but one that applies to all human beings whether they know it or not. Thus talk in terms of 'needs' appears to get the theorist out of the problem of imposing one's own individual value preference upon others. Needs talk has a scientific ring about it when the concept is used as though it were non-normative: it seems to open the way for objective expertise. If one talks as if a theory of needs were empirically established it gives the appearance of scientific utterance. This is especially important in a society where the language of science has considerable public authority and prestige.

Felix Oppenheim has recently argued that the 'inseparability thesis' (that is, the amalgamation of fact and value) and attempts to base normative principles on political facts are part of the trend towards certainty at any cost.[50] Moreover those philosophers and political theorists who deny that fact and value are separable tend to be the very ones who have revived the claim that 'ought' statements of political ethics can be derived from 'is' statements of political science, that is, that factual assertions can provide an 'objective' foundation or justification for value-judgements.[51] Needs talk and need theory, when looked at uncritically, appears to ground political oughts on factual statements about man and his condition. Looked at in this light the revival of need theory is part of the search for certain values and an objective political morality. The currency of 'need' can thus be seen in relation to its confusion of 'is' and 'ought'; its rhetorical and ideological effectiveness; and its seeming 'solution' to the pursuit of certainty. In particular the plausibility of 'need' comes from the possibility of exploiting its ambiguity.

However, we are still faced with the question of whether all of the above means that discussion of needs is to be excluded from the study of politics and from political theory. The answer would seem to be that we are still left in a dilemma.

It is incontrovertible that the way human beings behave and talk is commonly connected with 'needs'; moreover reference to 'needs' appears central

---

50 ' "Facts" and "Values" in Politics: Are They Separable?', *Political Theory*, Vol. 1, No. 1, February 1973, pp.54-68. J.S. Mill had a similar ambition to contain the world in a single theory and a faith in human beings to organise 'the good society' on rational lines while the Webbs had a similar dream of human perfection through politics and in particular through objective and efficient expertise. See Shirley R. Letwin, *The Pursuit of Certainty*, Cambridge University Press, London, 1965, especially pp.7-8, 244-318 and 321ff.

51 See, for example, Hannaford and Charles Taylor, *op.cit.*

to much imperative political theory. It has been convincingly argued that, traditionally, doctrines about how society should be constituted and how men should live have been developed in close connection with beliefs about human needs and purposes. These beliefs, in turn, are intimately related to more general conceptions of the nature of man. As different needs and purposes are distinguished as essential, different forms of society are prescribed.[52] Robert Lane, who has grappled with many of the theoretical problems involved in need theory, explicitly maintains that 'No one can write political philosophy without stating or implying what needs people strive to satisfy, often confusing real needs with some idealised version'.[53] Of course this interpretation, like that of Charles Taylor, depends on one's definition of what political theory and political philosophy entails. More importantly, it does not distinguish talk about human *propensities* from talk about human needs. While the former is normatively neutral, the latter, in use, is not.

Indisputably 'needs' is a significant item in political discourse and in the language of imperative political theory. Moreover, given its rhetorical possibilities it seems likely to remain so. However to admit to all this is not to accept a necessary connection between a theory of human needs and political 'oughts'. Granted its pivotal role in political rhetoric and in the manipulation of the language of politics (as an activity and as a discipline), what one cannot validly do is to use need statements or a theory of needs to establish necessary connections between an empirical situation and what one ought to do about it. Rather than being a bridge, an independent notion joining 'is' and 'ought', 'needs' is characterised precisely by being empirical and normative at the same time. The two elements may be distinguished analytically in formal theorising but separated only at the cost of destroying the character of the word and of denying ourselves the possibility of understanding its importance in everyday life. And this may stand as an emblem of the dilemma of contemporary political theory as a whole.

---

52 See Anthony de Crespigny and Alan Wertheimer, *Contemporary Political Theory*, Atherton Press, New York, 1970, Introduction, p.2. The authors however specifically include 'wants' in their discussion as does Charles Taylor.
53 *Political Thinking and consciousness, op.cit.*, p.24, cf. Taylor, 'Neutrality in Political Science', *op.cit.*, pp.41-2.

Wants or Needs, Choices or Commands

Antony G.N. Flew

— 'Now, if to be filled with what nature demands is pleasant, that
which is more really filled with real things will make a man rejoice
more really and truly with true pleasure; while that which receives what
is less real will be filled less really and certainly, and will receive more
untrustworthy, and less true pleasure.'
— 'That is quite inevitable,' he said.
— 'Then they who have no experience of insight and virtue, but spend
their whole time in revelling and suchlike ... cannot be satisfied inas-
much as what they are trying to fill is not the real and continent part
of themselves, nor is what they are putting into it real.'
— 'Truly perfect, Socrates,' said Glaucon, 'is your utterance regarding
the life of the vulgar.' — Plato: The Republic (585E-586B).

(1) I want to consider the relations and the differences between the notions
of want and of need. My main concern will be to bring out that an emphasis
upon needs, as opposed to wants, gives purchase to those who see themselves as experts, qualified both to determine what the needs of others
are, and to prescribe and enforce the means appropriate to the satisfaction
of those needs. Needs are in this respect, though not in all others, like
interests. Just as someone may want what is not in his interests to have,
or have some interest in securing what he nevertheless does not actually

want to obtain, so we may want what we do not need, and need what we do not want. The possibility of this lack of congruence, and its importance, can be illustrated at once in the former case by quoting two revealing expressions of what is often described, from a parochial Old World standpoint, as an 'Eastern' rather than a 'Western' conception of democracy. That the same applies in the latter case, and how this matters, should become progressively more obvious as we proceed.

The first statement was made by Janos Kadar, addressing the Hungarian National Assembly on 11 May 1957, the year after the ever-ready tanks of imperial normalisation had installed him in office. He said: 'The task of the leaders is not to put into effect the wishes and will of the masses ... The task of the leaders is to accomplish the interests of the masses. Why do I differentiate between the will and the interests of the masses? In the recent past we have encountered the phenomenon of certain categories of workers acting against their interests'.[1] The second statement was made on 7 July 1967 by Abdul Kharume, First Vice-President of Tanzania, addressing the annual foundation celebrations of the ruling and – of course – sole legal party on the Tanzanian mainland. He said: 'Our government is democratic, because it makes its decisions in the interests of and for the benefit of the people. I wonder why men who are unemployed are suprised and resentful at the government ... sending them back to the land for their own advantages'.[2]

These two statements suggest that we may usefully distinguish two different areas of meaning for the word 'democracy' in political discourse. In one – the 'Western' – the crux is what people themselves want, or at any rate decide. If some group takes decisions by a majority vote, then that is, as far as it goes, democratic. So too are institutions under which decisions are made by representatives, delegates, or officers, who have not only been voted in but may in due course also be voted out. It is today more than ever necessary, with an eye to the present pretensions of some Communist Parties, to underline that final clause. For the essential mark

1 Reported in *East Europe* for July 1957, p.56. I owe this reference to Sidney Hook, *Political Power and Personal Freedom*, Collier, New York, 1962, p.147.
2 I copied this one myself from reports in the Dar-es-Salaam press the following morning. I should perhaps mention that Kharume, who has since been assassinated, was a Zanzibari, and that, while mainland Tanzania has leanings towards China, his Afro-Shirazi Party, which maintains tight monopoly control of the islands, has been much advised and influenced by Soviet Germany. I certainly want to add that I myself have no difficulty at all in sympathising with those who preferred to go on scratching a wretched living among the not so very bright lights of Dar, rather than to be bundled back to the by comparison excruciating boredom of the villages from which they came.

of democratic ('Western') leaders or groupings is: not that they have already been popularly elected, or hope in the future to be so elected; but that, if and when they are voted in, they will maintain and promote arrangements to ensure that they can also be voted out. In the second of the two areas of political meaning the crucial reference is quite different. Arrangements may be said to be democratic ('Eastern') in as much as they are supposed to be in the interests of, or to the further good of, or to meet the needs of, whoever or whatever is here allowed to constitute the true and relevant people.

In the modern period Locke may be seen as the prime prophet of the first tradition. Rousseau is certainly the great protagonist of the second. His often deceived but never corrupted General Will is always upright, and necessarily directed to the collective good. Yet it is notorious that it is not to be reliably discovered, either in the hurly-burly of contested elections, or through the deliberations of collective assemblies. Precisely this is what gives such doctrines as his their strong appeal to all who think of themselves as members of an elite of Guardians, as adhering to 'a party of the vanguard'.[3] The word 'democracy' is also employed in a third sort of sense. All that needs to be said of this here is that it seems to have no necessary connection with either of the first two. In this third area of meaning the crucial reference seems to be to the absence of social barriers. Thus some will say that some organisation is in some sense democratic in its recruitment, without thereby implying anything at all about either its internal or its external political relations.[4]

That gives us a fundamental distinction between three families of senses. But notice that families of senses are not necessarily, and that these particular families of senses are not in fact, collections of species within a

---

3 See on this, in the French Revolution of 1789, J.L. Talmon, *The Origins of Totalitarian Democracy*, Secker and Warburg, London, 1952. It is interesting to notice that in his earliest presentations of proposals for 'a party of a new type' Lenin himself contrasted the extreme authoritarian centralism of what his followers now call democratic centralism with democracy; which word he appeared then to be construing, as his contemporaries in the then professedly Marxist Social Democratic parties of Western Europe construed it, in a sense of our first sort. For a development of this theme, with some quotations and more references, see my 'Russell on Bolshevism', due to be published in a two-volume collection of papers on Russell ed. George W. Roberts (Allen & Unwin).

4 It is, for instance, in senses of this third kind that the word is usually used both in John Dewey's *Democracy and Education*, Macmillan, New York, 1916, and in *Education for Democracy*, eds. D. Rubinstein and C. Stoneman, Penguin Education, Harmondsworth and Baltimore, 1972 (second edition). I have recently discussed the Dewey book, comparing it with the work of the Penguin Educationalists, in a lecture which I hope will eventually appear in print as part of a volume on Dewey edited by R.S. Peters.

wider common genus. It is, therefore, a shameful muddle to urge — what I have more than once heard from spokesmen of our new philosophical Radicals — that, while Canada or Britain is no doubt a democracy in a sense of the first sort, and while scarcely anyone could with a straight face say the name of the USSR or of any of its associated states, still these are perhaps, or surely, developing their own different — and higher — varieties of democracy. However, if A is φ in one sense of 'φ', while B is φ only in quite another sense, this gives us no grounds whatsoever for saying that A and B represent different species of φ.

2(a) I have so far made only one very obvious analytical point about wants and needs: that we may want what we do not need, and need what we do not want. Two other rather less obvious points of the same kind are suggested by the observation 'that an emphasis upon needs, as opposed to wants, gives purchase to those who see themselves as experts, qualified both to determine what the needs of others are, and to prescribe and enforce the means appropriate to the satisfaction of those needs'.

(b) The first is that the satisfaction of people's needs must be in their interests, or in some other way good for them. If you need medical attention, for instance, then getting this must be in itself, and all other things being equal, good for you; even if your likely conduct on your return to health is such as to make the whole business anything but either good for others, or good without qualification. Again, if I prescribe something which you definitely do not want, as what is required to meet some need of yours, then I must in consistency at least pretend that my prescription is to your ultimate advantage: 'What you need is a real thrashing, which will do you a power of good'; or, perhaps, 'What you need is a few months in an infantry training depot, which will make a man of you'.

(c) The second analytical point suggested by the same observation is that whatever is needed is needed not for its own sake but as a means to the fulfilment of some further function, purpose, or end. If I want to climb this particular route, then there may be no further answer to the question 'Why?'. Suggestions that I could get to the top more easily and more quickly by train or by helicopter may simply miss the point — that what I want is to climb, and to climb this particular route. Yet if I say that I need something it is never inept to ask 'What for?'. I need food and drink in order to maintain life and health; I need a lift in order to get me to Manchester in the morning; and so on. But if I claim just to need something, but not for anything further, then what I really have is not a need at all, but only a wish or a craving.

(d) A fourth analytical point is suggested by Kenneth Minogue's apophthegm: 'A need is legitimate or morally sanctioned demand'. He himself later quotes Simone Weil: 'Where there is a need, there is also an obligation'. But then he makes in his own person the much more cautious assertion: 'Desire may be capricious; need always claims to be taken seriously'.[5]

The truth, surely, is a little more convoluted. Certainly there is always something imperative about any idea of a need. For to say that this or that is needed is to say that it is a necessity for the fulfilment of some function, or purpose, or end. But this is by no means to say: either that that function, purpose, or end is 'legitimate or morally sanctioned'; or that this necessary means to it is also licit. Much less is it to say positively, that 'there is an obligation' upon everyone to assist all others to secure their every genuine need. It is not incoherent to assert that people need to do things, which ought not to be done, if they are to achieve objectives, which in any case they ought not to be pursuing: 'They needed to employ every instrument of terror if they were to secure their firm control over the countries which their armies had conquered'. Nor is it improper to speak of needing to do or to have this or that in order to successfully pursue what is admittedly only a pastime: 'You will need to do much better in the scrum if you are to have any chance of winning on Saturday week'.

On the other hand we do often contrast basic human needs – what is needed simply to sustain life, or to maintain whatever is taken to be the minimum tolerable standard of living – with luxuries and frivolities. No doubt it was with this contrast in mind that Simone Weil said what she said. For it would be hard not to accept that such needs, at any rate in so far as they are not being met, do constitute at least defeasible grounds of moral obligation upon the more fortunate. The whole situation can perhaps best be summed up by saying, that, while all needs are of their very nature imperative, most of these imperatives are merely hypothetical, only some are categorical.

3 The four essentials distinguished in the previous section conspire together to endow the notion of needs with much charm for anyone longing to belong to an authoritative and powerful paternalistic elite. First: because people's needs may be incongruent with their wants, whereas each individual is their own best judge of the latter, the former may be far more

---

5 *The Liberal Mind*, Methuen, London, 1963, pp.46 and 103.

satisfactorily determined by someone else. Second: because to meet my needs is necessarily in some way good for me, the person who directs or secures the satisfaction of these must be my benefactor; even though I may still, in my ignorance, resent or reject their surely well intentioned services. Third: because needs are necessarily means to ends, there must be room for expertise in determining what in fact is needed as the means to this or that end. Fourth: because needs are of their very nature imperative, and because their satisfaction is at least sometimes categorically imperative upon someone, those who are by profession engaged with such necessary matters must seem to be on that account important people, while their every prescription may in consequence appear to be inexpugnably admirable and mandatory.

In his percipient essay on *The Liberal Mind* Kenneth Minogue mentions some later substitutes from that esoteric vision of the Platonic Ideas, which qualified the original Philosopher Kings for absolute power: 'The notion of the general will, or . . . of the class-consciousness of the proletariat . . .' He then goes on: 'in each case a small set of people may establish themselves as experts in the pronouncements of these oracles . . . The concept of need is a less dramatic example . . . Most of its practitioners are mild social scientists, or benevolent welfarists, rather than wild-eyed fanatics like Robespierre or Lenin'.[6] Certainly it is, as such fanatics love to say, no accident that, in a period when so much is heard from the teachers' unions about the achievement of professional status, we also find that 'The concept of need is being increasingly widely used in educational discussions . . .'[7]

---

6 *ibid.*, p.109. In Britain at any rate the gulf between the 'wild-eyed fanatics' and 'the mild social scientists, or benevolent welfarists' seems to have narrowed considerably since 1963. After observing recent Labour Party conferences, and reading their latest election manifestos, Minogue could scarcely dismiss 'people for whom socialism is itself a dogma' as exotic varieties; or console himself with the reflection that most British 'socialists . . . would support a more experimental attitude to social reform' (*ibid.*, p.14).

7 R.F. Dearden, ' "Needs" in Education', in R.F. Dearden, P.H. Hirst and R.S. Peters, *Education and the Development of Reason*, Routledge and Kegan Paul, London, 1972, p.50. If the status model which the leaders of the school teachers had in mind was that of independent professionals acting on the instructions of their clients, then they would presumably be rooting for some sort of educational voucher system. For this alone can give all parents some measure of direct and effective say as to which teachers, or which schools, teach their children; and to what aims the teaching services of these teachers are to be directed. But the official Schools Council, dominated by representatives of the school teachers' trades unions, is in fact set to impose the opposite, Guardian model. See, for instance, Mary Warnock in *New Society* for February 11, 1976. Herself for many years a Headmistress, Mrs Warnock concludes: 'We should not be so frightened of our school teachers as to be unable to tell them clearly that, now we are grown up, we do not choose to be ruled by them' (p.548).

This raises, as it is intended to raise, the general question of the relation between professional or other people offering skilled services to the public, and those who may from time to time wish to make use of such services. A consideration of these relations will bring out: first, that, although our needs cannot be identified with our wants, it is nevertheless impossible to completely separate the former from the latter; and, second, that although some expert may be qualified to tell me what I need for this or that, there is no room for an expertise referring not to means only but to ends.

Suppose that I visit, as I did yesterday, my friendly neighbourhood storeman. I tell him about a job I want to do. He from his expert knowledge can, and did, help me. He explained what I needed and then sold me the necessary tools and materials. But no expert knowledge would have enabled him to discern what I needed had he been given no information about what I wanted. It would have been just the same had I visited a solicitor, or a surveyor, or an architect. They would have had to ask me what I wanted before they could begin to bring their expert knowledge to bear in order to advise me on my needs. The reason why a doctor is, generally, able to prescribe for the needs of his patients without first asking them what they want is that he can on almost all occasions take it for granted that they want to be as fit and as free from pain as they can be; and that they have come to him as patients precisely and only because they believe that he can and will help them to get better.

These are all simple and central cases of the employment of experts to determine needs, as means to the achievement of the actual and present ends of the employer. But there are, of course, also cases where the need or the supposed need relates to some want which cannot be expressed immediately, or which would or will be felt only on certain hypothetical conditions, or even one which it is thought ideally ought to be, rather than actually is or will be, felt by the person to whom that need is attributed. The first thing to stress about all such complicated and off-centre cases is that they do still manifest, in the various ways just indicated, the same logical link between a person's needs and that same person's wants.

The second thing to be emphasised, and more strongly, is that the further we get from actual and present desires, the more dubious becomes the status of the expert, and the more questionable his putative expertise. The first harmless step is when the need corresponds to a want which, although not in fact felt at the moment of prescription, will be felt as soon as the expert communicates some relevant item of his own knowledge: 'You need to have that treated at once, or the infection will spread and you will lose the whole arm'. But at the end of the road there is the Platonic guardian, whose absolute power is warranted by nothing else but a putative expertise consisting precisely and only in alleged privileged access to the objectives that everyone ought to have.[8] Deviation or defection from these ideal — indeed Ideal — objectives is in Plato's book necessarily an expression of psychological disease. Such disease must, of course, tend to discredit any conduct or conviction to which it gives rise, as well as being — like all disease — bad for the subjects themselves.[9]

Consider now two more or less off-centre examples. In the first a woman is lying injured and unconscious after a car smash. The doctor who steps forward to treat this victim both discerns and meets her need for such attention. For he can, and indeed must, assume that, were she able to ask for help, she would. In the second a man wants to kill himself. Choosing a time when he may reasonably expect not to be disturbed he goes to his garage, locks the door, shuts the windows, seals as best he can any cracks or crevices which catch his eye, starts the engine of his car, and lies down comfortably with his head hard by the car's exhaust. A doctor chances by, breaks into the garage, and rushes the now unconscious victim off for emergency hospital treatment.

No doubt this doctor too behaved exactly as both our laws and our conventional morality require. Yet it would be quite wrong for him to claim, as the doctor in the other case properly might, that he was acting simply as a professional man, rendering services to his patient/client. Our doctor was certainly not, on this occasion, acting on the instructions of the would-be suicide, who had made it as clear as he could that he wanted no interference. If, therefore, reference to the patient's needs is to provide justification for the drastic intervention in this case too, then those needs will have to be specified by reference to ideal rather than to actual desires. (In terms of his actual desires what our would-be suicide needed was nothing so much as a hole in the head!)

4 These two examples bring out the crucial difference: between, on the one hand, the independent professional expert as servant, determining needs by reference to the wants of the individual client; and, on the other hand, Platonic experts as masters, paternalistically prescribing needs by reference

8 See *The Republic*, 484A-485C and 487C-489C; and compare Renford Bambrough's 'Plato's Political Analogies' in *Philosophy, Politics and Society*, ed. P. Laslett, Blackwell, Oxford, 1956, reprinted in *Plato, Popper and Politics*, ed. R. Bambrough, Heffer, Cambridge, and Barnes and Noble, New York, 1967.

9 Compare my *Crime or Disease?*, Macmillan, London, and Barnes and Noble, New York, 1973, *passim*.

to their own judgment of what their subjects ideally ought to want. It is common today to excoriate elitism, without making clear whether the objection extends to every form of selection for quality. If it does then those who thus employ the word as a term of abuse betray education, and every other form of striving after excellence as well. Suppose that the epithet has to remain dyslogistic, then it would surely be much better to specify the obnoxiousness as being that of pretending to enjoy privileged Guardian access to ultimately authoritative values, and of claiming in consequence to possess the right by all available means to impose these uniquely authentic ends.

However sensible this suggestion may seem it is not, I am afraid, likely to be generally adopted. For, in a way which may remind us of those vociferous advocates of ever more equalisation of individual wealth and income who nevertheless manage to support enormously inegalitarian Leninist concentrations of all power in the hands of small and irremovable political committees, many of the most strident denouncers of elitism in non-socialist societies contrive at the same time to see no scandal in the monopoly power of socialist 'parties of a new type'.[10] However, whether or not my proposed definition of the word 'elitism' is acceptable, it certainly is worth citing some revealingly Platonic passages from two recent articles by one of the philosophically most distinguished of our new Philosophical Radicals. Kai Nielsen happens also to be both a former colleague of the writer and a fellow contributor to the present volume.

(a) The first of these papers asks 'Is Empiricism an Ideology?', in a mainly Marxist-Leninist understanding of the word 'ideology'. Nielsen begins by insisting, usefully, that empiricism in the sense of an insistence 'that all our knowledge ... of matters of fact ... is and must be ... based upon or derived from experience' not only is compatible with his own new-found secular religion, but also 'implies a constraint on theorising that any scientifically oriented realist, materialist or indeed any tough-minded

---

10 For instance: although the Penguin Educationalists mentioned in Note 4, above, are forever denouncing elitism as opposed to democracy, no one seems to notice any incongruity
in the presence among their numbers of Professor Brian Simon, who has been, and for
all I know still is, a member of the Executive Committee of the Communist Party (Muscovite).

11 *Metaphilosophy*, October 1972, pp.266-7. That this insistence is necessary can be appreciated by contrasting Robin Blackburn's editorial assertion in *Ideology and Social Science*,
Collins Fontana, London, 1972, that 'the assumption that there exists a realm of facts
independent of theories which establish their meaning is fundamentally unscientific'
(p.10). Compare 'Metaphysical Idealism and the Sociology of Knowledge' in my *Sociology, Equality and Education*, Macmillan, London, Barnes and Noble, New York, 1976.

person ought to welcome'.[11] What Nielsen is against is logical empiricism — defined here in terms of Hume's Fork plus the contention that 'For fundamental normative judgements ... there are no truth-conditions'.[12] This last is for Nielsen the stone of stumbling: '... such an account ... indirectly supports and reinforces pluralism and bourgeois individualism ... If someone ... takes this conception of valuation to heart, he is very likely to accept democratic pluralism as the most adequate political model and to be sceptical of ... what he is likely to characterise as "total ideologies" ... On such a model ... it is very difficult to talk about ... a truly human society, alienated labour and the like'.[13] So what Nielsen wants, as an enemy of 'bourgeois individualism' and (Western) democracy, is some materialist analogue to Plato's privileged access to the ideal Ideas: ultimate facts which are at the same time ultimate values; values for which there are exhaustive truth-conditions, and about which there could be experts.

The chief corollary drawn by Nielsen from rejecting this logical empiricist fundamental is, if possible, even more Platonic. Where Plato laboured to prove that the pleasures to be gained from satisfying disfavoured desires could not be real pleasures, Nielsen proposes to discount or to discredit various actual but unapproved wants, and, presumably, both the needs and the satisfactions arising from those wants, as artificial and hence not truly human. He complains that the defender of 'bourgeois individualism ... conveniently ignores considerations ... concerning the way wants are artificially created and sustained by the ruling classes to enhance and protect capitalism'.[14]

A full critique of Nielsen's position in this first paper would have to challenge two very different assumptions. Is it, for one thing, really impossible for his logical empiricist to provide good reasons why we ought to pursue some things and to eschew others?: 'On such an account ... No one can rightly tell us what we ought to want'.[15] Again, is it not mistaken — even paranoic — to suggest that in what Nielsen abominates as still capitalist countries 'the ruling classes' exercise the same degree of control as is normal in the already fully socialist countries?: 'wants are artificially created and sustained by the ruling classes to enhance and protect capitalism'. But what has to be said here is that it is ridiculous to dismiss actual

12 Nielsen loc.cit., pp.267-8. For explanation of the established nickname 'Hume's Fork' see my An Introduction to Western Philosophy, Thames and Hudson, London, and Bobbs-Merrill, Indianapolis, 1971, pp.383-9.

13 Nielsen loc.cit., pp.270-1.

14 ibid., p.271.

15 ibid., p.271.

wants simply 'as artificial and hence not truly human'.

Nielsen appeals for support to Marx and Engels, Marcuse and Gorz. It is curious that he makes no mention of Galbraith; but perhaps less curious is that he is, apparently, not able to think of any suitable citation from either of the Founding Fathers. Marcuse starts his essay 'Liberation from the Affluent Society' by categorically affirming that 'a better, a free human existence ... socialism *ought* to be'.[16] The problem as he sees it is that far too few of those people who have any choice in the matter actually want the kind of 'liberation' which he so longs to impose: for capitalism, in defiance of the Marxist prophecies, 'delivers the goods to an ever larger part of the population'.[17] So Marcuse contrasts 'objective need' — what he thinks people ought to want — with 'subjective need' — people's actually wanting what he thinks they ought to want. The latter, alas, 'does not prevail. It does not prevail precisely among those parts of the population that are traditionally considered the agents of historical change. The subjective need is repressed, ... firstly, by virtue of the actual satisfaction of needs, and secondly, by a massive scientific manipulation and administration of needs ...'.[18] In *1984* the slave Winston Smith for a moment saw hope in the proles: the master Marcuse now hails 'the intelligentsia as the catalyst of historical change'.[19]

It is remarkable, though maybe not surprising, that Marcuse finds it either unnecessary or impossible to deploy so much as one single illustration of this alleged 'massive scientific manipulation and administration of needs'. Turn, therefore, to J.K. Galbraith. Notwithstanding that 'Nothing in economics so quickly marks an individual as incompletely trained as a disposition to remark on the legitimacy of the desire for more food and the

---

16 In *The Dialectics of Liberation*, ed. D. Cooper, Penguin, Harmondsworth and Baltimore, 1968, p.175. Italics original.

17 *ibid.*, p.176. Compare similar statements in a notorious essay with the appropriately Newspeak title 'Repressive Tolerance'; in H. Marcuse, B. Moore and R. Wolff, *A Critique of Pure Tolerance*, Cape, London, 1969. Marcuse there makes it about as plain as he ever makes anything that his revolution requires 'the dictatorship of an elite over the people'. It is indeed for him and his followers a main grievance against the 'late capitalist' order that the silent majority does not want, and has no interest in, the revolution proposed: 'By the same token, those minorities which strive for a change in the whole ... will ... be left free to deliberate and discuss ... and will be left harmless and helpless in the face of the overwhelming majority, which militates against qualitative social change. The majority is firmly grounded in the increasing satisfaction of needs ...' (pp.107-8 and 134).

18 'Liberation from the Affluent Society', in *The Dialetics of Liberation, op.cit.*, p.182.

19 *ibid.*, p.188. I will not miss this chance of recommending Lewis Feuer's most illuminating studies of *Marx and the Intellectuals*, Doubleday Anchor, New York, 1969.

frivolity of the desire for a more elaborate automobile'[20], Galbraith wants to find some difference between fundamental and less fundamental wants and urgent needs. At least for certain purposes well he may: the possibility of some such distinction is, as we saw at the end of Section 2, an element in the logic of need.

But the basis he proposes will not serve: 'If the individual's wants are to be urgent they must be original with himself. They cannot be urgent if they are contrived for him. And above all they must not be contrived by the process of production by which they are satisfied ... The fact that wants can be synthesized by advertising, catalysed by salesmanship, and shaped by the discreet manipulations of the persuaders shows that they are not very urgent'.[21] A first objection to this piece of New Left conventional wisdom is that, with all the intellectual's characteristic contempt for the vulgar, Galbraith is vastly exaggerating the power of advertisers to generate fresh wants (he is not, I take it, maintaining that he himself and his Harvard colleagues are clay in the hands of Messrs Batten, Barton, Durstine and Osborn!). In any case if we do ever take the trouble to review all the advertising to which we are exposed in a week, we shall discover that precious little could be said to be even trying to create fresh wants out of nothing; as opposed to saying, or shouting, what is available; or persuading, or reminding us to buy one brand rather than another.

The more decisive, and more philosophical, objection is that only the most elemental and undifferentiated wants can be untainted by environmental dependence – for Galbraith the original sin of an affluent society. F.A. Hayek sees him off with a sharp brevity: '... innate wants are probably confined to food, shelter and sex. All the rest we learn to desire because we see others enjoying various things. To say that a desire is not important because it is not innate is to say that the whole cultural achievement of man is not important'.[22]

---

20 *The Affluent Society*, Houghton Mifflin, Boston, 1958, p.147. It was careless to write, without qualification, 'the desire for more food'; especially so soon after that fine phrase about 'the United States ... where ... now the food supply presses relentlessly on population' (p.123). He should reflect on his rather earlier saying that 'although the truth rarely overtakes falsehood, it has winged feet as compared with a qualification in pursuit of a bold proposition' (p.30).

21 *ibid.*, pp.152-3 and 158.

22 *Studies in Philosophy, Politics and Economics*, Routledge and Kegan Paul, London, 1967, p.314. Now that Galbraith has publicly acclaimed his socialist allegiance it would do less than justice to both men not to quote Hayek's immediate appreciation of the way the wind was blowing: 'For over a hundred years we have been exhorted to embrace socialism because it would give us more goods. Since it has so lamentably failed to achieve this where it has been tried, we are now urged to adopt it since more goods are not

(b) The second Nielsen paper, 'A Defence of Radicalism'[23], displays the author as a paradigm case of Popper's wholesale utopian social engineer. But our present interest lies in its further revelation of the self-image of a Leninist would-be Guardian. Nielsen is not, he assures us, 'suggesting that a small tightly-knit group of intelligentsia [and] class-conscious workers' should try to 'impose socialism from above'.[24] This clear denial seems, however, to be compatible with requiring 'that radical workers and intelligentsia should not be afraid to regard themselves as a vanguard, and should not lack the courage to insist on a vision of society — a positive conception of a truly human life — which does not correspond to the only one prevailing in our intellectually and emotionally drugged capitalist mass culture. And if the situation ever becomes ripe for this vanguard to translate such a vision of society into a social reality, they must not hold back from such a translation because they fear imparting or inculcating, through structural means, a set of values that some plain, but manipulated men, would not in their ideologically drugged state choose . . .'.[25]

Nielsen continues: 'This may sound — brought up as we have been in a liberal ethos — like an invitation to tyranny, but if it is done with integrity and with a full commitment to socialist and indeed egalitarian values, this must not and indeed will not be so'.[26] For sure this does sound like a prescription for absolutism. But — to parody a later and funnier Marx — do not be misled. It is.

When Plato was dreaming dreams of his own ideal city, stately as a Dorian temple, he did wonder for one uneasy moment how his guard dogs were to be inhibited from themselves preying upon the sheep. Plato then saw 'the chief safeguard' in their 'being really well educated'.[27] He never got around to suggesting any other. Nielsen, who claims to be no dreamer bringing news from nowhere but a 'scientifically oriented realist', a 'tough-minded man' possessing Marxist clues to history, can do no better than simply to assert that 'this must not and indeed will not' happen. For him

---

important. The aim is still progressively to increase the share of the resources whose use is determined by political authority and the coercion of any dissenting minority' (p.317).

23 In *Question Seven*, ed. H. Hawton, Pemberton, London, 1974. My own reply there concentrates upon that aspect, 'In Defence of Reformism'.

24 *ibid.*, p.65.

25 *ibid.*, pp.62-3. The passage concludes with a disclaimer against their attempting 'to achieve socialism without a mass base clearly supporting them'. But the remainder of the article makes it quite clear that this implicit prerequisite is not construed as involving actual majority support publicly revealed by freely contested secret ballot elections.

26 *ibid.*, p.63.

27 *The Republic*, 416A-B.

the sole but sufficient guarantee is not strict Platonic education but 'a full commitment to socialist and indeed egalitarian values'.

Nielsen, therefore, never gives a moment's thought to constitutional checks and balances, the institutional separation of powers: all such worldly-wise and Whiggish concerns are, no doubt, expressions of an 'ideologically drugged state' — a product of manipulations by the bourgeois! Yet the only guarantee he either asks or offers surely has been and is, in his view, provided by all actual Leninist parties; although certainly we should question the authenticity of an egalitarianism which can co-exist with their 'pitiless centralism'.[28] Faced by such a cry of blind and wilful faith from someone having access to all the lessons of this tormented age — the very century of the Bolshevik October coup and of the Gulag Archipelago — are we to laugh; or to weep; or to shudder?

5 It will not have escaped notice that all my specific contemporary illustrations of the Guardian mentality have been socialist. Of course it is perfectly possible to combine this authoritarian mentality with a rejection of socialism. Plato himself, while proposing in *The Republic* that his elite should constitute a commune, tax-supported as a fully salaried Guardian service, never suggested that any such arrangements should be extended to the vulgar, engaged in the banausic business of production. (Plato was — like General de Gaulle — perhaps too little interested in 'the baggage train' either to require or to forbid the public ownership of all the means of production, distribution, and exchange!) The fact remains, nevertheless, that in today's world the most numerous and the most powerful class of actual or would-be Guardians are socialists: indeed nearly all are — in the words of an old song — Lenin's lads.

It is in a brief final section just worth suggesting that this is something more than an ephemeral contingency. The concentration of control which is of the essence of socialism must by its very nature both attract and foster the Guardian mentality; while as a matter of fact a socialist economy seems to be difficult if not impossible to reconcile with either the political institutions of (Western) democracy or the liberties which this demands.

(a) Consider, for instance, the evergreen false antithesis between production for profit and production for use. It is at least as old as Aristotle's *Politics* and at least as new as tomorrow's Labour Party political broadcast. The antithesis is false, for what ought to be the very obvious reason that

---

28 Rosa Luxemborg, 'One Step Forward, Two Steps Back', in *The Russian Revolution and Leninism or Marxism*, ed. B.D. Wolfe, University of Michigan Press, Ann Arbor, 1961, p.84.

there can be no profit in producing what no-one has any wish to buy and, presumably, to use. Of course, what plain or not-so-plain folk choose to buy may not be what superior and right-minded — or, as the case might be, left-minded — persons believe they ought to want: it may be conspicuous waste or, to borrow a favourite word of the Mark I Harold Wilson, candyfloss. Again, much may be, and certainly should be, said about people who cannot earn enough to buy even the most minimal necessities of life and health. But none of this justifies any general opposition between, on the one hand, the profit system or production for profit and, on the other hand, production for use or production to satisfy human needs.[29]

The true antithesis here is quite different. A market confronts a command economy: in the former what is produced is ultimately determined by what people with the money to buy will be prepared to buy; in the latter the crux is what people in a position to enforce their commands, choose to command. This comes out as clearly as could be wished from a section on 'Profit or Planning' in John Strachey's *Why You Should be a Socialist*, a work which made or guided a whole generation of converts in a decade after its first appearance as a massively circulated Left Book Club pamphlet: 'Well, we all know what production for profit means ... Under Socialism ... you have got to arrange some other principles on which to decide what to produce. This alternative principle of regulation we call planning. There must exist in every socialist society ... a planning commission, which will decide year by year what kinds of things, and in what proportions, shall be produced. It has ... to make an estimate of the total needs of the population, and then another estimate of the country's total productive resources. Then it must see how best to fit one to another ...'.[30]

In another, longer work Strachey put it even more succinctly: 'As Mr and Mrs Webb write, "Once private ownership, with its profit-seeking motive of production for the competitive market is abandoned, specific directions must be given as to what each establishment has to produce" '.[31]

Strachey continues in the pamphlet: 'Is not this a very difficult job?', you may say 'Yes, indeed it is'.[32] Never fear. We do not and shall not

---

29 For references, and fuller discussion, see my 'The Profit Motive' in *Ethics*, Chicago, forthcoming.
30 Gollancz, London, 1944, p.68.
31 *The Theory and Practice of Socialism*, Gollancz, London, 1936, p.57. The Webb statement comes from somewhere in, aptly, *Soviet Communism: A New Civilization*, Chapter XIII. Compare Note 22, above.
32 *ibid.*, p.68.

lack for Guardians eager to pronounce on our needs, and, with a minimum of reference to any actual wants which might be expressed in the market place, to issue what they consider to be the appropriate commands.[33]

(b) Turning to the question of the practical compatibility of a fully socialist economy with the political institutions of (Western) democracy, it seems that those with any pretensions to a dual devotion are nowadays most reluctant to face the challenge as put, either in such books as Milton Friedman's *Capitalism and Freedom*[34], or by abundant experience of the now very numerous fully socialist countries. Certainly the only response which I myself have got from such people in recent months has been a smirking irrelevance: triumphant pointings to certain countries, currently objects of strong left-wing hostility, in which a pluralist economy is conspicuously not combined with a (Western) democratic political structure. The actual challenge, of course, concerns not a sufficient but a necessary condition.[35]

So I will end by emphasising, not for the first time, that the Leninists themselves have no doubts at all. Indeed they seem now to see the incompatibility as a main reason for pressing always for immediate and wholesale nationalisation. Thus in a document entitled *The Falsifiers of Scientific Communism*, published early in 1972, the Institute of Marxist-Leninism in Moscow sketched a programme for the seizure of total and irremovable power by Communist Parties following united front tactics: 'Having once acquired political power, the working class implements the liquidation of the private ownership of the means of production ... As a result, under socialism, there remains no ground for the existence of any opposition parties counterbalancing the Communist Party'.[36] It does not have, of course, to be called the Communist Party; nor to be Muscovite as opposed — say — to Pekinese or nationally autonomous.

---

33 It is salutary to read words written, after he had been driven into exile as an enemy of socialism, by the leading economist of the Prague Spring. Ota Sik in *The Bureaucratic Economy* tells a sad tale of what happened 'once market prices, competitive pressure, the freedom to shop around, and earnings tied to success on the market were done away with'; while, 'Esconced in their splendid isolation, totally indifferent to whether industries showed profits or losses, the bureaucrats supervised all the processes of production and distribution', International Arts and Sciences Press, White Plains, N.Y., 1972, pp.5, 4.

34 University of Chicago Press, Chicago, 1962. Compare, for instance, Samuel Brittan's *Capitalism and the Permissive Society*, Macmillan, London, 1973, or *The Case for Capitalism*, eds. M. Ivens and R. Dunstan, Joseph, London, 1967, or F.A. Hayek *The Road to Serfdom*, Routledge, London, 1944.

35 See, for instance, Friedman *loc.cit.*, pp.9-10.

36 Quoted in *The Economist*, London, June 17, 1972, p.23: I have since acquired a photocopy of the original Russian text.

The Politics of Needs — or, Who Needs Politics?

Neil McInnes

The attempt to mark off needs from wants is one version of the ancient distinction between Nature and Convention. The securing of needs is held to be natural, properly human activity whereas the securing of wants is merely conventional, artificial or 'socially determined' activity. It has happened before today that this supposed distinction was taken as basis for a social policy. One instance of that was the doctrine of Natural Law. In its eighteenth century version, that doctrine sought to separate what was natural to man (for example being 'born free') from what was historical, social or conventional (for example being 'everywhere in chains'). This led to the alliance of the doctrinaires of Natural Law with the enlightened despots, in a joint struggle against feudalism, the Church, the aristocracy, customary privilege and local liberties. The doctrinaires and despots were offering to promote everybody's natural needs, and in order to do so they said they must first limit or prohibit the artificial, conventional wants of certain classes.

Again today the Nature-Convention dichotomy, in the shape of the needs-wants contrast, is offered as foundation for a 'politics of needs'. The contrast that is suggested is not a simple one. Needs and wants are not held to be mutually exclusive. They partly overlap. That is to say, there are activities that correspond both to needs and wants: the individual wants the things that needs-theorists say he actually does need. However, there are also needs that he does not want, either because he is not aware of them (as our ancestors were not aware of vitamins) or for more complicated psychological and social reasons. The political problem in that case, according to the needs-theorists, would be to bring the individual to want those needs or else to promote them, administer to them, whether or not they were wanted. Finally there are wants that do not correspond to needs: the individual wants things that the needs-theorists say he does not need. It is this class of activities that will be called in this essay 'wants' simply; the other activities that are said to correspond to an objective need, whether wanted or not, will be called 'needs'.

A politics of needs would depend on making good the distinction between needs and wants and then proposing ways to promote the former. Such promotion of need-satisfying activities would be at the expense of want-satisfying activities whenever policy entailed allocating limited resources to certain 'priorities'; but even when no economic question was clearly raised, policy might still seek to deny the satisfaction of wants because their conventional origin was thought to show that they were superfluous, fatuous, nefarious or immoral.

The first point for such a proposed policy, then, would be to establish the distinction between needs and wants. (To avoid the cumbersome phrases 'need-satisfying activities' and 'want-satisfying activities', 'needs and wants' will be used for short, but the reference is always to certain concrete activities or enterprises.) The criterion for that distinction is a sanction which backs needs but not wants. At the level of simple bodily functions it has been argued that unless needs are met, sickness or death ensues, whereas that is not true of wants. At the level of more complicated activities the sanction proposed is not physical but mental ill-health, firstly individual neurosis, secondly, if many people are affected, social instability ('a sick society'). Of these two sanctions, it is the second, mental health, that is the more commonly discussed in contemporary needs theory, since that theory arose in prosperous societies that catered for most (though by no means all) people's basic physical needs, as these are described by needs-theorists. For example, the first two classes of needs that Maslow describes[1], namely physical or biological needs and survival or safety needs, have sickness or death as their sanction. They were the concern of earlier generations of needs-theorists, from the utilitarians to the socialists. It is the last three classes of Maslow's needs – the needs of belongingness, esteem and self-

---

1 Abraham Maslow, *Motivation and Personality*, Harper and Row, New York, 1954.

actualisation, which have mental ill-health (and social instability) for their sanction, that are the concern of contemporary needs-theorists. The reason they give is that militarism, violence, aggressiveness and all sorts of unhappiness flourish in societies that cater adequately for physical needs. These things, it was argued invoking modern psychology, arose because psychological *needs* were being denied or else satisfied in dangerous, vicarious ways. The clue to what genuine needs *are* lies in the study of individual and social derangement, for that study leads us to construct a picture of mental health (and hence of social health) such as might never have existed, but would if genuine needs were satisfied.

Thus needs, it is urged, are not simply wants supported by authority but activities that have, unlike wants, an objective necessity. 'If one of the basic [needs] has found no fulfilment, insanity is the result; if it is satisfied but in an unsatisfactory way [sic] — considering the nature of human existence — neurosis (either manifest or in the form of a socially patterned defect) is the consequence'.[2] In political terms, Fromm explains, this means that where needs are not met people become 'frightened, suspicious, lonely', unable 'to function effectively or intelligently'; they show 'apathy or such impairment of intelligence, initiative and skills that they gradually fail to perform [their social] functions'; *or else* 'they react by the accumulation of such hate and destructiveness as to bring about an end to themselves, their rulers and their system'.[3] Denied wants, it is implied, do not have these consequences. Needs are at one and the same time objective facts *and* the criteria or norms of mental health[4], and therefore the norms of a healthy society, one where policy is addressed to their satisfaction. This is the contemporary form of the politics of needs, which draws its notion of needs and of mental health from post-Freudian 'humanist psychology'.

It will be argued in this essay (1) that the criterion of mental health is too vague to be helpful in distinguishing two classes of activities, needs and wants. Secondly, it will be recalled (2) that individual psychology is of no direct relevance to political theory. On the contrary, the political is prior to the psychological and that is why theories of mental health include a reference to needs for something 'bigger than the individual', that is to an institution or social movement. It follows (3) that the effort to derive politics from mental health entails circular reasoning. Then it

---

2 Erich Fromm, *The Sane Society,* Routledge and Kegan Paul, London, 1973, p.68.
3 Fromm, *op.cit.,* p.18-19.
4 Fromm, *op.cit.,* p.193-4.

will be recalled (4) that the sanction of political opposition, carried to the point of revolt and 'social breakdown', has backed the most conventional and arbitrary of wants, wants that nobody would dream of calling requirements for mental health. Lastly, (5) we shall make clear some of the totalitarian implications of a policy based on one standard set of universal, unvarying and compulsory needs.

* * *

(1) It is a familiar figure of political rhetoric to present our demands as needs and another party's as mere wants, but orators would not claim to have an exhaustive list of needs in hand. The humanist psychologists do, but their lists are various and arbitrary. 'Security, intimacy and sexual satisfaction', says one[5]; 'relatedness, creativeness, rootedness, sense of identity, devotion and rationality', replies another[6]; basic biological needs, belongingness or rootedness, esteem and self-actualisation, counters a third.[7]

We are never shown how these lists (which are of both basic needs *and* the criteria of mental health) are arrived at, nor why there should not be other needs. They are simply thrown at our heads, often with the argument from authority that they come from 'long clinical experience'. In fact, their positive content is 'thin and indeterminate'.[8] When the humanist psychologists describe mental health, they deliver a sermon full of the weasel-words (qualifying and contradictory phrases) that empty it of pragmatic content. For example, when we are mentally healthy we are 'more fully human'[9]; 'fully born ... fully awake ... [know] our real but limited strength [and have ideas that are] truly ours'; that is five references to quantity without any standard of measurement being provided. Also, we 'love life ... accept death'; we know we are 'the most important ... and at the same time not more important than a fly'; we 'tolerate uncertainty ... have faith'; we like to be 'alone ... one with all'; that is, four contradictions. A nebulous 'conscience' and 'grasp of reality' complete this homily-definition.[10] Whatever use it might be to impressionable people in the clinical situation, it is too vague to found a politics. Yet Fromm claims to get from it a 'sane politics' that allows him to identify 'socially harmful'

5 H.S. Sullivan, *The Interpersonal Theory of Psychiatry*, Norton, New York, 1953, p.264.
6 Fromm, *op.cit.*, p.30-65.
7 Maslow, *loc.cit.*
8 *The Healthy Personality: Readings*, eds. Hung-Min Chiang and A. Maslow, Van Nostrand Reinhold, New York, 1969, p.24.
9 Maslow, *ibid.*, p.35.
10 Fromm, *op.cit.*, p.203-4.

activities, which he will have the state regulate, nationalise or put down.[11] (His examples of 'socially harmful' activities are earning profits, seeing American movies, and reading comic books and the crime pages.[12]) All that is certain about a politics based on vague but authoritatively decreed norms is that it would be repressive and arbitrary. Activities would be favoured or forbidden on grounds that cannot be clearly explained.

(2) The difficulty with a psychological approach to politics is that it leads to individualism. On the one hand, there are atomic individuals whose needs and wants spring from within themselves; and on the other hand, there is Society, which alternately provides and withholds satisfactions. This might be called *the view from the cradle*, for it is literally infantile in its contrast of Me with a World that now satisfies, now denies my cravings. Such a doctrine can give no account of the vast majority of individual activities, which are social, nor can it explain the origin and nature of society, if this is not those same activities seen, as they must be, independent of individuals.

The humanist psychologists have the customary trouble negotiating this *pons asinorum* from individuals to politics. They can show nothing against the proposition that a society composed entirely of mentally healthy persons would nevertheless be politically divided, and divided to the point of violence if those persons were deeply attached to irreconcilable social movements. Their argument is instructive, however, in that after dissolving society into individuals (*that* gives the psychologist his licence to discuss politics with authority), they smuggle society back in again, in the shape of certain basic individual needs for ... society. Now, since those needs were to determine a politics, they are caught in circular reasoning: the needs are already political. This fact is disguised by talking of needs for 'rootedness', 'relatedness', 'herd identity', 'status and conformity'[13] or 'feelings of belongingness and rootedness', devotion to 'some task, call, vocation, beloved work ("outside themselves")', feelings of 'duty, obligation or responsibility'[14] — all the time without saying that the unstated term of these relations of needing and feeling is nothing but a social institution or cause, something of a definite political colour. Maslow described very well, in his account of 'self-actualizing people' (the mentally healthy) what it feels like for the individual to be taken up into something 'bigger than himself'

---

11 Fromm, *op.cit.*, pp.334 and 361.
12 Fromm, *op.cit.*, p.334.
13 Fromm, *op.cit.*, pp.30-6, 38-60, 63.
14 Maslow, *op.cit.*, p.35-8.

but he avoids specifying that that something is a social, or even narrowly political, fact: a way of life or movement, which already has a policy.

(3) This deliberate vagueness, the repeated use of a relation without mentioning one of its terms, might well stem from the circumspection of the American psychologist, always anxious to 'keep politics out of it'. But also and more importantly it covers over a logical difficulty that lies at the heart of the politics of needs. Social policy was to be deduced scientifically from the needs of the mentally healthy person but it turns out that the mentally healthy person, by definition, already has allegiance to some social policy or other. This gets us nowhere. To offer to illuminate a social conflict between, say, capitalist enterprises and communes, or between Catholicism and Marxism, by deducing the correct policy from the needs of the mentally healthy is circular if you presuppose that the mentally healthy person is one who already has been 'taken up into' capitalist enterprise or a commune, Catholicism or communism. Perhaps a way out of the circularity would lie in saying that the mentally healthy had been 'taken up into' some *other* movement or institution. But then, apart from the fact that the other institution is never named, with the result that *its* policies are being advocated surreptitiously, there is the consideration that this only gets us to some other set of prior policies. The mentally healthy would be intervening in a political dispute with the opinions characteristic of a third political force. We would in no way have escaped from the battlefield of politics to some secure vantage point of non-political mental health and its basic needs. Social attachment *is* one of those basic needs, say the humanist psychologists (two millenia after Aristotle said man was *zoon politikon*). Accordingly we might as well study social affairs by staying with the various political things individuals are said to need, that is the various, concrete social movements or activities or enterprises that they 'need' to participate in, in order to be satisfied, healthy beings, instead of making the unnecessary detour via individual needs. Such needs are an otiose entity in politics.

(4) Needs are to be distinguished from wants by a sanction: if needs are not met, individuals become neurotic and aggressive, and this is said to lead to the political facts of revolt or social breakdown.[15] So if we could show that the suppression of mere wants also arouses opposition that can go to the extent of revolt and 'social breakdown', the distinction would fail. That would be easy to show, for human history is full of the wreckage of movements (including absolute government) that sought to put down

---

15 Fromm, *op.cit.*, p.18-19.

religious fanaticism or cruel social customs or bull-fighting or luxury or gambling or drug-taking or slave-owning — and were swept away, although none of those things corresponds to a need in the psychologists' sense (or perhaps in any other). Indeed, in one and the same society the suppression of apparently nefarious wants can encounter more political opposition than the denial of 'basic needs'. Napoleon I had more trouble curbing illicit distilling or Krushchev the abuse of vodka, than either had in denying their subjects' 'basic needs', whether for personal integrity or food. And the humanist psychologists propose to suppress wants more generally felt than that of alcohol. Fromm, for example, denounces as incompatible with mental health, profit-making (more generally even, 'the profit motive'), economic inequality and 'incestuous ties to clan and soil'[16] — that is, capitalism, hierarchy and patriotism. Yet the movements that oppose those three things, namely socialism, egalitarianism and cosmopolitanism respectively, have encountered, and will always encounter, serious resistance.

The needs-theorists are correct in trying to give their subject political relevance by arguing that needs have a sanction, a social might, for this is what politics is about, might against might. However, they are wrong to imagine that, among demands, only their needs have might. All social activities have their measure of might (and hence their *rights*, what they can enforce), and those of them that at a given moment have a high degree of efficacy we call political forces. It is innocent to wander on to the political battlefield proclaiming the discovery that the correct policy is the one that is ultimately backed by might, by opposition and revolt, for that is true of all the forces there, to varying degrees.

The needs-wants distinction fails, too, if we put it in terms not of the sanction but of social utility (of which, naturally, there are many different conceptions). Some want-satisfying activities that in a Marxist, humanist or simply demagogic view are 'less useful' than the need-satisfying activities can be shown to be essential prerequisites for them, in contemporary societies at least. That all should eat before there are feasts for the few is a principle still alive in Russia and China (whence the virtual absence of restaurants); and universal literacy used to be urged in India as a basic and thus more urgent need than superfluities like more universities. Yet luxury and higher learning are essential for, and causes of, a productive economy and an educated society. By seeking to satisfy 'everybody's needs' before 'some people's wants', a system can fail to satisfy either. Whereupon (to revert to the sanction) it is the opposition of 'some people' that is

---

16 Fromm, *op.cit.*, pp.69, 361.

more dangerous to the regime than the dissatisfaction of 'everybody'. That is why, for all their evident failures in the 'material sphere', the Chinese and Russian regimes are most vulnerable because they have caused a famine of enjoyment and intellectual undernourishment. Since wants are as politically efficacious as needs, the distinction either fails or is politically irrelevant.

*   *   *

(5) To find the totalitarian implications of this doctrine, we can recall the vagueness of needs-theorists about the actual social institutions that the healthy mind, by their definition, is devoted to. By not specifying them, one might hope to gloss over their multiplicity and their conflict, or even to give the impression that they are a unity, exemplifying one set of standards. In short, one could try to hide politics. Indeed, Maslow, in his later and more metaphysical work, actually speculates that the objects of the social needs of the healthy mind are all one: they are all 'equally potent' and 'form a unity of some sort', each being 'simply the whole seen from another angle'.[17] Significantly, he no sooner poses this 'unity of values' than he adds that 'values call for behavioural expression or "celebration"'[18]; they 'command adoration, reverence, celebration, sacrifice'. They are worth living for and dying for'.[19] If they are really one, then, this is the plan for the monolithic cult of a social dogma, the consecration of one set of social activities as expressing all healthy needs — the very cult and consecration practised by all totalitarian regimes. Maslow evaded that conclusion, which might have been personally distasteful to him, only by lapsing into religiosity.[20]

Needs-theorists cannot evade the inferences that, if there were a limited set of natural needs, then the activities that secure them would be promoted by all correct policies, and engaged in by all rational citizens. It would be obligatory for the state to foster them and, indeed, politically dangerous for it not to do so. It would be logical and proper for a citizen to engage in them and hence it would eventually be compulsory; if he did not do so, he would be deviating from the human norm or showing ignorance of what he needed, and on both scores stands to be corrected by his rulers. The totalitarian implications of this one set of universal requirements

17 Maslow, *op.cit.*, p.46-7.
18 Maslow, *op.cit.*, p.53-5.
19 Maslow, *op.cit.*, p.55.
20 Maslow, *op.cit.*, p.55.

THE POLITICS OF NEEDS — OR, WHO NEEDS POLITICS?   237

are more evident when the economic problem is borne in mind. Resources, including time, are limited, so the compulsory satisfaction of 'needs' must be at the expense of 'wants'. Certain activities would have to be curbed, or else priced out of the market. That is to say, even if they were not forbidden by the state, the massive diversion of resources to meet the demand for approved objects of need (and needs that are proclaimed universal and proper will come to be declared compulsory) would soon make unapproved activities impossible. Whatever materials they required would soon become impossibly expensive. It is enough to think of the impoverishment, and denial of other wants, that were suffered when unlimited demand was created for Swedish housing, British medical services or Soviet defence, that is, the needs of an earlier generation of needs-theorists which have secured state backing.

After the economic, there is the historical question. Natural needs would be unchanging, except in so far as human nature changed. That latter possibility seems not to be even envisaged by needs-theorists. 'Summing up, it can be said that the concept of mental health follows from the very conditions of human existence, and it is *the same for men in all ages and all cultures*[21], decrees Fromm. Maslow thought that the 'meta-needs' he had discovered corresponded to 'the eternal and absolute that mankind has always sought', because 'they are *per se*, in their own right, not dependent upon human vagaries for their existence. They are perceived, not invented. They are trans-human and trans-individual. They exist beyond the life of the individual. They can be conceived to be a kind of perfection. They could conceivably satisfy the human need for certainty'.[22] It is always hazardous to guess Maslow's meaning, but it seems he would agree with Fromm (and of course with the Plato of *The Republic*) that needs find expression in objective social activities which are fixed and unchanging.

In this respect, needs-theory is following in the footsteps of its ancestor, Natural Law theory. The static character of Natural Law — the fact that it began as a revolutionary challenge to unjust positive laws but ended by putting up other positive laws, its own, beyond the reach of amendment and criticism — came to be seen as a fatal fault. Thereupon there was invented the contradictory notion of 'Natural Law with variable content'.[23] Needs-theory has not yet, that I know, perceived this historical difficulty, and it is still seeking to base policy on an unchanging set of human needs.

---

21 Fromm, *op.cit.,* p.69. Italics mine.
22 Maslow, *op.cit.,* p.55.
23 Rudolf Stammler, *The Theory of Justice,* Kelley, Clifton, New Jersey, 1925.

In practice, that would place those entrusted with the application of that policy under the obligation to ensure that needs really did not evolve. To propose new needs, or to suggest that recognised ones no longer be given priority, or merely to press unofficial wants, would not be, as in capitalist democracy, a matter of moral criticism and market economics, but a political, indeed an institutional, question. At the limit, it would be subversion. How near that limit can be is suggested by the political crises that arise in the Soviet Union whenever revision of the accepted list of needs is proposed (as by Trotsky, Stalin, Malenkov or Krushchev), along with the consequent change in industrial policy.

The maintenance of an unchanging (or even slowly changing) conception of natural needs requires that economic enterprise and moral criticism be restrained, even outlawed, because they are forever proposing a 'revaluation of values', that is, a revision of needs. This problem was familiar to the authors of communist utopias, who all catered only for a short list of needs assumed to be fixed. Therefore they set their perfect static polity in a remote place (an island was best), forbade trade and cultural intercourse with foreigners, fixed the population size once and for all, banned changes in fashion, regulated technology (when they even thought of that explosive force) and looked with suspicion on poets, philosophers and similar agitators. As long as needs-theory embodies the same assumption of policy based on unchanging needs, it must propose similar precautions. (It is not always noticed that the illiberalism and suspicion of contemporary communist regimes in cultural affairs apparently remote from practical life are dictated not by ideological purity but by the necessity to prevent moral criticism calling in question the fixed list of economic needs on which official policy is based.)

Of course needs-theorists have seen the danger that their doctrine could be used to justify and enforce conformism. How could they overlook this, when the notion of 'mental health' arose in the same psychology schools as produced the blatantly political theory of 'adjustment'.[24] Their defence is a spirited attack on conformism – in the name of individuality. Having seen the political danger inherent in the single list of natural needs, they exclaim, 'But don't forget individuals differ!'.[25] However, when asked *how* they differ, the psychologists reply lamely, 'by occupation, social position, marriage and a host of other circumstances'.[26] This is the same effort to

---

24 Robert W. White, in *The Healthy Personality, op.cit.,* p.24.
25 Cf. Maslow's studies of individuals in *Motivation and Personality, op.cit.*
26 White, *op.cit.,* p.28.

hide politics that we encountered in the omission to specify the social facts to which healthy individuals are devoted. Unless the variety of moralities and policies has been stuffed away in that ragbag, 'a host of other circumstances', this presentation omits the fact that the politically important differences between individuals cut across occupational, social and marital status. They consist in an attachment to different moralities and policies.

Once the multiplicity of social standards is denied or hushed up, it serves nothing to seek to combat conformism by glorifying the self-actualisation of the individual. One is still left with, on the one hand, a unitary Society in which only one set of standards (normal needs) is admitted, and, on the other hand, atomic individuals dedicated to the private task of self-perfection — private, because it never questions the one set of public standards. One recognises here that combination of fake individualism and real conformism that was said to typify parts of American society before the 'values' of capitalist free enterprise were called in question in the 1960s.

It is necessary to look briefly at the notion of the 'supreme need', that for self-realisation, or what Fromm calls 'the total needs of man ... the unfolding of his powers'.[27] Firstly, this idea runs back to the radical humanism of the Romantics and of the young Marx, and hence it secures for needs-theory a measure of support from contemporary Marxist humanism. Secondly, as we have seen, it constitutes the defence of needs-theory from the charge that it encourages a totalitarian conformism: against the threat of a uniform set of compulsory needs, it glorifies one superior need, the need for the individuality of each 'whole man'. In other words, the conformism of a society in which only one set of needs was approved would be relieved by each person 'doing his own thing'. The vagueness of the expression is due to the vacuity of the idea. The offer to cultivate individuality without permitting a variety of social standards is bluff. What social activity would we have to engage in to secure self-realisation or the total satisfaction of all our needs? Where is the institution that caters not to one definable need but to 'self' or 'wholeness' or 'totality'? The notion is pragmatically empty, like the question, 'What must I do to be saved?'

A need (to use for a moment the relational manner of speaking of the psychologists, instead of the language of activities) must be of something specific. So a need of wholeness or totality is one of two things. Either it is a need of one more specific thing, whereupon it is another *part* of the self and has no way of winning sovereign power over needs for other specific things. Or else it is merely a governing principle or overriding

---

27 Fromm, *op.cit.*, p.29.

sentiment, and then it lacks a specific object, it has no force to command and no particular activity in which to manifest itself. One is obliged to suspect that 'self-realisation' is playing the familiar role of *ultimate objectives* in idealist theory: it is the one thing that all partial needs are 'really' aiming at, and therefore all those needs are 'really' identical since they are all needs of the one thing. This obliteration of differences would be in line with the hiding of political differences practised by the theorists of mental health — and remember that it was in order to avoid the totalitarian implications of that political monism that the notion of the unique whole self was introduced. We have lurched from political monism to psychological monism, from 'All social activities are really one' to 'All psychological needs are really one', but political plurality and moral conflict have not been recognised.

Before leaving the notion of self-realisation and the whole man, one might point out that nothing we have said weighs against the fact that individuals often achieve a nice balance or 'mix' of activities. They satisfy various needs or wants in what strikes them or others as harmonious proportions. If they do not, if the balance is perpetually shifting, we would say they were unstable persons, whereas if it is relatively steady we might call it their personality or character or destiny. It can happen that some such combinations seem to some observers especially felicitous, coherent and well-rounded. Before holding them up as examples of self-realisation, however, we would need to note that there is an indefinite number of such combinations (many of them socially incompatible with one another) and it is therefore not helpful to lump them all together. Secondly, it is quite misleading to suggest that the harmonious combinations came about by being willed, or by being needed, by some superior force, the drive for wholeness or self-realisation. Above all, it would be erroneous to pronounce any judgement as to wholeness or coherence in personality without taking account of the variety of moral and political standards that it was the purpose of self-realisation to gloss over. A person who may be said to have found a coherent and 'fully satisfying' life in business or in missionary work might be judged a stunted scoundrel by a person of different persuasion. Naturally, it is open to the psychologist to ignore such moral and political divergencies (as it is to the physician, pharmacist and undertaker) but then he cannot claim to have discovered the key to politics by ignoring its substance.

*   *   *

The latest — psychological — version of the politics of needs was elaborated by the post-Freudians during and soon after the war. However, as a political phenomenon its hour struck only in the 1960s, when it was taken up by the New Left. The transition from an older theory of needs to the latest one is described by Klaus Mehnert in these terms:

> All socialists . . . always assumed that freedom from material want would make mankind happier and more free. On that reasoning, wherever material hunger was satisfied, contentment must reign. Instead of that, Western youth is rebellious, and precisely the youth of these social strata that have not known physical hunger for a long while. Many young people turn away in outrage from society precisely when society achieves the age-old dream of mankind, the satisfaction of material needs. So there must be [i.e. on the socialist assumption] some other kind of need — intellectual and spiritual hunger. So far, so good. The West reached this conclusion long ago, and the New Left helped. Now Moscow picks it up. Just when the West has satisfied, without revolution, the material needs of hundreds of millions of people to an extent inconceivable to Marx, the Soviet ideologists prophesy a new revolution for the fulfilment of the intellectual and spiritual needs of the Western citizen.[28]

The coarse, propagandist version of that notion is: 'Capitalism need no longer pocket its profits at the expense of the masses' obvious [physical] needs, but it does use every opportunity to enrich itself at the expense of their chronic intellectual-spiritual needs. Only the form of the exploitation has changed; its essence has remained the same'.[29]

That way of telling the story may help show how the new theory of needs became popular, but of course we are under no obligation to look at the political problem of the needy from the sole point of view of socialist history. We could, as accurately if not more so, tell it as follows (with special reference to Britain).

A care for the needy has always been a part of western civilisation, notably in Britain. For centuries, this had little to do with politics, but was the concern of churches and charities. Even when, at the Reformation, the parish ceased to be solely a church institution and assumed secular functions (whereupon voluntary contributions were transformed into compulsory rates), this political benevolence remained a local (county) affair. Moreover, political benevolence was still secondary in importance to private philanthropy and free co-operation. The Benthamites provided the theory

---

28 Klaus Mehnert, *Moscow and the New Left*, tr. Fischer and Wilson, University of California Press, Berkeley and Los Angeles, 1975. I have thought it necessary to amend the translation slightly.

29 Mehnert cites this from two Russian authors (p.61; the translation has been slightly amended) but it is a commonplace of New Left, and now official Communist Party, doctrine.

for the gradual centralisation of benevolence in the hands of the state but it was not until the first World War that centralisation made great progress. During the war, also, the wartime mentality justified a concern on the part of the state not only for the needy but for certain general needs. The nationalisation of benevolence was carried through during the second World War, even before the socialist victory of 1945, but it was the postwar Labour Government that completed the transformation of benevolence from a concern for some people into a concern for all people's needs. The objects of that concern were no longer a particular group, *the needy*, but the totality of *needs* — needs of education, health, 'welfare' and 'security', the last two being open-ended concepts that could receive almost any content. At least the total approach was the theory; in practice, some distinctions still had to be drawn (in the shape of a means test) but this was done belatedly, reluctantly and, it was hoped, temporarily. The totality of needs was the ultimate subject of policy.

It is familiar that the unleashing of virtually unlimited demand for a set of approved, recommended services led to inflation, bureaucracy, the crowding out of other activities and various unforeseen social shifts whose consequences will take decades to appear. Less often noticed is the transformation of a universal need catered for by the state into a compulsory requirement that the state lays upon each citizen. Firstly, the need is, perforce, standardised according to bureaucratic norms that will not tolerate deviant wants. Then, once the state decrees that this standard object or service is needed, it often ceases to be wanted — and has to be forcibly administered. This may be seen most clearly in the case of education.[30] Learning is decreed to be a universal need, so it is presented in standardised, uniform, egalitarian services (such as comprehensive schools), which stifle local initiative and regional differences. The undiscriminating, total approach is even pushed to the point of dropping not only a means test but even a merit test, which might have shown which children *want* education. Thereupon education comes to be seen by many of its recipients as something the state purveys, like conscription or taxes, and which hence could not decently be wanted. So, many schoolchildren and students become the adversaries of educators. A need, a state requirement, has killed a want, which is a personal choice. By a similar process, much use of the health services is made by people who do not so much want to get well and stay well, as a matter of personal responsibility, as wish to settle

---

30 See Bryan Wilson's contribution to the pamphlet *Is Britain a Fair Society?*, London, 1976.

a score with the state, 'get their money back'. The adversary approach had led to the deliberate plundering of social services by some of the beneficiaries.

As against the total approach to universal needs, the tradition of care for *the needy* could well be maintained by a modern society. Not only could the familiar needy class (the poor who are always with us) be assisted in new ways (Milton Friedman's suggestion for a minimum *income* is one such) but new classes of needy persons could be identified. Neglected children, lonely old people, battered wives and alcoholics are examples of new classes of needy persons who have been clearly identified only in our day, sometimes by social work, more often by a change in sensibilities and standards. All can be helped without recourse to a general theory of needs and without massive intervention by the state.

This is a process that is bound to continue in societies with a long tradition of benevolence, and it is one that the post-Freudian[31] humanist psychologists could have contributed to. In their studies of aggressiveness, insecurity and various neuroses, the psychologists carried further our understanding of a new class of needy persons, people who suffer a lack that requires the help of others to fill. The psychologists thereby opened the way to a new benevolence to be exercised by a variety of institutions (not only or even primarily the state). Unfortunately, some of the psychologists chose another course. They drew up lists of the defects and lacks of their patients and said such a list constituted the catalogue of natural universal human needs, and then encouraged the illusion that the state could cater to those needs if only it adopted the correct policies. The guide to correct policy would be the ideal of 'mental health' — but since each psychologist elaborated this intellectual construction, 'mental health', by taking the opposites of the lacks of his particular patients, no two definitions agreed. To invite the bureaucracy to try its hand at a new and total approach to human needs on that arbitrary basis was to invite the threat of a collectivist, conformist and totalitarian polity.

---

31 Post-Freudian in the precise sense of following on from Freud's social reflections, notably in *Civilisation and its Discontents*.

The Quest for a Concept of Needs

Conal Condren

*'Now', seyde sir Gawayne, '... without longer abydynge, I shall laboure
in the queste of the Sankgreal ... and never shall I returne unto the
courte agayne tyll I have sene hit more opynly than hit hath bene shewed
here ...'**

1 Initially, the controversy with which this collection is concerned may
be summarised as follows: Can we conceptualise precisely the idea of human
needs, and then individuate and rank specific needs under the auspices
of such a conception for the purpose of giving more rational and just guidance to political activity? This needs controversy seems central to our
choices and priorities in, and even the legitimacy of our political
society.[1]

2 The controversy has been developed and sustained on a fairly abstract
level of discourse from a number of different perspectives. Nevertheless

---

* Sir Thomas Malory, 'The Tale of the Sankgreal: The Departure' in *Works*, ed. E.
 Vinaver, Oxford University Press, London, 1954.
1 See, for example, W. J. Meyer, 'Democracy: Needs over Wants', *Political Theory*, Vol.2,
 1974, pp.197-214; C. Bay, 'Needs, Wants and Political Legitimacy', *Canadian Journal
 of Political Science*, Vol.I, 1968, pp.241ff; H. Marcuse, *One Dimensional Man: The Ideology of Industrial Society*, Routledge, London, 1964.

the controversy has taken on a discernible character appropriate to 'political theory', this expression being both general enough to encompass diversity of approach, and specific enough to intimate some sense of community identity. The sense of identity amongst political theorists is not derived solely from the subject matter – politics – which is in itself a weak cement. It is derived primarily from certain shared procedures, general criteria of judgement, and orthodoxies of argument that are brought to bear upon, or are revealed through, consideration of any given problem. These I shall refer to as conventions, but I shall specify only those which are necessary for my argument.[2]

A relatively stable, self-conscious political theory community exists mainly in universities clustered generally in departments of politics, philosophy, sociology and history. It is by and large a professional community, and some sense of its identity may be due to this fact, perhaps as a sense of historical identity and community was fostered by the study of history becoming an established profession in the nineteenth century.[3]

In any relatively discrete community of activity there is not only a propensity towards studying an extrinsic subject matter, but also a propensity towards introspection, towards a concern with the character and the conduct of the community activity itself. This second propensity is of paramount importance in that without an assumed or explicitly accepted understanding of the character of the activity, it is not possible to participate consciously in its discussions, or to have any clear sense of its appropriate extrinsic subject matter.

3 In the light of these propensities we may delineate a typology of argument: (a) extrinsic and (b) reflexive. For an historian examples of the first might be the question of the madness of George III or the sanity of Rasputin, and of the second the question of how Burkhardt or Gibbon used their sources. Examples of (a) and (b) are easily connected, and problems initially or apparently subsumed under (a) may shift to or be better understood under (b). Problems in the history of the Renaissance may always change into problems in the historiography of the Renaissance, as the focus of attention shifts from the character of a period in time to the character

---

2 I do not mean that the needs controversy is sustained by those who teach political theory; simply that those who participate in the controversy, are, *ipso facto*, engaged in what we generally recognise as political theory, by virtue (primarily) of the conventions employed.

3 D. Forbes, *The Liberal Anglican Idea of History*, Cambridge University Press, Cambridge, 1952, p. 184.

of an historical concept.[4] When any (a)/(b) shift is made the purpose of enquiry changes, and the initial extrinsic problem becomes primarily one of a whole range of potential means to a reflexive end; an end of direct significance to all engaged in the activity, not just to specialists in a finite range of extrinsic problems. What is sometimes called the Wittgensteinian revolution in philosophy was primarily concerned with how philosophers should understand human verbal activity. It was (probably like all philosophic revolutions), a reflexive revolution. And it is doubtful if it had much more effect on non-philosophical verbal activity (the extrinsic raw material) than Lévi-Strauss' kinship theories have had on the mating habits of the Aranda. Again, the primary importance for historians and anthropologists of the work of Namier *(The Structure of Politics at the Accession of George III)* and Marcel Mauss *(L'Essai sur le don)* lay not in what each said, respectively, about political patronage amongst the English eighteenth century squirarchy or gift-giving amongst the Trobriand Islanders. It lay in the fact that each presented to his professional audience far-reaching arguments about the character and potentialities of a specific intellectual activity through the medium of the extrinsic subject matter. Reflexive controversies, by nature scholastic controversies, have wide-ranging ramifications within a given community as a whole. Such controversies are the means by which an iconoclast becomes a founding father; by which a community is cohered or fragmented, its purposes fixed or forged anew. The effect, however, of reflexive controversy upon the extrinsic subject matter of the activity is contingent upon the discretion between the subject matter and the established activity; the further removed the activity from the subject matter, the less the effects of reflexive controversy. The more stable the relationship is between activity and subject, the more calculable are the effects of reflexive dispute.

4 Political theory has a complex and incoherent intellectual character, revealing a blend of philosophical, historical and sociological conventions variously mixed with elements of political ideological commitment.[5] Elucidating the relationship of this activity with its extrinsic subject matter is less a case of delineating fixed contours than of plotting the ebb and flow of an uncertain tide. My suggestion here is that although the needs

---

4 J. Huizinga, 'The Problem of the Renaissance' in *Men and Ideas*, tr. S. Holmes and Hans van Marle, Meridian New York, 1959, p.245 and note p.364.

5 C. Condren, 'Three Aspects of Political Theory' in *The Pieces of Politics*, ed. R. Lucy, Macmillan, Melbourne, 1975, pp.67-103.

controversy may appear to be a species of extrinsic problem, and may most naturally be formulated as being about political activity (see above 1), it is best seen as a reflexive problem. It is primarily a series of arguments about the character and purpose of a fairly esoteric and neoteric activity. The arguments are vital to the activity as a whole, but they are likely to leave the ostensible subject matter of political theorising untouched or effected but capriciously. The controversy is a scholastic one.

If medieval theologians had really argued about how many angels could dance on the head of a pin, we would fall fundamentally into error if we took the dispute to be concerned with the nature of pins or the size of angels' feet.[6] Certainly the existence of pins is presupposed by the formulation of the problem, but if it had been discussed, it would have been because of certain implications and possibilities inherent in specialised concepts and modes of argument conventionally accepted by a coherent and self-conscious theological community. If there is a problem about human needs and political prescriptions, it is best seen not primarily as a matter of choosing between the manufacture of exploding heavenly bodies or pin-tables, but as a means by which a hitherto fragile intellectual community is seeking to stabilise and legitimise itself in the eyes of different judges. Despite the aura of political urgency attending much of the discussion about conceptualising and applying an idea of human needs, those to whom we normally refer as politicians may be relieved to know that this has less to do directly with their intentions, achievements and failures, than with those of a professional university community whose rhetoric helps identify its own members, hopefully fostering a more purposeful sense of community.[7]

5 We may begin to see the reflexive nature of the needs controversy by noting the lineage that is sometimes invoked to indicate the intellectual status of the task of conceptualising needs. Most communities, be they intellectual, economic or political, achieve and maintain a sense of identity and relative association with others through reference to a select and everpresent past — a microcosm of the family tree. This lineage functions

---

6 There may be such a theological *quaestio* as this concerning the implications of the concept of the incorporeal, but as far as I am aware, the angel/pin problem is a later parody. Robert Graves, *The White Goddess*, Faber, London, 1962, p.44, quotes an early medieval Welsh poem 'Room for a million angels/On my knife point, it appears', but as the text is corrupt and amended (vide Graves) this may be a later addition.

7 Essentially the same point about medieval 'historians' is made by R.W. Hanning discussing B. Lacroix, *L'historien au moyen âge*, Paris, 1971. See *History and Theory*, Vol.4, 1973, pp.424-5.

to catalogue and justify the activities, achievements and concerns of the community. The appeal to such a lineage, or more precisely to a relationship with it, is *ipso facto* an argument for propriety of conduct according to the standards of the community. The lineage that political theory has created for itself, partly from those of political history, partly from that of philosophy, is ever in the background of the needs controversy.

6 Thus Christian Bay, the most eloquent and persistent advocate for the imperative task of conceptualising and applying needs for the sake of our political salvation, asserts that it is only a present theoretical aberration that has dismissed this most central political problem from serious consideration. 'Classical political theory' (an expression reasonably intelligible to political theorists and political scientists but obscure to others) was acutely concerned with the problem of satisfying human needs, and now we need a return to authentic politics − a revolution in the old sense.[8] So familiar are political theorists with the community lineage that the significance of appeals or allusions to it are apt to be lost. They are markers, not of extrinsic but of reflexive dispute. Appeal to, and manipulation of, a lineage intimates (and fosters) a sense of community identity[9] − indeed only in this light are such lineal arguments in any community likely to be intelligible or persuasive. In precisely the same way, it is only in the light of a pervasive, potent and exclusive past that the archaic cry for revolution, *à la* Savonarola or Bay makes any sense at all.

Appeal and allusion to the past of a community (lineal argument) is not the only convention by which a community is cohered and distin-

---

8 See at length, C. Bay, 'Politics and Pseudo politics' in *American Political Science Review*, Vol.59, No.1, 1965, pp.39ff, and, (despite its apparent opposition to Bay's position) H. Eulau, 'Tradition and Innovation: On the Tension Between Ancient and Modern Ways in the Study of Politics' in *Behaviouralism in Political Science*, ed. H. Eulau, Atherton, New York, 1969, pp.13-14. The historical parallels between distant past political theorists and the present controversy are less between those who have (allegedly) been concerned with a concept of human needs, than with those thinkers who attempted to inject a new (any new) abstract issue into an existing structure of abstract concerns. I have in mind here, for example, Plato's elevation of *dikaiosyne* into the ethical structure of Athenian political discourse, and his re-defining of the ethical vocabulary of Athenian society; and the attempts by the spiritualist Franciscans and *fraticelli* to make 'poverty' a fundamental issue in religious/political discourse at the beginning of the fourteenth century. Conversely, there is but the most superficial and misleading connection between say, the platonic *ananke* or the Machiavellian *necessità* and contemporary needs theory.

9 W. Bluhm, *Theories of the Political System*, Prentice-Hall, New Jersey, 1965, is a thoroughgoing example of lineage manipulation, wherein a range of contemporary theorists, Strauss, Bay etc. are associated each in turn with a suitable forebear of lineal significance (Plato, Mill). Bluhm's purpose appears to be to use past and present reciprocally to legitimise each other in the eyes of the academic community and its initiates.

guished. A whole range of more specific conventions are exemplified (even crudely personified) in, and may be decoded by, reference to lineal argument. This is so with political theory.

7 In particular, a point of logic helps make a concept of needs difficult in political theory. The argument (in lineal terms associated primarily with David Hume) that it is impossible, licitly, to infer norms from positive premises is, according to most logicians, yet to be refuted. The belief in the categorical difference between normative and positive amounts to a philosophical (and more general academic) orthodoxy that is both well entrenched and subtly supported when challenged. Its acceptance underlies and gives distinctive character to theoretical discussions on many diverse issues. In the light of this orthodoxy needs becomes a problem because it is a word taken from diurnal discourse and habitually used in a manner which never clearly or consistently follows the conventions of logical argument, and systematically violates the Humean orthodoxy. Conceptualising needs then is in part a problem because the attempt appears either to involve flouting a logical convention or to involve stretching daily usage on a rack of logical precision. This, in its turn, violates, for many, another formal convention, to the effect that little is explained or understood about the extrinsic world by distorting it through logical analysis and precise re-definition.[10]

8 Thus far: community lineage and the importance of a logical convention indicates some distance between the diurnal world of political discourse, and the world of political theory. It is an intellectual distance (however it is maintained) that makes the distinction between extrinsic and reflexive important; it is equally distance that helps create the problem of needs in political theory.

9 If we overlook this intellectual distance we will be susceptible to two main dangers: (i) we may fall into the categorical error of mistaking the theoretical problems involved in conceptualising needs for political problems; the concept becoming seen as a panacea or a poison: (ii) extrinsic usage as a whole is then more likely to be taken as excessively homogeneous. Thus non-political usage may function simplistically to suggest the embryo of an adequate concept, which becomes in turn the means of solving the alleged problems of political needs usage.

---

10 In a most common form it is held to involve a fallacy of irrelevance, as Plato's account of *dikaiosyne* is held by some scholars (following Sachs) to be irrelevant to the questions initially posed in *Republic*, Books I and II, concerning the diurnal meaning of justice.

9.i In what we call political argument (encompassing slogans, manifestos, speeches, circulars, committee reports, newspaper letters, articles, editorials, interviews, public statements, press conferences and pamphlets) needs is a common and important word. It is a part of the ethical structure of modern political society constituted by the field of terms that are used to formulate, circumscribe and settle political arguments. The field includes such terms as *rights, justice, freedom, democracy, authority, obligation, individual, nation, progress, public interest, common good, totalitarian,* and *equality.* The list is not exhaustive, but it is difficult to imagine a political argument that does not employ and in different ways relate clusters of these terms. Equally, it is difficult to imagine a political theorist who does not take these terms as a significant part of his extrinsic subject matter.[11] Considered as a whole this rhetorical field is remarkably flexible. It constitutes a finite and highly organised sector of our abstract vocabulary which may be used to propound an almost infinite range of political utterances. Indeed diurnal political argument is persuasive (and recognisably 'political') primarily by virtue of the appropriate use of this cluster of terms including needs.[12] Now, by virtue of the fact that it conveys a sense of what is and what ought to be, needs may be seen (using Hume's law as no more than an image) as emblematic of the penultimate political problem, of the difficulty of transforming perceptions of what is into perceptions of what ought to be.[13] In this way, argument through the word needs is a particularly apposite vehicle for specific political problems. The distinction, however, between what is and what ought to be presupposes a prior distinction. Both general categories of fact and value rest on distinctions between necessity and contingency. In enumerating and appraising the facts of a given case it makes a great difference to our understanding and our actions

---

11 As a community engaged in circumscribed argument and persuasion, political theory has its own ethical structure, constituted by such terms as *originality, coherence, contribution, influence.* They are the means of organising significant utterance, and their successful use marks an effective argument: about say, freedom, and/or *x's* account of it.

12 My approach here draws on the language theory associated with F. de Saussure, *Cours de linguistique général,* Paris, 1916 and 1962, and the field theory of Jost Trier, on which see S. Ullman, *The Principles of Semantics,* Blackwell, Oxford, 1950, esp. pp.152-70, 309, 317. I have raised elsewhere, in a more general context, some of the possibilities of this approach to the study of political thinking, and to what I have called the ethical structure of political argument. See Lucy, *op.cit.,* pp.76-84 and 105-21.

13 See for example R.A.E. Fitzgerald, *Human Needs and Political Prescriptions: A Study of the Work of Christian Bay,* unpublished Ph.D. dissertation, University of New South Wales, 1975, pp.202ff, esp. 228; and the more general remarks of Michael Oakeshott, *Experience and its Modes,* Cambridge University Press, Cambridge, 1933 and 1966, pp.274ff.

which 'facts' we believe are or were determined and unalterable and which 'facts' we believe could have been otherwise. Moreover, it is only within the ambit of the contingent that it makes sense to talk about what ought or ought not to be. Thus imperatives ('ought' statements in their strongest form) are only intelligible *per se* in the context of alternative (contingent) courses of action. The designation of the necessary and the contingent underlies all needs claims, and helps explain the currency of the word within the structure of political rhetoric as a primary form of imperative.[14] Needs claims are formulated in a manner that virtually denies any alternative course of action. They present a contingency as if it were within the ambit of the necessary. Needs claims are compelling precisely because their grammar provides a means of conflating and appearing to settle the difference between necessity and contingency on the basis of which the politically problematic appears dissolved. That needs claims in politics reflect by seeming to conflate logically different categories does not mean that needs claims are in any sense a problem, or give rise to problems in politics. The categorical suggestiveness and ambivalence of the term needs is a source of neither political confusion nor incoherence in political argument. On the contrary, in one sense there is no problem of needs in politics. Argument through reference to needs is both widespread and non-contentious, being resorted to in different societies by many different groups. The idea of needs is simply a rhetorical device for carrying the contentious. To mistake the vehicle for the passengers is a significant categorical error, and one that lies beneath a good deal of the needs controversy.

To be able to formulate a grievance as a violation of a need is to go a good way towards establishing a right of redress[15]; to be able to wrap a specific policy in the garb of a need is equally to have, *a priori*, a strong case for its implementation. Resorting to needs claims is a potent rhetorical tactic; but like all such effective rhetorical forms, there is a conflict (an index of importance) over its possession. The conflict with respect to needs is worked out in two related ways: (a) if confronted with need claim $y,(yN)$ we may make a higher need claim for $x,(xN)$ arguing that x takes priority over y.

This however, is still to accept y as a legitimate need claim, and

---

14 Perhaps the best account of the rhetorical functioning of the term 'needs' is to be found in K.R. Minogue, *The Liberal Mind*, Methuen, London, 1963, Chapter 4, Section I.

15 On the relationship between rights and needs, and the shift from rights to needs claims see, A. Kaufman, 'Needs, Wants and Liberalism', *Inquiry*, Vol. 14, 1971, pp. 191ff.

may not be deemed a strong enough assertion (especially as need claims normally indicate urgency). Thus when confronted by yN we may deny y as a legitimate need and reclassify it. This in turn necessitates advocates of y re-establishing their claim as a need claim. This stronger tactic is above all facilitated by the existence of terms which function grammatically and lexically in a very similar fashion to needs, but which may carry a modified, if not an inverted, emotional resonance. Over time *wants* and, to a lesser extent, *desires* have come to function as such modifying classifiers for needs. It is partly because of the relationship between needs and wants (to take a simplified schematic relationship and to ignore the conceptual flummery of false needs), that the notion of needs retains its flexibility and common usage. The wide political appeal of needs claims is dependent upon wants (intimating mere volition) being an effective modifier, controlling all needs claims, prohibiting a permanent monopoly of needs predication, and thus insuring the general currency of the term. Together then, needs and wants form what might be called a self-modifying rhetorical compound. This compound is parallel to the liberty/licence compound. Liberty claims like needs claims, may be subjected to contentious hierarchical ordering (a). Or, they may be reclassified as highly pejorative licence claims (b).

Censorship may be formulated as a restriction upon liberty or a prohibition upon licence. Both compounds are a means of ordering political claims and demands and making counter claims by a process of association and minimal change. Both compounds share a similar economical structure. In political terms xN can be classified xW suggesting $\sim xN$ as a prelude to yN. Similarly we could replace N and W with symbols for liberty (L) and licence (L'), and we would find that arguments involving liberty and licence had the same basically reciprocal, biadic form. A liberty is a freedom of which we approve, which is (by the very use of the words liberty or freedom), given a high priority; a licence is a freedom of which we do not approve. Licence even more clearly than want or desire asserts the illegitimacy of another's claim: $xL' > x \sim L$. All such liberty/licence, needs/wants claims range within a presupposed or postulated area of contingency and it is within this area that specific imperatives, *qua* needs claims function. In political usage what signifies with needs claims is what we manage to classify in terms of them and not any concept of need itself. For the political theorist, however, modifying rhetorical compounds (because of their sortal instability) are theoretically unsatisfactory. *If* need can always be replaced by want and want by need, conceptualising one involves conceptualising the other as a distinction between synonyms is redundant.[16] Although 'a politics of human needs' and 'a politics of human wants (or desires)' seem different, it may only be a pattern of preferences irrespective of theoretical criteria of judgement that leads to the use of one expression rather than the other in any given context.

Moreover, what matters is the difficulty of conceptualising needs and only thereafter the question of what can be inferred from the given concept.[17] The difficulties are real enough, for as I have briefly indicated, whenever we come across needs in political discourse we founder on underlying (theoretical) rocks of categorical opposition and upon a complex pattern of reciprocity and controversial applications.

9.ii One initially plausible way around the difficulties of conceptualising needs is to start from the basis of non-contentious needs claims, and to extend (analogically) what implications we can into politics by use of a model. Need claims are least contentious when found in a context of clearly acknowledged rules and priorities. Thus in a context of playing poker, the statement 'I need a queen' (qN) asserts a necessity (given a specific end), accepts that getting a queen is contingent, but does not anticipate qN itself to be contentious. Given a hand of $9,10,J,K,4$ (of three different suits) the requirement of a queen is in fact explicable in terms of the rules of the game (the statement $\sim qN$ is what would require explanation) and its end. The acquisition of a queen is at the same time *(ceteris paribus)* a contingency, and 'a consummation greatly to be wished'. Here then, necessity, contingency, fact and value may all *seem* synthesised rather than just conflated in qN. The poker model and similarly circumscribed ones, however, are remarkably inappropriate to needs claims in a political context.

---

16 Sir Isaiah Berlin's essay *Two Concepts of Liberty*, Oxford University Press, Oxford, 1958, works within the Miltonic tradition by developing a theoretically spurious bi-fold distinction between an approved and a disapproved concept of liberty, which at the same time only inadvertently points to the rhetorical functioning of the term. Similarly, S. Benn and R.S. Peters, *The Social Principles of the Democratic State*, George Allen and Unwin, London, 1959, pp.141ff. attempt to distinguish needs and wants categorically by using the idea of detriment as a criterion for needs. As such this seems inadequate. We may imply detriment whenever we speak of needs, but this is true of what we designate our wants. It may simply be that an emphasis on detriment is one way in which we convert want claims into need claims, and thus detriment tells us something about the rhetorical compound, but this is not to point to a stable criterion for distinguishing and separating its components.

17 There is, of course, no obligation (from a theoretical perspective) to make this shift. Alternatively one may decide that what matters is the process of conceptualisation, in which case we have another reflexive shift (as is typical of the work of Quine for instance) reducing needs to a mere notational exemplum as a means of exploring the concept of a concept.

This is not because a political need claim is 'public', rather than 'personal', taking the form the community needs rather than I need (... to fill this straight/office): it is because in political situations — the ones in which it is thought urgent to apply an adequate concept of needs — the closely circumscribed and non-contentious context for a need claim is absent (9.i). It is almost, one could say, the absence that explains the use, and we have to ignore this absence (for which the whole rhetorical field of politics is in some way a substitution) if we are to extend qN statements to cover political situations. About the only thing that is non-contentious with xN and yN is N under which varying claims are subsumed. It is the means (together with a range of other items from the rhetorical field) by which people advocate different priorities, values and ways of achieving them. Needs usage in politics is almost the reverse of poker, chess, or fishing licence models.[18] Any desire to move from such needs claims models to the political theorists' extrinsic world of political discourse reveals a categorical misunderstanding almost as marked as the confusion of conceptual vehicles with itinerant passengers.

10 The quest for a politics of needs, perhaps on the inspiration of a Maslow, that is, for a non-contentious operational concept delineating the necessary and the contingent, and on the basis of established 'facts' expressing a set of universal priorities, is initially encouraged by closed models such as the poker one. It is however tantamount to asking for no politics at all. This may be considered futile, self-deluding or even dangerous; conversely it may be considered justifiable and plausible. We must, however, know what we are asking for, and we are certainly asking for a great deal; so much so that we must bear in mind the possibility that the quest has little to do with the parameters of extrinsic politics, that it is primarily reflexive, and perforce must be judged accordingly.

The non-contentious need claim, revealing an ordered set of priorities and firm guides for action, is as politically appealing as an ideal, as it is intrinsically theoretically interesting as a phenomenon. Superficially, at least, it holds out hope of a blueprint for ameliorating political conflict. In pursuing this possibility, however modestly, the political theorist *per se* asserts his relevance to the political world by means of, rather than irrespective of, his theoretical acumen. We have been concerned, albeit

---

18 Cf. the discussion between Kai Nielsen, 'On Human Needs and Moral Appraisals', *Inquiry*, Vol.6, 1963, pp.170-83; and P. Taylor, ' "Need" Statements', *Analysis*, Vol.19, No.5, 1959, pp.106-11. See also, M. Black, 'The Gap Between "Is" and "Should" ', *The Philosophical Review*, Vol.63, 1964, pp.164-81.

at a general and informal level, with some of the complexities of meaning and reference theory. Within political activity the question 'to what does a need claim refer?' may be answered (very largely) by saying it refers to a claim that an opponent may be anticipated to dismiss as only a desire, a wish or a want. But to what activity or to whom does the controversy refer?

11 We are now in a position to re-formulate this question under the auspices of a general reflexive problem: How far can a given term moulded by one set of (extrinsic) conventions be transported into the context of another set of conventions without either the term or the conventions of one's own activity being radically transformed? As a corollary and more specifically, how different are the conventions of political theory from those of diurnal discourse and how different should they be? The taxonomy of political theory together with its relationship to political activity is what is at issue, and the needs controversy is but one means by which the relationship is sustained as one of ebb and flow.

12 The fluidity of relationship is sustained by a tension between two common propensities roughly identifiable in terms of the *vita activa* and the *vita contemplativa*. The first calls for intellectual involvement in the conduct of the theorists' subject matter, the second for intellectual disinterest.[19] In political theory the most frequent justification for the activity has been in terms of its relevance to politics, and the not infrequent reshufflings of the names in the community's lineage have usually been both inspired by, and organised in terms of, ideological concepts pressed into pseudo-historical service.[20] At the same time however, political theorists like to picture their activity as a disinterested search for universal truths, and as an impartial analysis of political belief and utterance.[21]

13 I take the tension between the *vita activa* and the *vita contemplativa*

---

19 The *vita activa/contemplativa* distinction is not to be confused with the reflexive/extrinsic distinction (3) though they are related. The earlier distinction concerns the subject matter of enquiry, and the means by which it may be explored. It is a distinction appropriate to any form of intellectual activity. The latter distinction, (12) presupposing the former, concerns the nature and extent of a theorist's involvement in the main focus of his enquiry, and is not relevant to all forms of enquiry. Neither am I discussing the possibility of achieving 'objectivity' but simply the manifest importance of an academic ideal.

20 For example, Robert Blakey's initial study, *A History of Political Literature*, Robert Bentley, London, 1855; Y.W. Elliott and N.A. McDonald, *Western Political Heritage*, Prentice-Hall, New York, 1949.

21 A. Hacker, 'Capital and Carbunkles: The "Great Books" Re-Appraised', *American Political Science Review*, Vol.48, 1954, pp.775-86 esp. 783ff.

in political theory to be most recently and relevantly revealed in the aura of uncertainty emanating from political theorists during the 1950s and early 1960s. There was during this time considerable discussion on the alleged plight of political theory, conceived to be either dead or moribund. Apparently, political theory failed to deal rigorously and objectively, if at all, with the realities of political life, whilst its grand ideological edifices were either discredited in, or increasingly irrelevant to, current political activity. It was inadequate both contemplatively (the contemplative paragon being political science), and actively. Retrospectively, the whole 'crisis' in political theory was based on a series of misconceptions about political science; the importance of ideological thinking, and the character and history of political theory itself.[22] Primarily, perhaps, it was self-induced because of a lack of reflexive concern. But since then two things have happened. First, the aura of doubt has partially shifted to the adjacent and overlapping community of political scientists[23], and secondly (as one would expect) there has been a noticeable insurgence of reflexive theorising; this has helped to render the character of political theory contentious.[24] The lineage of political theory, though still largely accepted in some form, has been attacked as mythical and misleading and there has been an increased sensitivity to the exacting demands of historical understanding. Equally, an increased awareness of, and willingness to employ, rigorous philosophical criteria of judgement has developed. These changes, though perhaps as yet leaving the bulk of the community uncontaminated, have done something to refurnish credibility to political theory's claims to intellectual respectability as a disinterested and rigorous activity — a legitimate seeker after contemplative understanding.

---

22 For elaboration see C. Condren, 'The Death of Political Theory: The Importance of Historiographical Myth', *Politics*, Vol.9, 1974, pp.146ff.

23 See for example, *An End to Political Science: The Caucus Papers*, eds. M. Surkin and A. Wolfe, Basic Books, New York, 1970, at length; M. Lipsitz 'Vulture Mantis and Seal: Proposals for Political Scientists', *Polity*, Vol.3, No.1, 1970, pp.16ff.

24 See for example, R. Ashcraft, 'On the Problem of Methodology and the Nature of Political Theory', *Political Theory*, Vol.3, 1975, pp.5-25; J. Dunn, 'The Identity of the History of Ideas', *Philosophy*, Vol.43, 1968, pp.85-104; B.A. Haddock, 'The History of Ideas and the Study of Politics', *Political History*, Vol.4, 1974, pp.421-31; M. Levin, 'What Makes a Classic in Political Theory', *Political Science Quarterly*, Vol.88, No.3, 1973, pp.462-76; J.G.A. Pocock, *Politics, Language and Time*, Methuen, London, 1972; B. Parekh and R.N. Berki, 'The History of Political Ideas: A Critique of Skinner's Methodology', *Journal of the History of Ideas*, Vol.34, 1973, pp.163-84; Q. Skinner, 'Meaning and Understanding in the History of Ideas', *History and Theory*, Vol.8, 1969, pp.2-52; C.D. Talton, 'Historicity, Meaning and Revisionism in the Study of Political Thought', *History and Theory*, Vol.12, 1973, pp.307-28.

In contrast there has been a noticeable and lively resurgence in politically committed theories — each trailing by degrees its own sense of precedent. Anarchism, for a long while an unfashionable curiosity, seems likely, more than ever before, to become a credit to the once apparently futile enthusiasms of Godwin and Bakunin. Sophisticated arguments concerned with the feasibility of participatory democracy are rife; whilst advocates of sexual liberation ideologies, if they can find little in the way of a prestigious or palatable heritage (Plato too 'fascist'; Wollstoncraft too lightweight; Ockham and Averroes too Medieval), can claim urgency and a direct universal relevance. There is no scarcity of commitment, or more importantly, of explicit argument through commitment, and the belief that political theory is only vital when affecting the *vita activa politica*. If these impressions of the current state of political theorising are correct, then the possibility of synthesizing these opposing propensities seems remote, and the question of the potential character of political theory is acute. Herein lies the principal importance of, and rationale behind, the controversy surrounding the attempts to create a clear and stable concept of human needs.

14 In a singular manner the search for an adequate, operational concept of needs appears to hold out hope of satisfying two masters: a means by which political theory might be made more rigorous and more useful, balancing, as it were, *political* theory with political *theory*. The significance of needs theory to the different expectations of political theorists and to the reappraisal of the character of political theory can be indicated briefly under two related headings.

14.i *Needs and the parameters of political theory*   The impulse towards the *vita activa* is an impulse towards those aspects of an activity which afford making and justifying contingent choices within its limits. The contemplative impulse is, by contrast, directed towards the more stable, even necessary features of a given activity, and while it involves delineation of a range of contingent elements in the activity, it does not involve choosing between these elements or ordering a range of priorities. Similarly the active impulse has to reveal a cognisance of the necessities of the activity but only as a means towards, or prelude to, advocating preferences. Now needs connotes an element of the necessary and at the same time in political parlance expresses an imperative, and thus must be understood within a context of the contingent (9.i). In this way needs is a fitting focus for either propensity. The hope however that needs might appear to hold out for synthesising the contemplative and active propensities may be illusory.

It is one thing to stress the peculiar importance for the political theorist of the term needs; it is another to say that conceptualising needs through adherence to logical convention can encompass, or cohere with, all the diverse possibilities associated with the term and its lexical field in politics. What, to put the matter generally, is brought into focus here is the scope of any given specific set of conventions of argument in exploring needs. We may expect that insofar as the contemplative propensity (at least in the form most relevant here) is dominant, the logical difficulties attendant upon defining needs will take precedence over all else. To bring purely logical conventions of argument to bear on needs is quite feasible, but is unlikely (especially as political theorists are hardly pure logicians) to be seen as entirely appropriate to political theory. For logic, dealing with all relationships as necessary, or dealing only with necessary relationships is likely to prove by turns too restrictive, or too porous to capture the resonance and significance of a rhetorical compound. A logically rigorous concept of needs would be well removed from, and bear little resemblance to, the world of political activity. The best (from a political perspective) that we may hope for is a figurative extension of an otherwise irrelevant or arcane formulation. Conversely, in so far as the propensity waxes, rhetorical convention will become ascendant; conceptual problems will be minimised or avoided and ultimately they will be dissolved in diurnal discourse. The best (from a theoretical perspective) that we may hope for is a few glib and loose phrases preceding the real purpose of providing a political programme. The most likely possibility is a continued, though uncertain, balance of dispositions, a blend of antagonistic and mutually obscuring conventions seeking by turns to pull the whole discussion of needs in opposing directions.

14.ii *Needs and the perimeters of political theory*   If the emphasis is shifted from conceptualising to applying needs, in the context of what I have suggested (14.i) the discussion reveals the ascendancy of the *vita activa* impulse. Trying to enumerate and order specific needs, and discussing how and if at all specific needs follow from a concept of need (assuming we can jump the hurdle of conceptualisation) presupposes that such an enquiry is appropriate to the political theory community. To answer this fundamental reflexive question in the negative and to rule out of court the whole question of specifying needs, is an attempt to push political theory radically to the contemplative ideal. To answer in the affirmative — to the effect that the whole point of conceptualising needs is to be able to specify a rational set of political priorities, is to move as firmly in the opposite direction – to nudge the world of political theory entirely into the shadow of political action.

Under (14.i) and (14.ii) we can see that the question of needs (if it may be put in the singular) is a means by which a reflexive problem is formulated and disputed. Under (i) the needs problem focuses on the conventions appropriate to political theory, the parameters of community argument; under (ii) it focuses on the relationship of political theory to political action, upon the perimeters of the community's argument.

Conclusion

I have suggested a typology of problem, reflexive and extrinsic (3). Despite its natural extrinsic abridgement (1), the needs controversy is best seen primarily as a reflexive problem. Considerata may always be analysed according to different standards and intellectual habits – a point which may be made by way of analogy. Paul Klee[25] suggested that painting may be analysed in terms of three exclusive but complementary abstract categories: line, tone, and colour. One category alone cannot encompass a painting; complete analysis involves the use, in different measures no doubt, of all three categories. In an extreme case, we may say that an etching is without colour. Nevertheless the category of colour (even in this minimal way) is here being used to characterise the etching appropriately and without stigmatism. Although political theory as a reasonably well-established academic activity has its analogues of line, tone and colour, the analogy with painting soon reveals a significant contrast. The different patterns of convention found in political theory, and given strong geneological expression are arbitrary (within the realm of the contingent), and antagonistic (redolent with opposing values). Through the eyes of a Locke rhetoric is chaotic, incoherent, insecurely founded and 'a perfect cheat'.[26] Through the eyes of a Valla philosophy is narrow, inadequate, self-indulgent and irrelevant.[27] The qualities of rhetoric remain in the eye of philosophy, faults; the enthymeme, an ill-formed syllogism, as a configuration of lines can, never be poor colour. The precisions of philosophy continue to excite the impatience of oratory; philosophy's grey on grey is an obliteration of line and a craven use of pigment.

---

25 *On Modern Art*, tr. Paul Findley, Faber, London, 1948.
26 John Locke, *An Essay on Human Understanding*, Book 3, Chapter 10.
27 *Dialecticarum Disputationem, Libri III, Praefatio Book I*, cited in Linda Janik, 'Lorenzo Valla: The Primacy of Rhetoric and the De-Moralisation of History', *History and Theory*, Vol. 12, No. 4, 1973, p. 390.

Grey, dear friend, is all theory,
And Green life's golden tree.[28]

As was argued above (9.i) the very rhetorical strength of needs is a source of its theoretical unsatisfactoriness. The *vita activa* and the *vita contemplativa* are, in a way, the ideals of linear and chromatic reductionism. What does not conform to their conventions is condemned. The propensity towards either ideal, if unchecked, may be no bad thing and would result in a more coherent if more limited enterprise than political theory now is. In practice a balance is struck, an incoherent shifting pattern of compromise, which was in the 1950s seen to be vulnerable from quite different perspectives. The quest to conceptualise needs has been in large measure an attempt to overcome the apparent incoherences of established political theory.

It has been a means by which different dispositions have sought to dominate or re-direct the activity under the guise of an extrinsic problem. The categorical ambivalence underlying the common political use of the term needs (9.ii) makes it singularly suitable to this end. What in short it signifies is that when we are told that politics based on human needs is imperative and or uniquely legitimate, or conversely that such a politics is a dangerous illusion or a totalitarian danger, we are apt at first sight to think the dispute to be about what we usually understand by political society. It is not (14.ii): the size of angels' feet is of secondary significance.

The controversy surrounding politics and the concept of needs has been something of a grail quest, and like that of Arthurian legend, where 'every knyght toke the way that him lyked beste', it has been less for the benefit of the peasants who are passed in the night than for that of a noble order prone to internecine strife.

---

28 Goethe, *Faust*, I, 2038-9.

SELECTED BIBLIOGRAPHY

Works marked with an asterisk (*) indicate those which are perhaps of special relevance to contemporary need theory (Ed.)

T.W. Adorno, E. Frenkel-Brunswick, D.J. Levinson and R.N. Sanford, *The Authoritarian Personality*, Wiley, New York, 1950.

C.D. Alderfer, 'An empirical test of a new theory of human needs', *Organizational Behavior and Human Performance*, Vol.4, 1969, pp.142-75.

G.W. Allport, *Personality: A Psychological Interpretation*, Holt, Rinehart and Winston, New York, 1937.

G.W. Allport, *Becoming: Basic Considerations for a Psychology of Personality*, Yale University Press, New Haven, 1955.

* J. Aronoff, *Psychological Needs and Cultural Systems: A Case Study*, Van Nostrand, New York, 1967.

A. Aron-Scharr, 'Maslow's Other Child', *Journal of Humanistic Psychology*, scheduled for Vol.17, No.2, Spring 1977.

J.W. Atkinson (ed.), *Motives in Fantasy, Action and Society*, Van Nostrand, Princeton, 1958.

K.E. Baier, *The Moral Point of View: A Rational Basis of Ethics*, Cornell University Press, Ithaca, New York, 1958.

K.E. Baier and N. Rescher (eds.), *Values and the future: the impact of technological change on American values*, Free Press, New York, 1969.

J.E. Barnhart, 'Wants and "Real" Wants', *Journal of Value Inquiry*, Vol.6, Fall 1972, pp.226-33.

* C. Bay, *The Structure of Freedom*, Stanford University Press, Stanford, 1970 (first published 1958).

* C. Bay, 'Politics and Pseudopolitics: A Critical Evaluation of Some Behavioral Literature', *American Political Science Review*, Vol.59, No.1, March 1965, pp.39-51.

* C. Bay, 'Needs, Wants and Political Legitimacy', *Canadian Journal of Political Science*, Vol.1, No.3, September 1968, pp.241-60.

* C. Bay, 'The Cheerful Science of Dismal Politics' in *The Dissenting Academy*, ed. T. Roszak, Penguin Books, Middlesex, England, 1969, pp.187-205.

C. Bay, 'Human Development and Political Orientations: Notes Toward a Science of Political Education', *Bulletin of Peace Proposals*, Vol.1, No.2, 1970, pp.177-86. Full text in *Social Psychology and Political Behavior: Problems and Prospects*, eds. G. Abcarian and J.W. Soule, Charles E. Merrill, Columbus, Ohio, 1971, pp.148-82.

*C. Bay, 'Reshaping the Future Polity: Human Needs and Politics' in *Seeing Beyond: Personal, Social and Political Alternatives*, ed. D. Pirages, Addison-Wesley, Reading, Masachusetts, 1971, pp.267-79.

S.I. Benn and R.S. Peters, *Social Principles and the Democratic State*, Allen and Unwin, London, 1959.

J. Berthall (ed.), *The Limits of Human Nature*, Dutton, New York, 1974.

M. Black, 'The Gap Between "Is" and "Should" ', *The Philosophical Review*, Vol.LXXII, April 1964, pp.165-81.

T.B. Bottomore (ed.), *Marx's Early Writings*, McGraw-Hill, New York, 1964.

J. Bowlby, *Attachment*, Vol.1 of *Attachment and Loss*, Hogarth Press, London, 1970.

J. Bradshaw, 'The concept of Social Need', *New Society*, Vol.19, March 30, 1972, pp.640-3.

R.B. Brandt, 'Comments on "Wants, Needs and Liberalism"', *Inquiry*, Vol.14, Autumn 1971, pp.207-12.

*D. Braybrooke, 'Let Needs Diminish that Preferences May Prosper' in *Studies in Moral Philosophy*, ed. N. Rescher, Blackwell, Oxford, 1968, pp.86-107.

S. Budner, 'Intolerance of Ambiguity as a Personality Variable', *Journal of Personality*, Vol.30, No.1, March 1962, pp.29-50.

J.F.T. Bugental (ed.), *Challenges of Humanistic Psychology*, McGraw-Hill, New York, 1967.

H. Cantril, *Human Nature and Political Systems*, Rutgers University Press, New Jersey, 1961.

H. Cantril, *The Pattern of Human Concerns*, Rutgers University Press, New Jersey, 1965.

A. Campbell, P. Converse, W. Miller and D. Stokes, *The American Voter*, Wiley, New York, 1960.

H.M. Chiang and A. Maslow (eds.), *The Healthy Personality — Readings*, Van Nostrand, New York, 1969.

R. Christie and M. Jahoda (eds.), *Studies in the Scope and Method of 'The Authoritarian Personality'*, Free Press, Glencoe, 1954.

*J.V. Clark, 'Motivation in Work Groups: A Tentative View' in *Organisational Behavior and Administration*, ed. P. Lawrence and others, Dorsey Press, Homewood, 1961, pp.224-8.

C.N. Cofer and M.H. Appley, *Motivation: Theory and Research*, Wiley, New York, 1964.

C. Condren, 'Three Aspects of Political Theory' in *The Pieces of Politics*, ed. R. Lucy, Macmillan, Melbourne, 1975, pp.39-130.

W.E. Connolly, *The Terms of Political Discourse*, Heath Lexington, Massachusetts, 1974.

D. Cooper (ed.), *The Dialectics of Liberation*, Penguin, Harmondsworth, 1968.

L. Cronbach and P. Meehl, 'Construct Validity in Psychological Tests', *Psychological Bulletin*, Vol.52, 1955, pp.281-302.

A. Cunningham, 'Objectivity and Human Needs in Marxism', *New Blackfriars*, Vol.55, 1974, pp.112-23.

M. Czudnowski, 'Political Recruitment' in *The Handbook of Political Science*, eds. F. Greenstein and N. Polsby, Addison-Wesley, Reading, Massachusetts, 1974.

* J.C. Davies, *Human Nature in Politics: The Dynamics of Political Behavior*, Wiley, New York, 1963.

J.C. Davies, *When Men Revolt and Why*, Free Press, New York, 1971.

* R.F. Dearden, ' "Needs" in Education' in *Education and the Development of Reason*, eds. R.F. Dearden, P.H. Hirst and R.S. Peters, Routledge and Kegan Paul, London, 1972, pp.50-64.

* R. de Charms, *Personal Causation: The Internal Affective Determinants of Behavior*, Academic Press, New York, 1968.

A. de Crespigny and A. Wertheimer (eds.), *Contemporary Political Thought*, Atherton Press, New York, 1970.

A. de Crespigny and K. Minogue (eds.), *Contemporary Political Philosophers*, Dodd, Mead and Co., New York, 1975.

* W.J. Dickson and F.J. Roethlisberger, *Counselling in an Organisation: Sequel to the Hawthorne Researches*, Harvard University Press, Boston, 1966.

G. Di Palma and H. McCloskey, 'Personality and Conformity: The Learning of Political Attitudes', *American Political Science Review*, Vol.64, 1970, pp.1054-73.

G. Di Renzo, *Personality, Power and Politics*, University of Notre Dame Press, Notre Dame, 1967.

E. Durkheim, *The Division of Labor in Society* (1893), Free Press, Glencoe, 1947.

J. Elden, 'New Left Middle Class Radical Democrats: Peace and Freedom Party Activists Compared to Democrats and Republicans', UCLA Department of Political Science, Los Angeles, 1968.

E. Erikson, *Childhood and Society*, Norton, New York, 1963 (revised edition).

G.M. Erikson, 'Maslow's Basic Needs Theory and Design Theory', *Behavioral Science*, Vol.18, No.3, May 1973, pp.210-12.

A. Etzioni, *The Active Society: A Theory of Societal and Political Processes*, Free Press, New York, 1968.

* A. Etzioni, 'Basic Human Needs, Alienation and Inauthenticity', *American Sociological Review*, Vol.33, No.6, December 1968, pp. 870-85.

M.L. Farber, 'Politics: Under Maslow's Umbrella', *Contemporary Psychology*, Vol.18, No.5, 1973, pp.218-19.

L. Feuer, *Psychoanalysis and Ethics*, Thomas, Springfield, Illinois, 1955.

R. Fitzgerald, 'The Return to Authentic Politics' in *The Pieces of Politics*, ed. R. Lucy, Macmillan, Sydney, 1975, pp.32-8.

A.G.N. Flew, 'On Not Deriving "Ought" from "Is" ', *Analysis*, Vol.XXV, No.2, December 1964, pp.25-32.

A.G.N. Flew, *Evolutionary Ethics,* Macmillan, London, 1968.

A.G.N. Flew, *An Introduction to Western Philosophy,* Bobbs Merril, Indianapolis, 1971.

* A.G.N. Flew, *Crime or Disease?* Macmillan, London, 1973.

A.G.N. Flew, 'Philosophising about Education', *New Humanist,* Vol.88, No.12, April 1973, pp.482-3.

* A.G.N. Flew, 'In Defence of Reformism' in *Question Seven,* ed. H. Hawton, Pemberton, London, 1974, pp.67-80.

A.G.N. Flew, *Thinking About Thinking,* Fontana/Collins, Glasgow, 1975.

A.G.N. Flew, *Sociology, Equality and Education,* Macmillan, London, 1976.

P. Freire, *Pedagogy of the Oppressed,* Seabury, New York, 1970.

P. Freire, *Education for Critical Consciousness,* Seabury, New York, 1973.

E. Fromm, *Man for Himself: An Inquiry into the Social Psychology of Ethics,* Rinehart, New York, 1947.

* E. Fromm, 'The Psychology of Normalcy', *Dissent,* Vol.1, 1954, pp.39-43.

* E. Fromm, *The Sane Society,* Holt, Rinehart and Winston, New York, 1955.

E. Fromm, *Escape From Freedom,* Holt, Rinehart and Winston, New York, 1961 (first published 1941).

E. Fromm, *Marx's Concept of Man,* Ungar, New York, 1963.

J.K. Galbraith, *The Affluent Society,* Houghton Mifflin, Boston, 1969 (second edition revised).

W.B. Gallie, 'Essentially Contested Concepts' in *The Importance of Language,* ed. M. Black, Prentice-Hall, Englewood Cliffs, New Jersey, 1968.

A.W. Gouldner, 'Anti-Minotaur: The Myth of a Value-Free Sociology', *Social Problems,* Vol.9, No.3, 1962, pp.199-213.

A.W. Gouldner, *The Coming Crisis of Western Sociology,* Basic Books, New York, 1970.

G.J. Graham Jnr. and G.W. Carey (eds.), *The Post-Behavioral Era: Perspectives on Political Science,* David McKay, New York, 1972.

W.K. Graham and J. Balloun, 'An Empirical Test of Maslow's Need Hierarchy', *Journal of Humanistic Psychology,* Vol.13, No.1, Winter 1973, pp.97-108.

* F. Greenstein, *Personality and Politics,* Markham, Chicago, 1970.

M. Grene, *The Knower and the Known,* Faber, London, 1965.

M. Grene, *Approaches to a Philosophical Biology,* Basic Books, New York, 1968.

D.T. Hall and K.E. Nougaim, 'An examination of Maslow's need hierarchy in an organizational setting', *Organizational Behavior and Human Performance,* Vol.3, 1968, pp.12-35.

* C. Hampden-Turner, *Radical Man: The Process of Psycho-Social Development,* Schenkman, Cambridge, Massachusetts, 1970.

R.V. Hannaford, 'You ought to derive "ought" from "is" ', *Ethics,* Vol.82, 1971-72, pp.155-62.

*A. Heller, 'Theory and Practice: Their Relation to Human Needs', *Social Praxis*, Vol.1, 1974, pp.359-73.

R. Hofstadter, *The Paranoid Style in American Politics*, Knopf, New York, 1965.

D. Holbrook, *Human Hope and the Death Instinct*, Pergamon, Oxford, 1971.

D. Holbrook, *The Masks of Hate: The Problem of False Solutions in the Culture of an Acquisitive Society*, Pergamon, Oxford, 1972.

D. Holbrook, *Gustav Mahler and the Courage to Be*, Vision, London, 1975.

D. Holbrook, *Sylvia Plath: Poetry and Existence*, Athlone, London, 1976.

K. Horney, *Neurosis and Human Growth: The Struggle Toward Self-Realisation*, Norton, New York, 1950.

W.D. Hudson (ed.), *The Is-Ought Question: A Collection of Papers on the Central Problem in Moral Philosophy*, Macmillan, London, 1969.

I. Illich, *Deschooling Society*, Harper and Row, New York, 1971.

I. Illich, *Celebration of Awareness*, Doubleday, Garden City, New York, 1971.

D. Katz, 'The Functional Approach to the Study of Attitudes', *Public Opinion Quarterly*, Vol.24, 1960, pp.163-204.

*A.S. Kaufman, 'Wants, Needs and Liberalism', *Inquiry*, Vol.14, No.3, Autumn 1971, pp.191-212.

W. Kendall, 'Comment on McClosky's Conservatism and Personality', *American Political Science Review*, Vol.52, 1958, pp.506-10.

A. Keys and others, *The Biology of Human Starvation*, 2 vols., University of Minnesota Press, Minneapolis, 1950.

J.N. Knutson, 'Psychological Deprivation and Its Effect on School Behavior', *Bulletin of the Oregon School Study Council*, Vol.11, 1967.

*J.N. Knutson, *The Human Basis of the Polity*, Aldine-Atherton, Chicago, 1972.

*J.N. Knutson, 'The Political Relevance of Self-Actualisation' in *Public Opinion and Political Attitudes*, ed. A. Wilcox, Wiley, New York, 1973.

*J.N. Knutson (ed.), *The Handbook of Political Psychology*, Jossey-Bass, San Francisco, 1973a.

J.N. Knutson, 'The Long Term Effects of Personality on Political Attitudes and Beliefs', *American Political Science Association*, New Orleans, 1973b.

J.N. Knutson, 'Personality Correlates of Political Behavior: A Longitudinal Analysis', unpublished Ph.D. dissertation, University of California, Los Angeles, 1973c.

J.N. Knutson, 'Personality in the Study of Politics' in *The Handbook of Political Psychology*, ed. J. Knutson, Jossey-Bass, San Francisco, 1973d.

*B.P. Komisar, ' "Need" and the Needs-Curriculum' in *Language and Concepts in Education*, eds. B.O. Smith and R.H. Ennis, Rand McNally, Chicago, 1961, pp.24-42.

J.R. Kowski, 'Human Nature and Needs', *Dialectical Humanism*, Vol.1, Summer 1974, pp.103-13.

R.D. Laing and A. Esterson, *Sanity, Madness and the Family*, Tavistock, London, 1964.

R.D. Laing, *The Politics of Experience*, Penguin Books, Harmondsworth, 1967.

R.D. Laing, *The Politics of the Family and other essays*, Tavistock, London, 1971.

* R.E. Lane, 'The Need to be Liked and Anxious College Liberals', *Annals of the American Academy of Political and Social Science*, Vol.361, September 1965, pp.71-80.

* R.E. Lane, *Political Thinking and Consciousness: The Private Life of the Political Mind*, Markham, Chicago, 1969.

H.D. Lasswell, *Power and Personality*, Norton, New York, 1948.

H.D. Lasswell, *Psychopathology and Politics*, Viking Press, New York, 1960 (first published 1930).

H.D. Lasswell, *The Political Writings of Harold D. Lasswell*, Free Press, New York, 1951.

H.D. Lasswell, 'A Note on "Types" of Political Personality: Nuclear, Co-Relational, Developmental', *Journal of Social Issues*, Vol.24, 1968, pp.81-91.

* D.D. Lee, 'Are basic needs ultimate?' in *Freedom and Culture*, ed. D.D. Lee, Prentice-Hall, Englewood Cliffs, New Jersey, 1959, pp.70-7.

H. Lefcourt, 'Internal versus External Control of Reinforcement', *Psychological Bulletin*, Vol.65, 1966, pp.206-20.

* W. Leiss, *The Limits to Satisfaction: An Essay on the Problem of Needs and Commodities*, University of Toronto Press, Toronto, 1976.

S.R. Letwin, *The Pursuit of Certainty*, Cambridge University Press, Cambridge, 1965.

W. Liebrand, 'The Humanistic Approach in a Politico-Psychological Investigation', unpublished paper, University of Groningen, The Netherlands, 1974.

* L. Lipsitz, 'Vulture, Mantis and Seal: Proposals for Political Scientists', *Polity*, Vol.III, No.1, 1970, pp.4-21.

J. Loevinger, 'The Meaning and Measurement of Ego Development', *American Psychologist*, Vol.21, 1966, pp.195-206.

W. Lyons, 'Liberalism and Want-Satisfaction: a Critique of John Rawls', *Political Theory*, Vol.1, May 1973, pp.134-53.

* C.A. Mace, 'Homeostasis, Needs and Values', *British Journal of Psychology*, Vol.44, No.3, August 1953, pp.200-10.

D.C. McClelland, *The Achievement Motive*, Appleton-Century-Crofts, New York, 1953.

D.C. McClelland, *The Achieving Society*, Free Press, New York, 1961.

* H.J. McCloskey, 'Human Needs, Rights and Political Values', *American Philosophical Quarterly*, Vol.13, No.1, January 1976, pp.1-11.

H. McClosky, 'Conservatism and Personality', *American Political Science Review*, Vol.52, 1958, pp.27-45.

H. McClosky and J. Schaar, 'Psychological Dimensions of Anomy', *American Sociological Review*, Vol.30, 1965, pp.14-40.

C.A. McCoy and J. Playford (eds.), *Apolitical Politics: A Critique of Behavioralism*, Thomas Y. Crowell, New York, 1967.

W. McDougall, *Introduction to Social Psychology*, Methuen, London, 1960 (first published 1908).

* D. McGregor, 'The Need Hierarchy: A Theory of Motivation' in *Organisational Behavior and Administration*, ed. P. Lawrence and others, Dorsey Press, Homewood, Illinois, 1961, pp.224-8.

N. McInnes, *The Western Marxists*, Alcove, London, 1972.

C.B. Macpherson, *The Real World of Democracy*, Clarendon, Oxford, 1966.

C.B. Macpherson, *Democratic Theory: Essays in Retrieval*, Clarendon, Oxford, 1973.

R. Manzer, *Canada: A Socio-Political Report*, McGraw-Hill, Ryerson, Toronto, 1974.

* H. Marcuse, *One Dimensional Man: The Ideology of Industrial Society*, Routledge and Kegan Paul, London, 1964.

H. Marcuse, *Eros and Civilization: A Philosophical Inquiry into Freud*, with a new preface by the author, Sphere Books, London, 1969 (first published Beacon Press, Boston, 1965).

H. Marcuse, B. Moore and R.P. Wolff, *A Critique of Pure Tolerance*, Cape, London, 1969.

J. Martin, 'Tolerant and Prejudiced Personality Syndromes', *Journal of Intergroup Relations*, Vol.2, 1961, pp.171-6.

J. Martin and F. Westie, 'The Tolerant Personality', *American Sociological Review*, Vol.4, 1959, pp.521-8.

* K. Marx, 'Economic and Philosophic Manuscripts of 1844', tr. Martin Milligan, Foreign Languages Publishing House, Moscow, 1959.

K. Marx, *Early Writings*, tr. and ed. T.B. Bottomore, McGraw-Hill, New York, 1963.

* A.H. Maslow, 'A Theory of Human Motivation', *Psychology Review*, Vol.50, 1943, pp.370-96.

A.H. Maslow, 'Some Theoretical Consequences of Basic Need-Gratification', *Journal of Personality*, Vol.16, 1948, pp.402-16.

* A.H. Maslow, ' "Higher" and "Lower" Needs', *Journal of Psychology*, Vol.25, 1948, pp.433-6.

A.H. Maslow, 'Higher Needs and Personality', *Dialectica*, Vol.5, 1951, pp.257-65.

* A.H. Maslow, *Motivation and Personality*, Harper and Row, New York, 1954.

A.H. Maslow, 'The Instinctoid Nature of Basic Needs', *Journal of Personality*, Vol.22, 1954, pp.326-47.

A.H. Maslow, 'Deficiency Motivation and Growth Motivation', in *Nebraska Symposium of Motivation*, ed. M.R. Jones, University of Nebraska Press, Lincoln, 1955, pp.1-30.

* A.H. Maslow (ed.), *New Knowledge in Human Values*, Harper and Row, New York, 1959.

A.H. Maslow, 'Comments on Skinner's Attitude Toward Science', *Daedalus*, Vol.90, 1961, pp.572-3.

*A.H. Maslow, *Toward a Psychology of Being*, Van Nostrand, Princeton, New Jersey, 1962 (second edition 1968).

A.H. Maslow, 'Lessons from the peak-experience', *Journal of Humanistic Psychology*, Vol.2, 1962, pp.9-18.

A.H. Maslow, 'The Need to Know and the Fear of Knowing', *The Journal of General Psychology*, Vol.69, 1963, pp.111-25.

A.H. Maslow, 'Fusions of Facts and Values', *American Journal of Psychoanalysis*, Vol.23, No.2, 1963, pp.117-31.

A.H. Maslow, 'The scientific study of values', *Proceedings 7th Congress of Inter American Society of Psychology*, Mexico, 1963.

A.H. Maslow, *Religions, Values and Peak-Experiences*, Ohio State University Press, Columbus, Ohio, 1964.

A.H. Maslow, 'Criteria for Judging Needs to be Instinctoid' in *Human Motivation: A Symposium*, ed. M.R. Jones, University of Nebraska Press, Lincoln, 1965, pp.33-47.

A.H. Maslow, 'Self-actualisation and beyond' in *Challenges of Humanistic Psychology*, ed. J.F.T. Bugental, McGraw-Hill, New York, 1967, pp.279-86.

A.H. Maslow, 'Some fundamental questions that face the normative social psychologist', *Journal of Humanistic Psychology*, Vol.8, 1968, pp.143-54.

A.H. Maslow, 'The Farther Reaches of Human Nature', *The Journal of Transpersonal Psychology*, Vol.1, No.1, Spring 1969, pp.1-9.

*A.H. Maslow, *The Farther Reaches of Human Nature*, Viking, New York, 1971 (posthumous).

R. May, *The Meaning of Anxiety*, Ronald, New York, 1950.

R. May, *Man's Search for Himself*, Norton, New York, 1953.

R. May, *Love and Will*, Norton, New York, 1969.

R. May, *Power and Innocence*, Norton, New York, 1972.

A. Mehrabian, *The Structure of Non-Verbal Communication*, Aldine, Chicago, 1972.

D. Meier and W. Bell, 'Anomia and Differential Access to the Achievement of Life Goals', *American Sociological Review*, Vol.24, 1959, pp.189-202.

* W.J. Meyer, 'Democracy: Needs Over Wants', *Political Theory*, Vol.2, No.2, May 1974, pp.197-214.

L. Milbraith, *Political Participation*, Rand McNally, Chicago, 1965.

C.W. Mills, *The Sociological Imagination*, Oxford University Press, New York, 1959.

* K.R. Minogue, *The Liberal Mind*, Methuen, London, 1963.

H.A. Murray, *Explorations in Personality*, Oxford University Press, New York, 1938.

G. Myrdal, *An American Dilemma: The Negro Problem and Modern Democracy*, Harper and Row, New York, 1944 (first published 1942).

G. Myrdal, *Value in Social Theory: A Selection of Essays on Methodology*, ed. P. Streeton, Harper, New York, 1958.

*K. Nielsen, 'On Human Needs and Moral Appraisals', *Inquiry*, Vol.6, 1963, pp.170-83.

*K. Nielsen, 'Morality and Needs' in *The Business of Reason*, eds. J.J. MacIntosh and S. Coval, Routledge and Kegan Paul, London, 1969, pp.186-206.

K. Nielsen, *Reason and Practice: A Modern Introduction to Philosophy*, Harper and Row, New York, 1971.

K. Nielsen, 'On the choice between reform and revolution', *Inquiry*, Vol.14, No.3, Autumn 1971, pp.271-95.

*K. Nielsen, 'A Defence of Radicalism' in *Question Seven*, ed. H. Hawton, Pemberton, London, 1974, pp.53-66.

K. Nielsen, 'On the Diversity of Moral Beliefs', *Cultural Hermeneutics*, Vol.2, No.3, November 1974, pp.281-303.

J. O'Neill, *Sociology as a Skin Trade: Essays Toward a Reflexive Sociology*, Heinemann, London, 1972.

F.E. Oppenheim, ' "Facts" and·"Values" in Politics: Are They Separable?', *Political Theory*, Vol.1, No.1, February 1973, pp.54-68.

G. Parrott and L. Brown, 'Political Bias in the Rokeach Dogmatism Scale', *Psychological Reports*, Vol.30, 1972, pp.805-6.

R.S. Peters, *The Concept of Motivation*, Routledge and Kegan Paul, London, 1958.

M. Polanyi, *Personal Knowledge*, Routledge and Kegan Paul, London, 1958.

*M.G. Raskin, *Being and Doing*, Random House, New York, 1971.

J. Rawls, *A Theory of Justice*, Clarendon Press, Oxford, 1972.

C.A. Reich, *The Greening of America: How the youth revolution is trying to make America liveable*, Random House, New York, 1970.

*S.A. Renshon, *Psychological Needs and Political Behavior: A Theory of Personality and Political Efficacy*, Free Press, New York, 1974.

*S.A. Renshon, 'Psychological Needs, Personal Control and Political Participation', *Canadian Journal of Political Science*, Vol.22, No.1, March 1975, pp.107-16.

N. Rescher (ed.), *Studies in Moral Philosophy*, American Philosophical Quarterly Monograph, No.1, Blackwell, Oxford, 1963.

N. Rescher, *Introduction to Value-Theory*, Prentice-Hall, Englewood Cliffs, New Jersey, 1969.

W. Robinson, 'The Motivational Structure of Political Participation', *American Sociological Review*, Vol.17, 1952, pp.151-6.

C. Rogers, *On Becoming a Person*, Houghton Mifflin, New York, 1961.

M. Rokeach, 'Political and Religious Dogmatism: An Alternative to the Authoritarian Personality', *Psychological Monographs*, Vol.70, 1956.

*M. Rokeach, *The Open and Closed Mind*, Basic Books, New York, 1960.

M. Rokeach, *Beliefs, Attitudes and Values: A Theory of Organisation and Change*, Jossey-Bass, San Francisco, 1968.

*M. Rokeach, *The Nature of Human Values*, Free Press, New York, 1973.

M. Rosenberg, 'Misanthropy and Political Ideology', *American Sociological Review*, Vol.21, 1956, pp.690-5.

T. Roszak (ed.), *The Dissenting Academy: Essays Criticising the Teaching of the Humanities in American Universities,* Penguin Books, Middlesex, 1969 (first published Pantheon, New York, 1968).

T. Roszak, *The Making of the Counter Culture: Reflections on the Technocratic Society and its Youthful Opposition,* Faber, London, 1970.

J. Rotter, 'Generalized Expectancies for Internal Versus External Control of Reinforcement', *Psychological Monographs,* Vol.80, 1966.

J.J. Rousseau, *The First and Second Discourses,* ed. D. Masters, St. Martins, New York, 1964.

E.E. Sampson, 'Birth Order, Need Achievement and Conformity', *Journal of Abnormal and Social Psychology,* Vol.64, No.2, 1962, pp.155-9.

R.N. Sanford, 'Authoritarian Personality in Contemporary Perspective' in *The Handbook of Political Psychology,* ed. J. Knutson, Jossey-Bass, San Francisco, 1973.

I. Sarnoff and D. Katz, 'The Motivational Bases of Attitude Change', *Journal of Abnormal and Social Psychology,* Vol.49, No.1, January 1954, pp.115-24.

B. Schneider and C.P. Alderfer, 'Three Studies of Measures of Need Satisfaction in Organizations', *Administrative Science Quarterly,* Vol.18, No.4, December 1973, pp.489-505.

R. Schoenberger (ed.), *The American Right Wing,* Holt, Rinehart and Winston, New York, 1969.

J.R. Searle, 'How to Derive "Ought" from "Is"', *The Philosophical Review,* Vol.LXXIII, January 1964, pp.43-58.

*E.L. Simpson, *Democracy's Stepchildren: A Study of Need and Belief,* Jossey-Bass, San Francisco, 1971.

B.F. Skinner, *Beyond Freedom and Dignity,* Vintage, New York, 1971.

L. Sklair, *The Sociology of Progress,* Routledge and Kegan Paul, London, 1970.

P. Slater, *The Pursuit of Loneliness: American Culture at the Breaking Point,* Beacon Press, Boston, 1970.

M.B. Smith, J.S. Bruner and R.W. White, *Opinions and Personality,* Wiley, New York, 1956.

M.B. Smith, *Social Psychology and Human Values,* Aldine, Chicago, 1969.

*M.B. Smith, *Humanizing Social Psychology,* Jossey-Bass, San Francisco, 1974.

M.B. Smith, *The Psychology of Self,* McGraw-Hill, New York, (forthcoming).

T.A. Spragens Jr., *The Dilemma of Contemporary Political Theory: Toward a Post Behavioral Science of Politics,* Dunellen, New York, 1973.

L. Srole, 'Social Integration and Certain Corollaries: An Exploratory Study', *American Sociological Review,* Vol.21, No.6, December 1956, pp.709-16.

L. Srole, 'A Comment on "Anomy"', *American Sociological Review,* Vol.30, No.5, October 1965, pp.757-62.

S. Stouffer, *Communism, Conformity and Civil Liberties,* Wiley, New York, 1955.

C. Taylor, *The Explanation of Behavior,* Routledge and Kegan Paul, London, 1964.

*C. Taylor, 'Neutrality in Political Science' in *Philosophy, Politics, and Society*, 3rd series, eds. P. Laslett and W.G. Runciman, Barnes and Noble, New York, 1967, pp.25-57.

J. Taylor, 'A Personality Scale of Manifest Anxiety', *Journal of Abnormal and Social Psychology*, Vol.48, 1953, pp.285-90.

*P. Taylor, ' "Need" Statements', *Analysis*, Vol.19, No.5, April 1959, pp.106-11.

S. Tomkins, 'Left and Right: A Basic Dimension of Ideology and Personality' in *The Study of Lives*, ed. R. White, Atherton, New York, 1966.

*D.D. Van Fleet, 'The Need-hierarchy and Theories of Authority', *Human Relations*, Vol.26, No.5, 1973, pp.567-80.

*A.R. White, 'Needs and Wants', *Proceedings of the Philosophy of Education Society of Great Britain*, Supplementary Issue, Vol.VIII, No.2, July 1974, pp.159-80.

R.K. White, 'Motivation Reconsidered: The Concept of Competence', *Psychology Review*, Vol.66, 1959, pp.297-333.

B. Winer, *Statistical Principles in Experimental Design*, McGraw-Hill, New York, 1962.

D.W. Winnicott, *Playing and Reality*, Tavistock, London, 1971.

J. Yinger, 'Anomie, Alienation and Political Behavior' in *The Handbook of Political Psychology*, ed. J. Knutson, Jossey-Bass, San Francisco, 1973.

*J. Zinker, *Rosa Lee, Motivation and the Crisis of Dying*, Lake Erie College Press, Painesville, Ohio, 1966.

INDEX

affection (need for)
 x, 7, 36-8, 42, 45-6, 47, 48, 50, 75-6,
 77, 78-9, 112, 113, 114, 118, 121-2,
 205, 230
affiliation needs
 see affection (need for)
alien needs
 see false needs
alienation
 3, 9-10, 29, 32-4, 100, 104, 106, 108,
 110, 113, 118, 132, 139, 140, 151,
 161-3, 183

Allport, Gordon
 40, 72-3
Alpbach Symposium
 179, 184(fn)
ambiguity
 195-212
American Political Science Association
 xiii
anarchy
 see also political development
 80-3, 84, 85, 88, 93-4, 95
Anderson, John
 48
Aristotle
 52, 130, 158, 159, 166, 167, 168,
 172, 226, 234
artificial needs
 see also false needs
 x, xv, 26-35, 49(fn), 160, 164, 170,
 171, 222
attachment needs
 see affection (need for)
authentic needs
 see real needs
authoritarian
 see also elite

 xvi, 3, 23, 100, 107, 109, 111, 114,
 118, 210, 215(fn), 217, 232

Barker, Ernest
 31
Bay, Christian
 viii, x, xii, xiii, xiv, 35, 36-7, 46, 49,
 51, 55, 62, 71-2, 201, 203, 248
behaviour/behaviouralism
 see also political behaviour
 ix, 4-5, 10-11, 13-14, 16, 17, 18, 20,
 35, 43(fn), 46, 52-8, 71, 125, 133,
 165, 166, 171, 183, 208
being needs
 see also hierarchy of needs
 7, 39, 41(fn), 135, 137
belief systems
 8, 14-15, 16-17, 18, 66-7
belongingness (need for)
 see affection (need for)
Benn, S.I.
 see Peters, R.S.
Bentham, Jeremy
 29-32, 35
Berlin, Sir Isaiah
 253
biological needs
 see physiological needs
Bowlby, John
 43, 45, 48

Calvin, John
 74
Cassirer, Ernst
 189
Caucus for a New Political Science
 xiii-xiv
children
 see youth

Feuerbach, Ludwig Andreas
x, 144, 161, 166
First World
2, 20-5, 82, 149
Flew, Anthony
206, 209-10
Frankl, Viktor
179, 184-5, 192
freedom (need for)
see also personal control (need for)
xii, 2, 8, 11-13, 17, 19, 34, 38-9, 72,
151-2, 166-8, 176, 177, 183, 202,
250
Freire, Paulo
xi (fn), 21-5
Freud, Sigmund
14, 57, 59-60, 128-9, 130, 132, 171,
178-9, 184
Fromm, Erich
viii-xi, 37, 40, 42, 46, 128, 187, 193,
197, 231-3

Galbraith, J.K.
49(fn), 223-4
Galileo
186
Gallie, W.B.
see also essentially contested concept
142
Goldmann, Lucien
146
gratification (of needs)
33, 54-5, 58-64, 65-6, 68, 97, 170
Green, T.H.
27, 31
Grene, Marjorie
177, 185, 189-90

Habermas, Jürgen
143, 145, 150, 156
Harlow, Harry
45, 128
Hegel, G.W.F.
159, 161-2, 164, 168-9, 172
hierarchy of needs
see also Maslow, Abraham
x, xii, 7, 8, 11, 12, 15, 16, 26, 27,

34-5, 36-51, 57, 61(fn), 68, 68(fn),
75-6, 77, 94, 99, 135-8, 205
Hobbes, Thomas
26, 28, 82, 85, 86, 140, 158
Hobhouse, L.T.
31
Holt, E.B.
56(fn)
holy grail
72, 244, 260
human nature
xv, 1-2, 26, 35, 42, 72-3, 74-5, 81,
90, 97, 126-7, 134, 140-1, 161-2,
168, 205, 212, 237
humanistic psychology
see also psychology
7, 40, 42, 137-8, 231-2
Hume, David
see also is/ought distinction
ix(fn), 29, 153, 222, 249
Husserl, Edmund
174-7, 185-8, 194

induced needs
see false needs
irrational/irrationality
144, 181, 184, 191-2
is/ought distinction
see also Hume, David
ix, 40-2, 195, 197, 198, 199, 200,
202-8, 211-12, 222, 249-51

Jung, C.J.
128

Kant, Immanuel
95, 150, 166-8, 170
Kaufman, Arnold S.
50, 202-3, 251 (fn)
Keys, Ancel
44-5, 79(fn)
Kierkegaard, Sören
152, 153
Klee, Paul
259
Knutson, Jeanne
xii, 36, 37(fn), 45, 51, 68, 135, 207